KING AND QUEEN COUNTY, VIRGINIA

REV. ALFRED BAGBY, D. D.

Columbian College, Washington, D. C. (now George Washington
University), 1847 ; Princeton Theological Seminary, 1850-51.

KING AND QUEEN
COUNTY, VIRGINIA

By

Rev. Alfred Bagby, A.B., D.D.

ILLUSTRATED

Baltimore
REGIONAL PUBLISHING COMPANY
1974

Originally Published
New York and Washington
1908

Reprinted
Regional Publishing Company
Baltimore, 1974

Library of Congress Cataloging in Publication Data
Bagby, Alfred.
  King and Queen County, Virginia.

  Reprint of the 1908 ed. published by Neale Pub. Co., New York.
  1. King and Queen Co., Va.—History. I. Title.
F232.K4B2 1974   917.55'352'03   73-17399
ISBN 0-8063-7993-6

Reprinted from a volume in
the George Peabody Branch,
Enoch Pratt Free Library,
Baltimore, Maryland
1974

Made in the United States of America

To the gentle woman who for thirty-four years sat by my side, shared my joys and my sorrows, and nurtured my children; who for all these years has been an inspiration in mind and heart and life—

SARAH JANE (POLLARD) BAGBY—

this book is affectionately dedicated by the author.

FOREWORD

The planting and growth of a group of people in a new country is always an interesting story. It is regrettable, however, that great difficulties usually embarrass such a narrative; for a people in the process of rapid development oftener than otherwise permit the most essential facts in their history to drift into the limbo of the lost. And in addition to this common neglect, there has come upon the people of this county a civil war, destroying her most valuable public and private records.

But the author has made great compensation for the loss of so much original information by the diligence of his research and the faithful arrangement of his findings. His pages unfold before our eyes the pioneer settlement of this territory; its subsequent formation into the political division known as a county; the orderly development of this people under the law, customs, religion, and social life of a real English community; the names of many individuals and families who have added substance, culture, dignity, and luster to a brave and refined people; the arrest and almost overthrow of this civilization by a disastrous war; and the subsequent resumption of communal life under radically changed social and economic conditions.

This narrative will be of grateful and affectionate interest to the sons and daughters of this noble old county, and to Virginians everywhere; and, in after years, to those seeking information for a larger history of our race on these new shores.

A. J. Montagne.

Richmond, April 13, 1908.

PREFACE

The author has long since ceased to look for perfection in any production that is merely human,—much less can he make such claim for himself. The most anyone can claim is to approximate his own ideals. Our attempt has been to tell the truth, the whole attainable truth, and nothing but the truth; but we are mindful that the truth is not always the easiest thing to find, nor, when found, is it very easy to state it in a manner at once clear and attractive.

We are not conscious of any sinister thought, certainly not of any commercial thought, in the preparation of this volume. It has cost no little of time, expense, and labor, but it has been a labor of love. Himself a native of King and Queen, it has been his aim to set forth what he has seen and known of the nobility of the men and women it has sent forth as a legacy to the world. Omissions often and mistakes many will be observed, unavoidable from the inception, and for reasons but too obvious. Three times have the county records been swept away by fire, once during the Civil War. This is so disastrous that consecutive and detailed history of courts, transfers of real estate, and even county officers, is impossible. Hence much of our story is scrappy and fragmentary. I imagine that a parallel can hardly be found in the State.

The county is among the smaller ones, with no great fertility of soil; moreover, we are an isolated people with no great facilities for trading. The most that we can boast is in the character of our men and women, their culture, refinement, virtue, and devotion to religious ideals.

It has been my desire and ambition to do ample justice to every section of our county. I could have no motive possible to my discernment to do otherwise. As my own life has been in the middle section, things there have come more readily to my mind.

From my boyhood the Baptists have been predominant here. Every effort has been made to override all partiality to them. If some find their family names left out, it is surely not by design. Good men are not always responsive to appeals for family history and genealogy. An author is quite helpless in such matters. Even an honest man cannot write a history without data, nor ought he. The larger space given to the Clarks, the Civil War, etc., is not unfair, for they naturally and reasonably deserve a larger place in the public eye.

Anent the Colonial church,—the Church of England, —every possible effort has been made to get a representation worthy and satisfactory for our volume, but in vain. The author is greatly indebted to Hon. H. R. Pollard, Col. A. F. Fleet, Judges J. G. Dew, T. R. B. Wright, Charles T. Bagby, Esq., B. H. Walker, M. D., John Pollard, D. D., and notably also to W. H. Whitsitt, LL. D., for words of cheer and valued aid in various directions.

A. BAGBY.

INTRODUCTION

One of the happiest signs of the times is the awakening of the historic sense among our people. Much of the material of history goes to waste in every country; but in our Southern country a larger amount of it has been lost than in some others. We have been more solicitous to make history than to record and preserve it when made. Possibly that is true of every community at certain stages of its progress and development. In recent years a marked degree of interest has been aroused. The indifference of former years has passed away. That is one of the best features of the new day that has dawned upon us. Men are glad to cultivate a knowledge of families, municipalities, counties, States, and the whole country.

The county of King and Queen is truly ancient and honorable, and it is a concern to many people in many sections that its history should be collected and set in order. But there are certain obstacles in the way of such a consummation. The public records of the county have been destroyed by fire on more than one occasion. This is an incalculable loss. There are other sources of information, but none of these are so extensive and reliable as those once to be found in the clerk's office at the courthouse.

My honored friend, the Rev. Dr. Bagby, has devoted his attention for many years to the annals of King and Queen. He is sensible of the disadvantages under which he must labor, but he possesses a laudable ambition to preserve the things that remain, and to transmit an account of them to posterity. He is a diligent and careful student, and his interest in the subject has been earnest and continued for many years. I have enjoyed an opportunity to read over a portion of his work, and I consider it a very valuable and important contribution. I rejoice that he has decided to commit it to the press.

He will thereby render an excellent public service, and besides will perpetuate his own name for generations to come, by linking it with the history and fortunes of one of the most venerable and noble communities in our country.

WILLIAM H. WHITSITT.

RICHMOND COLLEGE,
September 12, 1907.

CONTENTS

PART I

PART II

PART III

DOMESTIC AND SOCIAL

PART IV

MISCELLANIES

ILLUSTRATIONS

PART I

THE PEOPLE: THEIR HOMES, WAYS,
WORKS, WORSHIPS

CHAPTER I

King and Queen is one of the tide-water counties of
Virginia, lying at its southeastern extremity, only some
forty miles from Chesapeake Bay. It adjoins the counties of Caroline, Essex, Middlesex, Gloucester, and
King William, being separated from the latter by the
Mattapony River. It lies on the northeastern shore of
the York and Mattapony Rivers. No student of this
portion of Virginia will fail to observe that all the eastern portion of the State is cut up into several narrow
strips—here called " necks "—by certain great rivers.
The dividing rivers are these: The Blackwater (a
branch of the Meherrin), James, York, Rappahannock,
and Potomac. The intervening necks are four, to wit:
beginning on the south, that of which Norfolk, Portsmouth, and Suffolk are central points; (2) that of
Jamestown, Yorktown, Williamsburg; (3) the neck
of Gloucester, King and Queen, etc.; (4) that which is
universally known as the " northern neck." To be yet
more distinct: we have the neck between the Blackwater
and the James; that between the James and the York;
that between the York and the Rappahannock; and
lastly, that between the Rappahannock and the Potomac.

Some future historian may disport himself in re-
counting the glories of each of these, and find a most
useful and enjoyable field.

1. Norfolk and Portsmouth will deserve superlative
praise. 2. Jamestown, Yorktown, and Williamsburg
speak for themselves, as being the cradle of the infant
colony and the home of Pocahontas, the white man's
only friend; and as furnishing, in the main, the scenes of
the exploits of that remarkable man, Captain John
Smith, who in the space of barely two years and five

months, almost by his single hand, saved the uncertain colony time and again from starvation and from the deadly tomahawk, and brought order out of chaos.

That wonderful little section of our State called " Northern Neck," is known the world over as the ancestral home of Washington, Madison, Monroe, and last, but not least, of the Lees,—among them that peerless citizen and soldier, Robert E. Lee.

This scant justice to our sisters of the other " necks " must suffice; our task is humbler. " Neck " No. 3, as above indicated, is subdivided longitudinally by a small stream, known near the Bay as Piankitank, while higher up it is nicknamed, with no regard to fitness, the "Dragon." This stream rises at a point some seventy miles from the Bay and flows down, first between Essex and King and Queen, and lower down between Middlesex and the latter county. The sluggish, fever-breeding stream might give ingress to steamers, and its banks might feed a large population if properly opened up. We thus locate the county of King and Queen as lying between the York and Mattapony on the south, and the Dragon (Piankitank) on the north.

The county, taking the Courthouse as its central point, is approximately in the same latitude, to the eastward, with Accomac across the Bay, Gibraltar, the renowned fortress at the entrance of the Mediterranean, and Athens, the venerable city of Greece; and with San Francisco and Yokohama to the west. The 77th degree of longitude west of Greenwich, passes through Ottawa (Canada), Washington city, and central King and Queen; it then passes southward through eastern North Carolina into the ocean, and crossing the Caribbean Sea, strikes the eastern end of the Isthmus of Panama, where is soon to be opened up the gateway between the two oceans. The county is one hundred miles south of Washington, thirty-six miles east-northeast from Richmond, forty miles northwest from Jamestown site, and fifty miles from the Bay.

The following names represented at Jamestown in 1608-9, are given on page 131 of Smith's History:

Smith, Behethland, Powell, Russell, Chashaw, Sickel-

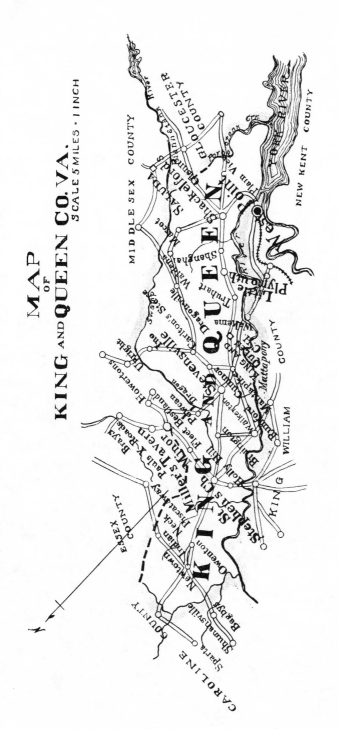

MAP
OF
KING AND QUEEN CO. VA.
SCALE 5 MILES - 1 INCH

more, Worlie, Todkill, Lone, Bentley, Shortridge, Pising, Ward, Persie, West, Phetiplace, Profit, Ford, Abbott, Tankard, Yarrington, Bourne, Burton, Colonel Dods, Brinton, Peacocke, Powell, Ellis, Gipson, Prat, Acrigyl, Read, Hancock, Wotton, Brooke, Nelson, Tyndall, Colson, Watkins, Fitch, Poole, Markham, Craddock, Brown, Janoway, Clarke, Skinner, Deale, Anthony, Baggly (Sergeant), Lambert, Pising (Sergeant), and others.

From Vol. II of the same history, at page 549, we obtain the following list of Jamestown settlers in 1620: Aston, Ashley, Archer, Anthony, Allen (4), Andrews, Abbot, Askew, Bowles, Button, Banks, Barber, Bonham, Brewster, Brooke, Bond, Beadle, Boone, Barnes, Badger, Britton, Bishop, Baron, Baker, Burley, Bromley, Barker, Bennett, Brewster, Bullock, Bayly, Butler, Burton, Baker, Beak, Bell, Blount, Cary, Calvert, Cecil, Corr, Chamberlaine, Cox, Cooper, Collins, Church, Camp, Cambel, Cooke, Conway, Cage, Cave, Crow, Chester, Cromwell, Drewry, Diggs, Dale, Denton, Dunn, Davis, Dobson, Dye, Drake, Dyke, Evans, Elkton, Finche, Farmer, Fox, Forrest, Farrar, Field, Francis, Fuller, Fleet (William), Gray, Gates, Gardner, Gilbert, Grave, Greene, Gore, Harris, Hicks, Hart, Hanson, Hill, Hinton, Hancock, Holt, Huntley, Harwood, Howell, Henshaw, Hooker, Hicks, Jones, Johnson, Toby, Jackson, Leigh, Layson, Martin, Moore, Miller, Oliver, Pit, Row, Robinson, Roy, Robins, Rolfe, Roberts, Smith, Spencer, Shelton, Scott, Shelley, Stone, Shipley, Shepherd, Stevens, Tracy, Turner, Tucker, Taylor, Thornton, Watts, Watson, Wilson, West, Webb, White, Westwood, Wright, Walker, Winne, Wilmer, Wood, Wells, Wheeler, Ward, Waller, Sir George Yeardley (Governor), etc.

The following names are taken from the old land books as those of settlers at Jamestown, from 1625 to 1670: Lasy, Spencer, Gather, Matheman, Cooke, Nelson, Hill, Powell, Woodyard, Yeardley, Combes, Hitchcock, Arundell, Grimes, Lyon, Younge, Davidson, Sharpless, Davies, Sands, Pierce, Hedges, Willard,

Moulston, Farmer, Lightfoot, Smith, Reuse, Gill, Cartright, Austin, Bricke, Rabenet, Andrews, Alder, Evere, Negar, Pott, Townsend, Leister, Kalloway, Howlett, Dickinson, Taylor, Sutton, Maericke, Rolfe, Lawson, Fouler, Waller, Boothe, Hamor, Clement, Langley, Greene, Addums, Ratcliffe, Gibson, Fremason, Pontes, Clarke, Raynolds, Hichmore, Riddall, Goldsmith, Gaill, Howell, Ashly, Blaney, Hudson, Hartley, Shelley, Bew, Ward, Mentis, Whitemore, Chauntree, Sheppard, Sawier, Danfort, Loyd, Orthway, Crouch, Starkey, Perry, Chapman, Granco, Snow, Isgraw, Ascomb, Buck, Porter, Jackson, Barrows, Scritten, Pasmore, Jeffreys, Hibbs, Duke, Hinton, Stephens, Rayner, Price, Spilman, Cawt, Manify, Holmes, Caleker, Sherwood, West, Barker, Scott, Carn, Hartl, Spalding, Hellin, Gray, Ocbourn, Pope, Constable, Jones, Johnson, Hall, Cooksey, Kean, Fitts, Reddish, Smallwood, Gicen, Southey, Painter, Webb, Gravett, Glover, Adams, Spence, Tooke, Roberts, Harlow, Sharke, Lect, Bennett.

Conjectural numbers of Indians in 1607 within sixty miles of Jamestown, 8,000.

Jamestown census: 1607, 100 to 120; 1608, 70 to 130; 1610, 200; 1617, 400; 1622, 3800; 1628, 3000.

CHAPTER II

PROGRESS AND EXPANSION FROM JAMESTOWN—
ORIGIN OF KING AND QUEEN COUNTY

It is easy to see how, by and by, there came a movement out from Jamestown to form settlements at various points around, the Indians, of course, receding before the whites. Under the impulse of their Saxon blood, men moved out and made new homes for themselves up the James, along Hampton Roads, across the Bay, and on the various rivers emptying into the Bay. It must be remembered that locomotion in that day was much easier and safer by water than by land.

Back, northward and westward from Jamestown, lay a vast wilderness trodden only by savages and wild beasts, while not infrequently the former awaited with his tomahawk or arrow any roaming white man. Thus it came about that even to pass through this boundless waste was perilous. On the other hand, it was easy to take a boat and row down the river, and through the adjacent waters. Indeed, Captain Smith, within the short space of less than two and a half years had largely explored the waters of the James, the York, the Rappahannock,* and the Potomac, and Chickahominy and

---

* John Smith, the colonist, was born in Lincolnshire, England, 1579; captured on Chickahominy, December, 1607; president of Council, 1608; saved the colony again and again from starvation by getting food from natives. He was painfully hurt by the sting of a stingray at the mouth of the Rappahannock, and soon after seriously wounded by an explosion of powder in a boat on James River, and sailed for England in October, 1609. He had just settled West's Colony at Powhatan, which he bought from that chief. Died 1631. Powhatan's domain extended from the Potomac south to the North Carolina line, and as high as the falls of rivers. This territory of Powhatan comprehended about 8,000 square miles, 30 tribes, and 2,400 warriors. Capt. Smith tells us there were 5,000 Indians within 60 miles of Jamestown, of whom 1,500 were fighting men. At first Powhatan held to Falls of river; subdivided (p. 387). James River to Patuxent was a patriarchial confederacy, each chief having his own council and council house. Beyond Powhatan's were the Matoacans and Manakins confederacies—all east of the Alleghenies. (Jefferson's Notes, pp. 143, 387.)

the Bay up to its northern extremity. These several waters gave welcome admittance to the new settlers, and thus the river shores were first preëmpted, and now began to be settled.

The York River was less than ten miles north from Jamestown in a direct line, and this naturally was among the first after the banks of the James, to be settled. About the year 1628 there was an understanding between the whites and the red men that York River was to be a dividing line between the two; the Indians holding the north bank, and the whites the south, and this line was reëstablished in 1646.

About this time, that crafty, uncompromising enemy of the whites, Opecancanough, chief of the Chickahominies, second in succession from Powhatan, moved his headquarters across the river to a point only some five miles obliquely across from the present West Point, and stationed himself on the soil of King and Queen, at a point called Matoax, or Mascot. The arrangement thus entered into could not stand against the Saxon blood, and the whites soon overran the line. Then the north bank of the York was occupied and held.

EARLY SETTLERS

We give the following names of settlers in that region, on the soil of the present King and Queen County, drawn from the antiquated books now in the land office in Richmond, counting from the year 1625 onward:

Major William Nash, Major William Lewis, Dr. Giles Mode, Anthony Haynes, Wyatt, Hodson, Loane, Chapman, Pigge, Colonel Nathaniel Bacon (Arioceo Swamp), Lockey, Austin, Peck, Diggs, Richard Harrison, Mozey, Birch (Hartquake Creek), Morris, Biggs, Hugh Roye, Jennings, James, Brund, Sexton, Woodward, Fuzey, Michel, Robert Pollard (near L. Creek), Clayborne, William Anderson (Poropotank Creek), Butler (Hartquake Swamp), Captain Thomas Byneton, Holmes, Williams (on Bestland, a branch of Piankitank), Robert Bagbie (1672), (joined Skipwith and Chapman), Robert Bagby (above tide, joined

Pigge and Hall, 1673), Henden, Key, Captain Lawrence Smith, Lieutenant-Colonel John Smith, Lightfoot, Roystin, Lewis, Hall (on Mattapony), Captain Robert Beverly, Garratt (Hartquake Creek), Mich, Robinson, Style, Story, Jones, Robert Spencer (joined Ed. Diggs), Captain Jacob Lumpkin (1682), Leigh, Madison (joined to Robert Bagbie, Miles, and Chamberlaine, near " Mantapike Path "), Colonel Richard Johnson, Echols, Bowden, Thomas Todd, Eastham, Taylor, Neal, Muire, Lane, Key, McKenney, Ed. Gresham (on Exall Swamp), Story.

1664, John Fleet, 1662, William and John Clarke, 1682, Thomas Harwood, John Clarke, Williams, Rogers, and Shackelford; 1693, William Todd, Robert Bird, Captain Joshua Story, Zackery Lewis; 1695, Ed. Gutharie, Alexander Campbell, Colonel Ed. Hill, Colonel Richard Johnson, Jennings, Carlton, Fox, Baylor, Watkins, Ware, Didlake, Pynes, Gardaner, Dunbar, Lyne, Thompson, Truman, William Bird, Gardner (Exall Swamp), Kemp, Temple, Roane, Crain, Captain William Fleet, Rowe, Dunn, Temple, Reuben Garrett, Charles Hill, Bayler, Temple.

Campbell's " History of Virginia " gives the following estimated population of Virginia for the various years, and other information of interest relating to King and Queen County:

1609—60 (reduced by disease and casualties).

1625—1500 (after massacre of March, 1622). These scattered over seventeen or eighteen places on James River. They had cattle, hogs, horses, and fowls now. Houses palisaded (p. 181).

When James I. died in 1625 there were only a few cabins in Richmond and nearly the whole colony was on James River and in Accomac.

1632—Williamsburg was settled, being at first the home of only one family.

1642—Berkeley came to Virginia.

1646—York River the boundary (p. 205).

1648—15,000, and 300 slaves (p. 205).

1701—40,000; (Connecticut, 30,000; Maryland,

25,000; Massachusetts, 70,000; New York, 30,000)
(p. 362).

1619—Women imported, and husband to pay 120
pounds of tobacco; negroes also imported. Taxation
by consent (p. 146).

1634—Captain Henry Fleet (pp. 185, 190).

1663—John and Theodore Bland (p. 264).

1664—Captain Dudley Diggs (p. 460).

1646—Rev. Steth, author of " Virginia History,"
lived at Varina, where Rolfe and Pocahontas had lived.

1664—John Robinson, Speaker and Treasurer for
twenty-five years; " Of cultivated mind and polished
manners." Christopher Robinson on the Rappahannock, his grandfather was nephew of an English Bishop.
The Speaker's father, John M. Beverly (pp. 535, 547).

1733—A horse worth $50.00, cow and calf $3.60

1775—Governor Dunmore's Council—Rev. P. Nelson, Page, Byrd, G. Corbin, Sr. and Jr. Richard Corbin was Deputy Receiver-General.

1782—Population, 567,614.

ORIGIN OF THE COUNTY

In the year 1634 the territory held by the Colony
was divided into nine shires—James City, Charles City,
Elizabeth City, York, Warwick, Henrico, Accomac,
Nansemond, and Isle of Wight. In 1654 a county was
formed from York, extending west to the headwaters of
Mattapony and Pamunky Rivers, to be called New Kent.
In 1691 another county was formed from the shire of
New Kent, including what is now King William, King
and Queen, and perhaps the whole of Caroline and
Spottsylvania, to be called King and Queen. The ori-
gin of the name is told in the following narrative:

In the beginning of the year 1688, James II., a son
of the Charles who was beheaded by Cromwell and the
Parliament, was reigning monarch in England. To
him the Virginia Colony was loyal—it was always loyal.
In November of that same year, William and Mary—
the latter the King's own daughter—came over from

Holland to England to claim the Crown against James, who had grown selfish and despotic. On July 1 (o. s.), 1690, a great battle was fought beside the River Boyne, in eastern Ireland, between the forces of James and those led by his son-in-law. It resulted in a victory for the latter, and William and Mary became joint sovereigns of the realm. The new county, being organized in the following year, was named for these illustrious personages, King and Queen.

It must be borne in mind that at this early date the population on the upper waters was quite sparse, and the Courthouse of the new county was located where it now stands.

CHAPTER III

RESOURCES, CLIMATE, ETC.

The following statistics of the agricultural and horticultural advantages of the county are compiled from memoranda prepared by the author in 1888, by request of Committee of the Agricultural Society of Virginia. They were designated to accompany an exhibit of county resources at the Virginia State Fair at the City of Richmond, in October of that year.

RELATIVE POSITION AND POPULATION

The county is part of the neck of land between the York and Rappahannock rivers, fifty miles from Chesapeake Bay, thirty-five north of east from the city of Richmond, and one hundred and fifty south from Baltimore, with both of which it communicates by steamers and railroad. It is fifty miles long by ten in width, with a population, in 1880, of 10,502, mostly homogeneous, being descendants of the original settlers.

MORALS AND CHURCHES

Taking it as a whole, its people are among the most refined, cultured and moral in the State. Very little whisky is sold. No liquor has been sold at the county seat for fifteen or twenty years, and but one case of disorder has been known to occur there within that time, and that between two belligerent colored citizens. In morals, our people will compare with those of any land.

Churches are numerous. It is not too much to say that this is a religious people. The Sabbath is held sacred, and Sabbath schools are largely patronized. There are Baptist, Methodist, Disciples, Christadelphian, and Episcopal churches. Indeed, most of the people are communicants in some church.

SCHOOLS

The system of public schools, supported by the State, is in full play here, and they are growing in utility. For the session of 1887 and 1888, there were forty-four schools, some graded, and 2000 scholars. The county is noted for its educational advantages, and for the general attention paid to the subject. Private schools and academies of excellent character and for both sexes abound. For higher education, facilities are at hand equal to any demand. Teachers and systems of teaching are of high grade. One or two high schools are in prospect.

HEALTH

This, to the immigrant, is a matter of prime consideration. The robust person, blooming cheek and incident cheerfulness, and in many cases advanced age of our people, refute the idea that this country is unfavorable to health. Indeed, our immigrants themselves contradict it. All tide-water sections have malaria, but it is by no means confined to tide-water. Timely precautions and watchfulness will almost uniformly prevent any trouble. It is also very much in our favor that typhoid fever, so common and fatal in higher climates, very seldom occurs here. Statistics show that the average of life in eastern Virginia is higher than anywhere else in the country.

CLIMATE

While subject to changes incident to countries near the sea, though by no means limited to them, our climate is exempt from the extremes of heat and cold occurring elsewhere. The needful supply of ice for summer seldom fails, but the thermometer rarely touches zero in winter, or rises above 95 Fahrenheit in summer. Floods and cyclones, which distress and overwhelm other sections, are almost unknown here. Occasional snows occur in winter, giving sport to the young with sleds and sleighs.

FIVE YEARS' AVERAGE OF KING AND QUEEN CLIMATE

	Rainfall, in.	Temperature.
January	3.192	38 to 44
February	2.049	41 to 47
March	3.95	48 to 54
April	3.68	56 to 62
May	2.83	63 to 70
June	3.75	71 to 78
July	4.49	77 to 82
August	9.15	76 to 81
September	4.76	69 to 74
October	4.63	62 to 66
November	2.61	47 to 53
December	2.87	43 to 48

SURFACE AND SOIL

Lying along the Mattapony and the Dragon, and stretching out to the distance of from several hundred yards to three-fourths of a mile, are extensive tracts of level land, mostly light and easily cultivated. Away from these waters the surface is undulating, sometimes hilly, with large fields and forests of level lands intervening. The character and constituents of the soil vary locally, and it is not uncommon to see one part of a farm heavy and stiff, and another light; grayish clay lands preponderate on the ridge. A clay subsoil generally prevails.

MINERALS

Gray and blue marls abound. These have been used upon the lands with marked results. The deposit frequently crops out from the surface, and is dug from the pit and applied at small cost. These marls are rich in carbonate of lime, and analyze 40 to 90 per cent. pure lime. The beds occur often, and are seemingly inexhaustible. Animal bones, shells, and Indian relics, in all stages of decomposition, are disinterred. Large beds of fine white sand are also common.

STAPLE CROPS

Corn, wheat, oats, rye, tobacco, potatoes (Irish and sweet), peas, beans, and occasionally buckwheat, are the staples. Peanuts and other truck are growing in favor;

sorghum and broom-corn are grown successfully. Tobacco raised here will compare well in quality with that grown elsewhere.

LANDS—PRICES AND CAPACITIES

Owners are beginning to realize the folly of attempting to cultivate so large an area as was in vogue here. Hence much land is on the market, at from $4 to $8, unimproved; and $8 to $20, improved; sometimes with a good dwelling and outhouses included. While considerable portions of these have been under cultivation, others lie in original forests.

The highlands, as well as alluvial and other bottom lands, respond easily and well to the hand of improvement; which is the great desideratum. There are many cases where lands which, under the wasting process of years of unskilled and neglected cultivation had grown thin, have been made to " rejoice and blossom as the rose." It may seem to some incredible, but is nevertheless true, that some of our lands which have been cultivated one hundred years or more with almost no return and no rest, are yet under the plow, and yield from ten to twenty bushels of corn to the acre. One large farm, which has been worked one hundred and fifty years, with only one moderate application of lime, and the respective fields grazed alternate years, still brings some fifteen bushels good corn. This shows well for the subsoil and the general constituents of the soil, and we challenge comparison with other sections. It is hardly a question what such lands would do in the hand of the skilled and active agriculturist. A large body of land skirting the Dragon and its tributaries, would well-nigh fill the granaries of Egypt, and only awaits the capital and energy needed to drain it! A company is already opening the stream below.

VEGETABLES AND FRUITS

An intelligent resident was asked, " Do you know of any good vegetable which cannot be successfully grown here? " The answer, after a moment's reflection, was,

" No! " The answer would be very much the same as to fruits, excepting those of the Torrid Zone only. Of course, certain varieties of each are better suited to our soil and climate, and in the selection regard must be had to this. We have apples—summer, fall and winter varieties—peaches, pears, cherries, apricots, quinces, damsons, plums; blackberries, growing wild in inexhaustible quantities, and very salable; strawberries, raspberries, melons, and last, not least, grapes. Soil and climate here seem specially favorable to the grape, though but little attention has hitherto been given to it. Yet it is growing in favor.

WATER

The abundant supply of pure, wholesome water, gurgling forth from almost every hillside, and readily accessible by wells to those who prefer it, is something marvelous. Strangers wonder at it, and admire. Scarcely a farm that has not enough and to spare for man and beast. In some cases artesian wells have been bored, at a cost of from $40 to $60, and to depths of 150 to 400 feet, with the result that a magnificent stream pours clear, sparkling waters into house and kitchen. The hamlet of Walkerton, alone, has eight of these in constant use.

TRANSPORTATION

Mattapony River, flowing into the York at West Point, is navigable for nearly the entire length of the county. A new steamer and sail vessels are constantly plying to and fro, giving ready access to Richmond, Norfolk, Baltimore, New York, and to foreign ports. From many parts of the county the Rappahannock is also easy of access, giving ready passage to Baltimore, etc. The Richmond and Chesapeake Railroad is projected, passing through the county to a point near the mouth of the Potomac, and thence to points North.

TIMBER

Assorted specimens of some of the best growths were

exhibited. Cypress is plentiful, affording the best shingles and weather-boarding in the world; chestnut yields the most durable fence-timber; black walnut is much in demand; oak, for railroad ties; pine, for fuel and general building purposes; poplar can be cut largely for the manufacture of paper; hickory, beech, ash, cedar, holly, dogwood, etc., abound. Immense quantities of these are annually exported, and in some cases purchasers have paid for their lands from this source alone.

FACTORIES—FACILITIES FOR

A number of steam mills are engaged in cutting shingles, laths, and other lumber, and there is room for more. Grist and flour mills give us meal and flour. Only one iron foundry exists in the county, but there are a number of shops for the work of the blacksmith. Factories for pickles and fruits are being established.

POULTRY AND EGGS

The demand for these increases annually, and is often above the supply, though this is enormous. One merchant sold $1,500 worth of eggs in a season. Poultry can be made very profitable. Brahmas, Plymouth Rock, and other improved breeds are now being introduced, and will pay even better.

STOCK

Our horses are mostly natives of the small breeds common to tide-water, though the demand is increasing for the higher grades. Of cattle, the Jersey cow is highly approved. One citizen reports three and a half pounds of butter daily from two cows, on pasturage alone. Much, it is thought, is to be made in the raising of colts, and with improved grades we see no reason to doubt its success. Of hogs, large numbers are slaughtered annually, and our bacon is equal in juiciness and sweetness to the best.

GRASSES

Our native growth, in many instances, gives good

grazing. Extensive tracts of marsh feed herds of cows and hogs, and on York River one gentleman gives no other feed to his cattle, even in winter, his herd subsisting and doing well on this alone. Clover, orchard grass, timothy, red-top and millet, succeed with necessary attention. During the present season large crops have been saved. One farmer, not far below us, housed one hundred and fifty tons, worth $12 to $15 per ton. This can be made a source of large revenue.

FISHERIES

Shad, herring, trout, pike, chub, sturgeon, and other varieties of fish are taken yearly, and give food and money to the people. From the York, on our eastern border, and from the Rappahannock, on the north, comes the succulent oyster, among the best, to our tables; while vast quantities are being shipped to market, and profitably.

TRADE

Our merchants buy in Baltimore and Richmond, and from the number of stores the trade must be heavy in the aggregate. Transportation being easier and cheaper, a very large proportion of our produce goes to the first-named city. When the new railroad comes much of this will be diverted to Richmond, or northward to Philadelphia and New York. From the port of West Point we have communication direct or indirect with all parts of the world.

LABOR

Labor is cheap as can be found elsewhere in the country. Native colored hands, by many considered the best in the world, can be had for eight dollars per month and board. To those who prefer it, white labor is obtainable.

SHEEP AND WOOL

This is a profitable industry. The yield for fleece may be set down at three to fourteen pounds. The

Cotswold, Shropshire, and other improved breeds, are coming in, and the yield increases. Lambs are always in demand in early spring and fall, and pay well. One gentleman reports a lamb dropped in March and weighing 100 pounds in July.

BEES AND HONEY

Bee-keeping can be made to pay. There were to be seen in our exhibit specimens from the hive of an enterprising lady of the county, surpassed by none, equaled by very few, in any section of the country.

GAME

From its comparatively isolated location, the county is well supplied with game. The deer, fox, rabbit, the wild turkey, goose and duck, quail, snipe, etc., are plentiful; while last, not least, the sora, that most delicious of all birds, gives life to our marshes and food to our palates in the fall. Try a specimen, fresh from the marsh and the spit, and be convinced.

ROADS

Our roads are good, except when affected by the rains and freezes of winter and spring.

FINANCES

The county's finances are in a healthy condition, the revenue meeting the annual expenses without trouble, and making a handsome return for State expenses. The tax rate is only eighty cents on the hundred dollars to both county and State. The county owes nothing.

MAIL FACILITIES

Mails pass and re-pass regularly and daily to and from Richmond, the morning papers from that city reaching parts of the county by or before 10 A. M.

POPULATION

Census Year	Total	White	Free Colored	Slave
1790	9377	4159	75	5143
1800	9879	4335	164	5380
1810	10988	4718	267	6003
1820	11798	5460	297	6041
1830	11644	4714	416	6514
1840	10862	4426	499	5937
1850	10319	4094	461	5764
1860	10328	3801	388	6139
1870	9709	4221	5488	....
1880	10502	4424	6078	....
1890	9669	4235	5430	....
1900	9265	4006	5259	....

CHAPTER IV

The author distinctly remembers that in the days
of his boyhood, there stood a dilapidated but still
tenantable house on a red-clay hill about midway between Stevensville and Cumnor, five miles above the
Courthouse. It was on land which was occupied for
years by Hon. H. R. Pollard, now City Attorney of
Richmond; but is at present occupied (1903) by Dr.
Thomas Latane. The place was known in 1830 all
around by the name of " Clark's."

This place is associated with two names which reflect
as much credit on the county in things material, as
Shackelford and Semple did in things spiritual. Historians and biographers agree in proclaiming that
George Rogers Clark was a native of Albemarle
County. This author ventures a decided opinion that
this is a mistake. Colonel John Pollard came to King
and Queen in 1818, from Goochland, the very year
of General Clark's death. Being an observing and
thoughtful man, and knowing something of the careers
of George Rogers Clark and his brother William, who
was only second to him, both being generals in the military service—he (Colonel Pollard) looked closely into
the question of their family lineage, birth, etc. From
his statement, oft repeated, it was agreed by the people
of the county that George Rogers was born at the place
indicated above, and was consequently a native of King
and Queen. Some of them knew the Clarks well.
While he was yet an infant his father removed to Albemarle, and it is easy to understand how historians have
made the pardonable mistake. The tradition at the
time of the death of George Rogers, near Louisville,
Ky., in 1818, as given by those acquainted with the

Clark family in King and Queen, was unanimous. This would seem decisive. The old house where he first saw the light of day disappeared many years since, and the site is now under cultivation.

We give below something of a family tree, compiled from the " Conquest of the Northwest ":

Before 1725 there settled in King and Queen an English immigrant named John C. Clark. He was unmarried. By and by, learning that a shipload of marriageable girls was to land at Yorktown—then a port of some importance—he went down to take a survey. It was easy then to go by boat from the Mattapony down the York River. The ship had just arrived. Mr. Clark was attracted by a red-haired maiden and married her.

We propose here to give a sketch of the Clark family, drawn in part from the " Conquest of the Northwest," and in part from William Kyle Anderson's sketches.

1. John Clark, Englishman, married red-headed Scotch girl, located in King and Queen after 1700 A. D.

2. Jonathan, his son, married Elizabeth Wilson, died 1734. In his will Jonathan Clark uses this language, in which it will be noted there is a recognition of the great God over all, and as well, of His Son, our Savior—the Lord Jesus Christ:

" Through the mercy and merits of Christ, our Savior."

3. John, oldest son of Jonathan, born 1724, married in 1749, Ann Rogers, daughter of Giles Rogers * and sister of Mrs. Donald Robertson.

4. George Rogers Clark, their second child, was born Nov. 19, 1752. The names of the brothers and sisters are, in order of ages, as follows: Jonathan, George Rogers, John, Richard, Edmund, Lucy, Elizabeth, William, and Frances.

Giles Rogers, Sr., was the grandfather, on the maternal side, of Ann (Rogers) Clark. Among the chil-

---

* Giles Rogers was an Englishman who settled on the Mattapony River in King and Queen in 1686.

dren of John, Sr., George Rogers and William were men of national reputation, and deservedly so. George Rogers, second son of John, Sr., emigrated to Kentucky when yet a mere youth. Kentucky in that day was a howling wilderness, inhabited largely by Indians hostile to the whites, and by murderous beasts of the forest. Immigrants were few and scattered. Roving bands of wild Indians often came across the Ohio, and these did not hesitate to murder any unlucky immigrants who happened to obstruct their way, nor even to attack their settlements or hinder their hunting. George Rogers Clark soon saw the condition, and finding the settlers at Harrodsburg—then a mere hamlet—practically defenseless, through the almost total lack of powder and ball, he determined to return to Virginia to procure arms and ammunition for the settlement. This was just after the Revolutionary War had set in. The pathway was long and tedious, but he found his family and visited the Governor and Council at Williamsburg, then the capital of the State, where, fortunately, he found that great and far-seeing man, Patrick Henry, at the head of affairs as Governor. After a delay, to him doubtless very tedious, he procured an order from the Governor requiring the military commandant at Wheeling to deliver to Clark ammunition—notably powder—to be transported down the river, for the purpose indicated, and to detail a certain number of soldiers to go with him as guard.

With a sagacity and vigor worthy of a man twice as old Clark took the powder down the river to a point some forty miles from Harrodsburg, and delivered it safely into the hands of the whites. The Indians laid an ambuscade on the road from the landing to Harrodsburg, and a number of his men were slain, but the object of the expedition was accomplished.

This put the colony in shape to meet the Indians on their raids, and a number of their lurking parties were broken up and scattered. And yet the raids grew more frequent and aggressive. It developed that a power, greater than the Indians, was behind them. It will be remembered that the war of the Revolution was being

waged in the East at this period.   The British had
pushed out their forces to several points on the Lakes,
and had built forts, notably one near Detroit, in Michigan.   From Detroit they extended their lines to and
down the Mississippi, erecting three forts on that river
—the southernmost at the town of Kaskaskia—and a
fort had also been erected at the town of Vincennes on
the Wabash.

The object had in view by the Governor-general of
Canada was manifestly to cut us off from acquisition of
territory north of the Ohio River and west of the Mississippi.   Canadian authorities incited the Indians, and
in some cases sent British soldiers along to direct their
raids upon the defenseless settlers in Kentucky.

With the keen eye of a strategist Clark saw that the
most effective means to stop these raids was to raise a
force, and, if possible, take and hold these forts.   With
this view he returned to Virginia and laid the case before
Governor Henry and his council, from whom he soon
received a commission as captain in the Virginia army,
with authority to raise a regiment and proceed to the
accomplishment of his object.

Let us pause a moment to fix in our minds the dates
of the events here recounted.   December 7, 1776, was
the date of the order for the powder; in October, 1777,
Clark returned to Virginia; January 2, 1778, he received orders and instructions from the Governor at
Williamsburg.   June 24, 1778, Clark leaves Louisville
in boats—an eclipse of the sun occurring just as he embarked—to go down the Ohio, aiming for Kaskaskia.
He has a force of only 175 men!   July 4, 1778, at midnight, he captures the fort at Kaskaskia, taking the commandant, Rocheblave, with all the garrison.   Next
morning he starts a subordinate with a small troop of
men, and in due time all three of the forts on the Mississippi were in the hands of the Virginians.

Clark next moves eastward across Illinois to the Wabash, some 160 miles, and captures the fort at Vincennes.   Then he returns to Kaskaskia, leaving a small
force at Vincennes.   But the British were not to be
foiled so easily.   The Vice-governor-general, whose

name was Hamilton, marched down from Detroit and recaptured Vincennes. Clark foresaw that unless Hamilton was checkmated he himself would be attacked in the spring at Kaskaskia. He determined to anticipate Governor Hamilton, and so in the freezing month of February, 1779, he leads a force back to Vincennes, in some places through waters up to their shoulders, outwits Governor Hamilton, and recaptures the fort with all its garrison. This was an amazing achievement— perhaps the equal of anything of its character accomplished during the Revolution. It added five great States, and a part of a sixth, to our Union—Ohio, Indiana, Illinois, Michigan, Wisconsin, and a part of Minnesota.

George Rogers Clark displayed a military instinct which was most remarkable, and that, too, without any previous training whatever. In our judgment, he ranks second only to Washington himself in the results he achieved.

William Clark was also a general, U. S. A. He was younger by some eighteen years than his brother, George Rogers. He was the Clark of " Lewis and Clark's Expedition " westward along the Missouri and by way of Columbia River to the Pacific. He was afterwards made Governor of the Louisiana Territory, with headquarters at St. Louis, and was highly honored by President Jefferson.*

The father and mother of these two men, as also the grandfather and grandmother, were King and Queen people.

* We are fortunate in having the following from the pen of our distinguished countryman, Col. A. R. F. Fleet: " I have pictures of George Rogers Clark and his brother William, which I shall probably present to King and Queen County as soon as I have time to prepare a paper on the two men. William, as you know, was the first Governor of Missouri, and stands in high repute in that State. Donald Robertson, whose life can be found in the Virginia Historical Library, taught James Madison and George Rogers Clark at his classical school in King and Queen. Thomas Walker, the ancestor of the distinguished Dr. Thomas Walker of Albemarle, and also of the Riveses and of Gov. Thomas Walker Gilmer, was also from King and Queen."

NOTES FROM ENGLISH'S "CONQUEST OF THE NORTHWEST."

Captain Edmund Clark.

Born September 25th, 1762, died 1817.

General Jonathan Clark.

Born August 1, 1750, died November 25, 1811.

Family.—Vol. I., pp. 29-31, 404. Pension, 785, etc. Surveyor, p. 59. Dunmore War, 64. Visits Kentucky, 65. Returned to Virginia and to Kentucky. Virginia Legislator. Sent by Patrick Henry with powder. Personal appearance, 165. Plans for conquest of N. W. Corn Island.

General George Rogers Clark.

Born November 19th, 1752, son of John Clark and Ann Rogers, born February 13th, 1718. Grandson of Jonathan Clark and his wife, *née* Bird.

Tributes to Gen. G. R. Clark.

In center of Indianapolis a bronze monument, a soldier of Revolution, dedicated 1895, 113th anniversary of Sackville. Vincennes 160 miles from Kaskaskia.

"For this great empire indebted to Clark alone."— Voorhees, U. S. S.

"Second only to Washington."—Turpie, U. S. S.

"A great Virginian—among the great and illustrious names of that magnificent State."—Sherman, U. S. S.

"Hannibal of the West."—John Randolph, U. S. S.

"Hard to find an officer achieving such results with a force so small."—Professor Hinsdale.

"Tall, commanding, full of resources, confidence and aff. of men."—Lyman C. Draper.

"Knew when to be mild, and when to stern and uncompromising."—Collins' History of Kentucky.

"Theater of exploits distant and unknown region." —Samuel Merrill.

" No hero of the Revolution a cleaner or better piece of work."—J. W. Daniel.

" Not twenty-six years old when Henry sent on great mission."—James Parton.

" The great territory of the Northwest due to one man."—President Garfield.

" Much credit due to the men, most to Clark himself."—President Roosevelt.

" One of the most daring and gallant exploits in our history."—Hoar, U. S. S.

" Our boundaries not Alleghanies, nor the Ohio, but Mississippi."—Judge Pickle.

" Majestic person, strong features, dignified deportment."—Judge Burnett (1779).

Both Jefferson and Henry his staunch friends and admirers.

Great feat accomplished in a wild country, without roads, in the midst of savage and British enemies, and in spite of depreciating currency.

Hamilton with strong force besieging Sackville fort, Helm and a private defending with a loaded cannon, demanding honorable terms, and gaining their point before surrender.

CHAPTER V

LEGISLATIVE ACTION CONCERNING THE FORMATION,
AND INTENDED TO ADVANCE THE INTEREST, OF
THE COUNTY OF KING AND QUEEN—HENNING'S
" STATUTES AT LARGE "

1.   In 1634 the Colony of Virginia was divided into
eight shires, " which are to be governed as the shires of
England.   The names of the shires are, James City,
Henrico, Charles City, Elizabeth City, Warwick River,
Warrosquyoake, Charles River, and Accawmack."
(Extract from the Judicial Proceedings of the Governor
and Council in Virginia.   I. Henning's Statutes at
Large, p. 224.)

2.   By an act of March, 1643, " Achommack " was
thenceforth to be known as " North'ton."   It was likewise enacted and confirmed that " Charles River
County " should be called " the County of York," and
that " Warwick River County " should be called " the
County of Warwick."   (I. Hen. St. at Large, p. 249.)

3.   It appears from a recital in the preamble of an
act passed at a session of the " Grand Assembly," beginning on the 12th of October, 1648, that there had been
another act (which I am unable to find) making it a
felony " To go to the north side of Charles [York]
River and make a settlement."   It was then enacted that
on and after the 1st of September, 1649, all the lands
lying on the north side of Charles (York) River and
Rappahannock River were to be open and free to settlement, and the said act making it a felony there to
settle, was repealed.   (I. Hen. St. at Large, pp. 353,
354.)

4.   On the list of " the names of the Burgeses for
each respective county," " New Kent " first appeared
November 20th, 1654, as represented at an assembly
held at James City on November 20, 1654, and Capt.
Robert Abrell appears to have been its Burgess; and

COL. JOHN POLLARD

(1803–1877)

Lieutenant-Colonel Virginia Militia, Commissioner of Revenue.
Lawyer and Commissioner in Chancery.

FACING 42

under the " Publique Orders of Assembly " the following appears:
   " It is ordered that the upper part of Yorke County
shall be a distinct county called New Kent, from the
west side of Scimino Creek to the heads of Pomunkey
and Mattaponie River, and downe to the west side of
Poropotanke Creeke."   (I. Hen. St. at Large, pp. 387,
388.)
   5.   Among the " Public Orders of Assembly " at the
session commenced March 24, 1655, is the following:
"ORDERED, That from Poropotank to Mattapony
upward (vizt) on the north side of Yorke River be a
distinct parish by the name of Stratton Major."   (I.
Hen. St. at Large, p. 404.)
   6.   By an act of the " Grand Assembly," held at
James City in March, 1661, the date of the holding of
the County Court of New Kent County was fixed for the
28th day of each month.   (I. Hen. St. at Large, p. 70.)
   7.   The County of King and Queen was formed
from New Kent County by an act of the " General Assembly begun at James Citty," on the 16th day of April
A. D. 1691.   The preamble of the act recites that:
" WHEREAS sundry and divers inconveniences attend
the inhabitants of New Kent County and all others who
have occation to prosecute suites there, by reason of the
difficulty in passing the river "; and it was enacted that
" New Kent be divided into two distinct counties, so
that Pomunkey River shall divide the same, and so down
York River to the extent of the county, and that the
part which is now on the south side of Yorke and Pomunkey River be called New Kent, and that the north
side with Pomunkey Neck be called and known by the
name of King and Queen County."   It was further
enacted, " That a court for the said King and Queen
County be constantly held by the justices thereof upon
the 12th day of the month in such manner as by the laws
of this county is provided."   (III. Hen. St. at Large,
pp. 94, 95.)
   8.   By an act of the " General Assembly begun at
His Majestyes Royall Colledge of William & Mary
Adjoyning to the City of Williamsburgh, the 5th Day

of December, 1700," it was recited as follows: " WHEREAS sundry and divers inconveniencies attend the inhabitants of that part of King and Queen County which lies within Pamunkey Neck when they have occasion to prosecute law suits at the ———, or to go to any other publick meeting by reason of the difficulty in passing Matapiny River"; and it was enacted that after the 11th day of April, 1702, "the said county of King and Queen be divided into two distinct countyes so that Matapiny River divide the same, and that that part of the said county which is and lyes on the north side the said Matapiny River and York River remaine and shall for ever hereafter be called and knowne by the name of King and Queen County, and that that part of the said county which is and lyes on the south side of the said river within Pamunkey Neck shall be called and knowne by the name of King William County. And for the due administration of justice,

" Be it further enacted by the authority aforesaid, and it is hereby enacted, That after the time aforesaid a court for the said King William County be constantly held by the justices thereof upon the 20th day of every month in such manner as by the laws of this county is provided and shall be by their commission directed. And whereas the towne land lying at West Point in Pamunkey Neck was purchased by the entire county of King and Queen as then it was, all the charges about the same being equally levied upon the whole number of tythables of the said county,

" Be it enacted by the authority aforesaid, and it is hereby enacted, That two thirds of the tobacco ariseing from the sailes of the said towne lands to the severall takers up thereof be repaid to the inhabitants that shall be for the time being on the north side of the said Matapany and York Rivers in King and Queen County upon the takeing up of the said towne land." (III. Hen. St. at Large, pp. 211, 212.)

9. By the " General Assembly Summoned to Meet at Her Majesty's Roial College of William & Mary adjoining to the City of Williamsburgh," begun on the 19th day of March, 1702, an act was passed entitled:

" An Act impowering the Court of King and Queen County, to purchase land for a Town." Unfortunately the text of this act has never been found or published. (III. Hen. St. at Large, p. 227.)

10.   Among the acts passed during the session of the General Assembly held in 1705 is one entitled: " An act for Establishing ports and towns "; but this act does not provide for the establishment of any port or town within the county of King and Queen. West Point was established as such a port by said act, which provided as follows: " That at West Point to be called Delaware, and to have Tuesdays and Satturdays in each week for market days, and the second Tuesday in September and four following days annually their fair." (III. Hen. St. at Large, pp. 415, 416.)

11.   By an act passed at the same session, entitled, " An act for the regulation and settlement of Ferries; and for the dispatch of public expresses," a ferry was established across York River from the Brick House to Graves's, " the price for a man one shilling, for a man and horse two and twenty pence halfpenny," and from West Point to Graves's, " the price for a man six pence, for a man and horse one shilling." (III. Hen. St. at Large, pp. 471, 472.)

12.   By another act passed during the same session the day of holding the County Court of King and Queen County was fixed for the fourth Monday in every month. (III. Hen. St. at Large, p. 507.)

13.   " At a General Assembly begun and holden at the Capitol, in the City of Williamsburg, on the second day of November, 1720," an act on the subject of ferries was passed, by which the following ferries were established over the Mattapony River: " From Samuel Norment's, over the said river, the price for a man, three pence, and for a horse, three pence, and for each hogshead of tobacco, six pence. From William White's over the said river, the price for a man, three pence, and for a horse, three pence, and for each hogshead of tobacco, six pence." (IV. Hen. St. at Large, p. 93.) The title of another appears as follows: " An Act for the vesting the fee simple estate of certain Lands in William

Beverley, of the county of King and Queen, gent., upon certain considerations therein mentioned." (IV. Hen. St. at Large, p. 116.)

14. By a session of the General Assembly begun and held on the 9th day of May, 1723, an act was passed entitled, " An act for dividing Saint Stephen's Parish, in the county of King and Queen." (IV. Hen. St. at Large, p. 141.)

15. At a session of the General Assembly begun on the first day of February, 1727, an act was passed entitled, " An act for erecting a new county, on the heads of Essex, King and Queen, and King William Counties; and for calling the same Caroline County." (IV. Hen. St. at Large, p. 240.)

16. By another act of the General Assembly begun and held on the 3d day of May, 1730, an act was passed in relation to the inspection of tobacco and the establishment of certain warehouses. The following public warehouses were established in King and Queen County: At Todd's, at Mantapike, and at Shepherd's in King and Queen County. (IV. Hen. St. at Large, p. 267.)

By a subsequent act the compensation of the inspectors at the public warehouses was fixed, and the compensation at the King and Queen warehouses was fixed as follows: At Todd's fifty pounds of tobacco per annum; at Mantapike forty pounds per annum; at Shepherd's fifty pounds per annum. (IV. Hen. St. at Large, p. 335.) By a subsequent act passed at the same session the rents of the public warehouses were fixed as follows: At Shepherd's twelve pounds of tobacco per annum; at Mantapike ten pounds per annum; at Todd's twenty pounds per annum; and the compensation to the inspectors at the said warehouses was charged and fixed as follows: At Shepherd's thirty-five pounds of tobacco per annum; at Mantapike thirty-five pounds per annum, and at Todd's forty pounds per annum. (IV. Hen. St. at Large, pp. 383, 385.)

17. By an act passed at the same session it was recited as follows: " And whereas the vestry of the parish of St. Stephen, in the county of King and Queen, have also lately purchased a good and convenient glebe,

for the parson of that parish, and his successors; and are desirous to sell the old glebe, which is inconvenient, and to apply the purchase money to other parochial uses "; and it was enacted that " The said old glebe, of the said parish of St. Stephen, containing, by estimation, near two hundred acres, with the appurtenances, be, and is hereby, vested in the present vestry of the said parish, and the vestry of the said parish for the time being, in trust," for the purpose of enabling the vestry to sell the same and convey a good title to the purchaser, " the purchase money " to be laid out and applied by them " in the purchasing of slaves, to be placed upon the new glebe, and such slaves, and their increase, so long as any of them shall be living, shall remain upon the said glebe, for the use and benefit of the present parson, and the parson of the said parish for the time being, for ever." (IV. Hen. St. at Large, pp. 441, 442.)

18. At the General Assembly held on the 5th day of August, 1736, the date of the County Court of King and Queen County was fixed for the second Tuesday in every month. (IV. Hen. St. at Large, p. 533.)

19. By an act passed by the General Assembly in November, 1738, it was enacted that Sir John Randolph, knight, treasurer of the revenues arising by two several acts, having departed this life, John Robinson, the younger, esquire, " be appointed " treasurer of the revenues arising from the duty upon liquors and slaves . . . " to hold the said office so long as he shall continue to be Speaker of the House of Burgesses, and from the time of his being out of that office, until the end of the next session of Assembly." His salary was fixed at " four pounds in the hundred, and so proportionably for a greater or less sum, . . . out of all and every the sum and sums of money by him received and accounted for to the General Assembly." (V. Hen. St. at Large, pp. 64, 65.)

20. Under section 35 of an act of the General Assembly, passed May, 1742, public warehouses for the inspection of tobacco pursuant to this said act were required to be kept " in the County of King and Queen at Shepherd's and Thomas Turner's, under one inspec-

tion; at Mantapike and Walker Town, on the lot of Mr. John Walker, under another inspection; and at Todd's." The salary of the inspector at Shepherd's and Thomas Turner's land was fixed at thirty-five pounds of tobacco, at Mantapike and Walker Town at thirty-five pounds, and at Todd's at forty pounds. (V. Hen. St. at Large, pp. 142, 144.)

21.   In May, 1742, an act was passed entitled, " An act for dividing the county of King and Queen, and adding the upper part thereof to the county of Caroline." By this act it was provided that after the first of December, next ensuing, " the said county of King and Queen be divided by a line to be run from the upper part of the land of William Wood, on the edge of Essex County, to the upper part of Captain Richard Tunstal's land, on Morocosick Creek; and that all that part of the said county of King and Queen, below the said creek, be one distinct county and retain the name of King and Queen County, and that all the other part thereof, above the said line, be thereafter annexed and made part of the county of Caroline." (V. Hen. St. at Large, p. 185.)

22.   In May, 1742, an act was passed entitled, " An act to vest certain entailed lands, parcel of a greater tract therein mentioned, in George Braxton, the younger, in fee simple, and for settling other lands of greater value, to the same uses." (V. Hen. St. at Large, p. 214.)

23.   In September, 1744, an act was passed, entitled " An act to empower the vestry of the parish of Stratton Major, in the county of King and Queen, to sell the glebe of the said parish, and to purchase a more convenient glebe in lieu thereof." (V. Hen. St. at Large, p. 251.)

24.   By an act passed February, 1745, " John Robinson, John Blair, and William Nelson, Esquires, members of His Majesty's honorable council; John Robinson, Esquire, Mr. Secretary Nelson, Richard Randolph, William Beverley, Beverley Whiting, and Benjamin Waller, gentlemen, members of the House of Burgesses, or any six of them, whereof two to be of the council

and four of the House of Burgesses," were appointed a committee for the revisal of the whole body of the laws of His Majesty's colony and dominion. (V. Hen. St. at Large, p. 321.)

25. In October, 1748, an act was passed entitled "An act for establishing county courts, and for regulating and settling the proceedings therein," and the county court of the county of King and Queen was required to be held on the second Tuesday in every month. (V. Hen. St. at Large, pp. 489, 490.)

26. In November, 1753, an act was passed entitled, "An act for clearing Mattapony River," by which act Richard Corbin, Esquire, John Robinson, Esquire, Lunsford Lomax, Edmund Pendleton, ThomasTurner, Henry Robinson, John Baylor, and Thomas Johnson, gentlemen, were appointed trustees and authorized and empowered to receive subscriptions and to contract with any person or persons for clearing the Mattapony River, by removing all stops which in anywise obstructed the navigation of the same, as far upstream as Burke's bridge, in the county of Caroline. (VI. Hen. St. at Large, p. 394.)

27. In March, 1762, the following act was passed by the General Assembly: "An act to empower the vestries of the parishes of Drysdale, in the counties of Caroline and King and Queen, and of St. Stephen, in the said county of King and Queen, to sell their glebes, and lay out the money in purchasing more convenient glebes."(VII. Hen. St. at Large, p. 513.)

28. By an act passed November, 1762, entitled, "An act for raising a Publick Levy," it is recited that, whereas a balance is due to the public from the county of King and Queen of $6,985.00, assessed on tobacco, the sheriff shall sell the said tobacco levied on for public purposes, to the highest bidder, etc. Presumably this tobacco was in the public warehouses of the county. (VII. Hen. St. at Large, p. 544.)

29. An act was passed November, 1762, establishing a public pilotage and regulating fees therefor, by which it was provided that from West Point to Shepherd's the pilot fee should be six pence, and from West

Point to Meredith's, Moore's or the highest landing up
the Mattapony River, one shilling. (VII. Hen. St. at
Large, pp. 580, 583.)

30.   In November, 1762, an act was passed entitled,
" An act for adding part of the county of King and
Queen to the county of Caroline, and for altering the
Court day of the said county of King and Queen," by
which it was provided that after the 10th day of February, next ensuing, the said county should be " divided
by a line to be run from Morocosick Creek, at the mouth
of Beverley Run, thence up the said run and the South
Fork which Beverley's mill stands on to the head thereof,
and from thence by a straight line to be run east to the
line between the said county and the county of Essex;
and that all that part of the said county which lies above
the said bounds shall be united to, and made part of, the
said county of Caroline."   It was also provided by the
said act that after the said 10th day of February, next
ensuing, that the County Court of the said county of
King and Queen was to be held on the second Monday
in every month.   (VII. Hen. St. at Large, pp. 620,
621.)

31.   An act was passed October, 1764, entitled,
" An act for establishing the landing place from Fraser's
Ferry to the causeway opposite thereto."   It was recited
in said act that the guardian of the infant children of
George Braxton, esquire, deceased, who were seized of
the reversion of the lands adjoining the said causeway,
had consented thereto.   (VIII. Hen. St. at Large, p.
49.)

32.   By an act passed October, 1765, the public warehouses at Shepherd's and Thomas Turner's were placed
under one inspection; at Mantapike, at Walker Town,
on the land of Mr. Baylor Walker, and at Waller's
Ferry in the county of King William, under one inspection; and at Todd's, under one inspection.   (VIII. Hen.
St. at Large, p. 78.)

33.   By an act passed November, 1766, the Speaker
of the House of Burgesses was given a salary of 500
pounds sterling per annum, and it was provided that
thereafter the offices of Treasurer and of Speaker of

the House of Burgesses should be separate and distinct. (VIII. Hen. St. at Large, p. 210.)

34. By an act passed November, 1766, it was recited that John Robinson having departed this life since the previous session of Assembly, the Lieutenant-Governor of the Colony had appointed Robert Carter Nicholas Treasurer in his place, and thereupon by said act he was appointed to hold the office during the continuance of the present General Assembly and afterward to the end of the next session of General Assembly. (VIII. Hen. St. at Large, p. 211.)

35. By the recital of an act passed in November, 1766, it appears that Robert Beverley, Esquire, then deceased, was, in his lifetime, seized of a valuable estate in lands, known by the name of Beverley Park, situate in the parish of Drysdale, in the counties of Caroline and of King and Queen, and containing 7,600 acres. (VIII. Hen. St. at Large, pp. 227, 228.)

36. In November, 1766, an act was passed entitled, " An act to empower the administrators of the estate of John Robinson, Esquire, deceased, to sell such parts of his real or personal estate as to them shall seem most convenient for the payment of his debts; " by which it was recited that John Robinson was greatly indebted for the balance of the public money in his hands, as well as to many private persons. By said act Peyton Randolph, Esquire, Edmund Pendleton, and Peter Lyons, gentlemen, administrators of the estate of the said John Robinson, were empowered to sell such portion of the said lands as they deemed most advantageous, etc. (VIII. Hen. St. at Large, p. 272.)

37. An act was passed November, 1769, entitled, " An act for the more speedy and effectual recovery of the debt due to the public from the estate of the late treasurer." (VIII. Hen. St. at Large, p. 349.)

38. By an act passed in 1769 it was recited that George Brooke was seized in fee simple of a tract of land called Mantapike, containing about seven hundred and eighty acres, lying on said (Mattapony) river, in the county of King and Queen, and by him purchased of Tunstall Banks; and by said act the fee-simple title was

vested in said George Brooks in lieu of an estate tail. (VIII. Hen. St. at Large, pp. 474, 475.)

39.   In February, 1772, an act was passed entitled, " An act to amend an act entitled an act for clearing Mattapony River."   By this act Richard Corbin and John Page, esquires, and Edmund Pendleton, Walker Taliaferro, George Brooke, William Aylett, Anthony Thornton, John Armistead, William Nelson, Jr., John Baylor, Jr., and John Jones, gentlemen, were appointed trustees to carry out the intent of the act, that is, to clear the river to Burk's bridge, etc.   (VIII. Hen. St. at Large, p. 579.)

40.   In February, 1772, an act was passed entitled, " An act to vest certain intailed lands, whereof Philip Ludwell Grymes, gentleman, is seized, in William Roane, gentleman, in fee simple."   (VIII. Hen. St. at Large, 630.)

41.   By an act passed February, 1772, entitled " An act to dock the intail of certain lands whereof William Todd, gentleman, is seised, and for other purposes therein mentioned," it was recited that Thomas Todd, formerly of the county of Gloucester, gentleman, was, in his lifetime, seised of a considerable estate in lands, and among others of a large and valuable tract of land lying on the Mattapony River, in the county of King and Queen, and of another tract containing about one thousand acres lying on the Dragon Swamp in the parish of St. Stephen in said county of King and Queen, etc. (VIII. Hen. St. at Large, pp. 631, 632.)

42.   In May, 1777, an act was passed entitled " An act for dissolving the vestries of several parishes."   It is recited in the preamble of this act that " there are such divisions in the parish of Stratton Major in the county of King and Queen that the affairs of the said parish have been for some time neglected," and by this act it was enacted, on that account, that the freeholders and housekeepers of the said parish should meet at some convenient time and place, to be appointed and publicly advertised by the sheriff of the county, at least one month before the 15th day of July, next ensuing, and " then and there elect twelve of the most able and dis-

creet persons, being freeholders and resident in the parish, for vestrymen, who should thereafter, being so elected, take and subscribe the oaths required by law." It was further recited in said act as follows: " And whereas the levies of the said parish of Stratton Major, for some time last passed, have not been laid by the vestry thereof, whereby the creditors of the said parish remain unpaid: Be it therefore enacted, That the vestry of the said parish, to be elected by virtue of this act, shall levy and assess upon the tithable persons of the said parish all such sums of money and quantities of tobacco, as ought to have been levied and assessed by the said vestry." (XI. Hen. St. at Large, pp. 317, 318.)

43. In October, 1779, an act was passed entitled, " An act for dividing the parish of Drysdale, in the counties of Caroline and King and Queen." By this division that part of the parish lying east of the line " to begin at the lower corner of the land of John Page, Esq., upon Mattapony River, and run along his lower line and those of Christopher Smith, Anthony Seale, and Frederick Phillips, to the corner of the lands of Edmund Pendleton, the elder, Esq., and Edmund Jones; thence along the lines between them to Morocosick Creek; thence up the creek to the mouth of Phillips' Run; thence up the said Run to Digge's upper line; thence along that line and the course thereof continued to the line of Essex County," was separated from the part lying west of the line described and was to retain the name of Drysdale. By the same act Edmund Pendleton, the elder, William Lyne, Anthony Thornton, Jun., Thomas Coleman, Mungo Roy, and James Upshaw, gentlemen, were appointed commissioners to sell and convey " the present glebe and buildings " belonging to the parish " for ready money or on credit, as to them shall appear most advisable," and " that the money arising from the sale thereof shall be equally divided between the said parishes of Drysdale and Saint Asaph " (the new parish formed), except that they were to appoint one or more disinterested persons to value the two churches then in the said parish of Drysdale and they were to deduct from the money any excess

of value of one church over the other.   (X. Hen. St. at
Large, p. 209.)

44.   In October, 1784, an act was passed entitled,
" An act to amend the act for clearing Mattapony
River."   By this act it was provided, " That as soon as
the trustees under the said former acts shall have removed all obstructions to the navigation thereof in the
manner therein directed, so that a boat carrying eight
hogsheads of tobacco can freely and safely pass as high
as Burk's bridge, from thenceforth the proprietors of
the land on both sides of the said river below the said
bridge, having notice thereof, shall be obliged to take
up, remove and destroy all artificial obstructions which
may be placed therein contiguous to or opposite his or
her land, under the penalty of forfeiting and paying
the sum of five pounds for every twelve hours the same
shall be or remain therein."   By the same act the trustees were authorized to open the navigation of the river
above Burk's bridge, under certain conditions.   (XI.
Hen. St. at Large, p. 530.)

45.   In October, 1785, an act was passed, entitled,
" An act to repeal the act of Assembly for establishing
the Town of Walkerton."   This act is in the following
language:

" BE it enacted by the General Assembly, That the
act of Assembly for establishing the town of Walkerton,
in the County of King and Queen, shall be, and the same
is hereby repealed.   That forty acres of land, which
were by deed bearing date the thirteenth day of June,
one thousand seven hundred and nine, given and granted
by John Walker, deceased, for the use of the inhabitants
of the said town, as a common, shall be, and the same
are hereby revested in the legal representatives of the
said John Walker in fee: Provided always, That nothing herein contained shall be construed to affect the right
of any person to a lot or part of a lot in the said place,
or to discontinue the public road to, or ferry across,
Mattapony River from the said town."   (Although
diligent search has been made I have been unable to find
the act establishing the town of Walkerton, referred to
in the above act.   (XII. Hen. St. at Large, p. 207.)

46. An act was passed October, 1788, entitled, " An act for opening and improving the navigation of Mattapony River," By this act Edmund Pendleton, William Nelson, John Baylor, Edmund Pendleton, Jr., John Hoomes, John Page, Mungo Roy, John Taylor, Francis Corbin, Benjamin Temple, Larkin Smith, Anderson Scott, Anthony New, and Lawrence Battaile were appointed trustees " for clearing, improving, and extending the navigation of the said river, from Todd's bridge, in the counties of King William and King and Queen, as far up the same as they may judge it practicable, so as to have a sufficient depth and width of water to navigate boats, batteaus, or canoes, capable of carrying four hogsheads of tobacco," and they were authorized to take and receive subscriptions for that purpose. They were authorized also to demand and receive, " for all commodities transported up or down the same, tolls not exceeding those imposed by the act entitled, ' An act for opening and extending the navigation of Potowmack River.' " The trustees were declared to be incorporated by the name and title of the Mattapony Trustees, and might sue and be sued as such. (XII. Hen. St. at Large, pp. 698-701.)

47. There was an act passed in October, 1791, entitled, " An act to amend the act for opening and improving the navigation of Mattapony River," whereby the board of trustees was reduced to eleven, who were named, as follows: " Edmund Pendleton, Francis Corbin, John Baylor, Edmund Pendleton, junior, John Hoomes, Mungo Roy, John Taylor, Nathaniel Burwell, Joseph Hilliard, junior, James Pendleton, and Thomas Martin," any five of whom could act. (XIII. Hen. St. at Large, pp. 286-287.)

CHAPTER VI

CHURCH HOUSES AND OLD HOMES

The fathers of the Colony had high ideals regarding their homes, and notably their church homes for the worship of God. Think of Greenway Court, Westover, Shirley, Brandon, and many others on the James. Settlers in King and Queen brought this high standard with them and lived up to it when their means allowed.

It will be borne in mind that the Colony was started under English auspices. It came naturally from this, forasmuch as the parent state and the church, which was the Church of England, were indissolubly joined in one, that the worship and forms of that church were paramount and that it stood without a rival in the Colony.

Citizens were taxed without discrimination, for the support of the one church, and the poor fellow who came short in paying was heavily fined. By and by, when Presbyterians, Quakers, Methodists, and Baptists began to show their faces and to assert what they regarded as their God-given rights, in the public proclamation of their doctrines, they were repressed with an iron heel. And so the Church of England had its own way in the Colony, and used in large part governmental aid in the support of its ministers, and in the erection of church houses. These last were built, truly, with a wise forecast looking to the future. Beginning at a point near the coast, there appears to have been a cordon of church houses erected about ten miles apart, houses of massive brick walls, not infrequently in the shape of a cross, with family pews raised to the height of four or five feet, a splendid pulpit at one angle, overlooking the entire floor, and a reading desk below, while the Creed, Lord's Prayer, and Ten Commandments were engraved in gilt letters on the wall at the east end.

Time, natural decay, and neglect have destroyed many

of these splendid edifices, but a few of them have been preserved, notably Christ Church and Abingdon, in Gloucester; and Mattapony, four miles above the Courthouse in King and Queen, the latter having been taken up and restored by the Baptists in after years. Some account of the last named, presenting it as it stood a hundred years ago, and as the writer saw it in his childhood, may be of interest. The walls were nearly three feet thick from the foundation to a point about three feet above the ground. It was constructed of bricks, most of them apparently moulded at the place. The walls, reduced somewhat in thickness as they ascended, rose to about twenty feet, where the roof was set on, a roof composed of timbers so massive as to excite wonder in the minds of beholders. The longer end of the cross in which the house was builded looked toward the west, and there apparently was the principal entrance, though there were doors also in the walls, looking to the north and south. The eastern walls were without any opening from the ground up. The floor was almost on a level with the ground. The walls and the roof were plastered in lime, the wainscoting reaching some four feet above the floor, and the walls rising thence to the curve in which they joined the roof. The plastering has long since decayed, and within the roof has been replaced by pine painted in oil; but the great walls seem built as for eternity. Here the Lumpkins, the Braxtons, the Corbins, the Harwoods, and many other honorable families worshiped—all of them now sleeping their last sleep.

The writer well remembers the high family pews,—with seats running round them on three sides, for patriarch, wife and children, and the stout door to shut them in,—the splendid pulpit, ascended by means of a balustrade and steps, the great sounding-board overhead, and the chancel, too, ornamented in gilt and gold, with table of the Law and Creed; and a reading desk on the floor under the pulpit. The scene which caught one's eye on entering the house impressed the mind of childhood with solemn awe and reverence, and could never be forgotten. Some of the aisles were paved with marble slabs. This house, we think we can say with confidence, was built as early as 1690. A marble slab, just outside the north door, covers the remains of Colonel Jacob Lumpkin, with this inscription:

JACOB LUMPKIN.

Obit 14 *die September,* 1708, *Ætatis* 64.
Dux Militum, Victor Hostium,
Morte Victus, Pax Adsit, Vives Requies,
Eterna Sepultis.

Near the south door, are two memorials of George and Mary Braxton, of Newington, parents of Carter Braxton, who signed the Declaration of Independence; while without in the capacious grounds lie the remains of a host of unknown dead. Monuments also are erected here to many who have died in later years, and the graves are often surmounted by structures more or less elegant.

It seems impossible for one to visit this spot without being reminded of verses from Gray's Elegy:

> " Beneath those rugged elms, that yew tree's shade,
>   Where heaves the turf in many a mouldering heap,
>   Each in his narrow cell forever laid,
>   The rude forefathers of the hamlet sleep."

> " Perhaps in this neglected spot is laid
>   Some heart once pregnant with celestial fire;
>   Hands that the rod of empire might have swayed,
>   Or waked to ecstasy the living lyre."

> " Some village Hampden, that with dauntless breast
>   The little tyrant of his fields withstood;
>   Some mute, inglorious Milton here may rest;
>   Some Cromwell, guiltless of his country's blood."

As was suggested above, this house is now held by the Baptists as a place of worship. The question is natural, How has this come about? It should be remembered that during the Revolution of 1776 the established Church of England, along with kingly authority, went down under the leadership of Jefferson and Madison. It followed from this that church houses of the Establishment were dishabilitated.

This house was for many years unoccupied and neglected. Tradition said that birds of the air built their nests, and beasts of the field had resort within its consecrated walls.

In the year 1803, Major Thomas Jeffries, Captain Robert Courtney, who afterwards served in the War of 1812, and other citizens, being at the time identified with no church, but feeling the need of the stated worship of God, came hither, and at some expense to themselves, cleansed the house, and invited the people to meet together in it, and worship the Lord God of Hosts. Rev. William Todd, then a young man of the Baptist faith, and deputy clerk, under his chief, Robert Pollard, Sr., was invited to lead in the worship. He was then a member of Bruington Church. By and by he was regularly ordained by a Presbytery of his brethren, and was privileged to baptize a few into the fellowship of this faith. Among these were Colonel John Pollard, Mrs. Mary Hall, and others.

From adjacent churches also, accessions were made, among the rest, Captain Courtney, John Redd, Captain Hall, Miss Priscilla Pollard, and some others.

In 1828, Colonel Pollard, with the encouragement and aid of other citizens, secured from the Governor of the State a warrant authorizing the Baptists to use and occupy the house with adjacent grounds, and a deed was given them to that effect. It should be remembered that glebe, and other property in the Commonwealth belonging to the Church of England, had long since been confiscated by formal act of the Legislature of Virginia.

The old so-called "Apple Tree Church," where doubtless the Robertsons, the Wilsons, and many about Dunkirk and Ayletts, attended worship, stood on the river road, some four miles above Walkerton, and on lands now held by John N. Ryland, Sr., Esq. It has long since become a mouldering ruin, and nothing remains but a few scattering bricks to tell of its ancient glory.   The so-called " Old Church " still stands some two miles below Little Plymouth, and is used by the Methodists.

There was also a church house of the Establishment on the land of Lieutenant Robert Roy, some miles still lower down, which has also gone into decay.   There were three parishes, each covering a part of King and Queen, Stratton Major below, and Drysdale above, St. Stephens intervening.

In more modern times, it is scarcely necessary to add, church houses creditable to the citizens, have been erected throughout the length of the county, by the Methodists, Shackelford's, (below Centreville), Providence (northward from Stevensville), Shepherd's, and Walkerton; by the Baptists, Poroporone, Olivet, lower King and Queen, Exol, Bruington, St. Stephens, and upper King and Queen; and Smyrna, by the Disciples. The Protestant Episcopalians have erected a neat chapel at King and Queen Courthouse, with ample grounds about it.   These houses are statedly filled with large congregations of devout worshipers.   As a rule, a devout religious sentiment, coupled with the spirit of worshipfulness, is a characteristic mark of the people, and has been for many years.

LOWER ST. STEPHEN'S PARISH CHURCH—NOW MATTAPONY

By Rev. John Moncure, D. D.

There is a section of Virginia where the Church once flourished; where, in Colonial days, our people from the motherland came to make their new homes, bringing with them the religious teachings handed down through the ages by their forefathers, and building houses of worship in the land of their adoption.   Time has wrought many changes, and among them the elimination alike of name and memory of many of these houses.

In the northern part of the county of Middlesex and throughout the counties of King William and King and Queen there is not one Colonial church where the services of the Book of Common Prayer are read to-day.

Yet time was when it was the book of worship of the country. In this section there are no less than six, and probably more, Colonial churches which are now occupied by other religious bodies, they having been abandoned by their original occupants more than a hundred years ago.

Among these venerable buildings is the Old Brick or Lower Church of St. Stephen's Parish, King and Queen County. It stands in the southern section of the county, near the King William line, about three miles from the Mattapony River, in a body of woods in which are many of the fine old trees that, like the church, have been identified with the lives of those who worshiped in the latter and now sleep their dreamless slumber under their branches and its walls. Could the whisperings of the winds through the branches of these giants of the forest be translated into words and become the story of long-gone days, many indeed would be the interesting lives which would be brought to light.

The building is of brick; whether brought from England in accordance with the prevalent tradition or not, is not known. For solidity of construction and architectural beauty it has not its superior, and probably not its equal, among the churches of Old Virginia. The walls are three feet in thickness. The brickwork is as nearly perfect as is known in the mason's art, the mortar being of adamantine hardness and looking as fresh as if it had been spread but a few months, showing the marks of the trowel with peculiar clearness. The bricks are alternately glazed and plain, this arrangement contributing greatly to the quaintness and beauty. The joists and the great timbers under the roof are of oak and poplar, some being so large that one's arms can scarcely more than span them. They are as firm and sound throughout as when first put in place: this after a duration of two hundred years.

The church is cruciform, of lofty proportions, and was built to seat about seven hundred people. Originally the aisles were laid with flagstones, but these have long since been removed. The ceilings are vaulted, in designs that are churchly and very attractive.

At the north angle of the cross once stood the old "three-decker" pulpit with the great sounding-board, without which no Colonial church was complete. These two have passed away. In the east end of the cross was the chancel, with its reredos, on which in gilt letters are painted the Lord's Prayer, the Apostles' Creed, and the Ten Commandments, with the name of God in Hebrew above them. It is Gothic in form, being surrounded and adorned at the apex and corners by representations of lighted tapers. The coloring is still rich and beautiful, and a retouch would make this reredos one of the most beautiful of its kind in Virginia.

The churchyard is not less interesting than the church itself. Here are the tombs of some, and the unidentified graves of very many, who were doubtless of the leading people of the State. At the southeastern corner of the church are the graves of George Braxton, Esq., and his wife, the parents of Carter Braxton, a signer of the Declaration of Independence. Over each is a marble slab, in which the inscriptions are scarcely decipherable, but with some difficulty one may read that of Mr. Braxton, as follows: "Here lies the body of George Braxton, Esq., who departed this life the first day of July, 1718, in the -1st year of his age, leaving issue a son and two daughters. He died much lamented; a good Christian, tender parent, kind master, a friendly, charitable neighbor."

Before the door leading into the north transept is a marble slab. One must almost step on it in entering the church. The inscription, thanks to interested friends of Virginia antiquities, has been rechiseled. It reads as follows: "Jacob Lumpkin, Obit 14 die September, 1708. Ætatis 64. Dux Militum, Victor Hostium, Morte Victus. Pax adsit, vives requies, Eterna Sepultis."

So many are the unmarked and entirely defaced graves that, to avoid digging into them, those who use the churchyard now must bury their dead quite a distance from the building.

There is very little to learn from the church in reference to its history,—only a fragment here and there.

LOWER CHURCH OF ST. STEVEN'S PARISH, NOW MATTAPONY CHURCH
Burial place of father and mother of Carter Braxton and tomb of Captain Jacob Lumpkin, obit, 1708.

On a brick over the southern or front door is the name
" David Minitree," and on another brick the letters
" W. L." The name, Thomas Hogg, is over one of the
windows. As to who these were, there is, as with the
sleepers in the churchyard, the great silence.

The Bible of the old church has been rescued from
the ravages of the past. It gives its testimony as to the
name and antiquity of the church, which might otherwise not be known. It is a well-preserved book, bound
in undressed calf. On the back is the name " Brick
Church." On a fly-leaf, in a very legible hand, the ink
being remarkably well preserved, are the words: " The
Lower Church of St. Stephen's Parish, in King and
Queen. Anno 1733, June."

The font is also among the articles preserved. It is
of attractive design, the bowl large enough to contain
about ten gallons of water. It was, many years ago,
presented to the Old Fork Church, in Hanover, where
it now is in use.

Little is known positively of the rectors and people
who worshiped in the old church. Bishop Meade mentions the parish and some interesting facts concerning
it, but his statements are based upon merely fragmentary
testimony. Among other things he says: " This parish was probably established in 1691, there being no
account certain of it." In a footnote he states that in
1724 the Rev. John Goodwin was minister. The parish
was thirty miles long, and had three hundred families
and sixty communicants. The first minister of whom
there is record was the Rev. John Skaife, who was in
charge in 1711. He is mentioned in Dr. Dashiel's
work on the " Councils in Virginia." Others were the
Revs. H. Dunbar, 1753, and Thomas Andrews, 1793.
There is a part of the county, called Dunbar, which can
trace its name to the clergyman. A remarkably fine
apple has been produced on this place, and is called the
" Dunbar." His name lives in a good fruit, typical, let
it be hoped, of a life fruitful in good works.

The names of Anderson Scott and Henry Young appear as lay delegates in 1785, and those of Thomas Hill
and William Fleet in 1796. The building was not used

much after the Revolution, and finally was entirely deserted, and remained so for fifty years. In 1824 the Baptists began using it, occupying it for twelve years before, by a grant from the Governor of Virginia, they became its owners. They have been in possession ever since, and some of the most aggressive and useful works of that denomination in Virginia have emanated from those who worshiped in the old church.

Many Baptist ministers in this and foreign lands have received their religious training here. The first minister of the body here was the Rev. William Todd, a man of great usefulness and consecration. His influence was so great that in the old Bible is written "Todd's Meeting House," as the name of the church when he was minister. It is now known as the Old Mattapony Church. One of the most useful laymen under Mr. Todd was Mr. Pollard, who, with his wife, was among the first members and most earnest worshipers. It was through his interest that his people became owners of the building after its abandonment, and it is through the kindness and courtesy of a descendant of his, Mr. Robert Pollard, who lives near by, and who is a deacon of the church, that much of the foregoing account has been obtained.

The interior of the church has been remodeled, the old floor being covered by one of plank raised two feet above the original foundation. The chancel is partitioned off, but behind it is the old reredos. In excavating beneath the chancel to arrange a baptistry, in 1855, human remains were found, supposedly those of the first rector. These were reverently reinterred beneath the church.

MATTAPONY CHURCH RECORDS

1842 Jan. 8th.—The term of Bro. Evans, who occupied our pulpit every 4th Sunday, having expired, Bro. R. H. Bagby, who had been licensed to preach, was called to supply his place and the call accepted.

1842 July 9th.—Bro. R. H. Bagby regularly ordained to the ministery.

Bro. Collins, of Pittsburg, Penn., a noted revivalist, being providentially with us, at his instance a protracted meeting was commenced. Preaching and prayer was held at the church during the day and from house to house at night. The religious feeling produced by the preaching of Bro. Collins and others was so great that nearly every family was brought under its influence, not only in this community, but throughout the whole surrounding country, and the interest continued to extend, until it became the greatest revival of religion ever known in this section of the country. Hundreds were added to the churches; to this church alone, on the 17th of July, 1842, were baptized 45 white and 37 colored, and on August 14th, 28 white and 25 colored,—total 135. The interest continued and many more were brought into the church.

1842 Dec. 10th.—Bro. R. H. Bagby dismissed to join Bruington Church, being called to the pastorate of that church. It seems that he continued to preach at Mattapony till Aug., 1843.

When Mr. John Bagby died he had over 50 grandchildren, many great-grandchildren, and one great-great-grandchild. This would be interesting to many.

By B. H. W.

I propose to write some account of the people, old colonial seats, and incidents connected with the people of long ago, on and near the Mattapony River.

" THE MOUNT "

If my information is correct, the home of the Todd family near Dunkirk, called " The Mount," is the oldest colonial residence on the upper waters of the Mattapony.

When the Todds first came to this country they settled in Gloucester County, at Toddsbury. One of the family accompanied Gov. Spottswood on his expedition over the Blue Ridge Mountains, and was one of the Knights of the Horse Shoe. One branch of the family moved to King and Queen and made a home near Dunkirk, which place at first was called Todds. There they acquired large possessions in lands and built on a very commanding bluff overlooking the Mattapony flats and river. The original owner was William Todd, who married a Miss Waring and died leaving a large family. The oldest son, also called William, inherited, under the law of primogeniture, all the landed estate, and Mrs. Todd was left comparatively poor with a number of sons. Being a woman of energy and judgment, she opened a hotel at Dunkirk, and, being successful, was enabled to educate her children, sending one son to Edinburgh, Scotland, to be educated as a physician.

There is a tradition that this place, now known as the "Mount," was the residence of Henry Edmond Washington (see Thackeray's "The Virginians"), and called by him "Fanny's Mount," after his wife, who was Fanny Mountain.

William Todd, 2d, left two daughters, one of whom married Samuel G. Fauntleroy, Sr., and the other Mr. Macon of Hanover. Mr. Fauntleroy was the last man in the county to use the coach and four. He continued to take his family to Bruington Church in his coach and four long after other families had discontinued the custom.

So this large landed estate passed from the Todds to the Fauntleroys, and some of it is still held by them.

"MONTVILLE"

On the King William side of the river is the village of Ayletts, founded by the family of that name. Philip Aylett did not build "Montville" on the river, but on the hills near the village of Ayletts. (It was not a colonial residence.) He married a daughter of Patrick Henry. His son, General William Aylett, inherited the old home, and after him, his son, Colonel W. R. Aylett.

On the hills overlooking Ayletts lived Robert (called Robin) Pollard, who for many years was clerk of King William. He was noted as a fox hunter, and for many years chased Reynard successfully. He wore on his hunting suit large silver buttons, which were objects of admiration to me in my early childhood.

" CHATHAM HILL."

Just below Ayletts on the King and Queen side was the residence of Joseph Temple, called " Chatham Hill," after the residence of Sir William Temple of England. His estate was a small one, but he raised a large family of children. Across on the King William side lived his brother, William Temple, in a large, commodious house, without children.

" PRESKILE "

Near by on the King William side is Preskile (or Presquile). I am unable to learn much of this old country seat. (Since writing the above I have become satisfied that Preskile was the residence of William Temple, brother of Joseph Temple of " Chatham Hill.") Early in the nineteenth century it was owned by Dr. Barrett, but I do not know that his family built the original home.

" NORTH BANK "

Opposite to this place is " North Bank," another old colonial building. The early history of this place is not known to me. Some seventy-five or one hundred years ago it was owned by Mr. Benjamin Pollard, brother of Robin Pollard of King William. He lost his wife in early life, and always after lived a widower with one daughter. He kept open house, and the sporting gentlemen of the surrounding country frequently resorted there for hunting, card-playing, etc. Among those who would come there for the good dinners and liquors was a man named Gatewood, who, though a member of the church, was fond of his dram. His conscience was not altogether easy on the subject, and he was accustomed to say, when taking his liquor, " What little I drink don't hurt me." Among others who frequented Mr. Pollard's house was Tom Redd, a wit and boon companion, who was too fond of his cups, but, taking the cue from Mr. Gatewood, would say, " What little I drink don't hurt me." He would repeat that in Mr. Gatewood's presence until it had become very obnoxious to him, and he had come to dislike Tom Redd very much. Upon one occasion, when a party of gentlemen were at Mr. Pollard's, Mr. Gatewood rode up. Mr. Pollard invited him in. He inquired if Mr. Redd was there, and the gentleman, in fun, assured him that he was not, while in fact he was, but had hid himself in a closet near the sideboard on which the liquors were placed. Being satisfied that Tom Redd was not there, Mr. Gatewood came in, and as he raised his glass to his mouth, Tom Redd poked his head out and said, " What little I drink don't hurt me." Mr. Gatewood instantly put down his glass without drinking his toddy, and mounted his horse and rode away.

" BEUDLEY " (THE RESIDENCE OF THE LATE BISHOP LATANE)

Near by on the King and Queen side is Beudley, built, I suppose, by Captain Mariott, a Scotch gentleman. He used to say that the place was called Beudley in " grandeur." He married the widow of John Walker, who was born a Baylor and left by her first husband three children, Baylor, Susannah, and Elizabeth. By her second marriage there were no children, and as her children were all in affluent circumstances, she left a part of her landed estate, called Smithfield, consisting of a thousand acres, to St. Stephen's parish, the income from it to be applied to the education of the poor children in that parish. Since the Civil War this land has been diverted from its original purpose and sold to individual parties.

Across the river lived the Roanes, an old and influential family, but they, as far as I know, had no colonial seat.

John Roane, Sr., represented his district in Congress for many years, and was succeeded by his son, John

Roane, Jr. The life of the latter was a very dissolute one, and, being exposed unrelentingly by John Gwathmey, was the cause of his defeat. I do not now remember the gentleman who succeeded him. His brother, Newman Roane, married the daughter of William Gregory. When they were standing before the parson he was asked for the license. He put his hand in his vest pocket and then said, "Total neglect." Though there was no license, the fathers of the bride and groom consenting, the ceremony was performed. The marriage was an unhappy one, and was dissolved by the legislature (the courts not having jurisdiction over divorce at that time) on the ground of cruelty. One son resulted from that marriage, Colonel Junius B. Roane. Another portion of the family lived at Goshen in King and Queen. Judge Spencer Roane, at one time one of the judges of the Supreme Court of Virginia, was a member of that branch of the family.

" CANTERBURY "

Situated near Beudley is Canterbury, the home of the Gwathmeys. That family has held it in possession for perhaps one hundred and fifty years, and still owns the old home, though much of the original farm has passed into other hands. Early in the history of the place it was owned by Owen Gwathmey. Between him and William Temple, who lived at Rose Mount, there was a bitter feud, and one night, as William Temple sat by his open window, he was severely wounded in his head and shoulder from a shotgun held by a negro. The negro was arrested and confessed that he was instigated to commit the crime by Mr. Gwathmey. At that day the testimony of a slave could not be taken against a white man, nor could a slave be hung, and so he was transported.

" WHITE HALL "

The next colonial house is White Hall, the seat of the Garlick family. It passed out of their hands some seventy-five or one hundred years ago. When I first knew the place it was owned by Mr. James Govan,

called at that time in some unaccountable way, " Giv-
ings." Mr. Govan married a daughter of Samuel G.
Fauntleroy, and was a man of considerable fortune and
very aristocratic in his feelings. His wife went to church
in her two-horse carriage, his children in a barouche,
and he in his sulky with fine horse and trappings. I
remember that my interest and admiration was excited
by his silver saddle stirrups. This fine old place is now
in the hands of foreigners, who have no regard for its
history and the honored dead who lie in its cemetery.

" LOCUST GROVE " (FORMERLY " RYE FIELD ")

After this old seat comes " Rye Field," now called
Locust Grove, the seat of the Walker family.

Late in the seventeenth century, Colonel Thomas
Walker, the third of that name, obtained from King
James II. of England a grant of land fronting for ten
miles on the Mattapony. Soon after settling there they
founded Walkerton, built a large stone house and gran-
ary, a large flour mill, cooper shops, cotton gin and com-
press, etc. Colonel Walker built his home on the second rise from the river, as in that early day there was
great danger of a surprise by the Indians to those living
immediately on the bank of the river. As there was
constant danger of an uprising of the Indians, he built
a fort or blockhouse near his residence for protection,
not only for his own family, but also for the neighbors,
who would flee to it when danger threatened. This
house was burned and then rebuilt on the banks of the
river a half-mile below the village of Walkerton.

While Colonel Walker was a member of the House
of Burgesses, his daughter, Mary Peachy, was married
to Dr. Gilmer of Williamsburg. He gave her a dowry
of £5000 sterling, and they moved to Albemarle county.
Her marriage was celebrated in St. Clemen's Church of
St. Stephen's parish. This church was allowed to go to
decay, and now even the brickbats have been carted
away. In some unaccountable way this church afterwards became known as " Apple Tree Church."

Colonel Walker left three children, Mary Peachy,

John, and Dr. Thomas Walker. The latter also moved
to Albemarle, and married, first, Mildred, widow of
——— Meriwether, and after her death, Elizabeth
Thornton, first cousin to his first wife and sister of Mil-
dred Thornton, who was the second of the five wives of
Colonel Samuel Washington, brother of General George
Washington. The family seat, Locust Grove, has up
to the present time remained in the Walker family.

Near Locust Grove was the home of the Tunstall
family. The original building has long since gone to
decay. The usual style of the colonial buildings of that
period was a square house with a large hall running
through, two stories high, and with four chimneys. But
the Tunstall house was in the shape of the letter U
with the ends next the river, and a court between the
wings. This place was sold by the Tunstalls to Robert
Temple, son of Joseph Temple of Chatham Hill.

The Tunstalls were prominent in the county and connected with the Brookes of Mantapike, Baylors, Walkers, etc. Some of the family were clerks of the county
for many years. The Mr. Tunstall who was the last
of the family to be clerk of the county, moved across
the county on the Dragon Swamp, and built him a home.
He died about 1790, and his family moved to Norfolk,
where his descendants still reside and have kept the
good family name untarnished. Mr. R. Brooke Tunstall, a prominent lawyer of Norfolk, some years ago
came up to King and Queen and visited the old Tunstall home on the Mattapony and the home of his grandfather on the Dragon. While there he met some negroes who told him that they worked the farm, but did
not remain there at night, and when he asked them why
they did not live there, replied that they were afraid
to do so because many years ago some old Tunstalls
lived there, and they were a frolicsome people, and still
came there at night and danced in the parlor. It is a
tradition that Mr. Tunstall was fond of the gayeties and
dissipations that prevailed at that day, and in building
his home made his parlor unusually large, so that there
would be room enough for persons to sit around, while
the dancers occupied the center of the room, and enjoy

watching the cotillon and the old Virginia reel. That was before the day of the round and hugging dances.

" ENDFIELD "

I failed to mention the large farm, Endfield, opposite Walkerton, owned in the early history of the county by the Berkeley family. The family never lived there, but it was kept for a " quarter," as such places were then designated. Some eighty or one hundred years ago a widow Berkeley married a Mr. Cooke, an Episcopal parson. An anecdote is current in regard to him, that he was a poor man, and even the horse which he rode was a borrowed one, and during the marriage ceremony, when he had to repeat the words, " And with all my worldly goods I thee endow," some one in the company said, " There goes the parson's saddlebags."

This farm is still owned by Parson Cooke's descendants.

" HILLSBOROUGH "

Next to the Tunstalls came Hillsborough, built by Colonel Humphrey Hill. He was a man of large means and carried on a large mercantile business, buying his goods in England and sending back cargoes of tobacco. Up to some twenty years ago the old tobacco warehouse was still standing. The foundation of this warehouse was laid on large solid rocks, brought from England as ballast. This house was well and substantially built. It has a handsome black-walnut stairway. In this house, as well as other colonial houses, the chimneys in the basement have an arched fireplace, but there is no flue passing upward from the arch. No one has ever explained to me why such places should be left in the chimney. They certainly did not strengthen the chimney, and very few bricks were saved by leaving the opening.

There was an arrangement on this house which I never saw on any other. Under the second-story windows there were earthenware martin nests in the shape of flower pots fastened to the house by wooden pegs. When visiting there, my early morning naps were often disturbed by the chattering of the martins. This place was sold by Mr. Charles Hill, the grandson of Colonel Humphrey Hill, to William Temple, who made a present of it to his sister, Mrs. Betsey Henley, the wife of T. M. Henley; and a member of that family still owns it.

" RICKAHOC "

The next colonial residence is Rickahoc (pronounced Rick-a-hoc, with an accent on the " hoc "). The building was destroyed by fire some thirty years ago. It was the seat of the Smith family more than one hundred years ago. Francis Smith represented that district in Congress prior to the time that the Roanes did so. An old gentleman, Charles Chilton, told me when I was a boy, that when he was a boy he visited Rickahoc during Mr. Smith's life, and that it was then the most elegant country residence he ever saw. The grounds were well laid out and ornamented, and the approach to the river, though steep, was graded and well kept. The interior of the house was painted in imitation of the President's house in Washington. The Smith family left the county perhaps one hundred years ago, and the place has passed through many hands since.

The Rickahoc building was a one-storied building, with four rooms and a wide hall on the first floor. The roof was very steep, and the upper rooms were large and comfortable.

" MANTUA "

Next to Rickahoc was Mantua. I cannot learn the early history of this estate. Carter Braxton, the signer of the Declaration of Independence, owned it once, and his grandson, Carter M. Braxton, at a later date owned it and lived there, but before that it was owned by Charles Hill.

Attached to the Mantua estate is a large marsh. Mr. Hill conceived the idea that it could be diked and made arable. He threw up a heavy dike around it and planted corn on it. The ditching, diking, etc., cost him $5000. The man who was his manager told me that the corn crop was by far the heaviest that he ever saw, and Mr. Hill realized $5000 from the sale of the corn. Next year he attempted to raise another corn crop, but the ground had sunk a foot or more and the muskrats cut his dike in so many places, letting the water in, that the crop failed entirely. Then he tried rice, but did not succeed in that, and so the attempt to make it arable failed; but since the marsh has returned to its natural condition, it is one of the finest grounds for sora on the Mattapony. I have sometimes fancied that as so much shot has been used over it, it might ultimately be used as a lead mine.

" EGGLESTON "

Across the river from Mantua is Eggleston, the colonial home of the Chamberlain family. It passed out of their hands many years ago, and the many acres of open land are now mostly overgrown in scrub oak and briars. One of the Chamberlain family became a sailor and vessel-owner. He loaded three vessels with grain and started one evening in March down the river with all three vessels, but neither he nor his vessels were ever heard of again. What became of them has been an entire mystery.

Adjoining the farm Mantua was many years ago a large manufacturing mill, built in colonial times, from which large quantities of flour were shipped to the West Indies.

" HOCKLEY NECK "

Just below this mill is the large farm Hockley Neck, owned many years ago by Mr. William Gregory, who at the time lived across the river at Sandy Point. This farm was always kept as a " quarter " and managed by an overseer.

" SANDY POINT "

Across the river from Hockley Neck was Sandy Point, at one time the residence of William Gregory. The colonial house there was built in 1758 by George Braxton, the father of Carter Braxton, as a home for his son. It soon passed out of the latter's possession, and Mr. William Gregory purchased it in 1820 from Mr. William Burnett Brown. This house was burned in 1830 and rebuilt by Mr. Gregory. There is an old tradition that while the house was burning Mr. Gregory was very solicitous to get his barrel (?) of silver out of the burning building. For that, however, I do not vouch. This information, except that about the barrel of silver, was given me by my friend, Judge Roger Gregory. Another tradition in regard to Mr. William Gregory is that he liked to go to King William Court, which occurred on the fourth Monday in March, and brag that he had finished planting corn. I know the fact that it was done at a very early day at his farm, Hockley Neck.

" MANTAPIKE "

Adjoining Hockley Neck is Mantapike, the home of the Brooke family for many generations. Colonel Richard Brooke, the last of the name who lived there, was a man of distinction and wealth. The building, of the usual colonial style of that day, stood on the banks of the Mattapony. Some fifty years ago it was pulled down and the timbers used in the construction of a more modern house away from the river. At this place was a large fishery, at which as many as a thousand shad were sometimes caught in a day. In the early history of the country there was a ferry and a road leading to Williamsburg. On the opposite side of the river, even now, can be seen the evidence of a wide roadbed through a long stretch of marsh or lowlands. The tradition is that it was a " national " road leading to Williamsburg. Mantapike was at one time a place of some commercial importance, and a shipping point for tobacco, having a large tobacco warehouse.

" NEWINGTON "

Adjoining Mantapike was Newington, established very early in the history of the county by the Lumpkin family. Very little is known of the family history. At the Mattapony Church there is a marble slab over the remains of Jacob Lumpkin, with the date 1708. On the same estate there still exists the foundation of a large building. The foundation walls are very thick, but nothing is known of its history.

The place came into the possession of George Braxton early in the eighteenth century, and he commenced many improvements on it which he never completed. Becoming involved in debt, he sold it to John Roane, who raised a family of twelve children; being a man of large wealth, he left each of the twelve a considerable estate. Newington he devised to his son, John Roane, Jr., who was addicted to drink. He had married a Miss Frazier, a lovely girl, but socially beneath him. This fact preyed on his mind, and one day, in a drunken condition, he cut her throat and then the throat of his butler and attempted that of his underbutler, but the latter hid himself in a barrel and so saved his life. Mr. Roane was promptly arrested, tried, and condemned to death, but the night before the day on which he was to be hung some friend supplied him with laudanum, and he died from the effects of it.

Across the river from Newington was the colonial home of another family of Hills. Colonel John Hill was perhaps the last of the family that lived there. My father, Temple Walker, and his brother, Baylor Walker, married two of Colonel Hill's daughters. At that day much of the journeying to visit among the old families living on the river was done in rowboats. One spring, when my father was going from his home to Colonel Hill's, a large sturgeon jumped in his boat, and when he arrived he told Colonel Hill if he would send to the landing he could have sturgeon steak for breakfast. This splendid old mansion was dismantled and the timbers used to build a modern house at Frazier's Ferry for Mr. Phil. Gibson.

" MELROSE "

Melrose is the next place in King and Queen on which was situated a colonial building. I cannot ascertain the

early history of this place. It was occupied some
seventy-five years ago by the Rowe family, but I do not
know that they were the original owners. This place
was bought since the Civil War by Mr. Jacob Turner,
and he dismantled the house and sold enough bricks
from the walls to pay the purchase money for the place.

" HUNTINGDON "

Across the river in King William is Huntingdon, the
seat of the Southerland family. It came into the possession of the Gregory family by bequest of Mrs. Fendal Southerland to her granddaughter, who was the
granddaughter of William Gregory and wife of Mr.
Thomas W. S. Gregory. Huntingdon has for many
years been abandoned as a dwelling.

" PLEASANT HILL "

The next colonial residence in King and Queen is
Pleasant Hill, built and for many years occupied by the
Robinson family. It was burned since the Civil War.
Here lived Henry Robinson, for many years Speaker
of the House of Burgesses. Upon one occasion, when
Colonel George Washington was addressing the House,
giving in a modest and hesitating manner an account
of his military operations, Mr. Robinson from the chair
said to him, " Sit down, Colonel Washington; your
modesty equals your courage."

" CHELSEA "

Across the river from Pleasant Hill is Chelsea, the
colonial home of the Moores, a family of considerable
distinction in the early days of the colony. There lived
Bernard Moore, who married a daughter of Governor
Spottswood, and accompanied the latter in his transmontane expedition. Chelsea was a splendid old country seat. It is now in the hands of strangers, and, I
hear, marred by late additions. Up to the time of the
Civil War it remained in the family, being owned by
Mr. Benjamin Robinson, who married a Miss Moore.

" LANEVILLE "

The next of the colonial seats, as far as I am informed, is Laneville, the home for many generations of the Corbin family. I do not know at what time it was built, but it must have been very early in the history of the country. At the beginning of the Revolution it is stated that Governor Dunmore sent many of the archives of the colony over to Laneville, where they were deposited in a subterranean cellar connected with the building. I do not know this, but it is probable if it be a fact (as it is said to be) that the Corbin who was then the owner of Laneville was a royalist. I spent a night at this old place some sixty-five years ago. It was then still owned by James Park Corbin, but occupied by Mr. Benjamin Robins. I was impressed with the length of the building. The middle portion was of two stories, square built, with four large rooms and a spacious hall passing through it, and flanked by two wings in which were pantries, storerooms, servants' quarters, bedrooms, etc. A tradition is that Colonel Corbin had his reception and sleeping rooms in one end of the building, while Mrs. Corbin occupied the other end, and that when he paid her a visit he ordered his coach and four and drove in formal style the length of the house to her reception room. Whether the royalist partisanship of the Corbin family in the days of the Revolution was a fact or not, Colonel Richard Corbin was a true man at the time of the War of 1812 with England, and presented the county of King and Queen with two brass cannon, which, during the Civil War, were sent to Richmond for the Confederate government. The Corbin family possessed great wealth, as wealth was counted in that day, and it was a common saying years ago, when speaking of a rich man, to say, " He was as rich as Corbin." Colonel Richard Corbin owned considerable property at King and Queen Courthouse; he or his father built the old tavern there, which was quite an imposing building at the time. It, along with every other building, both public and private, was burned by the Yankees during the Civil War.

On the Laneville estate, near the public road, there was a church building which long ago went to decay, and the bricks and tiles which floored its aisles were carried away. Some of the tiles were used as floors in the basements of private houses. This church was the parish church of Stratton Major parish, the register of which is still in the Georgetown Episcopal School, and a copy in the Virginia Historical Society in Richmond.

Mr. James Park Corbin was the last of the name who owned Laneville. It then came into the possession of Colonel Robert Bland, and is still held by some of his descendants. The original house has long since disappeared. I do not know whether the building at Dudley's Ferry, opposite West Point, was a colonial residence, but think it was not.

West Point and the farm back of it deserve some notice. If tradition is true, the farm was owned by Captain West. It was originally a very large one, containing some two or three thousand acres, and extending from river to river; yet it had only one house.

Early in the nineteenth century there was a considerable town of West Point, but it gradually decayed owing to the unhealthfulness of the location. When the railroad was built to the point there was only one house standing, and that unoccupied and dilapidated. I saw it when the land now occupied by the town was in cultivation. It was then owned by Hon. William P. Taylor, who sold a part of his farm to the West Point Land Company, at the time that the railroad came to West Point. It is likely that he was mainly instrumental in building the West Point Colonial Church, which stands, though in a dilapidated condition, with but few alterations from its original construction. It ought by all means to be repaired and restored to its original state. It is a shame on the State to allow such splendid buildings to fall to decay and become the home of moles and bats.

REMINISCENCES

It is well for us to ask now and then what others think and say of us; and Burns's couplet is still in force:

"Oh, wad some power the giftie gie us,
To see oorsels, as ithers see us!"

The writer, not long since, came across a book by William Kyle Anderson, of Detroit, Mich., which relates to the Robertson, Taylor, and Anderson families, formerly of King and Queen.   In 1897, desirous of gaining information regarding these families, of one of which he was a member, he made a trip from Detroit to Virginia.   Beginning on page 27 of his book, we read as follows:

"Three years ago we made a journey to the Old Dominion with the intention of running down to King and Queen and of having a look at the old stamping grounds, and locating the very spot where our ancestors lived and died.   How best to reach there was a question, for means of locomotion are still in a primitive condition down that way, and very much as they were a century ago.   There is no railroad in the County.   The Mattapony River extends along the southern border, and occasional boats from Norfolk and the Chesapeake ascend it, but that was too roundabout to our Mecca.   The way we had to take was across country and the means of locomotion such as we might find.   By the aid of friends in Richmond, the way was mapped out.   Taking a train on the York River Railroad, we alighted at a station, or rather a siding, known as Sweet Hall, which we found absolutely devoid of humanity either white or black.   After some search, we found a pickaninny who for a slight subsidy went in search of a neighboring farmer, who owned a good buggy and team and consented to drive us to Frazier's Ferry on the Mattapony, a distance of some seven miles.   There we were ferried in a skiff across the river, and some two miles down stream to what is known as King and Queen Court-House landing.   A warehouse once stood there, but now there is only a dilapidated shanty and a broken-down dock.   No human being greeted our arrival.   It was a broiling hot day, and we looked in vain for any means of transportation to the Court-House, three-quarters of a mile.   [Would it have hurt him to walk?]

" Seeing the dilemma in which we were placed, the ferryman offered, for a small fee, to take our bag and guide our steps to the Court House, by a shady path and through piny woods.   In this primitive fashion we journeyed to our destination.

"We found the village to consist of the following buildings: Court House and Clerk's office—both substantial brick buildings of one story—a diminutive ten- or twenty-foot jail in which one lone prisoner languished, a general country store, and a farmhouse of moderate size, dignified as "the Hotel." No hospitable landlord greeted us as we crossed the threshold. It looked like Goldsmith's 'Deserted Village'. An ancient, rheumatic dog wagged us a welcome, and soon a colored woman, bearing a pitcher of fresh water, informed us that 'de white folks soon be here, and glad to take care of yo'.

"The aged county clerk, who had held the office more than fifty years, had gone fishing, but we invaded his office, impatient to have a look at the records. Greatly to our dismay we could find none earlier than 1864. In that year, a raid from Norfolk (Gloucester Point) made by the Union force, burned the old Court House and clerk's office with all the old records. It was a sore disappointment, for we had hoped to find deeds of the Rogers, Robertson and Semple families. Also wills, marriages, etc.

"Balked in our expectations thus far, we determined, nevertheless, to prosecute our journey, and get *some* information. We were not altogether disappointed.

"Rosemount, the old Semple home, was easily found. It was a beautiful and extensive farm on a high plateau one mile back from the Mattapony River, but overlooking it, and much of King William on the opposite shore. It is about three miles northwest of Walkerton Village, and is now owned and occupied by Mr. William Dew, a gentleman who welcomed us with true Virginia hospitality. He pointed out the spot where the Semples were buried, but if there were any stones to mark the graves, none now remain.

"The residence stood in part on the foundation of a storehouse, and an immense spreading oak overshadowed the house. An old man of 80 years pointed out the site of the old Robertson place on the Mattapony River, four miles above Dunkirk. Nothing is now left to recall the very ancient homes of the Rogerses in the immediate neighborhood. The old Park Church is a pile of ruins, but we visited St. David's and (Old Cat Tail?) beyond the river; it must look back many years." (Pp. 27-31.)

So writes William Kyle Anderson, Esq., himself a descendant of Mr. Robertson. This is an unvarnished statement, and it is true, as he saw it. Our people and their fathers before them were poor, being aloof from marts and markets; but they bred what is better than gold—intelligence, virtue, and contentment.

Copy of an old paper saved from fires, furnished by Col. S. F. Harwood, June, 1905:

"The land at King and Queen C.-H. granted to Richard Tunstall

1667 was bounded by Mattapony river to the south, east by Apastocock branch, and on the west by Quintanoco creek. Edmund Tunstall and wife conveyed one acre for the use of the county where the C. H. now stands. In 1707 the land was divided, Richard Wyatt, in right of his wife who was the widow of the said Edmund, took the land next the river. Mary, the oldest daughter, took the land on the creek; Catharine, who was Mrs. Matthews, took the middle part; Barbary took two acres adjoining the C. H. land, and the residence on Apastocock swamp. 1713 Barbary conveyed to R. D. Wyatt all her right except the two acres above. Thos. Fox and Mary his wife conveyed to John Wyatt 134 acres, her part except the dower. 1720 John Baylor bought two acres at C.-H., and 404 acres from R. D. Wyatt. 1722 John Wyatt sold to Thos. Courtney 134 acres, also 66 acres, one-third of the widow's dower. 1728 John Matthews conveyed to Thos. Harwood 200 acres. 1739 Thos. Harwood willed (?) to his son John. 1739 John Baylor sold to Christopher Harwood two acres bought of John Wyatt. 1744 Christopher Harwood devised to his son William the same."

Attached to this paper is a cut showing the lands adjoining the Courthouse.

Smithfield was one thousand acres of land given to the county by Mrs. Mariott. She was a Miss Baylor of King and Queen or Essex County, and first married John Walker, who left two sons, John and Baylor, and two daughters, Elizabeth and Susannah, one of whom married Semple of Rose Mount, and was the mother of Bishop Robert Baylor Semple; the other daughter married Fleet, the father of Captain William Fleet, who was the father of Dr. C. B., Colonel Alex., and James R. Fleet. After the death of her first husband, Mrs. Walker married Captain Mariott, a Scotchman, who lived at upper Beudley on the Mattapony River. They had no children. She donated one thousand acres of land to St. Stephen's parish, the income from said land to be applied to the education of the poor children in the said parish.

Governor Lumpkin of Georgia was originally from King and Queen.

Also Hon. Alex H. Stephens was originally from King and Queen, and Stevensville was named for his family.

Colonel Robert M. Spencer, who lived at Clifton, was a prominent and highly esteemed man. Captain Robert H. Spencer, one of the best of men, served in the Confederate army. Alexander Dudley, a talented lawyer, was the founder of the Richmond and Y. R. R. R., and its president when he died.

There were many other worthy and valuable old citizens in the neighborhood—among them J. W. Courtney, Samuel Tunstall, Dr. and Thomas W. Garrett, Joel E. Bray, W. B. Bird, Samuel F. Harwood.

The Old Church, a half-mile below Plymouth, was built in colonial times. This house is about nine miles below the Courthouse.

Speaker Robinson built a magnificent home at Pleasant Hill, near Little Plymouth. Tradition tells us that as one approached from the highway, a noble colonnade with pilasters aloft, greeted him; and as he entered the colonnade, a tesselated floor, and doors and windows wrought in splendid mahogany delighted his taste and excited his wonder.

Richard Corbin, Esq., at one time Treasurer of the Colony, erected a commodious house, 150 feet in length, some miles above Pleasant Hill, at Laneville. They tell us that his wine cellar was kept filled with choice Madeira, and there seems reason to believe that a subway led out to the sloping bank near the river. This was his home in 1775, when Patrick Henry compelled a return of the value of powder removed by Governor Dunmore from the magazine in Williamsburg. Fine dwellings graced the river bank at Clifton, Melrose, Mantua, Newington, and various other places.

The following is from dictation by Captain R. H. Spencer: " Miss Polly Robinson, a daughter of Speaker Robinson, owned and lived at Clifton. Colonel Boyd married her. Dr. James T. Boyd owned and lived at Gainesboro, while Colonel R. H. Spencer lived at Clifton, in after times.

" Pleasant Hill was about four miles below Clifton, one mile back from the river. In Speaker Robinson's day Pleasant Hill was a place of great splendor. I think Governor Spotswood married a Miss Moore, sister to Mrs. Robinson. The house was magnificent. Tall, huge columns to greet the coming guests, porch floors wrought in mosaic, doors and windows of imported mahogany. Chelsea, Melrose, and Rural Felicity were old homes of the Rowes. The last named was sold afterwards to Colonel Spencer. Boardly was the old home of James Govan and Richard Raines. By the waste of time and of its adjutants, natural decay and destructive fires, many of our old homes have disappeared, and only the sites remain to tell their story. Pleasant Hill, Clifton, Melrose, Boardly, Mantapike, Newington, Mantua, Rickahock, Bunker's Hill (the old Bagby home), Locust Cottage, Spring Farm, have all suffered from one or all of these causes, though in some cases new buildings have taken the place of the old, notably at Clifton, Mantua, Melrose, Newington, Rickahock, and Locust Cottage."

The following interesting letter was written by James Southgate, Esq.:

In looking over some old papers a few days ago I came across some notes that I made in 1900 when I went through King and Queen in a visit to eastern Virginia, and among them I find the following in regard to Newington, about which we were talking when I saw you in Richmond and about which you had been unable to get any information from Mr. Harwood who lives there. If it will be of any use to you in getting up your book on King and Queen you are welcome to it. I don't know how how I secured this information, but probably from Robt. Spencer.

I never was there but once, and when a boy I went home with one of the Harwood boys on Friday afternoon to spend Saturday and Sunday, and the inducement held out for my going was that the water was to be drawn off from a fish pond in the neighborhood and we could get a good lot of fish. We went and rode a mule and arrived too late to get any of the best fish and had to take catfish, and you know they have terrible fins. We put a good string of them on the pommel of the saddle and both of us got up on this mule but we found the fish were too near so we moved them over on the neck of the beast, and, as the fish were fluttering still, the said shoulders got the benefit of these terrible fins, which so irritated the animal that he relieved himself of the fish and also the boys that were on his back. But as we fell in deep sand there were no bones broken, and we got the fish home and had to cook them for a late dinner, and I remember it was the most delicious dinner I ever partook of, but I have always thought that the keenness of the appetite was the reason. Newington was the original seat of the Lumpkin family. It was then owned by George Braxton, the father of the Carter Braxton who signed the Declaration of Independence. He died in 1736. It passed from the Braxtons to the Roanes, a family which were aristocratic and proud of their English descent. A son, John, married a Miss Frazier, a beautiful woman (from whose family Frazier's ferry is now called), but beneath him in point of family connections and standing in society. He so grieved over the mistake he made, that in a fit of desperation he killed his wife and the house servant, who tried to save the wife from the brutal attack of the husband. He was tried, convicted of murder, and sentenced to be hung, but before the time arrived he committed suicide in prison by drinking laudanum. This fine estate, of nearly one thousand acres, was afterwards purchased by the Harwoods, about 1810 or 1820, and is still in the hands of this family.

SCHOOLS AND ACADEMIES

The people of King and Queen were among the first in the State to give attention to the very important matter of the mental culture of their children.

Thomas Jefferson, after retiring from the office of President of the United States, set the pace for our people by starting a great university at Charlottesville. The Presbyterians had previously founded Washington College, now known as Washington and Lee University. In 1834 Richmond College was inaugurated by the Baptists. Up to that time the schools of King and Queen were few and, in the main, of low grade. But the people of the county in general (some exceptions, of course) have always shown great interest in the literary training of their children. Many of the youths of both sexes have had collegiate education, some of the boys going to William and Mary, some to Columbian University at Washington, to Randolph-Macon, and to Richmond College; and the girls to Hollins, Staunton, Charlottesville, etc. These and other high-grade schools, as the University of Virginia, Johns Hopkins, etc., have rendered us good service. We know of one resident of the county—we use the incident simply as an illustration—who, having five sons and eight daughters, educated all his boys at Columbian University, and the girls at schools of corresponding grade. We do not mention the name—modesty forbids—but it must be recorded to his everlasting honor.

A number of private schools were kept in different sections of the county, whose teachers in several cases made high reputations.

In the year 1753, Donald Robertson, a Scotchman quite thoroughly equipped, came over and began to teach, first as a private tutor. By and by, having bought land on the Mattapony River ten miles above Dunkirk, he there opened an academy for young men, and soon secured a patronage honorable to himself, drawing students from all quarters. He taught literature, mathematics, rhetoric, Latin, and perhaps Greek. It is likely that no teacher of his day deserved better of Virginians than did Donald Robertson. He taught the youth, James Madison, who said, after a distinguished and beneficent career, " All that I have been in life I owe largely to that man." It seems probable, also, that he taught General George Rogers Clark, whose aunt he married; as also other noted men.

About the year 1839, a Scotchman of culture and wise forecast, Mr. Oliver White, came to us and established an academy at Fleetwood, some six miles above Bruington Church. Mr. White deserves the everlasting gratitude of our people, within and beyond the borders of the county. He erected a standard which is telling to-day upon a number of pupils who do him honor, while he sleeps in his quiet grave, some four miles from Bruington and the same distance from Fleetwood.

About the same year (1839), Mr. John Bagby and Colonel John Pollard started an academy at Stevensville, near the center of the county, for the teaching of English and the classics and mathematics, and Major James G. White was employed as headmaster, followed by Rev. R. H. Bagby, D. D., W. J. Berryman, and others. These schools were largely efficacious in the preparation of the youth of the county for college training and business life.

COL. J. C. COUNCILL,
Twenty-sixth Virginia Regiment, Army Northern Virginia.

At Bruington, Captain Thomas Haynes opened an academy, of which Judge J. H. C. Jones was principal. Mr. Jones was a Marylander by birth, and came to us first from Columbian College. He did a good work in the schoolroom, afterwards studying law under James Smith, Esq., and by and by coming to be one of our most valuable and noted citizens. His invaluable wife —a daughter of Mr. James Smith—survives him, being now (1904) venerable in age and in honors. Judge Jones will long live in the memory of his pupils and his fellow-citizens, whose courts he presided over with so much of grace and skill, holding the scales of justice always evenly balanced.

About 1850 a very successful school was conducted at Newtown by Mr. Lewis Kidd, and in 1857 by Spencer Coleman. It was closed at the breaking out of the Civil War.

About 1856, an academy was established at Centreville, conducted by Prof. Gogerty, who was afterwards slain by a brother of a pupil he had disciplined in the school. Rev. A. F. Scott succeeded him in years after the war, and rendered a service highly efficient.

The training of our girls, also, was not forgotten. Miss Fannie Hughes, who taught a school in Gloucester, was largely patronized by our citizens. About the year 1837, Miss Myra A. Muse taught a school at Plainview, near the Dragon, for the Gaines family. She afterwards married Mr. James Southgate, and resided at Locust Cottage near Stevensville. Here she opened a school, which secured a large patronage and was highly approved. Rev. Robert Stubbs taught a school for girls some twelve miles below the Courthouse. A female school was kept at Newtown by E. Payson Walton. Also a private school, one of "Old Field" type. There was also a school for girls at Buena Vista, some miles below Centreville.

LOCUST COTTAGE

A female seminary was established at this place, situated about one mile east of Stevensville, in the late thirties, say 1836 or 1837, by Mrs. Mira Ann Southgate, wife of James S. Southgate, who moved her school from Little Plymouth. They were married in Gloucester County in December, 1828, and when they came to Locust Cottage had three children, Mary Anna, James, and Llewellyn, the two former having been born at Edge Hill, near Upton, now called New Upton, in Gloucester County, about ten miles north of the Courthouse, and the latter at Little Plymouth, in King and Queen. After locating at Locust Cottage, Thomas Muse and Cordelia Hunter were born, making in all five children. Mrs. Southgate was educated at a high school for young ladies in Richmond, Virginia, where she graduated with the highest honors. She at once chose teaching for a support, and in this way aided in the education of her brothers and sisters, who were left in dependent circumstances by their father, Colonel Thomas Muse, who for many years was clerk of the court in the county of Middlesex. Of her children, two only are now living, viz. James and Thomas Muse. Mary Anna married Richard Inge Wynne of North Carolina in 1861, and died in the town of Louisburg, N. C., April 27th, 1867, leaving one daughter, who grew to womanhood, married, removed to Texas, and died. Her four children soon followed.

James Southgate married Delia Haywood Wynne, sister of Richard Inge Wynne of North Carolina, in 1858, and six children were born of this marriage. Two boys died in infancy; one daughter, Annie, died in Durham, N. C., aged twenty-five and unmarried. James Haywood Southgate, the oldest child, is living (1904) in Durham, N. C. He married Kate, daughter of Bartholomew Fuller of Fayetteville, N. C., and four children were born to them, two dying in infancy and a daughter at the age of thirteen of appendicitis; the one left being a son, Thomas Fuller, aged eleven years. Lessie, the third child of James and Delia, married Prof. Simmons of North Carolina, and with her husband, the president, is teaching at Shorter College in Rome, Georgia. There are no children by this marriage. Mattie, the youngest daughter, married Thomas

D. Jones, a native of Virginia, though he was a citizen of North Carolina when he married; he lived in Durham and died there in 1889. There were three boys by this marriage, viz. Decatur, Southgate, and Lile. The first died suddenly at the age of six years; the others are living, their ages in 1904 being eleven and thirteen years.

Llewellyn Southgate married Miss Elvina Courtney, who died of pulmonary consumption shortly after her marriage; her husband soon followed her to the grave, by consumption of the bowels. He died at Boardly, a farm on the Mattapony near Gainesborough, May 23d, 1871, aged thirty-six years. He was a great sufferer, but met death bravely and with hope of a blessed immortality. There were no children by this marriage.

Thomas Muse Southgate married Miss Mary Portlock of Norfolk, Virginia, and has lived in that city ever since. By this marriage there were born four boys and four girls. The oldest two (sons) died in childhood. Mira, the oldest daughter, is married to Hiram H. Grandin, and they live on Staten Island, the family consisting of father, mother, and three children, one son (the oldest) and two daughters. A son, Thomas S., lives in Norfolk, and is a prosperous merchant. He married Miss Nettie Norsworthy, and there have been born to them four children, two now (1904) living, a daughter and a son, aged five and two years respectively. The second daughter married recently Mr. H. H. Bradley of Stateburg, S. C.; they now reside in Savannah, Ga. The two younger daughters, Frances Baylor and Helen Hunter, are unmarried, while Hugh, the youngest child, is a youth of eighteen years, living with his parents in Norfolk.

Cordelia Hunter Southgate, the youngest, who was the pet of the household at Locust Cottage, grew to be a woman of great worth, was proficient in music, and chose that for a support. She never married, but devoted her life to the good of others, and especially to work for the church. She died at the home of her brother James, in North Carolina, November 18th, 1894; at her request her remains were taken to Norfolk and laid by the side of her father and mother, to both of whom she was devoted, and by whose bedside she watched when they died.

We have been thus explicit in giving a history of this estimable family, because they were so well known and loved by hundreds of girls who went to this excellent school during the years previous to 1852, when they removed to Norfolk, Virginia.

Locust Cottage wielded a powerful influence for good in eastern Virginia, and there are scores of families now living whose mothers have sat at the feet of Mrs. Southgate to learn lessons of wisdom which have served them a good purpose in their lives. She was a teacher who taught because she loved to teach, and her thorough instruction and firm, though mild, discipline, endeared her to her pupils and made a telling influence upon their characters and lives. James S. Southgate, or, as he was familiarly called by the girls, " Marse Jeems," exercised on this great school a moral influence which was beautiful and healthful. While his estimable wife stored the minds of her pupils with useful knowledge, he looked after the commissariat, and his table was known far and near as " par excellence " for a boarding school. His influence for good was felt in King and Queen all the years he lived among this people. His walk was that of the true Christian, a " living epistle known and read of all men." His great desire was to preach the Gospel, but the school took so much of his time and attention that he had to be content with the license to exhort. He was powerfully gifted in prayer and most effective as an exhorter. Old Providence, in King and Queen, was the scene of his abundant labors in his Master's cause, and doubtless many are now living in that vicinity who can testify to the great work he accomplished among that people as superintendent of their Sabbath school and general director in all things pertaining to their spiritual welfare.

In 1852 Locust Cottage was sold to John N. Gresham, who lived there for several years, until fire destroyed all the original buildings. A small two-story cottage is all that now stands by the beautiful grove which in the old days sheltered beneath its grateful shade so many girls who, in after years, looked back with pleasure at the joyous times spent there. Desolation supreme marks this once lovely seat of learning, and naught remains to tell of its former greatness and beauty. Time has wrought many changes in this neighborhood, one of the happiest and most refined in the county for the happy years of which we write. After removing to Norfolk, Mrs. Southgate's health failed, and she ceased to teach. She died peacefully and calmly near Norfolk, on August 20th, 1862, and her remains now lie buried in Norfolk, by the side of those of James S. Southgate; who died, as he had lived, with a heavenly smile upon his face, at the home of his son James, in Durham, N. C., September 19th, 1877, nearly seventy-three years of age. Though dead, these two yet speak in the lives of thousands who have come under their influence. " Blessed are the dead which die in the Lord from henceforth: Yea, saith the Spirit, that they may rest from their labours; and their works do follow them."

A seminary for young ladies was conducted by Mrs. M. L. Fleet at Green Mount near Dunkirk. It was well patronized and did excellent work. She was largely aided by her accomplished daughters, Misses Lou, Florence, and Bessie. Mrs. Fleet is lovingly remembered by her numerous pupils.

HIGH SCHOOL AT STEVENSVILLE

In October, 1907, a high school for higher students was opened at Stevensville. This was done largely by the enterprise and earnest interest of Robt. N. Pollard and A. C. Eubank, trustees, and a band of earnest women coöperating with them. It is considered to be a very great success.

CHAPTER VII

RELIGIOUS DENOMINATIONS

There are two native qualities which have characterized our people perhaps more than any others; one the conservative spirit, the other the religious. The established church of the mother country had the right of way here as elsewhere; but already before the Revolution Methodists and Baptists began to appear, and in some cases were fined and imprisoned, or bonded. In order to have a fair and authentic representation, I have engaged one gentleman from each of the denominations to represent his own people in the county. Dr. B. H. Walker writes for the Disciples of Christ, Rev. J. W. Shackford for the Methodist Episcopal Church, and Rev. G. W. Beale, D. D., for the Baptist. Presbyterians have been represented here only by a few scattered members; Congregationalism and Lutheranism never had a footing in the county. A small number of persons near Little Plymouth identify themselves as "Christadelphians," under their leader, Dr. John Thomas.

The influence of certain ministers of the Gospel has been and is pronounced in the lives of the people. We name a few of these, but they are not exceptional cases. Revs. Shackelford, "Parson Mitchel" Shackford, R. Y. Henley, R. B. Semple, Andrew Broaddus, Sr. and Jr., R. H. Bagby, Thomas B. Evans, William and William B. Todd. These men have left a profound impression upon their respective communities—indeed their influence for good is still recognized, both within the limits of the county and beyond its borders. Eternity alone will disclose the splendid work which these men of God have accomplished. They are not dead, but only sleep, " and their works do follow them."

THE BAPTISTS

By REV. G. W. BEALE, D. D.

The frail barks which were wont to bear over the ocean our forefathers to these Western shores were wafted by winds of which it might be said none knew whence they came or whither they went. Often, perhaps, currents of air having separate and remote origins, and moving for long distances along different lines, united, and filling the sails of the adventurous craft, impelled them the more swiftly and surely to their destination. In like manner the agencies which brought at first the faith as held by the Baptists into King and Queen County, may not in every case be distinctly traceable. Different instrumentalities, starting in separate and remote quarters and entering the county from different directions, combined, it is believed, in sowing here the seeds of this faith and reaping fruits of its first harvest.

William Mullen, a native of Middlesex, who had made a temporary home in that part of Amelia that is now Nottoway County,—where, under the preaching of "Father" Samuel Harress and Jeremiah Walker, he had become a convert to their beliefs and a preacher of the same,—on a visit in 1769 to his kindred on the lower Rappahannock, passed through King and Queen, where he tarried for some days with his relatives. Here, in conversation with his brother, John Mullen, and James Greenwood, his brother-in-law, he satisfied them of the Scriptural warrant for his belief in regeneration. They soon afterwards professed their faith in Christ, and were immersed in witness that they had died to sin and risen to newness of life in Him. Both of them became Baptist ministers, and began to hold meetings, warmly exhorting their hearers to repent, believe, and be baptized.

In 1771, John Waller of Spottsylvania, accompanied by John Burrus, visited the county and preached the doctrine of the "New Lights," as the Baptist ministers were then derisively called. Under a sermon on the "New Birth," Ivison Lewis, who soon afterwards also became a preacher, was converted, with numerous others. Waller's preaching was powerful in demonstration of the Spirit, and many flocked to hear him. On February 11, 1773, a church was constituted, containing seventeen members, and called Lower King and Queen Church. This was the earliest Baptist church formed in the county.

The coming of Waller and the success of his preaching, particularly in the adjoining county of Middlesex, became the signal for a violent outbreak of persecution, which led, during the years 1771, '72, and '73, to the imprisonment in jail of a number of ministers for proclaiming the Gospel without having a license from the General Court. These severities were practiced more in several contiguous counties than in King and Queen; but here, in August, 1772, James Greenwood and John Lovall, while conducting a meeting (under a tree, probably) near where Bruington meetinghouse now stands, were arrested and confined within prison bounds for sixteen days. These indignities and hardships endured by the early preachers intensified their zeal, drew to them much popular sympathy, and greatly increased the effectiveness of their ministry.

An active colaborer with John Waller in these days of persecution was Lewis Craig, also of Spottsylvania. His itinerant labors were greatly blessed in that part of this county which lies nearest to Caroline, and there, in 1774, Upper King and Queen Church was organized with twenty-five members. The year following, at a place popularly known as "The Axle," a church called by that name was constituted with thirty members. This body has since been styled Exol.

These three churches—Lower King and Queen, Upper King and Queen, and Exol—had respectively as their first pastors, Robert Ware, Younger Pitts, and Ivison Lewis. Elder Pitts was, in 1780, succeeded in Upper King and Queen Church by Theodrick Noel, who served it as pastor for forty years, or until death released him from his charge. Ware and Lewis also retained their charges until dismissed by death, both of them having served for full thirty years.

Two of these persevering and faithful pastors lived to see two other Baptist churches organized in the county, Bruington in 1790, and Poroporone in 1807, the former with one hundred and fifty members and the latter with one hundred. Robert B. Semple began his useful and distinguished ministerial career by becoming the first pastor of Bruington at the time of its constitution, and he served in this capacity for forty-one years.

Elder James Healy was chosen an under-shepherd to the Poroporone flock, and continued as such until his decease in 1820. The Lower King and Queen Church, having been called to mourn the departure of their first pastor, Robert Ware, chose Elder William Todd as his successor in 1804 or 1805. His pastoral care of this body—the longest in the annals of King and Queen—covered a period of over forty-five years, continuing until interrupted by the infirmities of age which fore-shadowed his death, bringing it to pass in 1855. The popular and eloquent ministry of the Elder Andrew Broaddus began in this county in 1827, when he succeeded Dr. Semple in the care of Upper King and Queen Church, and here his labors were enjoyed for full twenty years, or until his death in 1848.

The long terms of pastoral service which have been thus particularly mentioned, betokening as they do the harmonious and loving relations that subsisted between the churches and their pastors, exerted a powerful influence in inculcating Baptist beliefs and practices in the minds and hearts of at least two generations in this county. Beginning in 1772 with seventeen members, in less than sixty years, or at the time of Semple's death in 1831, they had increased to 1,314.

The fifth church among the Baptists formed in King and Queen was named from the river which flows near to it—Mattapony. It was gathered through the labors of Elder William Todd, who at its constitution in 1828 became its pastor, and so continued for twenty-seven years. The church soon after its constitution repaired and remodeled the "Old Brick Church," a substantial colonial edifice of St. Stevens parish, built and used under the Establishment. This structure, it has been said, was probably at the date of its erection " the largest and best-built church in Virginia." Reared by Henry Gaines, the architect, at the contract cost of £1300, its dimensions were thirty by eighty feet, the walls being twenty-seven feet high and of " the thickness of five bricks at the foundation and four at the top." The building remains a commodious and comfortable house of worship.

St. Stephen's and Olivet, both constituted in 1842, organized the same year, complete the list of Baptist churches in King and Queen.

The year which witnessed the formation of these two churches was that also in which Richard Hugh Bagby, who had been ordained at the call of Mattapony, entered upon his labors as the successor of Elder Richard Claybrook in the pastoral care of Bruington. Early in his ministry the substantial brick meetinghouse of this church was erected, and here, under his consecrated and earnest labors, remarkable no less for his power to win souls to Christ than for his skill to train them for service after they were won, the church attained a degree of efficiency, influence, and prominence second to none other in the rural parts of Virginia.

Elder Bagby's labors on this field extended through twenty-eight years, and terminated only a few months before his death, which occurred October 29, 1870. His life, which had been eminently marked by holy zeal and consecration, rendered his dying hour almost seraphic. Among his last thoughts he reverted to the scene of his long labors, and said: " I would like to be buried at Bruington." Again he said: " Oh, in a few hours what indescribable brightness and glory shall I behold—never, never to leave it any more." A little later he exclaimed: " Give me one more draught of that cool water before I begin to taste the cool and pearly water of life, proceeding out of the throne of God and of the Lamb in the New Jerusalem. . . . Tell the brethren that I never realized as I do now the glories of the heavenly world. . . . I am happier, ten thousand times happier, than I ever was before in my life. My trust is in God." Summoning his fast-failing strength, he said to his dear companion, " Kiss me, my wife, kiss me "; and then his spirit gently departed to be with Christ and to behold the pearly fountain which he had already seen in beatific vision.

His dying wish as to the place of his burial met with loving and reverent compliance; his remains rest in the Bruington cemetery, not far from those of the sainted Semple, and, like Semple's, are fittingly commemorated with a marble gravestone.

In the lower part of the county, Elder John Spencer, who had the pastoral care of Poroporone Church, ended his career about the time that Richard Hugh Bagby's began. His labors in that field left an abiding impression for good. Elder Thomas B. Evans, at one time pastor of Exol Church, and for thirty-three years in a like relation to Olivet, rendered faithful and efficient service, of inestimable value, in lower King and Queen. Elder Alfred Bagby, for nearly thirty-five years the prudent and efficient pastor of Mattapony Church, was a recognized and potent factor in the support and progress of Baptist interests in this county.

If space allowed, it would adorn the annals of King and Queen to recount here the labors of the men who have in later years occupied in the ministry the fields where those earlier pastors, the pioneers, toiled so long, so patiently, and so successfully. Their record would embrace such names as W. B. Todd, Isaac Diggs, Andrew Broaddus, Jr., Southwood, Garlick, Land, S. C. Boston, J. W. Ryland, Moncure, Henning, W. A. Street, Fleet, Long, O. D. Loving, Crews, and F. B. Beale—all redolent of pious devotion and godly and useful service. The ministry of Andrew Broaddus, Jr., in connection with Upper King and Queen Church, where he labored for over forty years, was—when viewed in all its important aspects—one of the most successful and useful ever rendered by a pastor in Virginia. The large and well-constructed brick meeting-house of this church was reared in 1860, under Elder Broaddus' ministry, and it has sheltered as large, efficient, and cultivated a spiritual body as can probably be found in any hamlet in the State.

Any sketch of the Baptists of King and Queen would be too imperfect and inadequate that failed to notice the godly men and devout women among the private members of its churches, who have in their lives illustrated the doctrine of godliness and proved themselves influential in promoting the cause of truth and righteousness. Of such useful and honored members every church has had its quota. Benjamin Faulkner, Thomas Spencer, Robert Garrett, Thomas Jeffries have been among the names loved and cherished in Exol. The Eubanks, Webbs, Courtneys, Rylands, Bagbys, Fleets, Latanes, Joneses, Hayneses, and others have, by their zeal and piety, spread the name of Bruington afar. The Boulwares, Garnetts, Dews, Broadduses, and others, have borne the burdens and ennobled the annals of Upper King and Queen. Alexander Fleet, J. C. Council, and other colaborers have been pillars of moral and religious strength in St. Stephen's. The Pollards, Walkers, Greshams, Hundleys, and a list besides too long to enumerate here, have been prominent among the religious forces of this county at large in the Baptist ranks.

The list of men added to the Baptist ministry of this and other States from King and Queen has been both large and weighty. It includes, amongst those born and reared in the county, or else ordained at the call of one of its churches, such names as these: James Greenwood, Ivison Lewis, Henry Toler, John Courtney, William Hickman, William Todd, Robert B. Semple, Andrew Broaddus, John W. Hillyard, Robert Ryland, I. Lewis, John Bird, John Spencer, Edward S. Amory, William B. Todd, William Pollard, Thomas W. Sydnor, R. H. Bagby, Alfred Bagby, George F. Bagby, T. B. Evans, John Clark, George Schools, E. P. Walton, William Hill, R. F. Stubbs, Richard H. Griffith, Edward Gresham, James A. Haynes, John W. Hundley, Charles H. Ryland, William S. Ryland, John W. Ryland, Robert S. Jones, H. H. Jones, John Pollard, T. R. Boston, W. T. Hundley, George T. Gresham, R. R. Acree, Alexander Fleet, John R. Powers, and J. R. Murdock.

If regard be had to the long list here named and the high positions many of them have attained in denominational councils and service, it may well be questioned if any county in Virginia has made a larger or more influential contribution to our Baptist ministry.

The Baptists of King and Queen were among the foremost in the State in availing themselves of the advantages of organized efforts in the churches in behalf of reformatory, educational, and missionary aims. Temperance, tract, and missionary societies were early in existence. Female missionary societies were started as early as 1843, perhaps earlier, and are in active operation in all the churches to this day; their annual missionary days, observed with appropriate services and instructive and inspiring addresses, have enlisted a great degree of public interest, and accomplished an untold amount of good. These vigorous and aggressive factors of church life have not only fostered missionary and benevolent zeal, but also contributed largely to the excellent associational reports which have so long and so signally characterized the churches of this county.

A commendable zeal in the matter of education has all along been shown by the Baptists of King and Queen. Dr. Semple conducted an academy in early manhood, and later, in his relations to Columbian College, proved himself one of the truest and staunchest friends to collegiate training Virginia has ever had. Robert Ryland, as president of the Virginia Baptist Seminary, and later —for thirty-two years—of Richmond College, rendered inestimable service to the cause of sound learning. Alfred Bagby, as principal for three years of Stevensville Academy; James A. Haynes, as twice principal of Female Seminaries; Col. J. C. Councill, in his lifelong work at Fleetwood and Aberdeen Academies; Dr. John Pollard, as professor of English in Richmond College; Dr. Charles H. Ryland, as financial secretary of the same institution; Dr. Joseph R. Garlick, as principal of Bruington Seminary; Col. A. F. Fleet, as superintendent of large military institutes in both Missouri and Indiana; Garnett Ryland, as professor of Greek in

Georgetown College, Kentucky; Alexander Fleet, whose entire manhood, so far, has been devoted to the care of schools, while also laboring efficiently in the ministry;—these all have exerted a salutary and helpful influence on the Baptist households of King and Queen in behalf of the liberal training of their sons and daughters; and that for more than three-quarters of a century.

As a result of their influence, along with coöperating causes, the families of the county have, to an extent quite unusual, long exhibited a singularly beautiful refinement of manners, elevation of thought, progressiveness of spirit, and charm of mental and moral culture. Civic virtue and private worth have seldom, if ever, found truer exemplifications than in the men of this county; and its daughters, whether viewed as adorning their stations with their accomplishments and graces in the domestic, the social, or the religious fabric, well fulfill the poetic, but none the less practical, ideal of the Psalmist, " As corner stones polished after the similitude of a palace."

A few scattered incidents which may be mentioned strongly attest the high character and influence of the Baptist denomination in King and Queen. In Cathcart's Baptist Encyclopædia sketches are given of twelve or more of her sons,—more than find admission from any other Virginia county. During the eighty-one years the General Association has been in existence, eight of the sons of this county have been chosen to fill the president's chair in this body, and have done so for eleven years. The annual sermon before this distinguished assemblage has also been preached ten times by resident ministers or sons of this county. The Rappahannock Association in their annual meetings have been entertained sixteen times in King and Queen, oftener by four times than in any other county within their bounds; and during the sixty-one years of the association's existence (down to 1903) there has never been a year in which some worthy and efficient brother of King and Queen has not been chosen to fill one or more of their three offices.

The tide of prosperity has not flowed evenly for the

Baptist churches in this county during the past half-century. St. Stephen's has, during this time, increased fivefold; Exol has doubled its membership; Upper King and Queen has become one-third more numerous than it was, and Lower King and Queen has made considerable gains in numerical strength. Bruington has remained nearly stationary as regards numbers, whilst Mattapony, Olivet, and Poroporone have each fallen off in their membership.

The losses and want of growth thus indicated, however, are in no small measure due to the annual removal of members to the cities and other fields of service. The impoverishment of these churches has been the enrichment of others in Brooklyn, New York, Baltimore, Washington, Norfolk, Petersburg, Richmond, Danville, Lynchburg, Buchanan, Pine Bluff (Ark.), Atlanta (Ga.), and other places, to which the sons and daughters of this county have carried a rich inheritance of moral virtue and high attainments in religious training, and where, like hardy plants planted in new soil, they have taken root and flourished. These unforced exiles from the communities hallowed by the memories of Semple, Todd, Broaddus, Bagby, and other revered names, look back from their distant homes to the hearthstones and altars of this county with emotions as fond and loyal as ever the devout Moslem knew as he turned his face towards " The White Mountain " at Mecca, and with a pride and joy as humble and pure as ever the captive of Israel felt when in Babylon he opened his window towards the temple of his fathers and sang:

" If I forget thee, O Jerusalem, let my right hand forget her cunning;
If I do not remember thee, let my tongue cleave to the roof of my
mouth: if I prefer not Jerusalem above my chief joy."

THE DISCIPLES, OR CHRISTIANS

By B. H. Walker.

It is natural and right that anyone commencing to read the history of any people or county or religious body should wish to know what brought them into existence, and the reasons for their existence, and what claims they have to the notice of the reading public. Appreciating the reasonableness of such inquiry, I proceed to give the causes which brought the people known as Disciples of Christ, or Christians, into existence.

Some time between the years 1825 and 1828 *The Christian Baptist,* published by A. Campbell, by some means found its way to eastern Virginia, and some persons, who had been dissatisfied with certain prevalent doctrines of the churches,—such as special election, final perseverance of the saints, and special operation of the spirit of conversion independent of the Word of God,— were attracted by the sentiments expressed in that paper, began to talk and canvass them, and soon to question the scripturality of such doctrines, thus starting a warm discussion.   Dr. John Duval became an ardent advocate of the views which Mr. Campbell insisted on; on one occasion he preached a sermon in Bruington Baptist Church, proving from the Scriptures that the Holy Spirit operates only through the Word of God, and was promised as an indweller and comforter only to those who believed and obeyed the Gospel.   When he concluded his discourse, he asked Mr. Josiah Ryland, Sr., to offer prayer, and the latter prayed that the Church might be delivered from the false doctrine which had been preached them on that occasion.   Soon some of the members insisted that there was no scriptural authority for the so-called Christian experience which those offering to come into the Church were required to tell, nor for the practice of members sitting in judgment on the spiritual condition of the candidate, and whether or not they were ready to be received into the Church.   Another principle they insisted on was that only obedient believers could claim the promise of the forgiveness of sins, or, in other words, only those who, professing faith in Jesus, had repented of their sins and turned from them and been baptized, had the answer of a good conscience, the assurance of the pardon of their sins.   They also insisted that such churches only were scripturally organized as had a plurality of elders and deacons and celebrated the Lord's

Supper every Lord's day. Many of these positions, being new to the Baptists, were very strongly opposed and denounced, and because we as a sect denied that the Holy Spirit operated independently and apart from the Word of God, the charge was made (and with some is still insisted on) that we deny the influence of the Holy Spirit in conversion.

The discussion on these questions, especially the last, grew very warm. By a decree of the Dover Association in 1831 the new views were unscriptural and demoralizing, and the persons who advocated them were promoters of damnable errors; and the decree recommended the churches to withdraw from every one who still insisted upon these sentiments, which were contrary to the then prevailing doctrines held by the Baptists. Along with other Baptist churches, Bruington acted upon the advice of the Association, and withdrew from thirty-two members; who then, being without a place to meet in for religious worship, organized as a church, with R. B. Pendleton and Temple Walker as elders and John Draper and J. W. Watkins and others as deacons. As they had no house in which to worship, they erected a stage, as it was then called, across the road from Henry C. Nunn's residence, now owned by Mr. G. Tuck. There were only rude seats for the accommodation of the people. There were some splendid old oaks and hickories which gave abundant shade, and there the members and others met every Lord's day to sing and pray and to remember their Lord and Savior in the Supper. When the chilly days in the fall came on, they repaired to a vacant house, called the Cottage, on the land of P. B. Pendleton, now owned by Dr. Thomas Latane.

Next year, 1832, a church building was erected and dedicated. Soon Thomas M. Henley moved to the county, and he became the pastor and an elder, along with those first chosen; then James C. Roy, who had been a deacon, was chosen an elder after the death of P. B. Pendleton. Dr. John Duval preached for a long time for the Smyrna church, and also for the one at Rappahannock, but held his membership at Jerusalem in King William, where he also preached and acted as elder. Smyrna church, like all religious bodies, has had its days of prosperity and adversity, its days of joy and sorrow, but has steadily pursued its course, meeting regularly every Lord's day, keeping the ordinances as they were ordained by the Apostles, and standing for the truth, both in precept and example, as they understood it, and as they verily believe it taught in the Holy Scriptures.

Smyrna church, however, has not been as aggressive as the demands of the cause have required; has been too well satisfied to proclaim the Gospel and keep the ordinances as required by the divine standard, and has not reached out as it should to the regions beyond; still, the membership has been large for a country church, reaching as high as two hundred and fifty, and larger than any other church in the county.

Some time between 1845 and 1850 a church claiming to hold the truth as given by the Apostles was organized in the upper portion of the county, and called Horeb; sustained by Dr. William Dew, John Lumpkin, Roy Boulware, Richard Pollard, and others, it held regular meetings until during the war, when the Yankees destroyed it, and all the leading members dying or moving away, the organization was broken up and has never been revived.

METHODISM IN KING AND QUEEN

By Reverend Joseph W. Shackford. *

(Much of the information contained in this paper was gleaned from the diary of Mr. John Walker of Chatham Hill.)

The Methodist Episcopal Church was organized at the " Christmas Conference " held in the city of Baltimore, Md., in 1784; and Francis Asbury was chosen by

BEDFORD CITY, VA., June 9, 1902.

* REV. ALFRED BAGBY,
    Richmond, Va.

MY DEAR BROTHER:

Enclosed I send you the paper on " Methodism in King and Queen." Owing to lack of data for the lower part of the County, my account that body as the "Itinerant General Superintendent," or Bishop. For about twenty years prior to that time, itinerant Methodist preachers had been at work along the Atlantic slope from New England to the Carolinas. At first these men were few in number, irregularly distributed, and greatly handicapped by their distance from Mr. John Wesley in England, by whose authority they were generally directed. Now, however, with a regular organization of their own, and with a resident Bishop of fervent piety and indomitable energy, they " greatly multiplied."

King and Queen County, like many others, early became the traveling ground of these Methodist " circuit riders." Without houses of worship at first, they preached at private residences, under brush arbors, at camp meetings, or in any place where they could get a congregation to hear the Word of the Lord.

The early " circuits " were not defined by any natural or political boundary lines; but were composed of an irregular number of " appointments," or preaching places, including often the whole, or large portions, of several counties. In this way King and Queen, for some time prior to 1829, was in the " Gloucester circuit "; from that time to 1834 it was in the " Caroline circuit "; it was then put in the " Essex circuit "; and, a few years later, was called by its own name, the " King and Queen circuit." Under these fluctuating conditions it is difficult to trace the growth of Methodism here separately

in that direction had to be brief and only of a general character. It may seem that undue prominence is given to Mr. John Walker and my father. It is true I had more material at hand respecting them than respecting others, but I think the facts will support the position given them.

I have not signed my name to the paper, because I do not know your wish as to that. You can do as you wish about that. Of course there are many other features, such as the relations of Methodism to other denominations in the County, etc., which are not to be mentioned in so brief a sketch. I trust the paper may be serviceable to your work; and wishing you much success therein, I remain,

Yours fraternally,

Jos. W. Shackford.

and apart from the contiguous regions with which it has been so intimately associated.

About 1790 Stephen Roswell preached in King and Queen. The first Methodist preaching in the upper part of the county was at the home of Mr. William Shepherd, Sr., the great-grandfather of Mr. Melville Walker of Walkerton. Among the first Methodist members in that neighborhood was old Mrs. Clayton. The first Methodist church there was originally built about three miles east of Clarkston Postoffice by Mr. William Shepherd, Jr., in 1800, for a schoolhouse. In 1802 this was turned into a Methodist "meeting-house" and called "Shepherd's," after the name of its builder. This small wooden structure was replaced by a brick building (33x39 feet), completed on the 23d of October, 1838, and dedicated by Rev. Harry B. Cowles on the 25th of the following December.

It cost $468.36, the most of which was paid by Mr. John Walker of "Chatham Hill," son-in-law to Mr. William Shepherd, Jr. This house, it seems, was badly constructed, and in 1859 it was pulled down and the present large brick edifice was built just across the road, opposite the old site; the new house was dedicated to the worship of Almighty God May 27th, 1860, by Rev. Henry B. Cowles.

About 1835 "Providence" meetinghouse was built, a plain wooden structure, which was succeeded in 1890 by a large brick church. "Paces" was a preaching place very early in the nineteenth century, and the brick church now standing was built about 1836.

Still lower in the county the "Old Church," "New Hope," "St. Andrew's," and "Shackelford's" very early became rallying points of Methodism. In 1885 a Methodist church, called "Mizpah," was built in the village of Walkerton and added to the King and Queen circuit. Many other places from time to time have been used by the Methodists for assembling the people to hear the Gospel; but the above churches, or meeting-houses, as they were originally called, mark the principal spots in the county where they have established strongholds for the Kingdom of the Lord Jesus Christ.

Among the active ministers of the first half-century of Methodism in this field were the following: Stephen Roswell, Samuel Gerrard, Lewis Skidmore, Hezekiah McLelland, John Hersey, Rufus Ledbetter, Samuel T. Moorman, William H. Starr, Thomas S. Campbell, Moses Brock, George W. Nolley, Edward Cannon, Richard Corbin, David Fisher, Thomas Crowder, Richard Bennett, Richard Mitchell, Thomas Durham, William Davis, John W. White, John P. Gregory, James McDonald, James W. Lewis, Henry B. Cowles, Robert Michaels, William E. Grant, Richard Hope, Isaac M. Arnold, James E. Joyner, Gervis M. Keesee, and Abram Penn.

Within the last fifty-five years, the following preachers, in the order given, have labored in that part of the county lying above Little Plymouth, and now known as King and Queen circuit:

Joseph H. Davis, Joseph Lear, Stephen W. Jones, Thomas H. Briggs, John Bayly, John B. Laurens, B. H. Johnson, Charles H. Boggs, Joseph R. Griffith, William H. Starr, Lloyd, Moore, John G. Rowe, Hezekiah P. Mitchell, Thomas M. Beckham, George M. Wright, Josiah D. Hank, Charles E. Watts, John W. Shackford, William E. Evans, Benjamin C. Spiller, William W. Lear, William A. Crocker, John T. Payne, Joseph W. Shackford, Robert E. Barrett, John P. Woodward, Robert E. Bentley, and Frederick G. Davis. In addition to these, the presiding elders of this period did a great deal of effective work in the county; among them were William B. Rowzie, E. P. Wilson, Thomas A. Ware, Jacob Manning, Leonidas Rosser, James D. Coulling, Joseph H. Davis, J. Powell Garland, Francis J. Boggs, George H. Ray, William E. Payne, Charles E. Watts, and Joseph H. Amiss. Of all these preachers named, only two, Hezekiah McLelland and John W. Shackford, settled in King and Queen; the others were nearly all transient itinerant pastors.

Mr. McLelland, having served in the Virginia Conference for many years, located after his marriage with Miss Mary Temple, daughter of Mr. Humphrey Temple, near Walkerton, where he lived until his death,

November 9th, 1832. His funeral eulogy was preached
November 27th, 1832, by Rev. Lewis Skidmore, from
the text II. Corinthians, vii. 2.

While living in the county he labored earnestly, and
so long as his strength lasted, for the salvation of souls
and the cause of Methodism. He was survived by his
wife, three sons,—Thomas Cole, Benjamin Whatcoat,
Enoch George,—and two daughters, Susanna Benson
and Martha Cole. The last named, Miss Martha Cole
McLelland, on February 10th, 1846, was married to
Rev. John William Shackford, while he was on the King
William circuit. In 1847 Mr. Shackford traveled the
Westmoreland circuit, and in November of the same
year he retired from the Virginia Conference, of which
he had now been a member for five years, and located
on his farm near Walkerton, to which he gave the name
Orange Grove.

At that time he was only 28 years of age, and was
ardently devoted to the cause of Methodism. Thenceforth for more than thirty-five years he labored " in season, out of season," throughout King and Queen, and
often in King William and Essex Counties, for the
cause of Christ. He preached often at " Shepherd's,"
" Providence," " Paces," and the " Old Church," and
many souls were converted under his ministry. He never
lost his devotion for his itinerant brethren; his house
was their home, they sought his counsel, loved him cordially, and he labored with them in their meetings, and
for their support in all the practical work of the church.
Acting under the authority of the Quarterly Conference
in 1873, he raised the money to buy the first parsonage
for King and Queen circuit. He was class-leader, superintendent of Sunday school, and preacher, all in one.
He loved God's people of every name; and no minister
ever labored in King and Queen who did more to estab-
lish Methodism in the county. For the last fifteen years
of his life he was too feeble in body to preach much;
but he did what he could to help on the little church
which had now been built at Walkerton, and to which
he gave the name of Mizpah. He died in his eighty-
first year, on July 10th, 1900, and was laid to rest in

the family burying ground, lamented by a great number of neighbors, relatives, brethren, and friends. Very tender and impressive memorial services, at which loving tributes were spoken by ministers and laymen of his own and other denominations, were held at Mizpah on July 22d, 1900.

The total number of Methodists in King and Queen probably never exceeded a thousand at any one time. They number now (1902) seven hundred and ninety. Among this people there have been many, both men and women, who were faithful and devoted followers of Christ, shining as lights before the world. There may be mentioned Mr. William Shepherd, Jr., the founder of "Shepherd's Church," where he was the leading member for more than forty years. He died April 5, 1842. Mr. John DeShazo, a member of the same class with Mr. Shepherd for twenty-eight years, died November 5, 1834. Mr. John Walker, of "Chatham Hill" for nearly fifty years, first joined the Methodist Church in 1818 in Nashville, Tenn., where he was then engaged in business; but he returned to Virginia and united with the "Shepherd's class" at a meeting held by Rev. Samuel Gerrard at the house of Mr. William Shepherd, Jr., in December, 1819. From that time until his death in February, 1867, he was a faithful and devoted Christian. No member of the denomination in King and Queen ever exerted a more positive and abiding influence for Methodism than did this godly layman. Truly he was "diligent in business, fervent in spirit, serving the Lord." The Bible was his guidebook. He daily held prayers with his family and servants, for whose spiritual welfare he showed the deepest concern. He was kind to the poor, generous to the weak and erring; but he had no toleration for duplicity or meanness of any sort. Cato the Censor was not more strict in his ideas of rectitude; nor was John, the beloved disciple, more affectionate and tender towards his Christian brethren. On June 19th, 1826, returning from a camp meeting, held at "Old Church," in the lower end of the county, he wrote these words: "I feel thankful to my Maker I am yet striving for the King-

dom of Glory. Lord [grant] that I may hold out till
death and be crowned with life eternal in Heaven!"
When the end came, more than forty years afterwards,
his loved and intimate friend, Rev. John W. Shackford, inquired of him: "Brother Walker, what are
your prospects now?" As his spirit was passing through
the gates he answered back: "O, Eternal life! Eternal
life!" So lived and died one of the pillars of early
Methodism in King and Queen. His wife, Margaret
W. Walker, a faithful, godly woman, survived him,
with her two sons, Watson and Melville—she for
nearly twenty years. Watson died in 1900; Melville
in 1904.

There were many others who faithfully served God
and went to their reward. Space is left to mention only
a few. At Shepherd's, besides those already given, were
William Dix, Sr., Dr. Moore Fauntleroy and family,
William J. Clarkson, Charles R. Evans, Charles Burgess, Peter Toombs, Philip Hodges, Joseph T. Brown-
ley, Franklin Simpkins, Mrs. Elizabeth Carlton, Mrs.
Elizabeth Hundley, with her sons, John and George
K., Mrs. Mary McLelland, Miss Martha Wilson, Miss
Mildred Perryman, Miss Susan Crowe, and many others
who have fallen asleep. In more recent years Watson
Walker, Melville Walker, Thomas Sterling, William
Trice, John F. Trice, Lewis P. Fryer, Willie Cook, and
others, have served the church there officially. Of
these, Watson and Melville Walker, sons of Mr. John
Walker named above, deserve special mention. For
fifteen years after their father's death they were the
strength and support of Shepherd's. When Mizpah
was established at Walkerton, they, together with Lewis
P. Fryer, Mrs. William H. Walker, and the Shackford
family, transferred their membership to that place, and
there wrought for Methodism with such faithful co-
workers as Captain George P. Hudson and wife, Captain B. F. Eaton and wife, Mrs. J. W. Caldwell, and
others.

Among the laymen at "Providence" in the long-ago
were: James Southgate, Robert S. Nunn, Henry Nunn,
Thomas DeShazo, John DeShazo, Low Brown, Quarles

Nunn, and Richard Williams; more recently, William C. Anderson, Richard B. Nunn, Joseph G. Nunn, Thomas J. Crouch, William Brown, Samuel P. Latane, John C. DeShazo, and Charles W. Porter. Some of these are still living, but most of them have fallen asleep. Of the last two named it ought to be said that for more than thirty years they have toiled with unceasing fidelity for their church. Mr. DeShazo, merchant and farmer, and Mr. Porter, treasurer of King and Queen County for the last thirty-four years consecutively, are truly such material as men are made of, reflecting credit not only on themselves but on the church they have served so well, earning thereby the confidence and love of the whole community.

But the time would fail me to speak of many more " whose names are in the book of life."

At Paces there were William Watts, Lambeth Hundley, Thomas W. Garrett, Dr. James B. Garrett, Jimmie Gibson, Alfred Carlton, Isaac Carlton, and others.

At Old Church and Shackelford's many of the large family of Blands,—including Colonel Robert Bland, Dr. William Bland, Dr. James Bland, Major Bland,— Mr. Beverly Anderson and his son, Dr. Garrett Anderson, with a large number of Roanes, Shackelfords, and others, followed the Methodist faith.

The increase in membership has usually come through special revival meetings in the churches, or through camp meetings, so frequent in the earlier days. At a camp meeting in 1827 in Gloucester there were more than a hundred conversions; June 20-24, 1834, at Shepherd's there were about thirty conversions; August 23, 1838, under preaching of Rev. Robert Michaels, there were ninety-four conversions at Providence; July 20-28, 1850, there were sixty conversions at Shepherd's, and likewise at other places multitudes of souls were turned unto the Lord. Thus it will appear without the least disparagement of other Christian denominations that Methodism has contributed liberally to the number of godly men and women in the good old county of King and Queen, the noble lives and conduct of whose people prompted the public statement made by Bishop

James A. Latane at Antioch in 1880: " I have traveled," said he, " in many parts of the country; but I
have never been in any other place where the people
have so much of the fear of God as they have in this
community."

BRUINGTON CHURCH

We give here some extracts from an interesting sketch
of Bruington Church, written by Judge J. H. C. Jones;
Bruington being one of the oldest of the churches in
our county:

" The earliest account we have of Baptist preaching
in the neighborhood of Bruington is that in August,
1772, James Greenwood and William Stovall were
preaching not far from the place, when they were seized
by virtue of a warrant,* and immediately taken to prison
in the common jail of the county, where they remained
sixteen days, at the end of which period they were released upon giving bond for good behavior.

" It seems probable, however, that previously in
1772, and even in 1771, John Waller and other Baptists
from one of the upper counties had already preached in
this neighborhood. After them, Greenwood and Ivison
Lewis held meetings here. But while there were Baptists living around Bruington as early as 1772, they were
not organized until 1774, when they formed some connection with Piscataway Church in Essex.

" About 1780 a church was constituted at Bruington
under the care of William Jones, but in consequence of
some charges against him it was thought advisable to
dissolve, and the members returned to Piscataway and
were regarded as a branch of that church until 1790,
when, having been favored with a revival in which several influential persons were baptized, they formed a
church of their own. At its organization on the fourth
Saturday and Sunday in September, 1790, it was com-

* James Greenwood was seized while preaching near Bruington
Church and imprisoned in the County jail. There, the historian says,
" he preached, and prayed, and wept ".

posed of 150 members. Robert Semple,* being then in his 21st year and having been previously baptized, was unanimously chosen pastor, and accepted the call. It is said that on the 24th of the same month in which he was baptized, he and the late Andrew Broaddus, Sr., both made their first attempt at preaching at the house of Mrs. Lowrie in Caroline. He was publicly ordained to the Gospel ministry on the 26th of September, 1790, by Elders Ware, Noel, and Lewis. On the same day Lewis Smith, Thomas Nunn, and William Whayne were ordained deacons. In 1791 they built their first house of worship, which stood on the opposite side of the road to the present building. It was a wooden structure, plain, unplastered, and uncomfortable, with no heating appliance, and no glass lights save one narrow window at the pulpit.

" Under Semple's ministry the church soon began to grow in influence, and took high rank for efficiency. Some were added by baptism every year, and then at the close of 1799 a work of grace was manifested which continued through many years, and was so remarkable that it was the subject of special notice in the Dover Association for the year 1800. It is said that the revival was due, not to preaching, but to singing, prayer, and exhortation by private members, and to the ordinance of baptism as most effectual; it was administered nearly every Lord's Day, and some of nearly all ages and ranks and both sexes were baptized. About one hundred and thirty were brought into the church, among them the late Elder William Todd, who soon afterward began to preach. On the third Sunday in March, 1804,

---

* Robert Baylor Semple was of Scotch descent, born 1769, educated by Mr. Taylor and Rev. P. Nelson. He was teacher, lawyer, and preacher; was baptized in 1784 by Rev. Theodoric Noel. Semple had a keen knowledge of human nature and was well instructed in righteousness; he " aimed his darts at the conscience, not at the head". In 1820 he was president of the old Baptist Triennial Convention. He was made D. D. by Brown University and William and Mary College. The last year of his life there was a great revival at Bruington and over a hundred persons were baptized. His last sermon was upon Exodus xv. 11.

he was dismissed, with about one hundred others, who resided in the lower vicinity of the church, to join Lower King and Queen Church. On the first Sunday in August, 1804, Josiah Ryland, William Fleet, William Holt and Thomas Courtney were ordained deacons. In 1809 a membership of three hundred was reported to the Dover Association, and between this date and 1816 Moses Nunn, Justin Beadles, William Hill, Lewis Howerton, and Robert S. Jones are mentioned as deacons; later the names of Joel Willis, Thomas Garnett, and Hugh Campbell appear. William Fleet was Clerk in 1812, and Thomas Nunn was Treasurer. In 1816 a day of fasting and prayer was appointed on account of the low spiritual condition of the church, and also on account of a prevailing drought. On the Wednesday following fast day one of the best rains of the year came, in answer to prayer. At a church meeting in February, 1817, a sister was cited before the church to answer the charge of leaving her father's house and marrying against his consent, she being under age. She appeared and apologized, and a committee was appointed to intercede with her father for a reconciliation.

"On November 27, 1817, James Webb, a deacon of Piscataway, had been received by letter and recognized as a deacon of this church. As early as 1816 it was proposed to build another house for worship; the work was discussed and laid over until July 4, 1818. The first service was held in the new house on the fourth Sunday in June, 1820. It was a brick structure, 70x33 feet, and stood upon the site of the present building. It had a gallery, a door at each end, and another door on the south side of the house, opposite to which on the north side stood the pulpit. About this time two things caused some trouble; one, the failure of members to attend service, and especially business meetings; the other, the failure of members to contribute to the support of the church. Measures more or less stringent were adopted to remedy these evils.

"On the 29th of May, 1825, Robert Courtney, John Bagby, and John C. Richards were ordained deacons;

27th of May, 1826, Hugh Campbell resigned as clerk and John Bagby was elected in his stead. On the 26th of April, 1827, Robert Ryland was publicly ordained to the Gospel ministry. In 1828 John Duval was elected as associate pastor and accepted (the pastor, Dr. Semple, had changed his residence to Fredericksburg, and Dr. Duval filled the pulpit on the third Sunday in his place).

" Dr. Semple died December 25th, 1831, having served the church from the time of its constitution to the day of his death. This eminent servant of God deserves our highest testimonial of gratitude and thanksgiving. Under his ministry the church was uniformly happy and prosperous. A few years before his death he was called to a high and important position; but remained pastor here until he died. His annual salary probably did not exceed $100. In 1814 the membership was three hundred; in 1824, three hundred and fifty. In 1818, fifty baptisms were reported, and in 1831, one hundred and two. In December, 1818, a plan was devised for increasing interest in, and securing contributions for, missions. Revs. John Clark and Robert S. Jones belonged here. The Dover Association met with the church in 1792, 1805, and 1820.

" Elder Richard Claybrook * was chosen as Dr. Semple's successor April 14th, 1832. He was a most worthy man, and seems to have been greatly loved by the church. He died December 4th, 1834, having had a most successful pastorate. In 1832 the membership was four hundred and sixty-five; in 1834, four hundred and eighty-three. Rev. Robert Ryland preached at the church one Sunday in each month for a period of fourteen months. About this time a fund was established for the maintenance of the poor.

" Claybrook was succeeded by Rev. Eli Ball, who was chosen December 27, 1834, to preach two Sundays in each month and on Saturday before the first Sunday. July 4, 1840, Elder Ball resigned, having been called to an important work for the denomination. This pastorate seems also to have been remarkably successful,

---

* Richard Claybrook, b. 1785, in King William.

the church reaching a membership of five hundred and eighty-six. The church during this period was active, too, in works of practical benevolence. A Sunday school was begun; as also temperance agitation, tract distribution, and an educational society. Regular weekly prayer meetings also were established; these were held mostly at private houses. It was in this pastorate, also, that regular collections were first taken for missionary purposes. It is notable that Mr. Charles Hill, a gentleman in the neighborhood of exemplary character, though not a professor of religion, gave his cordial help in the Sunday school. In 1836 brethren Thomas Haynes and Samuel P. Ryland were appointed superintendents of the Sunday school; brother Haynes acted in that capacity for the most part until 1846, when he removed to Washington city, brother Ryland succeeding him. Meetings were also arranged for the benefit of the colored people, and a committee appointed to supervise these meetings. In 1837 Thomas Haynes, S. P. Ryland, and Alexander Fleet were elected deacons.

"The church being now again without a pastor, a day of fasting and prayer was observed, looking to the election of some one as under-shepherd. Elder William Southwood * agreed to supply the pulpit for one year from August 1st, 1840. August 29th Elder T. W. Sydnor was elected pastor and accepted for one year. He began work in January, 1841. The treasurer reported for this year (1841) $755.82 collected for benevolent objects. Twelve baptisms are reported. Elder Sydnor declined to serve a second year. By arrangement made in January, 1842, Elder William Southwood was to fill the pulpit on the first and fourth Sundays, R. H. Bagby on the second, and John O. Turpin on the third. June 11th, 1842, R. H. Bagby was elected pastor. By many he was regarded as an answer to the prayers of the church. December, 1852, the church engaged with its pastor for preaching every Sunday, and

---

* William Southwood, pastor in the latter part of 1840, was b. in England, October, 1783; d. October, 1850, and was buried under the church at St. Stevens.

HON. J. H. C. JONES

Judge of the County Court of King and Queen, President of the
Baptist General Association of Virginia.

fixed his salary at $500. On the first Sunday in January, 1853, Alfred Bagby was publicly ordained to the ministry; July 28th of the same year William S. Ryland was ordained. In 1856 the church resolved not to retain in fellowship a member retailing ardent spirits.

" In January, 1858, Joseph Ryland, James R. Fleet, and Leland Cosby were elected deacons, and on Sunday George F. Bagby was ordained to the ministry. During 1858 $900.77 was collected for benevolent objects. May 31, 1863, Charles H. Ryland was ordained to the ministry; December 31st John W. Ryland was ordained. A Sabbath school for the colored children of the neighborhood was organized in 1863, with John Bagby, Jr., as Superintendent, and Alexander Fleet, Jr., as assistant. The school was conducted under an arbor in the churchyard. The Rappahannock Association met with the church in 1858 and 1866.

" Elder Bagby's pastorate was counted a great success, and when he resigned, in 18—, to enter upon work as field secretary of the State Mission Board, it was a matter of universal regret. His death on October 29th, 1870, was a sad blow to the cause. His body and that of his wife, as also those of Dr. and Mrs. Semple, repose in the church cemetery near by."

THE WINNING OF RELIGIOUS FREEDOM.

The following sketch appeared in the Richmond *Times-Dispatch*, November 11, 1906, under the heading:

" VIRGINIA'S FIGHT FOR FREE RELIGION."

With a few verbal corrections it is inserted here as a valuable contribution to the ecclesiastical history of Virginia, and thus, by its subject matter, of broad interest to the history of King and Queen County.

" A collection of specially interesting and important manuscripts will be put on exhibition in the portrait gallery of the State Library this week by the Department of Archives and History. This collection is that of ' religious petitions,' which were presented to the General Assembly during the momentous years of the Revolution and the years succeeding.   These documents will be so arranged, with accompanying cards, that the progress of the struggle which ended in complete religious freedom may be studied from beginning to end. A number of these religious petitions will be included among the State Library's exhibit at the Jamestown Exposition.

" Interesting as the history of the overthrow of established religion in Virginia is, the majority of people are ignorant of it.   The story of the struggle is told in these petitions with a fullness seldom found, and consequently the collection will have a more than usual interest for those who love the history of the State.   In fact, the religious petitions are the only source for certain phases of the religious conflict in Virginia, and this is the first time that they have been exhibited.

" *Origin of Petitions.*—For a proper understanding of their value, it is necessary to know something of the conditions which produced them and the grievances that they endeavored to remedy.   It is difficult for us, with our acquaintance with the present condition of things in Virginia, spiritual and temporal, to appreciate the conditions existing in the State at the beginning of the Revolution.

" There was an established church in Virginia, the Church of England.   The people were required to attend its services, and were taxed for its support.   In return the people received the services of a somewhat inferior clergy, which was criticised as being unlearned, unenthusiastic and generally acquainted with the world, the flesh, and the devil.   The criticism was probably overdrawn, but there can be no doubt that the clergy exercised little influence upon their parishioners.   The burning zeal of the dissenting preachers, their rivals, may have thrown the clergy of the Established Church into a different relief from that in which they would stand to-day.

" At all events, things religious were out of joint in Virginia for some years prior to the Revolution.   The spirit of rebellion against authority was on foot throughout the Colony, and applied to religion as well as to politics. The Established Church, the Church of England in Virginia, became unpopular with many people because of its connection with royal authority, the character of its clergymen, and, not the least, because of the taxes extorted for its maintenance. The local tyranny exercised by many vestries in church matters did not enhance the popularity of the Establishment. Indeed, some writers attribute the deficiencies of the Established Church to its lack of ecclesiastical control and the corresponding power of the vestries. The church, they say, was not episcopal.

"*Wonderful Awakening.*—Popular discontent with the church found expression in the celebrated ' Parsons' Cause,' in 1763, when the youthful Patrick Henry began his fine agitating career. The clergy of some parishes attempted to collect their tithes of tobacco, as fixed by the law at so many pounds, at a time when tobacco was high. The law was appealed to; the parsons were legally right, but Henry's tongue confounded them.

" Conditions were ripe in Virginia for the growth of active dissent. The means of growth were supplied by one of those religious movements which have so often convulsed the British people. This was the great revival of the Wesleys, Whitefield, and Edwards. The conception of religion as a conscious and intimate relationship between the soul and God was preached as never before, and awoke the slumbering religious instincts of the English-speaking people.

" The Presbyterians were the first dissenting sect to enter Virginia as a sect. They were chiefly Scotch-Irish, of the West, and they did not all at once affect eastern Virginia. But some years before the Revolution the Presbyterians began to make headway in Hanover and the adjoining counties, and presently Baptists, Quakers, Methodists and others entered the Colony and propagated their doctrines. The Baptists, especially, grew rapidly, and disturbed the conventional and unemotional Virginia of the eighteenth century to its depths.

" Indeed, the effects of a burning evangelical Christianity, preached crudely, but with utmost sincerity, were marvelous. The old Virginia of that day was used to dull and sleepy lectures upon morality, delivered unenthusiastically to high-backed pews and powdered dignity. Into this drowsy land the itinerant exhorters flocked and vividly painted heaven and hell, disturbing the peace of mind of the whole community.

"*Persecution Followed.*—The first case of imprisonment seems to have taken place in Fredericksburg in 1768. John Waller, Lewis Craig, James Childs, and others, were hauled up before three magistrates, who offered to release them if they would promise to spare the county their sermons for a year and a day. They refused, and were marched to jail, singing as they went through the streets: ' Broad is the way that leads to death.' Some of the natives believe that the curse of this persecution stopped the growth of the town for a hundred years.

" A number of similar cases of imprisonment followed, and legal persecution was sometimes accompanied by mob outrage, as the powerful emotions awakened by the religious revival antagonized those whom it did not attract. Persecution, as is sometimes the case, but not always, aided the growth of the persecuted sect.

" The Baptists increased in numbers, as did the Presbyterians, while many Quakers and other sectarians came into the State from the North.

" It was now the beginning of the Revolution. The chief questions that strained the relations between King and Colonies were political, and religious matters might not necessarily have entered into the conflict to a great extent. This was certainly the preference of a majority of the leading patriots, who were churchmen, while they were rebels. But revolutions sometimes accomplish more than they aim at. The dissenters, now largely outnumbering the churchmen, were determined that religious as well as political liberty should be secured, and the dissenters had the sympathy of some of the strongest men of the day.

" A political motive for assisting the dissenters lay in the fact that the State would need their warm support in the coming struggle. To men as broad as Jefferson, Madison, and Mason, the occasion called for the general assertion of liberal principles. When the Convention of 1775 met as a convention, and no longer as the House of Burgesses, the dissenters began to send in petitions, and it was by petitions attacking or defending the Established Church that the struggle was chiefly waged.

"The Baptists, in a petition dated August 14, 1775, expressed sympathy for the patriot cause and asked that their ministers might have the liberty of preaching to the Virginia troops. The Convention could not well refuse this request, and passed a resolution permitting dissenting clergymen to preach to the soldiers "for the ease of such scrupulous consciences as may not choose to attend divine services as celebrated by the chaplain."

"The dissenters had not yet begun to attack the church in their petitions. The first move for complete religious freedom came from the convention of 1776, in the Bill of Rights. In this notable body sat Archibald Cary, Robert Carter Nicholas, Patrick Henry, Richard Bland, Thomas Ludwell Lee, John Blair, Meriwether Smith, James Mercer, Edmund Pendleton, Edmund Randolph, Henry Tazewell, James Madison, George Mason, and other men of mark. Some of them were strong defenders of the Establishment, but the genuine love of liberty which animated Mason, Madison, and their followers, as well as the necessities of the moment, prevailed, and the famous sixteenth article of the Bill of Rights was passed. It reads: ' That religion, or the duty we owe to our Creator, and the manner of discharging it, can be directed only by reason and conviction, and not by force or violence; and, therefore, all men are equally entitled to the free exercise of religion according to the dictates of conscience; and that it is the mutual duty of all to practice Christian forbearance, love and charity towards each other.'

"*Baptist and Presbyterian Onslaught.*—This article was adopted June 12, 1776, and on June 20 the Baptists attacked the Establishment in a petition asking that they be allowed to maintain their ministers and enjoy the ministrations of these without the necessity of supporting the clergy of ' other denominations '—meaning, of course, the clergy of the Establishment.

" The first General Assembly of Virginia met in October, 1776. The attack on the Establishment then became general, and many petitions, chiefly from the Presbyterians, poured in upon the legislature. The Presbytery of Hanover asked for the repeal of laws countenancing religious denominations and enforcing taxation for their benefit. One immense petition, signed by 10,000 names, and many yards in length, attested to the number and unanimity of the dissenters.

" The Assembly bowed before the public will, and passed a law on December 9th, 1776, exempting dissenters from the support of the church. This bill was carried only after a severe struggle, in which Pendleton and Nicholas led the conservatives.

" Dissenters were relieved of the burden of supporting the Establishment with their taxes, but the question of State interference in religious matters was not yet settled. It was still a debated question whether there should be taxation for ecclesiastical purposes. Meanwhile, the opponents of the Establishment secured a postponement of the payment to it of any taxes at all. This condition of abeyance lasted through the years 1776-1779, in which time a number of petitions were presented, asking for the overthrow of the Establishment, or opposing the system of church taxation, which was called assessment.

" *Jefferson's Act Held Up.*—In the session of 1779 the opponents of the Established Church made a determined assault upon it, and succeeded in crippling it seriously, although they were not able to secure their full demands. Taxation for the benefit of the clergy of the Establishment had been suspended for three years. Five suspending acts were passed, and in 1779 the laws for the support of the clergy were repealed. It now became impossible for the old Establishment to hope for an exclusive benefit from taxation, although the question of taxation itself still remained undecided.

" The settlement of the latter could have been accomplished by the passage of Jefferson's ' Act for Establishing Religious Freedom in Virginia.' The bill for religious freedom was reported in the House of Delegates in June, 1779. It was held up, the enemy being too strong. The act, as finally passed, reads: ' Be it enacted by the General Assembly, that no man shall be compelled to frequent or support any religious worship, place or ministry whatsoever, nor shall he be enforced, restrained, molested or burthened in his body or goods, nor shall he otherwise suffer on account of his religious opinions or belief, but that all men shall be free to profess and by argument to maintain their opinions in matters of religion, and that the same shall in no wise diminish, enlarge or affect their civil capacities.'

" The bill was not passed, however, at this session, and for a number of sessions to come. The bill failed to pass for several reasons. In 1780-'81 the State was deeply involved in the progress of the war. After the establishment of peace in 1783, the old church, which had been paralyzed by the war, began to show signs of reviving. A plan was brought forward to secure the property still held loosely by the church, by means of an act of incorporation, and to provide for the support of the clergy by a system of general taxation of all the citizens of the State for the benefit of the various churches.

" This law would give each person the right to choose the church which should receive his tax. In this way the Presbyterians, Baptists, Methodists—if they considered themselves separate—and other sects, would be established, as well as the Protestant Episcopal Church, which was the successor and heir of the old Establishment.

" *Several Makeshifts.*—The plan was formidable through its leading advocate, who was none other than Patrick Henry. Time and responsibility had cooled the once ardent radical and he had become the maintainer instead of the upsetter of systems. A number of Presbyterians, and perhaps some other dissenters, seem to have favored this plan, which would have had the merit of making preaching a somewhat less precarious profession than it was.

" A large part of the Assembly was Episcopalian. It

was accordingly possible to do something for the battered old church. As a result, a law was passed in 1784 providing for the incorporation of the Episcopal Church.

" By this law vestries were empowered to acquire property of a certain income; they might indulge in lawsuits or be sued, and (principally) they might hold the glebes and other church property formerly belonging to the Establishment, and now claimed by the Episcopal Church as heir. This act was followed in December, 1784, by ' A bill establishing a provision for the teachers of the Christian religion.' The bill embodied the plan for the general support of religion and religious sects by means of taxation.

" It was true that this bill gave the same right to all sects which called themselves Christians, a term that in those days was largely inclusive. It was not, however, in the line of religious freedom, and small consolation would the irreligious taxpayer have found in the privilege of choosing a destination for his unwillingly paid taxes. Immediately the war of petitions was renewed as never before, and from almost every county of the State came denunciations of the plan, or fervent appeals for its support.

" *Madison to the Rescue.*—James Madison was the leader in the fight against incorporations and assessment. He put forth his famous ' Remonstrance,' which at once had great effect throughout Virginia. The balance went decidedly against the taxation plan. The Presbyterians, who had in some instances favored assessment, now closed up solidly against it, and the Baptists, who had been solidly against it all along, refreshed their zeal. Madison seized the opportunity to bring forward once more Jefferson's bill for religious freedom.

" Modest James had proved to be a trusty guardian of the bill which his great and good friend, Jefferson, had fathered, and had stood by it through many disappointments. The bill passed the House on December 17th, 1785, and put an end to all church establishment, general or particular.

" But the Episcopal Church was still incorporated,

and the other religious sects sent in petition after petition opposing it, signed apparently by nearly all the inhabitants of the State. As long as the church continued incorporated, its title to the old glebes and other property handed down to it remained good. The Legislature bowed again before what was mainly the popular will, and in 1786 repealed the incorporating act. The glebes continued to remain in the hands of the vestries, where there were any vestries, but they were held by a very uncertain tenure.

" It was the object of the Baptists to change this uncertain possession into certain dispossession. The principle of republican equality was on their side. From 1786 until the end of the century the Baptists, and possibly other dissenters, continually put in petitions for the sale of the glebes and the appropriation of the proceeds for other purposes than the support of religious denominations,—*delenda est Carthago!*

" The Episcopalians struggled pathetically against the loss of this last privilege, which appeared to them as an absolute right. ' That conceiving their society hath under laws passed more than a century previous to the Revolution,' said one of their petitions, dated in 1797, ' the same right to their glebe and church as each individual has to his property legally vested during the royal government, they have continued to hold and use them for their appropriate purposes: in all other respects considering themselves in a state of perfect equality with their brethren of other societies,—ardently wishing to live in peace and harmony, and the intercourse of benevolence and charity, with all.' This was a strong plea, but the opponents of the Episcopal glebes were able to put forth the argument that the glebes in many cases represented the taxation of all the inhabitants, dissenters as well as churchmen, for the benefit of the old Establishment alone, and, therefore, that no single church had the right to property so gotten; consequently that the State should use the property for purposes which would benefit all.

" The unfailing supply of petitions at last produced their effect. In January, 1802, the Assembly passed an act directing the sale of the glebes, and the proceeds were devoted chiefly to the poor. The last scene of the religious drama in Virginia was thus played, and the Establishment totally passed away."

The supporters of ecclesiastical establishment and taxation had argued that the withdrawal of all State support from religion would mean the overthrow of religion; that religion in this world of evil cannot stand alone. Dissenters retorted with a reminder of the friendless but healthy condition of the primeval church. In the early years of the nineteenth century the former seemed to have the best of the argument, for religion was in a sad state of decline. This came about, however, from other causes than disestablishment. It was chiefly due to the license bred by war and upheaval, and to the propagation of " French principles " in the State. Virginia became full of skepticism and atheism. Curiously enough, skepticism and atheism flourished as a green bay-tree,—and yet withered, for before many years had passed there was a great and general revival of religion in the old commonwealth, and the French influence lingered as only a memory.

PART II
CIVIL WAR ANNALS

CHAPTER VIII

THE WAR STARTS—THE HOME GUARD

It is easy to understand that the great events of this period constituted a crisis in our county as well as in all the Southland. Our people—at least an overwhelming majority of them—were for the Union so long as there was hope left. Our representative in the Virginia Convention was a Union man until President Lincoln called for troops to overrun our sister Southern States; then everything underwent a change, and with few exceptions the county voted to oppose Mr. Lincoln's measures and voted for secession. With great unanimity and cordiality our people assumed the gigantic responsibility which fell upon them. Could General McClellan's views have been carried out, his great army would have landed at Urbanna and passed through the county with Richmond as the objective point. This, I believe, is undisputed history. Mr. Lincoln overruled him, and Fortress Monroe became his base. Up to late in the spring of 1862 we had not suffered any material hardships from the war. We were separated from the great armies by the York River below, and the Mattapony higher up. This circumstance saved us from untold trouble which afflicted other people more remote from Richmond than ourselves.

So soon as Mr. Lincoln's election was announced, we witnessed a great upstir; the militia had more frequent drills, under Colonel J. R. Bagby, Lieutenant Colonel T. R. Gresham, Major Roderick Dew, etc. Lincoln was inaugurated, Sumter was taken, and the government called for 70,000 soldiers to retake forts. The State Convention at once passed a vote of secession, General Lee was made commander-in-chief, and soon Virginia joined her sisters in the South.

When the tocsin of war was sounded our people showed their metal in the sending of five infantry companies to the war, besides several cavalry companies.

King and Queen County from first to last sent five infantry companies into the field. We give those companies in order: June 24, 1861, Twenty-sixth Virginia Regiment; regular officers, Colonel Powell Page, Lieutenant Colonel J. C. Councill, Major J. S. Garrett. Company H, Captain R. A. Sutton (died since war), First Lieutenant J. D. Taylor, Second Lieutenant W. C. Gayle. Company C, Twenty-sixth Regiment, Wise Brigade (see paper by Lieutenant J. W. Hundley). Company I, Twenty-sixth Virginia Regiment, Captain Spencer (see paper by Captain James Pollard). Company K, Thirty-fourth Virginia Regiment, Colonel Goode, Lieutenant Colonel Harrison, Major J. R. Bagby, Captain A. F. Bagby, etc. (see paper by Orderly Sergeant Dr. John Bagby).

Many from the county joined various companies recruited in other sections, and we feel it to be a duty to mention among these last the following names which appear to us to shine resplendent in the ranks of Lee and Stuart. There are other names worthy of mention had we space for them:

Captain Thomas W. Haynes (Company H, Ninth Virginia), son of Captain Thomas Haynes of Bruington, joined the Lee Rangers. He was as gallant a soldier as ever drew sword. Dashing and fearless, he received a desperate wound from which he never recovered, though he lived to be treasurer of King William County. He married a Miss Hawes, and died many years ago. William Campbell, now an honored resident of Dunsville, Essex County, and once representative in the legislature of Virginia, was a native of King and Queen. He married Miss Janett Latane. When the war came on he was in the far Northwest, and on his way back to King and Queen visited an uncle in Illinois, who made every effort to detain him, but failed. He then joined the cavalry, and proved himself among the bravest of the brave. An incident is told of him in Stewart's Raid in rear of McClellan,

May, 1862. Near Old Church he came face to face with an accomplished Northern cavalryman, trained at West Point in all the arts of sword practice. The conflict was severe and ended in the complete disarming and capture of the Federal soldier. Presently the captive said to Campbell: " I can't understand how you succeeded in disarming me." Campbell answered, " I am *left-handed.*" " Now I understand," said the captive. That left hand was, and still is, dangerous. Colonel Thomas Smith was a son of Hon. James Smith of Smithfield, King and Queen, and a brother of the late Captain James W. Smith of the Twenty-second Virginia Battery, and was noted for soldiery conduct. P. E. Lipscomb, at present doorkeeper of the House of Delegates (he married Miss Imogen Hawes of Poplar Grove), fought well and lost a leg in battle.

A CITIZEN'S DIARY

The extracts below are from a diary kept by one of the most venerated citizens of the county during the war, and present a vivid picture of the status here during the whole of this eventful period. So far as we know, this is the only diary extant of that period in the county. The author begs pardon in advance if these extracts should seem to relate to one section of the county, and largely to the soldiers in that immediate vicinity. What is said here in commemoration of the soldier boys from Stevensville may be understood to apply with equal force to every company from King and Queen. It would be a pleasure to give details from each company in turn, but that is not practicable, for want of necessary data.

It must be borne in mind that our county is separated from Richmond by the two branches of the York River, Pamunkey and Mattapony. This fact doubtless saved our people from numberless and nameless worries. We were by no means, however, exempted from the common perils and conflicts incident to the situation. The people were in full sympathy with the Confederate Government, and did what they could for the common cause. In addition a home guard was organized by and by, composed of men and youths who for one cause and another were exempted from service in the army. Rev. R. H. Bagby, D. D., was made captain of one company, and the rank and file was made up of some of the first citizens of the county,— Joseph Ryland, James R. Fleet, B. T. Taylor, W. P. Courtney, Sylvanus Gresham, Robert Pollard, Jr., Halbach, Porter, and others,—making in all a company of a hundred cool, daring men, ready to pursue, to stand on defense, and, if need be, to suffer for their people. This company never failed to strike at the public enemy when he came our way, and it is reported that a distinguished Federal general remarked that he had met no such spirited opposition in any other county in the State as in King and Queen. It will be seen in the sequel how these old men distinguished themselves in encounters with Union forces.

Kilpatrick's Raid.—General Kilpatrick, commanding a body of horse, came into the county May 5-6, 1863, and camped in a field opposite Locust Cottage (Stevensville). That night our people had a new experience, and there occurred at Locust Cottage, the home of Mr. and Mrs. John N. Gresham, a scene which, withal, was highly amusing. The General sent word to Mrs. G. that he and his aids would take tea with her. She made ready, and the company sat down. As the lady of the house poured out the tea, she boldly remarked, " Did I ever think it would come to this, that I should be pouring out tea for Yankee soldiers, come to waste and destroy? " The General, not at all disconcerted, coolly remarked: " Never mind, madam, we have only come to seek and to save that which was lost." The cavalry did no special harm, save that numerous horses were taken, and next morning went on its way. Stragglers from the ranks, however, not under the eye of the General, were very offensive. Old citizens, notably Samuel P. Ryland and James Robert Fleet, were unhorsed, robbed, and beaten.

The Spears Raid, so-called.—On July 8th, 1862, a

squad of cavalry came up from Gloucester Point and camped at King and Queen Courthouse, the object being to break up boats and prevent crossing the river on the road to Richmond. We give here an interesting account by Dr. B. H. Walker of an encounter next day between them and the home guard at Walkerton. The account in Dr. Walker's diary runs:

" So soon as we learned that the Yankees were coming up the road towards Walkerton, Major Bagby [at home on furlough], and I arranged a plan to capture them. I was to go the Ridge road by Butler's Tavern, gather all the men I could, and make for Walkerton. When I reached that village, I found several of the home guard, and others, including Mordecai Cook, a youth, eight in all. In half an hour a Yankee lieutenant, with five men rode up, inquired for the ferryboat; but the ferryboat had been hastily taken down the river. Presently the lieutenant walked into the store. My gun was lying on the counter. He and I scuffled over the gun. William Turner shot him with a pistol, but he ran out into the yard, and Alfred Gwathmey shot him with buckshot. A fusilade began between us and the remaining four men. One man was shot from his horse and another from behind a tree by Mordecai and killed. The rest were scattered. I then agreed to go up to Richmond and post the authorities about conditions in our county. Colonel Goode at White House was ordered by General Lee, through myself, to send soldiers to our aid. Before he could do so, the enemy had retired to Gloucester Point."

Major Bagby and Holder Hudgins.—Pending all this, Major Bagby had come into the river road near Mantua Ferry, where a citizen from Mathews named Holder Hudgins, with a wagonload of provisions on the way to Richmond, had been halted by a squad of Union cavalry. The major, without disclosing his identity, remonstrated against the arrest of private citizens, and the soldiers were evidently intimidated. The major withdrew, and taking a position just below, awaited developments. Presently two soldiers came down at a rapid pace, and refusing to halt when summoned, the major fired, killing one of them. The rest of the squad were captured by the home guard. Thus ended the first raid into King and Queen County.

Dahlgren Raid, March 2-3, 1864.—Lieutenant Colonel Ulric Dahlgren, a son of Admiral D., U. S. N., was young, dashing, and chivalrous. We here subjoin a succinct account of this notable raid from a painstaking statement of the facts compiled by Prof. John Pollard, D. D.:

"In the winter of 1863-4 the Army of North Virginia lay near Orange Courthouse, the Army of the Potomac (General Meade) in Culpepper County, the Rapidan separating them. In February an expedition, supposed to be planned by government in Washington. General Kilpatrick, with four thousand cavalry, to pass General Lee's right flank, destroy railways, and dash into Richmond. February 28th, 7 P. M., Kilpatrick left Stevensburg, crossed at the lower ford (Ely's) to Spottsylvania. Here Dahlgren with four hundred picked men was detached to go by Frederick Hall (C. & O. R. R.), capture a park of artillery there, cross James River to south side, release prisoners at Belle Isle, arm them, set city on fire, etc. The colonel picked up a negro guide to lead him to a ford over the James, and was carried to Dover Mills. He reached Dover Mills at 8 A. M., March 1st—two nights and one day on road—say ninety miles. Thus far, all well, though tired. But at Dover the poor negro could not point out a ford, and was hung for his pains. When Dahlgren, turning then down the river to rejoin General Kilpatrick, reached neighborhood of city, Kilpatrick had been driven off and moved down Peninsula. Dahlgren came within three miles of city, lost forty men, and was compelled to retire and escape as best he could. He moved around to Hungary station (R. F. & P.), came to Brooke Turnpike, and moved northeast. Meantime his force separated—some moving after Kilpatrick, and one hundred or one hundred and fifty under Dahlgren to cross Pamunkey and Mattapony and so retire to Gloucester Point. Entered King William at Hanover Town, King and Queen at Ayletts. This county is sixty-five miles long, running along the Mattapony, with not a single settlement larger than a village. Average of virtue and intelligence far above usual, [the people] ardently devoted to Confederate cause and ready to assert their devotion. Young men were at the front; old men organized a regular company (officers commissioned regularly), as home guard for local defense. R. H. Bagby, D. D., captain,—one of the ablest ministers in Virginia. In addition to home guard there were fifty or seventy-five troopers from army in the county recruiting. So soon as it was known that Colonel Dahlgren was crossing the river above, the defense began to gather in squads. It was now March 3, 1864. Half mile above Bruington his rear attacked by twenty-five men, and one man killed,—a corporal,—just at Bethlehem, a colored church. "The blood of the martyrs is the seed of the church," said a Confed-

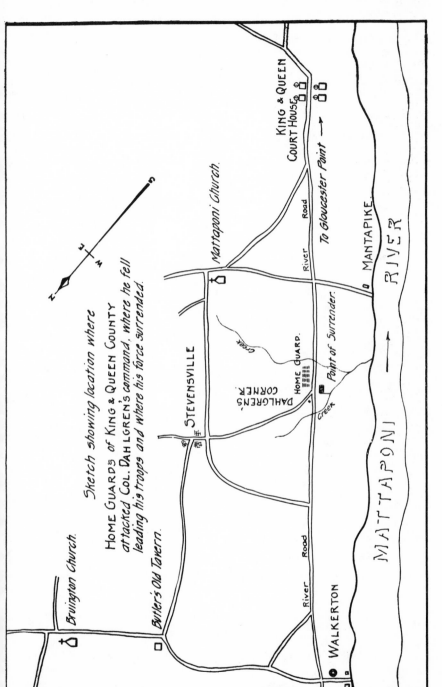

Sketch showing location where HOME GUARDS of KING & QUEEN COUNTY attacked Col. DAHLGREN'S command, where he fell leading his troops and where his force surrendered.

Bruington Church.

Butler's Old Tavern.

STEVENSVILLE

DAHLGREN'S CORNER

HOME GUARD.

Point of Surrender.

Creek

Mattaponi Church.

River Road

To Gloucester Point →

KING & QUEEN COURT HOUSE

MANTAPIKE

WALKERTON

River Road

MATTAPONI ← RIVER

erate. Below Bruington the road branches, one fork passing down toward and along the river, the other by Stevensville, rejoining the first a mile below that point. At point of junction is the "Dahlgren corner." The home guard and some sixty soldiers having moved ahead, stationed themselves in a wooded thicket here, about nightfall, and awaited Dahlgren's approach.

" Captain Fox was in supreme command (Major Pollard sick at Mr. Bagby's), his men posted on northeast angle of the two roads. Night without moon, but not all dark.

" Just about midnight Dahlgren moved slowly down upon corner. Discovering his enemy, there was a recoil, but Dahlgren drew his pistol, called to his men, and moved up, resolutely demanding surrender. The flash of arms broke upon midnight shadows, and Colonel Dahlgren, young, ardent, brave, enthusiastic, fell over into a ditch, pierced by five bullets. The column then withdrew into a neighboring field. Christopher B. Fleet and A. C. Acree scouted around and located them. Next morning all surrendered save officers, who escaped but were captured afterwards by Captain R. H. B. The captures amounted to one hundred and thirty-five soldiers, forty negroes, besides horses and arms. Major Cook, second in command, left with four or five others during night, but was taken as aforesaid.[1] Colonel Dahlgren's watch, memorandum-book, and ring were taken; and there was some mutilation, which was afterwards regretted. A lock of his hair [2] was preserved by Mrs. Juliet Pollard, and afterwards sent to his father. [He was signally avenged by General Kilpatrick in the burning of the county courthouse, clerk's office, etc.] The morning following, a rude coffin was made, and by and by a grave dug. A few gentle friends were in the act of lowering the body into grave, when orders came to send body to Richmond. This was done and he was buried at Oakwood. Thence it was secretly removed, through Miss Van Lew, a Union sympathizer, to the neighborhood of Laurel, whence again it went north into the hands of his family after the surrender. The admiral wrote to the government immediately after the surrender, inclosing one hundred dollars in gold and asking for the body. As it had been moved from

---

[1] This is interesting: Thirty years after this a young man entered a hotel in a western city and recorded the name Bagby. The eye of a stranger fell upon the lettering. He asked the young man if he was from King and Queen County, Virginia. On receiving an affirmative answer he proved to be the identical Major Cook, and the young man before him a son of his old captor. They had a kindly chat together.

[2] This was taken from his head by Moore B. Wright, a member of the home guard, and was left in the keeping of Mrs. John Pollard, Sr.; after Appomattox the hair was left in charge of the provost at Stevensville, to be transmitted to Admiral Dahlgren.

Oakwood by secret Federal sympathizers, the government was greatly perplexed. Evacuation solved the difficulty. Thus the colonel was buried four times.

After Colonel Dahlgren was killed the officers of his command, six in number, with Major Cook in the lead, escaped. Next day, March 4th, they came, well-nigh starved, to the overseer's house on farm of Captain R. H. Bagby, some two hundred yards from the dwelling. The preacher-captain at once seized his pistol and followed by his son, Dr. J. B., and a colored servant, Jim Boler, rushed into the house where the officers were seated waiting for supper, no guard as yet being stationed, and the officers at once surrendered to his summons. The whole party were sent prisoners to Richmond.

Confederate force at Dahlgren Corner on night of March 3, 1864: Cavalry, Pollard, twenty-five men; Captain Fox, fifteen men; Captain Todd, nine men; Captain Magruder, seventy men. Captain Bagby's home guard, thirty-four men; Captain Halbach (schoolboys), fourteen.— one hundred and sixty-seven men in all. Only about one hundred of Dahlgren's men were captured, some were killed enroute, and probably some escaped. After the capture large quantities of silverware, rings, and watches, with other valuables, which had been taken from wealthy families, were retaken from the persons of the prisoners."

Second Kilpatrick Raid, March 10, 1864.—General Kilpatrick, at the head of a large cavalry force, came up from Gloucester Point March 10, 1864, to avenge the loss of Dahlgren and his force. The Courthouse, clerk's office, tavern, and private property were burned. Kilpatrick was opposed by General Beal with the Ninth Confederate Cavalry, and lost some of his men, but soon returned, leaving smouldering ruins in his track.

Sheridan's Raid.—Part of Burnside's corps passed through the upper portion of the county May, 1864, but made no tarrying. Later, General Sheridan, returning from his engagement with Hampton at Trevillians, came into the county and camped at the Courthouse, but returned the next day and rejoined General Grant on the Chickahominy. Our people suffered more from this raid than perhaps from any other during the war. Our people were greatly overwhelmed, in common with their fellows, when tidings came of the surrender at Appomattox. Sheridan camped, both going and coming, at Farmington, five miles above Walkerton. He burned Walkerton Mill and otherwise inflicted great damage.

(By Spottswood Bird.)

A Major Wilson of the Fifth Regiment, Pennsylvania Cavalry, U. S. A., was in command of the first Federal force which came up the county in 1862. On June —, 1862, he captured three Confederate soldiers at Frazier's Ferry (on King and Queen side), and brought them to the Courthouse, where he kept them until the afternoon of that day. He sent a party of about twelve men with a lieutenant to Walkerton, where they encountered some youths and citizens who had hastily gathered there for defense. The encounter resulted in the death and wounding of several of the enemy and the capture of all the rest, except one man, who escaped and reached the Courthouse that afternoon, on whose arrival and report of the disaster to them, Major Wilson hastened his force back to Gloucester Point as rapidly as possible. He took a wagon and pair of mules from Mrs. Martin in which to carry the three captured Confederates, promising her to return the wagon and mules, which, to the surprise of us all, he did in about a week or ten days later, sending them by a citizen of Gloucester County, who at his request took a receipt from Mrs. Martin for the return of the wagon and team. The demeanor and gentlemanly conduct of this Major Wilson and his men while at the Courthouse were in the highest degree commendable, and in luminous contrast to the vandalism which ever afterwards characterized the raids under officers of a far different type, who spread terror and destruction in their path.

Colonel Spears of the Eleventh Regiment, Pennsylvania Cavalry, burned all the buildings, public and private, at King and Queen Courthouse on the morning of March 10th, 1864.

The following were members of Company F, Twenty-fourth Virginia Cavalry, organized at King and Queen

Courthouse in spring of 1863:   L. W. Allen, captain;
Preston Bird, Spottswood Bird, T. N. Jones, and James
E. Hooper.   There were two other companies of cavalry organized at the same time and place, one commanded by Captain Richard Hord of Gloucester
County, and the other by Captain ————, afterwards
by Captain James Jeffries.

CHAPTER IX

ROSTERS OF KING AND QUEEN COUNTY IN THE CIVIL WAR

Officers of Twenty-sixth Virginia Regiment: Colonel, Powell Page; Lieutenant-Colonel, J. C. Councill; Majors, Joseph Garrett and N. B. Street.

COMPANY C, TWENTY-SIXTH VIRGINIA INFANTRY.

(Wise's Brigade).

[Supplied by Rev. John W. H. Hundley].

Captain,	N. B. Street
First Lieutenant,	James R. Houser
Second Lieutenant,	John W. Hundley
Second Lieutenant,	James R. Hart
First Sergeant,	Andrew B. Cauthorn
Second Sergeant,	Benjamin F. Eubank
Third Sergeant,	Lemuel S. Roane
Fourth Sergeant,	Joseph Tucker

Corporals: Robert Bland, William Didlake, Thomas Dike, Robert Lumpkin.

(At the reorganization in 1862 Lieutenant Hart was succeeded by Andrew B. Cauthorn; James Thurston was made First Sergeant.)

Company C was mustered into service at Gloucester Point, June 12th (I think), 1861.

PRIVATES:

Adkins, John	Burbank, Jacob [2]	Collier, Robert
Ainsley, William	Burton, Cornelius [2]	Collins, John
Allen, William	Carlton, John	Corr, D. F.
Bland, James Polk	Carlton, Richard 1st	Creswell, John [3]
Booton, Benjamin [1]	Carlton, Richard 2d	Davis, ———
Booton, Henry	Carlton, Robert	Davis, Benjamin
Booton, William	Carlton, Wm. Henry	Eubank, John [2]

[1] Killed at Nottaway Bridge, 1864.
[2] Killed, ———————, June 15, 1864.
[3] Taken prisoner, June 15, 1864.

Evans, Cyrus
Fleet, James
Flemming, Dennis
Fletcher, Robert
Garrett, Joseph
Garrett, Lemuel
Garrett, Montgomery
Gibson, George
Good, John
Hart, Jos. W. (Rev.)
Hilliard, Quint [3]
Hoskins, John B.
Hurt, Buck
Jesse, Richard
Kerr, Harvey
Kidd, W. H.
Lucas, Thomas

Lucas, William
Lumpkin, Quint
Moody, W. H.
Muire, James
Muire, Samuel
Newbill, George T.
Newbill, William T.
Oliver, Frank [3]
Oliver, Leslie
Parron, Henry
Pendleton, George
Prince, James
Purcell, R. B.
Redd, George
Redd, John
Richerson, Andrew [4]
Richerson, Elias

Richerson, W. J.
Smither, ——
Smither, William
Shelton, —— (1)
Shelton, —— (2)
Taylor, ——[5]
Taylor, Philip
Taylor, Richard
Trice, Edward [4]
Tyler, Benjamin R.
Tyler, Lewis A.
Watkins, Corbin
Watlington, James
Williams, Calhoun
Williams, Charles (?)
Williams, Junius B.
Wilson, ——[6]

COMPANY G, TWENTY-SIXTH VIRGINIA INFANTRY.

[By W. S. Courtney.]

Captain, R. H. Spencer (captured, Petersburg, June 15, '64)
First Lieutenant, R. B. Roy (captured, Hatcher's Run, April 7, '65)
Second Lieutenant, M. B. Davis (wounded and captured, Petersburg, June 15, 1864; killed, Hatcher's Run)
Third Lieutenant, A. P. Bird (wounded, died at home)

First Sergeant, J. W. Turner; Second Sergeant, William H. Jackson (captured) ;Third Sergeant, William J. Eubank; Fourth Sergeant, F. A. Morsball (killed) ; Fifth Sergeant, J. M. Bew (wounded, Howlett House, May 20, 1864)

Corporals: G. F. Hart, G. W. Hayes (killed, June 15, 1864), G. W. Turner (killed), James H. Turner.

[3] Taken prisoner, June 15, 1864.
[4] Killed, July, 1864.
[5] Mortally wounded, June 17, 1864.
[6] Died near Chaffin's Bluff, 1863.

CAPT. EDWARD CAMPBELL FOX

Fifth Virginia Cavalry, Army Northern Virginia, in command at
Dahlgren's Corner; killed in battle at Yellow Tavern.

PRIVATES:

Acree, Horace
Acree, W. N.
Bew, Hezekiah
Bew, Jno.
Bland, Dr. J. E.
Bray, W. T.
Brooks, William G.
Brown, George
Brown, J. L.
Burton, R. C.
Burton, R. E.
Burton, Robert B.
Callis, Charles
Cardwell, George W.[1]
Cardwell, J. N.[2]
Carlton, Ira
Carlton, Levi
Carlton, W. B.[3]
Carter, Frank
Carter, Robert
Cauthorn, G. W.
Colly, James
Colly, Jno.[4]
Courtney, W. S.[4] *
Crittenden, S. S.
Davis, Albert
Davis, James A.
Davis, Joseph A.
Diggs, R. D.

Donovan, Jno.
Edwards, Alfred [5]
Edwards, Dunbar
Egar, J. H.
Estis, F. B.[4]
Estis, J. S.
Eubank, A. W.
Gaines, Jno.
Garrett, Augustin
Garrett, Richard [4]
Garrett, Thomas C.[4]
Gibson, Adolphus
Gibson, George [2]
Gibson, Jno. C.
Groom, Benjamin
Guthrie, B. E.
Hilliard, Allen
Hogg, William
Huckstep, Charles H.
Hurt, W. H.[4]
Knapp, Joseph N.
Landrum, Joseph [4]
Marshall, Jno.[4]
Mirick, Newton [4]
Murphy, W. A.
Norman, J. G.
Norman, James J.
Oglesby, George [4]
Oglesby, Richard [4]

Oglesby, William
Parker, Albert
Parker, S. P.
Rives, James
Seward, Ed.
Seward, John [5]
Seward, R. B.[4]
Smith, Lewis W.
Spencer, Gideon L.
Spencer, James R.
Spencer, T. B.
Thurston, F. A.[3]
Thurston, William
Tuttle, Edw. D.
Tuttle, Jerome
Walton, L. R.
Walton, Reuben [1]
Wheeler, Baylor
Wyatt, Andrew
Wyatt, Jno. R.
Wyatt, Levi
Wyatt, Robert S.
Wyatt, Thomas W.
Wyatt, W. N.[3]
Yarrington, Andrew [6]
Yarrington, James [5]
Yarrington, R. H.

COMPANY H, TWENTY-SIXTH VIRGINIA INFANTRY.

[By Lieutenant J. D. Taylor.]

(Wise's Brigade).

Mustered in June 24, 1861, Gloucester Point, Va.

Captain, R. A. Sutton (died since war)

* I never missed a day's duty in four years, two months, ten days.
Never had furlough, except captured June 15, 1864.—W. S. C.

[1] Wounded.
[2] Killed.
[3] Captured.

[4] Captured, June 15, 1864.
[5] Killed, June 15, 1864.
[6] Killed, 1864.

First Lieutenant, J. D. Taylor
Second Lieutenant, W. C. Gayle (died since war)
Third Lieutenant, G. P. Lively (died since war)

First Sergeant,	J. W. Bland
Second Sergeant,	M. C. Meredith [1]
Third Sergeant,	Thomas Bowden [2]
Fourth Sergeant,	Rodney Bland [3]
First Corporal,	J. M. Shelton [3]
Second Corporal,	A. T. Bland [4]
Third Corporal,	Thomas Fary
Fourth Corporal,	Joseph Williams [3]

PRIVATES:

Anderson, L. E.[3]
Anderson, R. H.[3]
Booker, B. T.[6]
Bowden, R. E.
Bowden, Thomas
Bristow, A.
Broach, Benjamin
— Brown, George [5]
Brushwood, L. C.[4]
Cook, J. R.[3]
Cook, Paskal
Corr, M. W.
Didlake, John [3]
Didlake, Joshua [7]
Didlake, Nathan
Edwards, Alfred [3]
Edwards, D.
Elliott, Alexander
Elliott, Paskal [3]
Elliott, Powell [3]
Fary, G. T.
Fary, W. E.

Fleming, Henry[3]
Gains, B. T.
Gains, J. A.[3]
Gains, R. H.[3]
Garrett, Alfred [3]
Garrett, Gustavus [3]
Groom, Beverley [3]
Groom, L.
Groom, Richard [3]
Hall, Robert
Hall, William
Johnson, John
Jones, William
Kemp, Thomas [3]
Kilingham, Thomas
Likins, Joseph
Mason, Thomas
Mason, Windon [2]
Massey, William
Milby, C.
Milby, H.[8]
Milby, J. T.[6]

Milby, L.
Milby, Malachi
Morris, A. S.
Moss, George
Pierce, Phw.[3]
Riley, G. D.[3]
Riley, J. L.[e]
Riley, J. T.[6]
Roane, E. N.
Roane, L. M.[3]
Roane, Richard
Russell, W. H.
Shelton, James
Skates, A.[9]
Walcott, A. J.[3]
Ware, Gustave [3]
Ware, J. T.
Ware, James [1]
Williams, R.
Wood, T.
Yarrington, E.[10]
Yarrington, T.

[1] Killed at Petersburg, June 17, 1864.
[2] Killed at Osborne Turnpike.
[3] Died since the war.
[4] Died at Chaffin's Farm, 1862.
[5] Killed June 15, 1864.
[6] Died in prison.
[7] Killed at Petersburg, on picket.
[8] Died at home during war.
[9] Killed near Five Forks.
[10] Killed, battle of the Crater, July 30, 1864.

COMPANY I, TWENTY-SIXTH VIRGINIA INFANTRY

[By Captain Josephus Pollard.]

Captain,	J. W. Smith
First Lieutenant,	S. P. Latane
Second Lieutenant,	A. C. Walker
Third Lieutenant,	A. F. Fleet
First Sergeant,	Josephus L. Pollard
Second Sergeant,	George L. Owens
Third Sergeant,	Richard Jeffries
Fourth Sergeant,	Griffin Longest
Fifth Sergeant,	Bernard Eubank

PRIVATES:

Alexander, Harvey
Allen, Joseph
Atkins, Thomas
Baldwin, W. B.
Ball, G. W.
Ball, Harry
Ball, James
Bradley, George
Chilton, C. D.
Clark, Howard
Cooke, Carr
Cooke, Claiborne
Cooke, Henry
Cooke, Joseph
Cooke, Thomas
Elliott, W. I.
Gatewood, W. H.
Graves, D. T.
Harper, Mac
Harper, W.
Hutchison, Thomas
Longest, Howard
Longest, I. T.
Longest, John
Longest, Younger

Loven, W. L.
Lumpkin, W. H.
Martin, ———
Martin, C. D.
Martin, C. H.
Martin, Howard
Minor, Philip
Minor, Robert
Mitchell, William
Montague, W. V.
Mundy, L. G.
Mundy, William
Owens, B. H.
Owens, R. D.
Owens, W. G.
Parker, Elijah
Prince, Baylor
Prince, James
Reed, Edmund
Reed, I. W.
Reed, Richard
Rouse, T. B.
Rouse, Tazwell A.
Rowe, E.
Sale, A. J.

Schools, R. B.
Schools, T. A.
Schools, Thomas
Schools, W. G.
Simpkins, I. F.
Simpkins, Lawrence
Skelton, Granville
Skelton, I. H.
Skelton, James
Skelton, W.
Smither, L. R.
Stouse, Richard
Trice, George H.
Trice, James W.
Trice, Jno. F.
Trice, P. P.
Verlander, Jno. L.
Verlander, Mordecai
Watkins, Edward
Watkins, Hugh
Wilson, C. L.
Wilson, Calvin
Wilson, Seymour
Wilson, Thomas H.

Officers Thirty-fourth Virginia Regiment: Colonel, T. F. Goode; Lieutenant-Colonel, ——— Harrison; Major, J. R. Bagby.

COMPANY K, THIRTY-FOURTH VIRGINIA INFANTRY.

[By Dr. John Bagby, O. S.]

Captain, A. F. Bagby (wounded on retreat from Petersburg)

First Lieutenant, J. Ryland (wounded, June 17, 1864, at Petersburg; captured, October 28, 1864)

Second Lieutenant, William T. Haynes (discharged, March 13, 1865, to join Mosby)

Third Lieutenant, B. H. Walker (killed, December 18, 1864)

First Sergeant, Jno. Bagby (wounded, March 31, 1865, near Five Forks)

Second Sergeant, Jno. W. Ryland (wounded at Seven Pines, May 31, 1862)

Third Sergeant, E. F. Acree (promoted to Color Sergeant)

Fourth Sergeant, T. C. Segar (killed, June 17, 1864)

Fifth Sergeant, J. L. Cosby (wounded, December 7, 1864)

Corporals: B. F. Cooke, A. V. Daniel (wounded), George W. Didlake (wounded, October 13, 1864), H. T. Lumpkin (died September 13, 1865)

PRIVATES:

Ashley, C. B.

Bagby E. (killed, July 30, 1864)

Bagby, Richard

Bagby, T. (wounded, May 18, 1864; retired, December 8, 1864)

Berkeley, N. (wounded and died, May 30, 1864)

Booker, I. D. (wounded, Nov. 2, 1864)

Booker, J. W. (retired for six months)

Broocke, W. R.

Brushwood, I.

Carlton, Benj. (wounded, May 31, 1862 [at Seven Pines], and May 18, 1864)

Carlton, Fountain (died of typhoid fever, 1862)

Casey, William (wounded, July 24; died, July 25, 1864)

Cashen, M.

Chaplin, P. B.

Coleman, R. L. (captured)

Cook, G. W.

Cooke, I. M. (wounded, June 26; died, August 14, 1864)

Corr, George T. (died of pneumonia, March 12, 1865)

Crossfield, J. A. (wounded, May 18; died, May 21, 1864)

Crouch, G. W. (wounded, June 16, 1864)

Crouch, T. J.

Davis, J. S. (wounded, March 28, 1865, and died)

Deshazo, J. M.
Didlake, Charles (wounded October 16, 1864 and died)
Didlake, J. H.
Didlake, R. S. (wounded, March 28, 1865, and died)
Drudge, Joseph
Easley, M. (wounded, Dec. 7; died, Dec. 15, 1864)
Eubank, J. H. (wounded, March 31, 1865)
Flournoy, D. (retired, Feb. 21, 1864)
Fogg, J. U. (wounded, Nov. 26, 1864)
Gleason, R. H.
Gleason, W. W. (died, Sept. 8, 1864)
Graham, S. L. (wounded, Aug. 26, 1864)
Gresham, J. A. (wounded, July 9, 1864)
Gresham, J. H. (wounded at Seven Pines; promoted to Sergeant)
Gresham, R. H. (wounded, July 8, 1864)
Harper, C.
Harris, J. (killed, August 13, 1864)
Harrison, J. B. (discharged)
Howell, J. C. (captured, June 15, 1864, and died in prison)
Hundley, J. T. C. (captured, June 15, 1864)
Hurt, G. H. (captured, June 15, 1864)
Jones, S. V. (wounded, March 31, 1865)
Kelley, T. C.
Kemp, J.
Kemp, J. B. (killed, July 6, 1864)
Lumpkin, T. F. (captured, June 15, 1864)
Lyne, R. A.
McLelland, B. W. (captured, June 15, 1864)
Moore, J. S.
Moore, L. (deserted, December 1, 1864)
Myrick, J. T. (wounded at Seven Pines, May 31, 1862, and retired)
Nunn, C. R.
Nunn, J. G. (captured on retreat)
Nunn, S. S. (captured)
Parks, J. W. (wounded, July 29; died, December, 31, 1864)
Patterson, George A. (wounded, November 27, 1864)
Pendleton, H. C. (wounded, May 18, 1864)
Perkins, M. C. (wounded, December 13, 1864)
Phillips, George (wounded, March 31, 1864)
Porter, C. W.
Powers, J. F. (killed, September 11, 1864)
Pynes, J. A.
Pynes, W. M. (wounded, May 18, 1864)
Reed, J. R. (wounded)
Ryland, N. (wounded, May 20, 1864)

Ryland, S. (wounded, July, 1864; was in the last of fight at Appomattox, April 9, 1865)

Sale, B. P.

Sale, J. C.

Sanford, H. (wounded)

Scott, B. S. (wounded, May 18, 1864)

Scott, T. W. (wounded, June 16, 1864)

Segar, F. V. (received seven wounds at Seven Pines, May 31, 1862)

Segar, H. G. (wounded, May 18, 1864)

Silverthornes, I. C. (wounded)

Smith, L. R.

Smith, W. R. (died, August 20, 1864)

Spencer, W. M. (died, August 2, 1864)

Temple, W. (made corporal September 16, 1864, and captured)

Terry, J. H.

Terry, S.

Thornton, F. (wounded, July 30, 1864)

Thweatt, W. G. (wounded, May 18, 1864)

Tillage, W. J. (deserted)

Turner, E. (died of pneumonia)

Turner, L. (transferred, August 8, 1864)

Vaughan, W. H. (wounded, August 3, 1864)

Walker, J. W.

Walker, T. N. (made corporal, September 16, 1864)

Walker, W. H.

Walton, J. W.

Walton, Z. (wounded, May 18; died, June 7, 1864)

Wessels, J. T.

Willroy, J. W. (transferred, December 15, 1864, to Mosby's Battery)

Wiltshire, J. M.

Wise, J. H.

Wright, J. F.

Young, H. H.

Young, J. M.

In addition to these we have to report a number of cavalry companies, as follows:

ROSTER OF COMPANY E, FIFTH VIRGINIA CAVALRY.

CAPTAINS:

Marius P. Todd, Campbell Fox, Richard Hoard, William C. Nunn

LIEUTENANTS:

W. C. Nunn, W. S. Dicks, William Hoskins, William P. Bohanan, Robert B. Hart

SERGEANTS:

Campbell Fox, Robert B. Hart, H. K. Evans

PRIVATES:

Acree, Alexander
Albright, Mathias
Blake, Cisero
Blake, Llewelyn
Bland, B. F.
Bland, Joel
Bray, Joel
Bray, James [1]
Bristow, Andrew
Brooks, William G.
Bourno, Theo.
Bourno, Thomas
Butler, Flemming
Buckner, John
Bulsman, Leroy
Burch, William R.
Burton, Robert
Brown, Hyte (Hite)
Callis, James
Cardwell, William
Carlton, Granvil
Carlton, Isaac
Carlton, Leroy
Catlet, Bradly
Cauthorn, Ira B.
Clark, Temple
Clayton, Enoch [3]
Cloudis, E. C.
Collins, George A.
Cook, Fountain [1]
Cook, Monroe [2]
Cook, William
Crittendon, George D.
Daniel, George
Daniel, Robert
Davis, Robert [1]

Davis, Stage
Dew, Benjamin
Dew, William
Dudley, Thomas [1]
Eastwood, A. W.
Eubank, J. C.
Fauntleroy, Garnet [1]
Fleet, Jno. A.
Folliard, Jno. P.
Garret, Adolphus
Garret, James W.
Garret, Robert
Gibson, James
Gibson, Philip
Gregory, Fendal
Gresham, Charles
Gwathmey, Alfred
Gwathmey, Archie
Gwathmey, Charles
Gwathmey, Llewelyn
Harwood, Archie
Hobday, Charles E.
Howlet, John
Hutchinson, Paine
Johnson, James
Kemp, Thomas
Lane, Oscar
Lane, Rucker
Lipscomb, E. P.
Machen, Thomas
Machen, William
Marchant, " Wash "
Martin, George
Martin, William [1]
Minter, J. W.
Mitchell, John

Monghaw, James
Muire, Marcus A.
Muso, W. S.—" Buck "
Oliver, Frank [1]
Purcell, J. H.
Revere, Peter
Revere, Thomas
Richardson, J.—
" Pungy "
Richardson, Jas. H.[4]
Richardson, Thos.
Richardson, W. T.
Roane, William E.
Rowe, James
Rowe, Laurence
Rowe, Thomas
Saunders, L. A.
Savage, Thomas K.
Skelton, Philip
Smith, Lewis A.
Smith, Richard
Sorrel, Hiraus
South, Robert
Stone, Andrew
Turpin, Archie
Turpin, " Jack "
Tyler, Thomas
Walden, Frank
Walker, Melvin
Walker, Watson
Watkins, Charles
Watkins, "Clayborn" [5]
Watkins, J. Polk
Watkins, Townley
Wayn, Joseph [1]
White, William H.

[1] Killed. [2] Disabled. [3] Deserted. [4] Died in prison.
[5] I think that was his name. He was an up-county man, with light hair and florid complexion.

We are unable to give Rosters of two other cavalry companies made up largely from King and Queen, to wit, Capt. Allen's and Capt. Magruder's.

COUNTERSIGNS

Some persons will be interested in the following daily countersigns given out by officer of day on dates mentioned:

At Gloucester Point, 1862: January 4th, Davis; 8th, McLaws; 10th, Richmond; 20th, Chericoke; 23d, Selma; 26th, Yorktown; 29th, Hampton; February 8th, Sumter; 16th, Charleston; 24th, Maryland; March 6th, Davis; May 1st, Asia; 15th, Portsmouth; 25th, Fairfax; June 5th, Ceylon; 15th, Morgan; 25th, Gloucester; 28th, Damascus; August 22d, Arcola; September 2d, Forest; 12th, London; 24th, Vandome; 28th, Leesburg; October 4th, Natchez; 5th, Egypt; 8th, Lee; 11th, Rhodes; 13th, Leesburg; 23d, Cadiz; 29th, Page; November 4th, Kinston; 12th, Fayette; 19th, Tyler; 25th, Centreville; 30th, New Orleans; December 3d, Virginia; 8th, Phillippi; 12th, Abingdon; 16th, Missouri; 20th, Shelby; 25th, Mobile; 28th, Charlotte; 1863, January 2d, Augusta; 6th, Raleigh; 12th, Macon; 18th, Monroe; 23d, Vandome; 28th, Johnston; February 2d, Kinston; 8th, Keokuk; 15th, Grafton; 18th, Pekin; 24th, Paris; March 2d, Preston; 8th, Charleston; 15th, Augusta; 21st, Vance; 27th, Bragg; April 2d, France; 13th, Quincy.

At Diascon Bridge, 1863: April 20th, Wise; 30th, Virginia; May 5th, Heath; 7th, Acoquan; 13th, England; 20th, Pekin; 25th, Egypt; 30th, China; June 5th, Ney; 10th, Merida; 15th, Nestor; 21st, Eipley; 25th, Pocotaligo; July 2d, Cairo; 7th, Dover; 13th, Hagerstown; 20th, Generic; 27th, Raleigh; August 3d, Goshen; 11th, Winton; 16th, Nashville; 20th, Braxton; 24th, Bedford; 28th, Gauley; September 7th, South; 16th, Vicksburg; 29th, Murfreesboro; October 8th, Mississippi; 15th, Johnston, etc., etc.

CHAPTER X

Captain A. F. Bagby's brief memoir of his cousin, Major John R. Bagby, and his account of the company in command of which he succeeded his cousin, is the first historical sketch I have seen of this gallant major and his gallant command; and I hope that Captain Bagby's example will be followed by others in bringing to notice the services of other organizations which have not been duly noticed in our histories and essays.

KING AND QUEEN ARTILLERY COMPANY

Captain Bagby's Account of Its Work at Battle of Seven Pines— Marched in Mud and Water—Official Records Show the Good Work of Men of King and Queen.

" The King and Queen Artillery " is not named as such in the general orders of the war records. We find, however, Bagby's Company, Fourth Artillery, mentioned, and there are several official recognitions of its valiant and efficient service. There is no doubt whatever that " The King and Queen Artillery " company is the organization referred to.

" Bagby's Company, Virginia Volunteers, serving as heavy artillery," is designated as part of the command of Colonel C. A. Crump, under Major General John B. Magruder, at Gloucester Point.—War Records, Series I., Vol. IX., p. 37.

The report of Captain John R. Bagby, Fourth Virginia Battalion, of the operations of that organization at Seven Pines, May 31st and June 1st, 1862, appears in Series I., Vol. II. (first part) of the War Records, at page 968, where Captain Bagby recites that " the battalion, without any regular organization, having been together but a few days before they were ordered into battle, and having no opportunity to acquaint themselves with infantry drill, with the exception of Captain White's company, a temporary organization was effected, without authority, by the election of Captain C. C. Otey as lieutenant colonel and Captain John R. Bagby as major."

In the battle of Seven Pines the Fourth Battalion lost in killed and wounded six (6) commissioned officers and eighty (80) enlisted men; and played a worthy part in the action, serving alternately as infantry, artillery, and infantry again. Captain Bagby says in his report:

" On the morning of May 31st, 1862, after a fatiguing march through mud and water of several miles, we were formed in line of battle on the right of the Williamsburg Road. From thence we passed through the woods to an opening in front of the enemy's intrenchments on Barker's farm. We were then ordered to charge the enemy through some felled trees, which we did without encountering any serious resistance, and reached the enemy's intrenchments in good order, some four or five of the battalion being wounded. At this juncture one of the companies (Captain Bagby's) was ordered to take charge of three pieces of artillery left by the retreating foe. This duty was discharged, firing into two regiments of Yankees forming to attack us, with considerable effect. Also a portion of Captain Montague's company was detailed to assist in Captain Carter's battery, many of his cannoneers having been disabled. The battalion was then ordered forward, Captain Bagby's company again taking its position in the battalion, and ordered to charge the enemy in ambush among felled trees on the right of Barker's house. We passed through the enemy's tents, wheeled to the right, and upon reaching the edge of the felled trees threw ourselves on the ground and fired upon the enemy whenever they showed themselves. After being in this position some fifteen or twenty minutes, some officer in our front ordered his regiment to retire, and when they reached our position Captain Otey (acting lieutenant-colonel) gave a similar order; when we retired through

DAHLGREN'S CORNER
At which Colonel Dahlgren fell.

the enemy's tents, and about half of the battalion stopped at the intrenchments; the balance retreated farther. The portion of the command that stopped at the intrenchments remained there until after dark, when they were ordered to the rear and bivouacked for the night. They remained in this position during the next day."—War Records, Series I., Vol. II., Part I., pp. 968-9.

Brigadier General R. E. Rhodes, in his report of the battle of Seven Pines, speaks of Captain C. C. Otey of the heavy-artillery battalion, as one of those who had been conspicuous for their gallantry and efficiency, and who fell while pushing forward with their men in the thickest of the fight. And he mentions also " the gallantry and coolness " of Captains Bagby and White and Lieutenant Yeatman of the heavy-artillery battalion. General Rhodes also notices the conduct of the King William Artillery, which was commanded by Captain (afterwards Colonel) T. H. Carter, as " equaled by no one in the history of the war for daring, coolness, and efficiency." With General Rhodes's report is a statement showing that three officers and thirteen men were killed and three officers and sixty-four men wounded in the heavy-artillery battalion, of which the King and Queen Artillery was a part. (See War Records, Series I., Vol. II., Part I., pp. 975-6.) Colonel C. C. Pegues's Fifth Alabama Regiment speaks highly of the artillery " under the management of Captain Bagby," and of the Fourth Virginia Battalion, which did severe execution upon the retiring enemy.

We find a reference to Captain A. F. Bagby and his company, which had become Company K of the Thirty-fourth Virginia Regiment, in the report of Major General Bushrod R. Johnson (War Records, Series I., Vol. XL., Part I., p. 792). This report recites the events of the action of Saturday, the 30th of July, 1864. On that day the mine was exploded under the Confederate works near Petersburg, the enemy rushed into the breach, and there was a heavy engagement, known as the battle of the Crater, in which the losses of Johnson's division,

—killed, wounded, and missing,—were 922. And it appears that some of the companies of the Thirty-fourth Virginia Infantry, under Colonel J. Thomas Goode, proved very handy in taking charge of artillery pieces, which otherwise would have been unmanned. General Johnson refers to one of these companies, under Captain Samuel D. Preston, and then says: "It is proper here to state that Captain Preston was wounded and Edward Bagby, aid-de-camp to Colonel Goode, commanding the brigade, was killed whilst serving its gun (a gun of Davidson's Battery), and that then Captain A. F. Bagby, of Company K, Thirty-fourth Virginia Regiment, took charge of it, and served it with fine effect until near the close of the action."

The Virginia Heavy Artillery has had but scant attention, and any communication of facts respecting it would be acceptable.

MAJOR JOHN R. BAGBY

Captain of King and Queen Artillery

Major John Robert Bagby was born November 13th, 1826, near Stevensville Post Office, King and Queen County, Virginia. His father was John Bagby, of Scotch descent, and a soldier in the War of 1812. He was a graduate of the Columbian College at Washington, D. C., taking a high stand in his class. For many years he very successfully conducted a mercantile business at his native place. He was for several terms elected magistrate in his county, and was made colonel of militia previous to the Civil War.

At the breaking-out of the war he raised a volunteer company known as the King and Queen Artillery, and afterwards as Company K, Thirty-fourth Virginia Infantry, which company he commanded until 1862, when he was made major of the above-mentioned regiment. He was conspicuous in the battle of Seven Pines, having his horse killed under him, and in several fights was known to kill one of his foes with his own pistol or gun. He was wounded around Petersburg in the spring of 1865; from which he did not recover for many months.

Major Bagby died March 26th, 1890, highly esteemed by all who knew him. In fact, no man ever lived in his county more loved and honored than he was, as was evidenced at the unveiling of his portrait, which now adorns the walls of the Courthouse of his native county.

THE KING AND QUEEN ARTILLERY

This company was organized at King and Queen Courthouse about the 1st of May, 1861, by the election of John R. Bagby, captain; Josiah Ryland, Jr., first lieutenant; A. F. Bagby, second lieutenant; and Josiah Ryland, Sr., third lieutenant; and was mustered into the Confederate service at West Point, Virginia, May 29th, 1861. The company was called King and Queen Artillery, and expected to be supplied with light guns, but being unable to procure them, was placed in charge of the heavy battery at West Point. It remained there four weeks, when ordered to Gloucester Point and put in charge of a heavy battery at that place. It was here that the company was subjected to its first fire from the enemy, and had the honor and distinction of sinking the first and only Yankee boat ever sunk in York River, so far as the writer knows. The company remained at Gloucester Point until the evacuation of Yorktown, when it was divided into two sections, one in command of J. R. Bagby, with two small cannon, and the other with muskets, under Lieutenant Bagby. The company met General Johnson's army below Richmond, and was hastily organized, with other companies of heavy artillery, into what was known as the Fourth Virginia Heavy Artillery, with Captain C. C. Otey as lieutenant-colonel, and J. R. Bagby as major. With this organization the company went into the battle of Seven Pines, carrying sixty-five men and leaving twenty-six. The battalion did effective work in this battle, capturing a battery from the enemy, which Bagby's company soon turned on them with telling effect. (See Official Records of Union and Confederate Armies, Vol. XI., pp. 968, 972, 973, 975, 978.) After this fight the company was placed in charge of heavy guns below Chaffin's Bluff. A. F.

Bagby was made captain, First Lieutenant Josiah Ryland having joined Mosby's command. Josiah Ryland, Sr., was made first lieutenant, and Benjamin H. Walker, third lieutenant. The company remained at Chaffin's Bluff until the spring of 1863, when it was attached to the Thirty-fourth Virginia Infantry, Wise's Brigade, and designated as Company K of that regiment, and sent to South Carolina, near Charleston. It remained there until Petersburg was threatened in 1864, around which place the brigade was ordered, and where it remained until the evacuation.

The company was under almost constant fire from the time it reached the vicinity of Petersburg until the surrender at Appomattox, gaining special distinction at the battle of the Crater. (See Official Records, Vol. XL., p. 792.) It was called on to take charge of one of our own batteries near the Crater, where at least four detachments of men had been killed or driven away, owing to the exposed position. The guns were so successfully worked that much damage was done the enemy by the incessant rain of shot and shell.

The company surrendered eighteen men at Appomattox, in command of Sergeant John W. Ryland, all the commissioned officers having been previously killed, captured, or wounded. Captain Bagby was wounded at Sailor's Creek, and taken prisoner. Lieutenant Josiah Ryland, Sr., was captured near Petersburg; Lieutenant W. F. Haynes resigned his commission the March previous on account of ill-health, and Lieutenant B. H. Walker was killed near Petersburg.

The company was composed of unusually good material, having in it some of the best men in the county, and numbered from first to last one hundred and sixty-five men, about one-half of whom were killed or wounded.

A. F. BAGBY

Late Captain of Company K, Thirty-fourth Virginia Infantry

(From a Soldier's Diary.)

The author is fortunate in being able to give here extracts from a diary kept in excellent form by an old and prominent gentleman, who was an almost life-long resident of the county. It is entirely reliable:

"*May* 24, 1860.—Election to-day of county officers, with the result following: Justices, Thos. Haynes, J. R. Bagby, Thos. Latane, E. S. Acree. State Atty. J. M. Jeffries [afterwards Judge].

"*July 5th, Court day.*—An address by Major B. B. Douglass. Capt. Haynes fell on the Courthouse green with apoplexy and died. He was much loved, having begun life as a school-teacher. Heard to-night of death of Wm. F. Pendleton, of King and Queen, in Washington City. He had lived an eventful life, belonged to the army and to the State Council; a vain man, assuming great influence in affairs of State and nation, claimed to know all the celebrities, and could entertain one by the hour. Clay and Webster frequently consulted him.

"*Sat., May* 4, 1861.—Col. J. R. Bagby, who returned to Baltimore last Tuesday to look after his goods, got back yesterday. He went from Richmond to Baltimore on steamer *Geo. Peabody.* She was stopped at Old Point by an officer from Cumberland, but finally allowed to proceed. Returned on steamer *Adelaide,* but she was compelled to drop her passengers at Pt. He managed to get to Norfolk, thence to Richmond, and home. His goods were shipped by a Baltimore steamer, and got there safely.

"*May* 7, *Regimental Muster.*—Large attendance, 2 Co.'s organized and officers elected. May 10, the old men organized a Home Guard. Col. John Pollard, Capt., T. N. Fogg and J. N. Gresham, Lts. [Col. P. afterwards declined; Rev. R. H. Bagby, D. D., was made Capt. and served through war.]

"*May* 23, 1861.—Vote taken on ratifying ordinance of Secession. Not a negative vote in the county.

"*May* 24.—Home Guard met and fully organized. I am in the squad of J. N. Gresham, R. H. and A. Bagby, etc. Troops rapidly coming into Richmond.

"*May* 25.—Union troops occupied Alexandria. Our army at Manassas, 15 miles away. Col. Ellsworth killed by Jackson.

"*May* 26.—Dr. Sampson of Washington came down to help ordain J. Pollard, but as certain parties objected to his acting, he passed on to Richmond.

"*May* 27.—A Military Company organized and drilled. Many present.

"*May* 29.—Everyone in the neighborhood helping to fix up soldiers for the war, and everyone present to say good-bye. Refreshments served at the School House, Stevensville, also religious services by Revs. Land and Diggs.

"*May* 30.—Company marched to Mantapike to take ship, the writer with them. Band struck up Dixie as the schooner moved off. Capt., J. R. Bagby; 1st. Lieut., Josiah Ryland, Jr.; 2d Lieut., A. F. Bagby; 3d, J. Ryland, Sr.; 4th, Benj. Walker; 1st Sergt., W. T. Haynes, etc." [A roster of this company will be found in its place.] "They numbered 84 in all. Reached West Point, and it was amusing to see the boys make first attempt to cook supper. We found at West Point the Taylor Grays, New Kent artillery and infantry; Bagby's company changed to infantry.

"*June* 5.—Went down to Pt. and found Co. on parade. Quite a number of men have been sick, caused, I think, by water.

"*June* 10.—Went to C. H. to witness departure of the Carlton Store Rifle Co.—Capt. N. B. Street, J. R. Howser, J. W. Hundley, and Jas. Hart, Lts.

"*June* 12.—Hear that a battle has been fought at Bethel Ch., York Co., some 150 Yankees killed. Our loss, one killed, five or six wounded.

"*July* 23.—Papers bring particulars of a great and glorious battle near Manassas—Federals completely routed by Genls. Beauregard & Johnston.

"*Oct.* 23.—Prices: Coffee 30c, sugar 15 and 20c, powder $4 per lb., sole leather 75 and 80c.

"*Oct.* 24.—Housewives getting yarn for carpets and dresses for servants and children.

"*Nov.* 20.—Richmond City crowded. Men from every Southern State.

"*Dec.* 25.—Mrs. T. W. L. Fauntleroy and Wm. H. Courtney died. No gaieties this Christmas.

"*March* 7, 1862.—Forts Henry and Donelson in Tenn. have been captured by the Yankees.

"*March* 11.—News of naval fight in Hampton Roads, between ironclad Virginia and a fleet of U. S. Ships. The ironclad acquitted herself with great credit.

"*March* 21.—In Richmond. Salt $10 per bushel, Bacon 25c, brown sugar 25c, sole leather 90c to $1. Visited Confederate Senate but was not favorably impressed. They did not seem to be sensible of their responsibilities, disputing about their pay. Stonewall Jackson on the scene.

"*April* 3.—A meeting of our people at the Court House, and it was unanimously resolved under no circumstances to take the oath to the U. S. Government.

"*April* 8.—At Gloucester Point, spent night at Hickory Fork.

"*April* 10.—Went over to Yorktown. Visited Fort Magruder. While leaning over parapet, heard the whistle of the first Yankee bullet. Presently they were coming too fast to be pleasant. A soldier said: ' Gentlemen, you had better not expose yourselves; a man has just been killed down the line.' Witnessed for the first time the firing of a cannon, a 12-lb. rifled gun fired by Capt. T. J. Page; directed at a battery being erected by Yankees some two miles away. Shell did not reach battery. In a short time, walking down the line we saw the dead soldier, shot in the neck; struck the carotid artery,—a sad, solemn sight. Enemy had occupied a peach orchard some five or six hundred yards from our line—a heavy chestnut railed fence in front. I could distinctly see them run under cover and presently fire at our men.

"*Apr.* 11.—Returned to Yorktown with Josiah and Chas. Ryland and C. Brown of Mathews. Capt. Carter's Art Co. had arrived from King Wm. Met Lieut. Robt. Ryland and others. Enemy's sharpshooters concealed in peach orchard annoying, two regiments drove them out, and the trees were cut down and defences burned.

"*Apr.* 13.—Dined with Capt. Councill's mess to-day.

Particulars of battle of Shiloh.   In evening attended a very pleasant prayer meeting in Capt. Bagby's tent.

"*Apr.* 14.—Visited K. & Q. Cav.   Met Mrs. Dix, Archy Harwood, Tom. Tyler, Watson, Walker, T. R. Gresham, and Capt. Todd.   Steamers and gunboats below throwing shells.   Presently came in range of our battery; Capt. Page gave them a shot from a rifle gun. One of their shells fell in parade field and I got a piece of it.

"*Apr.* 15.—Heard the boom of a cannon and whistling of shell, another and then another,—continued all day.

"*Apr.* 16.—Yankees still shelling all night last night. Returned home.

"*May* 3.—Orders to evacuate Yorktown and Gloucester Pt.

"*May* 5.—Mr. John Bagby and I sent wagon to help troops along with provisions—found them camped this side Mill at C. H.   The soldiers seemed very grateful.   They left G. P. Sat. night.

"*May* 6.—Met advance of column at Mantapike swamp—some came by Mattapony, some on River road,—met them again at St. Stephen's.

"*May* 7.—Alarm that Yankee gunboats were at C. H. and Mantapike.   Went down the road towards M. and saw steamer with flag as she turned down river. If a Yankee soldier should reach my house sick, I should feel bound to give him shelter and relieve his wants.

"*June* 5.—News of battle Seven Pines.

"*June* 7.—On Sat., 31st May, our Stevensville Co., being part of a battalion,—Col. Otey, J. R. Bagby, Maj.,—Genl. Rhodes's brigade, were marched out, as they supposed, to do picket duty.   Marching two miles, they were ordered to strip and prepare for battle. About 12 o'clock came upon Yankee outpost and drove it in.   Emerging into a field of nearly one mile, they faced an intrenchment with a triangular redoubt, a deep ditch in front and 6 field pieces mounted.   Our company, commanded by 2d Lt. Jos. Ryland (Alexander Bagby sick), charged in splendid style, waded the ditch waist-deep in water, drove the enemy from his guns, and turned them upon him. Soon they charged the enemy a second time in a thick wood. They retired presently to intrenchments and held them. The Co. acted most nobly. Capt. B. (now Major) mounted the breastworks, and taking off his hat waved his men on. He lost five men killed on the field and two dead since; Saml. Hoomes, Jas. Courtney, Bacon, Cornelius Pines, Jas. Butter, John Chilton, R. C. Hart, Kelly, Tom. Myrick, Valvin Legar, B. P. Sale, Benoni Carlton (severely wounded), Wm. H. Meyer (died after), Bolivar Lumpkin, J. W. Ryland, McLellan, G. Prince, Shallen Sale, J. W. Walton, John Wilroy, John H. Gresham, Sam Dollins, John Crossfield, and J. L. Cosby, wounded.

Col. Otey was killed. Capt. Bagby's horse killed under him. They captured a large amount of stores, two hundred tents, wagons, small arms, 28 or 30 cannons, 800 prisoners, among them a wagon loaded with lemons. Yankees afterwards claimed a glorious victory.

"*June* 11.—Very cool and cloudy—reinforcements going up constantly to McClellan.

"*June* 18.—Hear of a cavalry reconnoissance in rear of McClellan by Genl. Stuart; came round Hanover C. H., encountered enemy near Old Church, killed a number, destroyed great deal of stores, captured 175 prisoners and lost only one man killed, the gallant Capt. Wm. Latane. Returning they swam the Chickahominy and constructed a rude bridge for heavy guns. News comes too of splendid victories by Jackson in Valley. A few negroes escaped to the enemy. Prices: Sugar 65c, coffee $2, gaiter shoes $12, boots $30, chickens $1 to $1.50, eggs $1. Cabbage 75c, salt 25 to 50c lb. We used parched corn, wheat, rye, and sweet potatoes for coffee.

"*June* 30.—Jackson is certainly in rear of McClellan, while Genl. Lee presses him back. Jackson has been at White House.

"*July* 1.—Tuesday. About 10 o'clock heavy firing to about 9. It was awful, even to listen to.

"*July* 3.—Crossed at Walkerton. Went to Mrs.

Sutton's and crossed Pamunkey en route to Richmond.—
Dr. G. W. Pollard's at night near Hanover Town.
Sam Roane has been killed, Friday evening. He was
a very fine man."

We subjoin extracts from diary of private W. S.
Courtney of Company G, 26th Regt., and from letters written by him during the war:

"I again head my letter in old Virginia, having
been in the State one week to-morrow. When I got to
Hick's Ford, Greenville County, the Yankees took possession of the railroad between us and Petersburg so
that the train could go no further. We had to guard
the bridge there and sent Captain Street's and nine
other companies of the 59th Virginia to guard the
bridge over Nottoway. The Yankees attacked them
with a great force, and a fierce engagement succeeded,
leaving us in possession of the field. Our loss was one
killed, six wounded and five taken prisoners. Ben
Boughton was killed and Wm. Smither wounded. At
this writing I am about four miles from Petersburg. I
am tolerably well clad for a soldier. There is no chance
of my getting home before the Yankees are cleaned
up. As I do not desire to say anything about our movements, I must close."

The next is dated Elmira, N. Y.: "Dear mother,
I received your letter of 24th Aug. I am a prisoner
of war. I am very well. We have lost two of our boys
since we came here—James Cardwell and Bob Seward.
Frank Marshall was killed and so was John Seward.
Wm. Jackson is here, and Wm. Carlton. Tell Mrs.
Guthrie Ben is here. I have gotten a suit of clothes
since I came here. Would like very much to hear from
the Co., and hope I shall be with them again.—W.
S. C."

Extracts from a diary by the same soldier, beginning
September 14, 1863, and running to July 15, 1865:

"We left Burton's Farm near Petersburg for Charleston, S. C., Sept. 14th. Got to Petersburg same day,
left 15th for Weldon, and that evening left for Wilmington. Reached Wilmington on 16th; on guard that
day. 17th passed Florence, S. C., and reached Charles-

ton 18th, camped two miles from the city. There we stayed until Feb. 9th, 1864, when we left camp for John's Island. Had a brush with the enemy there on the 11th, in which Lieut. A. P. Bird and Geo. W. Cardwell were wounded. I was covered up by the explosion of a shell. Left Johnson's Island 13th. 23d Feby. left camp for Florida and reached Savannah 24th. Visited Forts Brown and Bartow. Left Savannah 27th, passed through Valdosta, and camped on the Withlacochy River. Got to Madison, Florida, March 1st. Passed by Lake City on the 2d, Baldwin the 3d, and got to Camp Milton same day. Left the 2d of March and got to Waldo the 4th; left on the 5th and came back to Camp Milton on the same day. April 17th left for Charleston, S. C., reached Quitman 21st, passed Valdosta and got to Savannah 22d, passed Camp Wapoo and got to James Island on the 23d. May 4th left for Virginia, got to Wilmington 5th, passed through Goldsboro and got to Hicksford the 7th, left the 10th and reached Petersburg 11th, spending the night in the city. Camped there 12th until the 15th, and reached Ware Bottom Church, fighting with the enemy, on the 17th. Adolphus Gibson was killed on 16th. Brushes with the enemy on 18th, 19th & 20th of May, and on the 2d of June Ed. Tuttle wounded. Left Ware Bottom on 11th and got to Petersburg same day; camped on Jordan's Farm, two miles from town, where we had a great fight on 15th June, in which I was captured. I was taken to General B. Smith's headquarters, and from there to General Butler's headquarters, and on the 16th was put on a boat, reaching Old Point the 18th, and got to Point Lookout on the 19th. 27th July left on a boat and reached New York 28th. Reached Elmira, N. Y., June 29th [1864]. Left Elmira for home July 11th, 1865, passed through Baltimore and got home 15th July, 1865."

In a letter to the author, dated Little Plymouth, April 14, 1903, Mr. Courtney says: "Find enclosed the two old army letters. I had promised them to the Confederate Museum. I have just read them again, and I could not keep back the tears. My heart goes out yet to the Lost Cause, and swells with emotions I cannot utter. I feel like I was parting with a dear friend. They bring back before me so vividly the days that tried my soul."

An amusing incident under circumstances solemn and impressive: In May, 1861, Company K, Capt. Bagby, 34th Virginia, was drawn up in line, about to start to the front—some of them never to see home again. As they stood in line on the schoolhouse lot at Stevensville, a crowd of friends and relatives were present to say good-bye. Among others, a most estimable Christian woman passed down the line shaking hands, with a word of cheer for each one, while the sternest faces were moved and eyes suffused with tears. Presently she grasped the hand of a half-witted fellow named B. C., and said, "If God be for us, who can be against us?" "Nobody but the Yankees, madam," answered the soldier.

DIARY OF CIVIL WAR, BY DR. B. H. W.
1862

July 5-6.—After an early breakfast visit Camp of 26th Va., and from there to the forts of Chaffin's Bluff,—seemingly very strong, made of heavy beams 10x12 inches, and on them nailed oak planks 4 inches thick, and then come plates of iron 2 inches thick, and the same reversed; shots strike at an acute angle and glance over. Also earthworks and rifle pits. Sent for to see John H. Gresham,—wounded by a ball in the calf of the leg.

7th.—Visit camp of 55th Va., thence to Mechanicsville, and Ellerson's Mill. Yankee fortifications very strong. Our men advanced to attack across a field swept by artillery, then down a hill and across a boggy meadow in which trees had been felled, then had to ascend a hill two hundred yards before reaching intrenchments. This was the scene of the fights of Thursday and Friday, June 26th and 27th.

8th.—Met Major Bagby in the road, he being at home on furlough, who told me that eleven Yankee cavalry had passed Stevensville going to Walkerton. We arranged at once to capture them—I to go by Dickie's Bridge and Butler's Tavern, he to follow after them to Garnett's mill. I reached Walkerton and found several men already there, including Mordecai Cooke, eight in all. In half an hour a Yankee lieutenant rode up with five men, inquiring for the ferryboat (they had come up for the purpose of destroying boats on the river) ; but the ferryboat had been taken down the river and hid. The Yankees had reported a regiment coming on behind them. All at once the lieutenant entered at the front door, we being in the counting-room in rear. My gun was lying on the counter between us. I caught it up and demanded his surrender; he stooped under the counter, and suddenly springing up caught hold of the gun and we scuffled over it. William Turner then came up behind and shot him with a pistol; he ran out at the front door and just then Alfred Gwathmey shot him with a load of buckshot. He ran up the road towards the mill; we called upon the four Yankees remaining to surrender, but they began firing upon us; several of them were wounded and one killed, all the rest mounted horses and fled.

Meantime Major Bagby had encountered a squad of the enemy at Mantua Gate, killing one; one escaped, and the rest were captured. I started to Richmond at once to secure help. General Lee gave me an order for Colonel Goode to go down with a regiment of cavalry.

14th.—Entering Richmond I had an interview with General Lee. I never met a man who more completely won my heart,—unaffected and simple, no stiffness or bluntness. He said that as soon as he could arrange matters he would send us help; that it was the duty of every man to be in the army if possible, for we had everything to lose. The enemy conducted the war upon barbarous principles. In their retreat from Richmond they had destroyed everything in their reach, even things necessary to their own sick and wounded. So much General Lee.

28th.—Mistress Mary E. Gresham died this morning, leaving three children, one an infant. Her sister, Mistress John N. Gresham, took the baby, Mistress B. Carlton the oldest, and R. H. Bagby the middle one (Andrew).

Sept. 4th.—Hear to-day that Jackson has got in the rear of Pope's army causing immense destruction; and when Longstreet came forward and rejoined him they inflicted tremendous losses on the Union army.

13th.—Prices: Coffee $2.00, Salt 35 to 50 cents, Boots $35.00 to $40.00, Ladies' Gaiters $12.00 to $20.00, Spun Cotton $69.00 per bale, Pine $1.50 to $2.00, Calico $1.25 to $1.50, Sugar 75 cents to $1.00, Tobacco $1.00 to $2.00, Bacon 50 to 60 cents.

16th.—Twelve soldiers came here this evening to stay all night. All belonged to " Holcombe Legion " of South Carolina. They are named in honor of Mrs. Governor Pickens, who was Lucy Holcombe. I met her some years ago at Old Point.

26th.—Christopher Brown with a drove of cattle and sheep stopped here to-day. He is carrying them to Ayletts for the Governor.

27th.—Hear of the death of Dr. Geo. William Pollard of Ayletts, a most valuable and estimable citizen; also James Christian, and Thos. Bagby, a son of Mr. Travis Bagby.

Oct. 3d.—Dr. J. M. Evans arrived here from Richmond bringing the body of Mr. Pratt Smith, a son of Mr. Frank Smith, of Covington, Ky. He came to Virginia at the beginning of the war and joined William Christian's company. Mr. Smith was wounded in the right side in the battle of Manassas; was removed to Warrenton, where he had camp fever. Mason at his urgent request went up to Warrenton and brought him down to Richmond, hoping to be able to get him to Middlesex. He died, however, between Richmond and this place. We buried him at Hamstead, the old family home in Middlesex.

8th.—Dick B. and his wife came down from Petersburg bringing us a barrel of sugar worth about $200.00.

11th.—Some wagons from the lower part of Gloucester, belonging to Dick Hoard and loaded with wheat, passed going up to Richmond. Wheat is worth there from $3.00 to $4.00 per bushel.

14th.—Am hauling my sugar cane (sorghum) to Tom Henley's to be made into molasses. He charges one-half for making. He invented a mill with which he can make fifteen gallons a day, and if he had more boilers could make much more. An ox-cart load makes about six gallons, and it is selling at the mill for $3.00 per gallon.

15th.—Last night two men from Gloucester brought a negro man named Coleman belonging to Mr. John Bagby, and a man and his wife belonging to R. H. Land. They were trying to get to Yorktown.

30th.—Mr. William Beckwith, formerly of Gloucester, but lately of Florence, Ala., dined here. He once belonged to the Fourth Alabama regiment, but was discharged on account of ill health; has been to Gloucester to visit old friends. Was in the first battle of Manassas, in the seven days' fight around Richmond, and in second Manassas; his clothes were pierced again and again, but he has not received a scratch otherwise.

31st.—Heard of the death of cousin Mary Peachy Pollard, wife of Dr. George William Pollard. She was a woman of rare accomplishments and great beauty. Her health, however, was delicate. Her heart and soul and hands have all been engaged in allaying the troubles and pains of soldiers. The Yankees have been often in her house, but she always maintained her dignity and independence, demanded protection, and omitted no occasion to express her devotion to the South. She thus greatly helped her husband in saving his property.

Nov. 4th.—To-day elections are held in New York and some eight other States north. Between the Democrats and Abolitionists at the North is as between the Devil and the deep blue sea—that is, one is about as bad as the other; for the Democrats even wish to force us back into the Union. An effort was made to-day in a public meeting to raise money to buy shoes and other comforts for our suffering soldiers. Mr. Jos. Ryland led in the effort, and proposed to be one of twenty to raise $1000.00 each. There were seven pledges.

6th.—Last night a gunboat came up to Mantapike and lashed to the wharf. Some one going to Richmond had been stalled on a hill near by, and hearing the noise, the captain of the boat thought it prudent to take to his heels. They made a most precipitate retreat down the river, apparently thinking the enemy was upon them.

10th.—A very heavy frost and considerable ice. Mr. Oliver White dines with us to-morrow.

21st.—Up to Richmond with R. H. B. While here I learned that Misses Nancy and Baldwin Hill, daughters of the late Baylor Hill, together with Miss Lizzie Haynes of this county, daughter of the late Captain Haynes, have given themselves most nobly to the work of helping sick and wounded soldiers. They deserve a monument. Visit camp, return home to-morrow. The President calls for men between the age of thirty-five and forty to join the army. There are very few left in the county. Congress has exempted magistrates, wheelwrights, millers, doctors of five years' practice, also clerks, sheriffs, commissioners, and those who have charge of twenty negroes.

22d.—My wife has had woven three hundred and sixty yards of cloth of all kinds during the year to clothe ourselves and the negroes. I had no idea that so much was required. It becomes now quite a burden.

Dec. 1st.—(Monday.) Yesterday and to-day people with their families were passing on their way to Richmond, among them Doctor Walker Jones and Richard Hoard. Sold my wheat to Ryland & Carlton for $2.00 per bushel.

2d.—Encountered in the road to-day a drove of sixty-three hogs being brought from Mathews County and taken to Richmond. This drove will probably bring from three thousand to four thousand dollars. It is rumored in the papers that France has proposed to England and Russia jointly to offer mediation to the U. S. and the Confederate States, but England and Russia decline to act.

4th, Thursday.—Salt is a scarce article, and much of what we have is indifferent. The salt made from water in the Chesapeake Bay down in Mathews has been tried and keeps meat very well.

5th.—Confederate bonds bearing 8% int. are in demand, and bring a small premium.

6th.—Called to see my old friend, G. W. Quarles, and found him very ill with pneumonia. Poor fellow! he passed away during the night; unfortunately he died as he had lived, without preparation.

7th.—Thermometer down to twenty degrees.

9th.—Some people getting out.

10th.—For eighteen months or more now we have been holding interdenominational prayer-meetings at the various churches around. We had to-day a faithful and touching exhortation from R. H. B. on the great importance of uniting effort with our prayers. These meetings are sometimes very interesting and impressive.

11th.—Attended to-day the sale of Samuel H. Roane's property, which sold at high figures. A yoke of oxen brought one hundred and two dollars, spinning wheel seven dollars, old ox-cart fifty dollars.

12th.—P. E. B. has lost three children with diphtheria. This disease has been common of late. Papers say that the enemy are throwing bridges across the Rappahannock at Fredericksburg.

13th.—Rapid firing has been heard to-day northward towards Fredericksburg—especially in the afternoon and towards night. The distance is perhaps sixty miles. The town has suffered very severely, some of the citizens killed and very many houses struck by balls. We anxiously await the result.

14th.—Reports reach us that the Yankees are advancing in large force from Gloucester Point. They came as far as Barnes Lawson's, burning his dwelling, and then retired. There has been a most remarkable appearance of the sky to-night. About nine o'clock a light appearance towards the north, and in a short time there shot up therefrom white pillars similar to the tail of a comet. Each successive one shot up higher and higher until a few reached the meridian. Nearly all these appearances were in the north, and continued until nine o'clock, then disappeared.

15th.—We thank the Lord for his mercy in giving us the victory at Fredericksburg. Oh! that our people might feel a proper degree of humility and thankfulness to our Heavenly Father.

16th.—Intended to go up with R. H. B. to General Lee's army to carry two hundred and forty pairs of socks, one hundred and sixty flannel shirts, thirty comforts and blankets, gloves, etc., contributed by our ladies for the poor fellows in arms. I was too unwell to go. Sorry to hear that Generals Cobb and Gregg were both killed in the battle.

19th.—A deserter from the Union army reports that Burnside ordered the attack to be renewed Sunday morning, but his leading generals protested and it was not done.

21st.—Thermometer at sunrise was twelve. Two soldiers, Lieut. Lee and Mr. Sinclair, of Gloucester cavalry, stayed with us last night.

24th.—Capt. A. B. and my sister Fanny were married at my house to-night. The company was small, but pleasant; eight couples of waiters. Company broke up at a late hour.

28th.—My neighbor, Mrs. B.———, taking dinner with us to-day, reported that some one had broken into her house and robbed her to a considerable amount. It is probable that there are one or more gangs of negroes depredating around.

29th.—Went with a company last night to Mrs. M. A. Hart's. While there a negro ran out of her kitchen, and refusing to halt when ordered, C. D. shot him twice, but not fatally. A party also broke into Major B.'s house Saturday night, but did little damage.

1863

January 1st (Thursday).—At the sale of W. F. P.'s estate negroes brought high prices. One valuable man (T. H.) was bought by J. M. J. for eight hundred and forty dollars. He is fifty-six years old. Heard yesterday that a lady in Essex gave fifty barrels of corn for one sack of salt. I myself have just paid forty dollars for a sow and nine pigs.

3d.—Papers report to-day that a very large mass meeting was held in New York in which resolutions were passed calling on the government to propose an armistice looking to peace. It came to nothing.

6th.—Reports of successes in Kentucky, but General Bragg has retired from Murfreesboro saving captured property and prisoners. A monitor was sunk off Hatteras, and other gunboats had to throw their guns overboard.

7th.—Major Bagby at home.

8th.—A case of smallpox in our neighborhood, and patient in a terrible condition, both blind and delirious.

9th.—Yankees made a raid into King William yesterday and captured some wagons at White House.

11th.—Collection for Fredericksburg sufferers.

12th.—The *Harriet Lane,* a Yankee steamer, captured in Galveston Bay.

13th.—Papers report that Democrats at the North wish to know on what terms the South will return into the Union. The answer was returned, On no terms whatever.

Order in which the States seceded:

Dec. 20th, 1860, South Carolina;
Jan. 9th, 1861, Mississippi;
Jan. 11th, 1861, Alabama and Florida;
Jan. 19th, 1861, Georgia;
Jan. 26th, 1861, Louisiana;
Feb. 1st, 1861, Texas;
April 17th, 1861, Virginia;
May 6th, 1861, Arkansas;
May 20th, 1861, North Carolina;
June 8th, 1861, Tennessee.

15th.—Heard of the death of Colonel Bartlett Todd, of Petersburg, from cancer, aged seventy-five; a man of high sense of honor.

17th.—Board of Examination of conscripts for the county met here to-day; quite a number of friends dined with us. Thermometer down to eighteen degrees.

27th.—Mr. Jno. N. Brown, belonging to the Sussex cavalry, has come down to select camping grounds for General W. H. F. Lee's brigade; he spends night with us. I have subscribed for the *Semi-Weekly Enquirer,* for which I pay eight dollars.

29th.—Quite a number of other cases of smallpox in the neighborhood.

30th.—Prices in Richmond: Turkeys $10, Sheep $15, Coffee $5 per lb., Sugar $1, Meal $4 per bushel, Apples $35 to $45 per bbl., Butter $1.25 to $1.50 per lb., Eggs $1 per doz.

Feb. 1st.—At meeting to-day I enjoyed especially the singing of the old hymn " Whilst Thee I seek, protecting power."

2d.—Weather fine, wind N. N. E.

4th.—General W. H. F. Lee's cavalry brigade is stationed near Bestland.

5th.—I sold a beef in Richmond for two hundred and seventy dollars.

7th.—Heavy frost, ground frozen, and much ice in the road. Persons sick with smallpox are said to be in fearful condition; two have already died. One of the soldiers who was with us in 1861 was killed in the battles around Richmond. While here he commended himself to us very much. His name was E. E. Knight.

13th.—Paid a visit to-day to General Lee's camp and found them located on the road between Miller's and Bestland. The roads were in a horrible condition.

14th.—Six Marylanders belonging to our army spent the night with us; names: Forbes, Roby, German, Riddle, Gorman, Decatur; they were from St. Mary's and Charles counties and Baltimore.

16th.—G. P. bought a horse from a soldier for sixty dollars, and sold him liquor for forty dollars per gallon. The horse is said to be worth one hundred and fifty dollars. The Marylanders who were with us are in pursuit of forage, especially fodder; they got some in Middlesex.

17th.—Rumors of French mediation, and dissatisfaction reported in Northwestern States.

19th.—A poor negro belonging to Mr. Boughton near Miller's, having a bad case of smallpox, ran out the other night and went two miles up the road before he could be caught. He is delirious.

20th.—The French minister has recommended a conference between commissioners from the North and South, with a view to settle trouble, but Mr. Seward rejected it.

22d.—Snow six or eight inches deep; wind north, thermometer twenty-two degrees.

27th.—Hear of several handsome affairs, among them the capture of the *Queen of the West* and another steamer called *Indianola*.

March 1st, Sunday.—Meetings to-day in accordance with President Davis' proclamation, appointing to-day for fasting, humiliation, and prayer.

March 5th, Court day.—A number of persons at court; not much business. At least half a dozen wagons appeared with blockade goods, and it is reported that almost as many pass by every day.

6th.—Several sales have taken place of household goods at high prices. A man told me to-day that he had sold a barrel of apple brandy for thirteen hundred and fifty dollars.

8th.—R. S. Ryland and Mr. Golden, of Lee's Rangers, with us to-night. They are returning from Gloucester Point, hoping to surprise the place, but were disappointed. There were several gunboats there.

10th.—An old lady (Mrs. Gresham) told me that a bride some years back spun and wove her own wedding dress. After it was warped it was so fine that she passed it through a gold finger-ring.

13th.—Have had frequent snows of late.

17th.—Hear of a handsome affair between Yankee and Confederate Cavalry near Kelly's Ford; the former were finally routed. Major Puller, of Gloucester, and the noted Major Pelham, of Alabama, were killed.

22d.—Our people took a collection to help the sick in General W. H. F. Lee's brigade. I find that the horses in his brigade are in a very bad condition.

26th.—A case of scarlet fever at P. E. Brooks's.

30th.—A negro man named Jacob, belonging to J. R. B., who had run off to the Yankees, but had come back to the county, was caught last night.

April 5th.—I have forebodings; articles of life are very scarce, and the poor are sadly straitened. Army wagons carried off nearly all of the corn in the country. Twenty-five dollars per barrel has been offered for it; indeed you can get almost any price. Bacon, too, commands $1.50 per lb., shad $3.00 to $5.00 each, eggs $1.50 to $2.00 per doz. There is distress, too in Richmond. Wearing apparel and things edible are higher and higher. A barrel of fish sold when I was in town a day or two ago for $100.00.

11th.—On a visit to Petersburg I find soldiers, mainly cavalry, occupying log huts along the roads. Visit Chaffin's Bluff also, crossing the James on a pontoon bridge.

13th.—Rode to town on horseback with a pair of saddlebags across the saddle, in each end of which was stuffed a bale of cotton, and a tin bucket tied behind. I carried also a carpetbag and an umbrella. It was indeed ludicrous.

14th.—Went down on York River Railroad and learned of the illness of Mrs. L. F. H. She subsequently died,—but the most triumphant death I ever witnessed.

16th.—Called to see Tomlin, who was wounded in the attempt made last Friday at Gloucester Point.

20th.—Sent for to see Captain Tomlin, and found that mortification had occurred in foot and ankle. Dr. F. Taylor, Dr. Vaughan, and I consulting, determined to take off the leg; which was done, but without suitable instruments.

29th.—Tomlin, poor fellow, died last night.

May 1st.—Papers bring intelligence that General Hooker has crossed the river above and below Fredericksburg.

2d.—Firing was heard yesterday and again to-day. A man from Newtown says it was distinct there, continuing all day. Another case of scarlet fever,—one of my own daughters.

4th.—Heard on the road to-day that a force of Yankee cavalry was crossing at Piping Tree early yesterday morning; thought lightly of the report.

5th.—Yankees in large force crossing at Walkerton. I deemed it best to leave home; started up the road about ten o'clock towards the Mill Gate, and spent the night with my old friend N. D. A note from R. H. B. informed me that fifty cavalry passed Stevensville, stating that they had been whipped at Fredericksburg. After breakfast, passed through the Smyrna neighborhood and came home. On the way I met a member of the Gloucester cavalry, H. R. P., and C. B. F., with two Yankee prisoners (one Lieut. Mitchell), belonging to 12th Illinois Cavalry, whom they had captured. I passed on, in company with R. H. B., G. F. B. C. W. P., and P. E. L, to Carlton's store. Three prisoners had been captured in that neighborhood, but on the other hand Yankees had captured two Confederate wagon trains. Returning homeward, I found the Yankees were still passing down the road in squads. I thought it best to get out of the way, and started up from my house toward the Mill Gate. Reaching a point about a hundred yards of the latter, I found myself face to face with a squad of Yankees. They were coming down on the Providence road towards Stevensville. I turned my horse immediately upon seeing them, and fled back towards the store. Was fired at quite a number of times, but fortunately escaped, and reaching the store, turned up the road towards Bruington. Some five or six Yankees pursued me, and one followed me a quarter of a mile. Perhaps it is very well for both of us that I did not know it. Made my way through the woods to the cottage on the road to Mr. George Pendletons, but did not enter the house. Spent the entire night in the woods.

6th.—The Yankees are scattered about in various directions, stealing horses and negroes. They have taken two of my horses, one worth four hundred, the other two hundred dollars. R. H. B. lost three, J. B. two, I. D. one, Col. P. two, Col. Wm. B. Davis seven, Col. Fleet three, J. R. Fleet five. The Yankees camped on the land of J. N. Gresham, ate at his table, and drank his liquor.

7th.—Learn that the Yankees were a part of General Stoneman's command, which had passed Louisa and Hanover and Ashland, and having been attacked near there, crossed and came over into our county. They destroyed considerable stores and treated some of our citizens very rudely,—notably Mr. S. P. Ryland and J. R. Fleet,—because they would not readily surrender their personal property, like watches, horses, etc.

10th.—By special request, Dr. S. S. H. read at Smyrna to-day a dying exhortation of Mrs. Margaret Campbell (the first wife of Alex. Campbell), a most admirable production.

11th.—Very warm, thermoneter 85. Mr. A. W. R. of Gloucester dined with us to-day, reporting that he has been a great sufferer by depredations of the enemy.

12th.—Replanting corn. Heard with great regret of the death of Stonewall Jackson.

13th.—Shad are beginning to run in Mattapony. We got fifty to-day.

19th.—Took my wife to see Col. Charles H. Carlton, a son of B. C. He is an old acquaintance and full colonel in the Confederate army.

20th.—Herrings are being gotten from the river, and are very helpful.

23d.—Called to see A. B., whose fractured arm has failed to unite. Other cases of scarlet fever,—at Elder I. D.'s this time.

27th.—Reported at Stevensville that the Yankees are at King and Queen Courthouse and advancing.

28th.—Election day, but very many persons deterred from going to the polls.

June 1st.—Exceedingly harassed and perplexed by unpleasant reports and prospects; am anxious to get something out of the way of the vandals, but do not know where to put it, or whom of my servants to trust. I think I have some that are faithful, but am not sure.

2d.—Heard late last night the Yankees are retiring. They came into Middlesex and Essex from Gloucester Point.

3d.—R. H. B. started with a wagon of hospital stores to Richmond; the people brought more than he could carry. Dr. J. M. E. came up from Middlesex; he reports that the Yankees boarded transports at Urbanna and crossed at Carter's Creek.

4th.—Yankees carried off very large number of negroes, notably Dr. Roy's, Thos. W. Garrett's, Lotty Moore's, Mrs. Col. Spencer's, etc.

5th.—Report comes this morning that the Yankees are in force at Walkerton, setting fire to houses, mills, etc.; could see smoke ascending from three or four different points. About two o'clock heard the booming of cannon, evidently from gunboats returning down the river. About four o'clock Halback, Tommy Ryland, and I started toward Walkerton, passing through by Mrs. Cook's, McLelland's, and Dr. Henley's. Near Dr. Henley's a shell passed near us and exploded. We turned towards Hillsborough, and pretty soon saw three boats, all shelling the bluffs on King William side; as they passed Hillsborough, they fired a volley of small arms at Mr. H. and the children standing in the yard. Several balls struck the end of the brick dwelling, and one passed through a window and struck a door. Shells were thrown at citizens at various points, one at Mrs. R. Douglass, sitting in the porch at Frazier's Ferry with a child in her arms.

6th.—Yankees reached Walkerton Thursday night about one o'clock; landed four hundred infantry, seizing horses as they advanced by land towards Ayletts. At this place they burned foundry, store, dwelling, and granaries. An immense deal of property was destroyed, negroes taken away, horses stolen.

9th.—Learn to my regret that Harriet, a daughter of Rev. I. D., was dying. He has been sadly afflicted,—diphtheria.

12th.—A party of gentlemen assembled at Stevensville, notably Col. Wm. B. Davis, Elders R. H. Bagby, and R. H. Land, Capt. M. P. Todd, Rodney Dew, J. M. Jeffries, to devise measures to protect ourselves. Our enemies are adopting a barbarous warfare; we must defend ourselves. Hear of several cavalry fights near Brandy Station,—enemy finally driven across the river.

15th.—Very warm and dry. Lucy Fleet left with Tom. Henley to go to Middlesex.

16th.—Another meeting of citizens at Providence to confer about defense. The enemy in some cases force women and children to take the oath or leave their home. Col. A. Fleet called to order and Elder R. H. Land prayed. There has been a large peace-meeting in New York city,—thirty thousand people present. They acknowledge that they have been whipped.

17th.—General Ewell has captured Winchester, storming the works, capturing cannon, stores, and prisoners.

21st.—Reported to-day that Yankee cavalry was advancing from Gloucester Point; our company assembled, thirty strong, and took a position to attack them in case of an advance. They turned off, however, passing up by Carlton's store, and then took the direction of Ware's Church. We have now three companies of home guards; one at Newtown, one at Stevensville, and one at the Courthouse, commanded by Captains Lumpkin, Bagby, and Todd.

22d.—All three companies of home guards met at the Courthouse, also one company from King William. It has been rumored for a day or so that the Yankees were again advancing, and we feel very well prepared to receive them, for we have one or two companies from the regular army now in the county.

24th.—Several gunboats at West Point creating some alarm in the county.

26th.—Yankees making a raid by Old Church, Hanover Courthouse, and enter King William at Nelson's Bridge.

27th.—Company in camp at Dunkirk, slept on blanket and oilcloth, with saddle for pillow. Twice during the night ordered to saddle up, but a heavy rain led us to desist. About day we started across the river, marching in the direction of Hebron Church, where we joined Douglass' and Croxton's companies, all under Col. Douglass. At Hebron entered the church, built up a good fire in the stove. Just as we began to get comfortable, in dashed pickets reporting that the enemy were almost upon us. The report proved deceptive, for the enemy had turned off on another road towards Brandywine. Col. Douglass moved in that direction on another road. I, with Albert Hill, Bennie Fleet, Boone Dew, and Wm. Samuel, left as a picket near the chapel. After a while we rejoined Col. D., striking the Brandywine road, but the Yankees had passed down ahead of us. Our battalion subsequently ran into the enemy near Sharon Church, but as it was found the enemy were too strong, we fell back before them. That night my company recrossed into King and Queen. (We ascertained later that there was a considerable force of infantry with the cavalry which we had encountered; it was fortunate we were not seriously engaged with them.) On Saturday night (27th) I reached Walkerton, together with T. McLelland, W. C. Anderson, Jos. Griffith, Henry R. Pollard, Chas. Didlake, John Thurston, Moore Wright, Robt. Woodward, E. S. and Alexander Acree. Nothing occurred during the night.

30th (Tuesday).—We have been cut off from Richmond and have no mails. Yankees are certainly landing a heavy force at White House.

July 1st (Wednesday).—Rumored that the Yankees are advancing in heavy force through King William. Attend prayer-meeting at Bruington; exhortations from R. H. B., J. R. G., Col. Fleet, and Arthur Temple.

3d.—Sultry. The Yankees are in considerable force in King William, camped on Jas. Roane's land, and can be distinctly seen from this side. Heavy and rapid firing heard from 6:30 to 7 yesterday evening. Our company go into camp at Rosemont, and picket river from Walkerton to Dunkirk.

5th.—Yankees at Walkerton in gunboats.

8th.—A boy born to Mrs. L. T., weighing nine pounds. Delightful rain to-day, first since May 8th.

9th.—Capt. Bagby's company (home guards) had weekly meeting to-day. We find that there are two deserters, who had hid themselves in a cave; caught one; the other escaped.

10th.—Hear depressing news of the fall of Vicksburg.

11th.—Weather of most remarkable character—air humid and thick like Indian Summer,—sun hardly to be seen at all; has the appearance this P. M. of sun in eclipse. Wind south.

12th.—Same appearance of the atmosphere and of the sun to-day. Basement of dwelling very damp. (This weather continued through next day,—yet no rain, though heavy dew.)

14th.—Capt. B. [R. H. Bagby] returned from Richmond, reporting that his company was accepted by Department, and he got all the ammunition he asked for. Heavy rain.

20th.—Port Hudson on the Mississippi capitulated on the ninth, after garrison had eaten their last mule. Tremendous riot in New York, but Lincoln suspended the draft.

22d.—Appropriate and excellent exhortation from Dr. Robert Ryland of Richmond.

23d.—Three Baltimoreans spent night,—Berryman, McGee, and Adams. The first was wounded in first Manassas.

27th.—Little Mary D. is very ill. She subsequently dies, leaving a mother greatly afflicted.

31st.—Dined at A. B.'s with wife, Mr. Jeff., Sue, and Mollie, Mrs. Col. P. and Mrs. Dr. and P. Woodward.

August 4th.—Up early to go to Richmond with Dr. J. M. E., who wishes to consult a physician. Saw Dr. Pettacolas.

Prices: Calf skins sixty to sixty-five dollars, Brown Sugar two, Loaf four, Bacon $1.75, Boots sixty to seventy-five, Salt five, Calico three to four, Corn ten per bushel, Meal twelve, Flour thirty, Bale Cotton No. 6 twelve per bale.

5th.—Spend the night at Old Church, and reach home by nine o'clock.

8th.—Mercury ninety degrees.

11th.—Diphtheria and scarlet fever still raging. Intense heat modified by a splendid rain.

13th (Thursday).—Company met and drilled. Peaches very fine.

21st.—Fast day. Had notice that the Fifth Virginia Cavalry would be along, and Col. Rosser wished breakfast for himself and officers.

24th.—Part of the Fifth Regiment came by, returning from lower Middlesex, and bringing fifty-odd Yankees captured from two gunboats Saturday night by marines under Lieut. Wood. The boats were lying in the river below Urbanna. We had one man wounded. The Yankees one or two killed and several wounded. Marines took possession of the boats and moved down the river in quest of other boats. People of the neighborhood furnished dinner to Capt. Fox's company and the prisoners, under the large oaks near Mr. John B.'s ice house.

27th.—Fifth Regiment returned and encamped near McLelland's. Walter Burke, only seventeen, took supper with us,—a Baltimorean.

Sept. 7th.—Heard to-day of the death of D. L.—he was about seventy. Poor old man, he died without any hope in Christ. I have known him all my life, and never heard him speak in praise of any man. He scoffed at religion and watched for failings of professors.

15th.—Put down sorghum machine, ground four barrels of juice to be converted into molasses.

18th.—Was aroused during the night by G. R. F., who announced that the Yankees were encamped just below Carlton's store in large numbers. He reported that he, Drs. W. and H., W. R. C., and J. P., had scouted below the store, and that W. R. C., being in advance, had been fired upon and perhaps killed; that he, also, had been fired upon, but had escaped, with difficulty. (This afterwards turned out to be all a hoax gotten up on F.)

25th.—News of Bragg's victory at Chickamauga.

28th.—At a sale an ordinary pair of oxen sold for more than four hundred dollars, and common cows brought one hundred and fifty dollars.

Oct. 10th.—Received of Mr. B. seventeen gallons of very nice molasses made from three loads of cane.

23d.—No mails to-day, stage did not leave Richmond.

25th.—Cold wind, north. Heard of the death of old Mr. T. M. He was eighty-three years old, a most remarkable man in personal appearance, in disposition, and habits. From an accident in his early youth, injuring his spine, his body was remarkably curved,— breast-bone almost, if not quite, down to the pelvis: the shortest body and the longest legs I ever saw. Owing, I think, to his disease, he was exceedingly peevish and quarrelsome, and had during his life more disagreements and lawsuits than any man I ever knew. I suppose that for thirty or forty years there was no time that he did not have one or more suits on hand. He contested the lines with each one of his neighbors, spent thousands of dollars, visited no one, and no one visited him. Indeed, he rarely spoke to any neighbor, and kept the neighborhood in constant turmoil. In early life he wrote in the Clerk's office, and afterwards preached. Strange as it may seem, he married three times. One son is married, an amiable and highly respected and esteemed citizen.

28th.—Heard a week ago to-day that Capt. T. W. H. had been severely, perhaps mortally, wounded. Great sympathy is felt for him. Apprehensions, however, were not verified, for Capt. H. lived for years, and became treasurer of King William County after the war. I knew him very well; he was kind, generous, amiable, full of fun, sprightly; never studied much, but always stood well in class; a favorite in school and out. When war broke out he joined a company made up by W. H. F. Lee, and was made O. S., was promoted to Lieutenant, and afterwards Captain; one of the bravest of the brave, and enjoyed the confidence and esteem of all.

31st.—Dined at Mrs. R. P.'s with Thomas Wood of Kentucky. He had to leave his home at Lexington in consequence of sympathy with and aid to Confederate army.

Nov. 5th.—Paid State and County tax, which, together with one-tenth of my crops, in money, would amount to upwards of six hundred dollars. Bought a mare at public auction, very poor and worn down, with sore back, and paid three hundred and eighty-five dollars,—worth thirty.

6th.—Attended drill of home guard, with court-martial.

8th.—Bishop Johns preached at St. Paul's, confirming thirty-four, among them M. J.

14th.—Yesterday evening Logan G., a granddaughter of Mrs. P. B., on horseback with E. B.: the former cutting the horse, it sprang off and both the girls fell backward to the ground. Miss G. sprang up quickly; when, seeing that she was pale, the girls came to her help, but in a few moments she died. It was indeed a distressing affair.

19th.—Dr. T. L. came to court to-day wearing a pair of shoes with wooden soles. They attracted much attention; leather is very scarce.

22d.—Mordecai C. reached home from Charleston to-day, sick. Company K of 34th Virginia has been South now for some weeks.

27th.—Thomas has defeated Bragg at Chattanooga, —thus come the lights and the shades.

Dec. 4th.—Yankees are reported retiring before our army in the West, and so is Meade before Lee.

7th.—Salt has been bought by the county for the people.

11th.—Got my share of salt to-day—198 lbs.

17th.—Last night at 7:40 we heard a rumbling sound, which shook the house severely; in two or three seconds this was repeated. Presently other persons from outside the house came in, asking what was the cause. This was repeated again about 4 A. M. (Probably explosions of magazines at Yorktown.)

25th.—A very dull Christmas, no gaiety or joyousness apparent.

30th.—Men hired to-day for $400, women for $100 to $150. At present rates this would make the total cost of a man about $1000.

1864.

Jan. 1 (Friday).—Pleasant to-day, but colder towards night.

2d.—Mercury 11 degrees.

3d.—Getting ice.

4th.—Mr. J. N. G.'s house burned. Very little saved from the fire, some of the girls losing everything.

7th.—Three Marylanders, Johnson, Childs, and Lithicum, with us.

13th.—R. H. B. was thrown from his sulky yesterday, and again to-day as he rode with Mary R. He was quite badly hurt.

19th.—Left home for Richmond.

Prices: Sugar $5.00, Coffee $18 and $20, Bacon $3.50 to $4.00, Turkeys $2 lb., Eggs $3 doz., Flour $200 bbl., Meal $18 bu., Calico $6 to $8, Domestic $5 and $6. Medicines are enormously high.

22d.—Saw General John H. Morgan and members of his staff. He is a quiet, gentlemanly-looking person, would not strike one as a dashing officer. Charges at the hotel $20.00 per day (Ballard House). Meeting to-night to raise funds for soldiers losing limbs. (Bought a horse about this time, near fourteen years old, for $450.)

27th.—Organized a society, auxiliary to the one in Richmond mentioned on 22d.

31st.—Government prices for Corn $20, Wheat $5. In Richmond, Corn $20 per bu., and wheat $30. The times appear to me to be very much out of joint, and I fear the people demoralized. I hear of some dancing in this neighborhood, and more in other neighborhoods.

Feb. 4th, Court day.—Heard a speech from R. L. Montague on the momentous questions before the people. He exhorted the people to sell everything at government prices, and to use and wear only such things as could be made at home; his words were with power. Appropriations were ordered to-day for soldiers' families. $15,000 in county bonds were sold. A colored man in the woods to-day saw two hawks fighting at top of a tree; in a short time they clinched and fell to the ground. He found they could not extricate themselves and killed them both; he pulled them apart with difficulty.

6th.—Mrs. P. Brooke died this morning. She was calm in the prospect of death, and sang with earnestness and feeling " 'Tis Religion that Can Give."

7th.—Heard from a picket at Mantua Ferry that the Yankees were in King William in large force; sent message to Captain B. (This turned out to be a hoax.)

15th.—Snowing. One of Yankee officers, named Driscoll, escaped from Richmond; was captured by J. B. and others.

17th.—Intensely cold with high winds.

18th.—Thermometer 6 degrees above at sunrise.

21st.—Sent for to see Dr. J. Lewis of King William. River has been frozen for some days, but is open to-day.

24th.—In Richmond. Paid $10 for dinner at Ballard House.

25th (Thursday).—Merchants ask $180 bu. for Clover seed. Saw bacons sold for $8 lb.

March 2d.*—Yankees reported crossing Pamunkey at Dabney's Ferry and coming this way. Capt. Bagby ordered his company to meet at Bruington at 5 o'clock. Capt. Magruder's and Capt. Blake's companies, of regular army, with us. Passing up the road over Dickie's Bridge I met a man at the fork, one mile this side of Bruington (Capt. Charles G.), who reported the Yankees at Bruington. We laughed at the report, but in a few minutes heard firing and saw members of the Home Guard fleeing toward us, and Yankees pursuing. The latter halted, and soon began firing at a squad of our men near Butler's old tavern. The interval was a half-mile or more, but one of our men was struck, though not seriously hurt. (Have heard since that Col. Dahlgren fired the shot.)

Retiring before the Yankees, most of the Home Guard, with Capt. Magruder's command, took the direct road towards Dickie's Bridge and Stevensville. As we came down it was suggested to send a scout in the direction of the River road. Capt. Harrison of Ma-

---

* This and the next following entry give an account of the famous Dahlgren Raid.

gruder's company volunteered to move across the fields and count them as they passed down the other road. Passed through B.'s & T. M.'s and Philip Bird's into the Cow Trap woods below Belmont. In about five minutes after we reached our point of observation, the Yankees came along and I counted them,—one hundred and seventy men, mounted. We gave them a shot apiece, which they returned. Presently they stopped and seemed to be feeding in Gaines' old field, but we have since learned that it was at Hocklineck. We moved back from the woods into the road, and passing by Stevensville, we joined Magruder, augmented by some of the King and Queen cavalry under Capt. Fox, the Home Guard, etc. Capt. Bagby had already drawn up his men at the forks of the road above Mantapike. Capt. Fox was requested to take charge of the entire force, and arrangements were made to fight them should they attempt to pass. About 10:30 P. M. the enemy were reported moving. Some of our men at the same moment were moving down towards the fork on the Stevensville road, and came in contact with the enemy just as they reached that point. Col. Ulric Dahlgren, seeing the men in the road, rode up and demanded a surrender, snapping his pistol. The man, or men, immediately fired return shots, and then a fusillade began from the northeast corner of the woody slope upon the head of the Yankee column; the enemy hastily retreated. Then our boys gave a tremendous shout and rushed into the road. I noticed a horse struggling in the agonies of death and a man under him, and in a short time another man lying in the ditch with his feet up against the fence and tree; this last was Col. Dahlgren. Meantime the Yankees were in considerable commotion,—we on our part expecting another attack,—but as they did not advance, we feared an effort would be made to flank us, and so get by. So Lieuts. Nunn and Acree, Cris. Fleet and I moved out to learn about their intentions. We soon became satisfied they were still in the field. We moved down to where the Mantapike road crosses the River road and raised a barricade, awaiting the enemy the rest of the night. Next morning the whole force surrendered,—it produced a thrill of joy. The field presented a disorderly sight,—horses running loose, arms, saddles, haversacks, canteens, silverware, blankets, etc., scattered in confusion. Most of the arms and many of the horses were appropriated by our soldiers. I got a broken-down horse marked " U. S.," Spencer rifle, saddle, etc. My little boy brought in another horse. During the day many prisoners were brought in.

5th (Saturday).—Last night Capt. Bagby sent for me to come to his house to help guard six prisoners captured by him. Maj. E. F. Cooke, Lieut. Merritt, Lieut. Bartley, Privates Hogan, Williams, and Litchen, came to the house of his overseer (McFarland), and asked Mrs. M. to prepare them some supper. She immediately began preparations, but privately dispatched a negro girl to acquaint Capt. B. of their presence. The overseer's house is about one hundred and fifty yards from the dwelling. Capt. B. and his son John, at home on furlough, seized their pistols, ran down to the overseer's and rushed into the room, presenting their pistols and demanding a surrender. Maj. Cooke hesitated, when Capt. Bagby said, " Surrender, or I will kill you," at the same time presenting his pistol at the major's head. It was indeed a trying moment,—two men against six, and all heavily armed. The major, with great reluctance, threw down his arms, and the rest followed his example.

As I could not get up last night I hurried to go this morning, and found the prisoners snugly in bed in Capt. B.'s parlor. Soon after reaching there, news came that two more Yankees were in Capt. B.'s woods not far away.

I hurried off, along with McF., J. N. Gresham, Jr., and John Lawson, to look after the two. Taking a position which commanded a view of the meadow just below, I awaited their appearance. In about fifteen minutes they came in sight, and coming up to a small stream of water, stooped to drink. I drew up, halted them, and demanded a surrender, with which they complied. I carried them to Capt. B.'s, where we all got breakfast, and marched the eight prisoners to Stevensville, there awaiting the arrival of the other prisoners, who had been carried to Camp Exol. In the evening they were taken forward toward Richmond, numbering ninety-one. Three were unable to travel, one on account of a wound through the knee, and two from being hurt by horses. These three were Daniel Denis, from Lafayette (or Marshall), Indiana; a second was Michael Madden; the other John H. Remsen. Remsen was the man whom we found lying under the horse when Dahlgren was found lying in the road at the corner.

7th.—Rumors of the advance of the enemy, and Home Guard ordered out.

8th.—Home Guard assembled at Stevensville about sunrise, but learning that the enemy had retired, we disbanded. Two of the men wounded came to my house and were cared for, and one of them was lodged with Rev. I. Diggs.

9th.—Yankees were certainly at Centreville yesterday.

10th.—Home Guard met again at sunrise, and very soon we could see smoke arising from houses burning at the Courthouse. Our scouts came in and reported that the Yankees were advancing. Scouts further reported that they had burned the Courthouse, jail, clerk's office, tavern, storehouses, barns, stables, and mill, and the private residences of Wm. Martin and Robt. Pollard. After perpetrating this vandalism, they moved to Carlton's store, where they did other mischief, then went to Camp Exol and burned that. Soon after, Col. Beale came up with the Ninth Regiment and skirmished with them, but the Yankees retreated so rapidly towards Little Plymouth that Col. Beale failed to do them any serious damage.

11th.—Ground saturated from the rain of yesterday. Everything in disorder, horses in the woods, cows and hogs loose in the field, and negroes indisposed to do anything. Got dispatches that Col. Beale wanted all the information he could get, as the Yankees were lingering below. Capt. Bagby went to Richmond with prisoners and has just returned.

12th.—Company out and under arms all day. Bought fifteen bushels of oats at $10 per bushel.

18th.—Winds south, high and warm.

22d.—Very cold, windy, and unpleasant. Commenced snowing about one o'clock, and continued for some hours. Wind blowing a severe gale from N. E. It is now positively certain that Gen. U. S. Grant has been made lieut.-general, and has succeeded Gen. Halleck as commander-in-chief of the Yankee armies; that for the present he will be in command of the Army of the Potomac. Indeed, there seems to be a general change of commanders of Yankee armies all around, and, among others, Sherman is to succeed Thomas at Chattanooga. General Forest has just defeated Grierson and Smith with their cavalry forces, they having seven thousand against his twenty-four hundred.

23d. Snowing all night, but about nine o'clock this morning sun came out and it grew pleasant. In some places it was from three to five feet deep. Shad are just beginning to run.

26th (Easter).—A very blustering day. Almost all the snow melted.

27th.—Called to see Mr. P. Bird, who is sick.

28th.—John W. Deshazo died yesterday.

31st.—Home Guard are to meet second and fourth Thursdays at 10 A. M., Pyne's old shop. Dined at T. H.'s with Maj. John Henley and his wife and sister (Mrs. Susan Copeland), refugees from Williamsburg, who have suffered very much by the Yankees.

April 5th.—Miss Kate M. is ill at W. D. G.'s, and P. Bird at his own home. Wind very high.

11th.—Had the pleasure to-day of meeting Alexander C. Jones, formerly of this county, now of Arkansas; he is just from the army of Gen. Longstreet.

12th.—Mr. Philemon Bird died this morning about day. His physician worked hard on him, but failed to arrest the disease.

20th.—Sent a hog to Richmond weighing 273½ lbs., which brought me $1094.

22d.—Hear to-day that Maj. J. R. B. is in Petersburg, suffering seriously with dyspepsia. News that

Gen. Hoke has captured Plymouth, N. C., with twenty-five hundred prisoners, thirty-five cannon, one hundred thousand pounds of bacon, etc.

26th.—Dentis, a Yankee prisoner at my house, left for Richmond. He seemed reluctant to go, and we were sorry to part with him, though he was an enemy. His education is limited, but he has considerable natural shrewdness.—A few shad.

May 4th.—The horses, saddles, guns, etc., captured from the Yankees were appraised to-day, so as to make an equal distribution among the men engaged. The men who held the horses should be allowed to retain the minor articles.

5th.—Sent to Mr. B. Carlton 199 lbs. bacon for families of the soldiers.

8th.—Mercury 89 degrees.

9th.—Great anxiety to learn issue of battle between Lee and Grant.

10th.—Hear that Yankee army landed at Bermuda Hundred, advanced towards Petersburg Railroad, and were driven back with some loss. [About this time the Yankees had constructed a high tower at a point some ten miles from Petersburg, from which to spy over into the city. One morning General Butler, who was in command, had gone up to the top of the tower to see what he could see. While he was up there a cannon ball from a Confederate battery two miles away came over and struck the tower. The people around said, " The old general came down quicker than he went up."] Medical Board assembled here yesterday.

12th.—Attended drill, and Home Guard was ordered to rendezvous at St. Stephens.

13th.—Most of the company from St. Stephens were ordered out on picket at Walkerton, Ayletts, and Dunkirk. Spent the night in the church.

14th.—Went to Ayletts to picket the ferry, along with H. Cox, J. McF., A. C. Coleman, and Z. Carlton.

15th.—Spent last night in the ferry house and was relieved this morning. Mr. T. W. L. Fauntleroy, John and Joseph Ryland, Mrs. P. Smith, Edwin Watkins,

W. H. Berkeley, etc., were very kind and liberal in sending provisions.

16th.—Got home tired and sleepy. Heard yesterday, to my deep regret, of the death of Capt. E. C.
Fox, Polk Watkins, Jos. Wayne, and Robt. Davis, all
of the King and Queen cavalry, in a battle with Sheridan at Yellow Tavern. Alex. Acree is very badly
wounded,—and others.

17th.—Gen. Beauregard had a heavy fight with the
Yankees below Drewry's Bluff yesterday, and drove
them back, taking a large number of prisoners (Gen.
Hickman, etc.). It is said also that Gen. Breckenridge
has whipped them at New Market in the Valley, and
Gen. Joe Johnston driven them back from an attempt
on the fortifications at Dalton.

18th.—Put up herring and a few shad at Mantapike
this morning.

About this time there were strong indications that
the enemy would cut us off from Richmond, and perhaps overrun all this part of the State. Grant was coming down from Spottsylvania Courthouse in the direction of Cold Harbor, and already a cavalry force of
some 3000 men had appeared in upper King William.
A very large infantry force passed through the upper
part of the county, together with, as it would seem, the
entire wagon train of Grant's army. They crossed over
at Dunkirk and other points above. The Home Guard
was called out, and moved up towards Clarkston, but
finding the enemy in very strong force, they were smart
enough not to attack, yet, as far as was in their power,
to prevent straggling. We camped at Shuter's Hill, belonging to John Ryland, Saturday night, and Sunday
night on Joseph Ryland's land. Saturday John A. Fleet
and myself were sent on a scout, and reaching a certain
position, saw a large number of wagons, some on each
side of the river, with cavalry and infantry. They had
camped on John Fauntleroy's field beyond the ferry.
Some two hundred or three hundred cavalry had before
this crossed to our side of the river; having built a good
bridge, we supposed the whole body intended crossing,
but next morning the two hundred recrossed, the bridge

was taken up, and they went on their way. There is no doubt that Burnside's corps passed down by Newtown and crossed the Mattapony below. The Home Guard watched them, and there were but few stragglers.

Here, with May, 1864, this interesting journal closes, with the exception of a few items that would not interest. Events ripened so fast from this time on that the journalist suspended his writing and seems to have turned his attention more in other directions. It was during the month of July that Sheridan, with a cavalry force of some ten or twelve thousand, moved out from General Grant's lines, flanking Richmond first northward, and then westward along the line of the Chesapeake & Ohio Railroad. His objective was to join General Hunter, who was moving southward towards Lynchburg, with a view to capturing that city. Each of them failed of his object. Early was sent to Lynchburg to head off Hunter, and General Hampton intercepted Sheridan some ten miles above Louisa Courthouse, the latter making haste to get out of his way. In retiring, Sheridan came down into our county, bringing with him the largest force (save Burnside, who simply passed through) that ever set foot on our soil. He came down as far as King and Queen Courthouse, where he camped. Naturally there were a great many stragglers, and immense mischief was done by parties along the line of their march. Fortunately for us, it was of brief duration, for next day being Sunday, they passed back up the county and retired across the Mattapony and Pamunkey, rejoining General Grant. These fellows visited well-nigh every house of note on all the roads within five miles of the Mattapony River. They got pretty much all they wanted at each place, and in some instances behaved very rudely towards women and children. Many of them were foreigners, as one could easily detect from their speech. We were certainly as glad to be rid of them as they were to quit us. This was the last raid into our county, but we shared to the full in the distresses about Petersburg, doing what we could to alleviate the sufferings of the poor fellows in the trenches; and when Richmond was evacuated—especially when Appomattox came a week later—we were as much distressed as any of our unfortunate people. One Monday afternoon (it was, I think, the third day of April, 1865) the author had walked across the road to visit his wife's father. As he came back, entering the road to recross, he saw a negro man coming down the road, dressed in a fantastic costume, and reporting as he passed down, " Richmond has gone up." It was to very many hearts like a wail from the lower regions. Still, we were not without hope that the matchless man who was leading our armies would find some way to save our declining cause. Appomattox, of course, settled the matter, and left us struggling in the waves of Reconstruction. Our county people had acted their part wonderfully well. We had surrendered husbands, brothers, sons, and treasure to sustain the banner of General Lee, and when Reconstruction came it just happened in the good providence of God that we suffered less than very many of our fellow-citizens of less fortunate communities.

Such incidents as that of the Dahlgren lock of hair—given on a previous page—are an index of the feeling and motive of our people in their part of the great conflict. They were not actuated in their defensive measures by feelings of malice, or jealousy, or a vindictive spirit, but they stood manfully for the defense of their rights as they saw these, under the Constitution of the United States.

CHAPTER XI

FROM RICHMOND TO APPOMATTOX

A Narrative of the Operations of the Twenty-fourth Regiment of Virginia Cavalry,—Gary's Brigade, Army of Northern Virginia,—April 3-7, 1865.

By S. BIRD.

After the stirring campaign of the summer and fall of 1864, the cavalry brigade of General M. W. Gary, A. N. V.,—composed of the Hampton Legion, the Seventh South Carolina, Seventh Georgia, and Twenty-fourth Virginia regiments of cavalry, and Harkerson's Battery of artillery,—found itself in the month of January, 1865, at " Camp Gary," about four miles below or east of Richmond City, near Fair Oaks station on the York River Railroad.

This cavalry brigade was at that time about the only Confederate force of consequence to offer resistance to any advance which might be made by General Ord's corps of the Federal army, which occupied Fort Harrison on the north side of James River, several miles below our camp.

In February, I think it was, a part of General G. W. C. Lee's division of infantry moved to that side of the river. Fortunately for us, the enemy seemed content to remain quiet for a time, at least during this severe winter, and we improved the time left us from the vigorous and trying picket duty along the White Oak Swamp, in making rude tents with pine poles, splitting the poles as best we could for roofs, which we supplemented with strips of any and all kinds of cloth or old blankets that we could gather to protect us from the freezing and almost incessant rains of that trying winter.

Rations for the men, as well as food for our horses, grew sadly and feelingly less with each succeeding week, until about the middle of February, I think it was, we learned that our regiment, the Twenty-fourth Virginia Cavalry, would probably be allowed, as a matter of necessity, to move by companies to localities nearest the homes of the men, from which points the men would go to their respective homes to recruit both themselves and horses, for a week or two at least, so as to return in good shape for the spring campaign, which we all knew would be desperate and decisive. The sequel proved that it was more than that; it was " short, sharp, decisive," and ended in despair.

In pursuance of this plan, our company (F), commanded by the venerable and chivalrous Captain L. W. Allen (who at the age of sixty years and more shared all the hardships and dangers of camp and march and battle with a degree of cheerful endurance surpassed by none of his men in the ranks), received orders late in the evening of one of the coldest days in February we ever felt, to move the company to Taylorsville, in Hanover County, a distance of probably twenty miles.

Just about sunset we were ordered to " saddle up," and in thirty minutes or less we were on the march. Who of our number could ever forget that night? Our line of march was directly over the ground nearly every foot of which had been cut and worked up by the two armies during the preceding summer, in the campaign from the Wilderness to the James River, followed during the fall and winter by our wagons in quest of supplies for our army, until the surface was now a frozen mass of mud, spikes, and gullies. I have never been able to determine which suffered the most that night, the men from the piercing, freezing cold,—poorly clad as they were,—or the horses literally treading on spikes at every step, until many of them could go no further; when their riders would stop, kindle a fire in the woods, and wait for daylight to enable them to choose the way, if indeed there was any choice even then.

My brother and myself, whose horses had never failed us, were among the few who continued the march to the end that night; keeping our feet from freezing, and aiding our horses at the same time, by dismounting and leading them for hours. About daybreak we

reached Taylorsville, found good log tents which some
infantry had lately vacated, and which were like pal-
aces to us,—roomy, with log chimneys, and plenty of
clean straw for our beds. We lost no time in kindling
fires and thawing ourselves out, not forgetting to unsaddle quickly our poor suffering horses, and cover them
with all our blankets, while the fire and straw sufficed
for us indoors.

In such luxurious quarters, we did not then envy the
poor fellows who had dropped out by the wayside that
night, and who were straggling in until late that day,
their horses footsore and limping, themselves half-
frozen and famished.

We remained there three or four days, for our horses
to rest their lacerated and swollen feet; when in groups
of four or five we were ordered to our respective homes
in the adjacent counties, to remain and recuperate man
and beast for about two weeks, and then return to the
vicinity of Taylorsville, or such other place as the command might assemble at; meantime keeping ourselves
in readiness to obey any orders for special duty which
might reach us, or to return promptly to our command.

When we consider the suffering which had to be endured that winter, when there was no place we could
call winter quarters, shelterless when moving from place
to place, poorly clad, and withal reduced almost to a
state of starvation with only about four ounces of
bacon and a pound of corn meal or flour for a twenty-
four hours' ration,—it might be well to reflect a moment and ask the question, "Who but Confederate
soldiers could have been trusted to go to their homes,
and return to their commands, only to be better prepared to meet the ' overwhelming numbers ' which we
all knew the enemy were losing no time nor resources
to marshal against us?" Some of the boys said we
were only going home to fatten up and return in good
" killing order," and there was really more truth than
wit in the expression.

The men were simply placed on their honor, and
right loyally did they honor the confidence reposed
in them. Not only did they, with scarcely an exception,

return in a few weeks, but many who (for what they considered good reasons) were already absent without leave (for no furloughs were permitted under any circumstances) returned also.

Sergeant C. H. Carlton (noble Christian soldier), my brother Preston and myself were instructed to proceed to our homes in King and Queen County; and after resting our horses a few days my brother and myself were to scout the Rappahannock and Piankitank Rivers down the south sides, and returning home continue the scout up to the vicinity of Fredericksburg and Richmond,—unless in the meantime some movement of the enemy should render it in our judgment important to report promptly to Richmond.

We executed the first part of the programme, discovering no movement of the enemy, except some activity of the Federal gunboats in the lower Rappahannock and Piankitank,—nothing to indicate the landing of any considerable force. We found, however, many of our men who were absent without leave, and told them we were authorized to inform them all that if they would return voluntarily to the regiment within a week or ten days, the army regulations would be suspended and " play quits " as to them. They readily consented to this, as they said it was their intention to do anyhow, and carried out their promise, while our guarantee as to regulations was sacredly kept by the officials.

On our return to our home, where we expected to rest our horses a week or more, we learned that orders had been sent through Sergeant Carlton for us to return as promptly as possible to our regiment, which would rendezvous somewhere in the vicinity of Hanover Courthouse. Remaining at home about two days for necessary rest, because nearly all of our time since leaving Taylorsville had been occupied in the scouting duty assigned to us, we started to rejoin our command.

Reaching the Pamunkey River we found it swollen over its banks, with a rushing current caused by recent heavy rains. It was perilous to venture swimming our horses, which we would have done under ordinary circumstances, when there were no boats, although the stream is usually narrow and high up the river. We also learned that a column of the enemy had been seen on the opposite side that day, which for the time would likely cut us off from reaching our command, if indeed we should be able to escape capture. We therefore determined to wait a day or two in hopes that both the river and the enemy would resume their proper places. Accordingly we ventured to our home, about twenty miles distant, which we reached that night.

How little did I dream of the impending blow about to fall on me with the first crushing sorrow of my then vigorous and buoyant youth. With the exception of some fatigue from our recent scout and exposure, my brother and myself were in perfect health.

The following morning my brother rode over to spend an hour or two with one of our nearest neighbors, whom he had not seen during the few days he had spent at home. To our surprise he did not return that evening or night, as we knew was his intention. On the following morning a messenger rode up and informed us that he was quite sick. My father, not thinking he could be seriously ill in so short a time, immediately went over to this neighbor's and brought him home in a carriage. Never shall I forget my horror and amazement, and the indescribable feeling of despair which seized and almost paralyzed me, when I went up to the carriage to assist him out and looked into his pale face, the expression of which told me in silent but unmistakable tones that he was already in a dying condition.

The nearest physician was hastily summoned and every effort made to revive him,—without avail. He had made his last scout and by some strange destiny had been turned back from reaching his command, where he could be brought *home* to die that night. He had suddenly fallen into a stupor the day before while sitting with his friends around their hospitable fireside. Thinking it was simply the result of fatigue and exposure, or a chill, they had put him to bed expecting that he would awake refreshed from sleep and well in the morning. It proved, however, that the sudden stupor was delirium, from which he did not rally or regain consciousness. This is the short pathetic story of his sudden death, the disease or immediate cause of which has always been and will continue to be a mystery. No language could express my crushing grief and deep despair.

After more than thirty-five years have intervened, my heart almost sinks within me now and bleeds afresh at every pore as memory reverts to that dark, dismal, desolate hour when relentless death claimed the only brother of my soul. He had been all that a devoted brother could be to me. From earliest childhood we had been inseparable, slept together, started to school together the same day, pursued the same studies, in the same classes,—until the school was broken up by the call to arms in the spring of 1861, when the teachers enlisted the larger boys into the company of which they were elected officers, and turned our playground into a drill ground.

We were both too young then for military or service duty, nor were we separated until the summer of 1863, when my brother, at the age of eighteen, joined the army around Richmond. The following year I joined his company. He was a veteran then and watched over me with the tender solicitude of a mother; nor were we ever separated again until his death.—Two days later, on a bleak, dreary evening in March,—the earth wrapped in snow and ice,—we laid him in the quiet graveyard by the side of our precious mother, with her to await the resurrection morn. Among the thousands of heroes who offered and yielded their lives for our Southland there were none more heroic and chivalrous than he.

Could he have chosen the manner of his death it would have been in his accustomed place in the forefront of the battle, his gleaming saber flashing inspiration to his comrades and defiance to the foe; in obeying his last order and performing faithfully his last duty; not like the galley slave, scourged to his dungeon at night, but as one who " wraps the drapery of his couch about him and lies down to pleasant dreams." Alas, brother of my soul, that my pen falters and words fail me to pay the tribute due to your noble life! I cannot pen this narrative for my children without this humble and inadequate tribute to your memory, commending to them your noble life as an inspiration and example for them to obey the call of duty.

On the morning after his burial I set out, disconsolate and desolate, to join my regiment, which, on the second day of my journey, about March 25 I think it was, I found at " Old Gary," where it had just camped after some slight skirmishing with the enemy several days before, they having retired to the vicinity of Fort Harrison without offering battle.

I should be recreant to my duty if I failed now to mention the tender and sincere sympathy with which the members of my company, as well, indeed, as the whole regiment, greeted me. Especially as brigade scout, my brother Preston was well known and esteemed by all; his modest bearing, quiet disposition, kind and sympathetic heart, were no less admired than his dashing, intrepid bravery in battle or whenever cool courage and discretion were demanded.

As I rode into camp with my unspeakable grief reflected in my countenance, the greeting which came from everyone was " Where is Preston? " I made a supreme effort to answer *dead,* for I knew at that moment I could only give utterance to that one word. I could not speak, but chokingly leaned over on my horse and sobbed for utterance; they knew too well the answer I was trying to utter and with eyes filled with tears gathered around me, took me from my horse, assisted me to a rude tent, mingling their tears with mine, striving as best they could to comfort and calm my bursting heart, until I could find utterance and relate the sad, simple story of my brother's sudden death. Noble fellows, your sympathy for me was sincere and heartfelt, but your tears and grief were your best and spontaneous tribute to the noble young soldier, whom you so much loved and who would now return no more. It was unusual for those veterans to give such visible expressions of sorrow at the death of one of their number. They had often seen their comrades fall so thick and fast that they would become discouraged, and lose their spirit for the grewsome work which duty demanded of them in active warfare.

General Gary sent me a message of sympathy, and expressive of the loss he had sustained in the death of his trusted and chivalrous young scout. In the fall of 1863, when Preston first received his " baptism of fire," General Gary had been impressed with his dashing bravery and gallant bearing in battle, and selected him for some important duty requiring the highest order of courage and discretion. This speedily resulted in his appointment as independent scout, with credentials to go and report at will; he knew the peril and responsibility of his mission, which he promptly accepted, proceeding at once to spend most of his time in the enemy's line and around their outposts.

He frequently captured the enemy's couriers with their dispatches, which of course he promptly reported. At other times, eluding the hostile pickets (generally at night), he went into the enemy's camp, thus keeping informed as to their movements, strength, etc. It may be interesting and instructive to my children to mention one or two of his experiences as illustrative of the perils of a scout.

On one occasion in the fall of 1864 he, with two other scouts, crept between the enemy's pickets at night, after first hiding their own horses in a convenient thicket, and cautiously crept into the enemy's camp. Their purpose, as well as I remember, was, if possible, to capture a certain Federal officer in his tent.

They approached close to the coveted tent (which they had previously located) without being detected, but found to their disappointment that it was surrounded by a strong cordon of guards (something unknown with us), which it would have been supreme folly to attack in the midst of their camp with any hope of making the coveted capture, even if they succeeded in capturing the guards, as it would have aroused the camp and resulted in their own capture or death.

The next thing to do was to withdraw and escape

as quickly as possible. Although everything had been quiet up to that moment, they suddenly discovered some movement from a part of the camp, which made their position perilous, if not for the moment hopeless. As they stealthily approached the main road leading through the camp, watching for a favorable moment to dart across it unobserved, a loaded wagon drawn by four large mules approached. Detection seemed certain then, for they could not retrace their steps and they only had a few moments to determine what to do, but it was enough; their only hope was to pass out with this wagon, which they (in a whisper) decided to do. Crouching close by the roadside, as the wagon came up with their revolvers in hand they sprang up, one on each side of the driver, who, before he could realize the situation, was warned in a whisper, emphasized with two pistols at his head, that if he spoke or moved it meant death. Of course he was " struck dumb." He was then ordered to let his team proceed, and in this way they passed the camp sentinels, who did not hail them, thinking doubtless that the wagons were moving under orders.

A short distance beyond the guards, and before any other wagon or troops came up, they ordered the driver to turn his team into an opening in the woods; proceeding in the woods a short distance, until out of view from the road in the darkness, they quickly and quietly unhitched the mules, threw some of the contents of the wagon (they did not know then what) across their backs, and led the mules with their prisoner through the woods to the track by which they had entered the camp and which they now followed back to the spot where they had left their horses. By this time it was day, and, hurrying to elude pursuit, they reached camp in due time, hungry and sleepy, but with four large sleek fat mules and a Yankee sutler prisoner, who for the first time fully realized " where he was at."

The capture proved to be a sutler with his stores, which he said he was moving to another location; of course without the faintest idea of locating his wagon and wares at a secluded spot in the woods, his mules in the hands of the " rebel " scouts, and himself in Libby prison.

On another occasion, after having satisfied himself of the route which the couriers of the enemy were in the habit of taking, my brother crept into their lines and selected a favorable spot near the roadside, where he secreted himself at night and awaited the passing of the first fellow whom he might take to be the bearer of dispatches. He said experience had taught him that couriers usually rode alone, and at greater speed than the ordinary soldier, especially at night; thus enabling him to spot them. On this occasion everything was so quiet as the night wore on, and he became so benumbed with cold, that he was about to leave his hiding place, and retrace his steps through the pickets, when he heard the footsteps of a horse rapidly crossing the pontoon bridge which the enemy had made across the James River for communication between their forces on the north and south sides of the river. He was confident that the rider was the dispatch-bearer for whom he had so long been shivering in the cold, and that he would take the route past the spot where he was secreted. He accordingly left his hiding place and crouched close on the roadside. The rider approached, lowly humming a tune, and increasing his speed after crossing the bridge. As he was passing the spot Preston sprang in front of him, and seizing the bridle stopped the horse, while with the other hand he covered the rider with his pistol, and ordered him to throw up his hands, and dismount quickly and quietly. The horseman obeyed without the least controversy, and the next moment was marching from the road, a prisoner with his hands up in front of his captor, who led the horse a short distance, then halted a moment to disarm the prisoner, and proceeded to a place of safety, where he could be searched for the coveted dispatch. Imagine the scout's chagrin and disgust when instead of the dispatch he found the prisoner's pockets full of chips, or devices used by gamblers. The prisoner had been over the river indulging in a game of cards with some of his chums on that side until the " wee small hours " and was returning in happy mood when captured. The captor, in relating the incident to me, said he felt so thoroughly chagrined and disgusted at his "water haul," that his first impulse was to release the poor fellow, whose repining at fate had excited his sympathy, and content himself with keeping the fine horse, arms and accouterments, as a reward for the night's work; but this would never do, as the prisoner, if released, would of course reveal to the enemy the story and location of his capture and thus enable them to guard this road, so as to defeat future attempts on that line; whereas if held as a prisoner his fate would be as profound a mystery as the identity of the fellow who "hit Billy Patterson." The horse, however, was a fine animal, with splendid saddle, bridle, etc.; the arms of the best,—patent repeating carbine, revolver, etc. The prisoner's uniform and splendid equipment indicated clearly that he was more of a "sport" than a soldier.

After being kindly treated, he agreed, as he was being taken to prison, to exchange his magnificent long cavalry boots with his captor, as he would have little use for them in prison.

These two incidents, of many, are related simply to give some idea of the life and perils of a scout, whom the enemy made every effort to capture, and who knew from their threats which reached his ears that if captured he would receive no quarter.

THE EVACUATION

Sunday, the second day of April, 1865, dawned bright and clear; which was welcomed and appreciated by the men after the protracted cold and wet of the winter and early spring, as they were but scantily protected by the improvised tents, so-called, at old "Camp Gary," to which they had returned less than two weeks before, as already related.

About midday it was so warm and bright that Apollas Luck, who in the tenderness of his brave soldier heart had striven in every way to comfort me by his constant presence and companionship since the death of my brother, proposed that we take our horses out under the hills about a mile distant in the direction of Richmond to nip any grass which they might find.

While our horses were strolling along in search of anything they could find to eat, we were lounging on the hillsides. Richmond was in view, and everything as calm and quiet as a zephyr. We were impressed with the serenity of the surroundings, and talked about the absence of everything resembling war or the desperate struggle which for four years had continued around the environments of the devoted city. Truly it was the ominous calm preceding the storm.

Late in the evening we bridled our horses and returned to camp, where we gave them their scant feed of corn, and blanketed them as we thought for the night. I gathered up about half a dozen canteens and proceeded to the spring, a few hundred yards distant, for the water supply of our mess for the night and for picket duty at daylight the following morning, as was our custom, while Uncle John Flippo, as we called him, started the fire to cook our morsel of bread; which, however, was never cooked. On my way to the spring, just about sunset, a horseman dashed by at headlong speed in the direction of brigade headquarters; I took no special notice of him at the moment, thinking it was some fellow who had spent the day in the city and was returning with a full stomach and lighter heart than the rest of us. In about fifteen minutes I was returning with the canteens filled, and as I reached the top of the hill was amazed to see everything in confusion, the improvised tents pulled to pieces, men mounted and rapidly forming by companies. I hastened forward, saddled up as quickly as possible, and in a few minutes was in line, just as the order to move forward was given, with no time to inquire the meaning of it all. Nor did anyone know that we were ordered to move.

We marched two or three hours east in the direction of Fort Harrison, and crossing the nine-mile road, if I remember correctly, halted about 9 P. M., dismounted and formed into line of battle, with orders to make no noise. About midnight we were permitted to lie down in our tracks, keeping in line with hands on our carbines. Thus we remained on the wet ground, shivering as the night grew cold, until about the first streak of dawn, when we mounted noiselessly and proceeded in nearly a direct line towards Richmond.

While in line that night we whispered our respective opinions of the meaning of the movement, the prevailing opinion being that the enemy was advancing in our front and that about dawn we would rush forward to attack and surprise them.

No one thought for a moment, or ventured the suggestion, of the evacuation of Richmond. The one and only thought we permitted ourselves to entertain in this connection was that it was our business to defend the beloved city, around which still clustered the hopes and destiny of the Confederacy. Just as the sun rose clear and bright we reached the outer earthworks below the city, when to our horror and surprise we saw a white flag on the top of the parapet by the roadside, two persons in citizens' dress standing by it, and a carriage near by. At the same moment a glance westward brought the city in full view except as it was enveloped by the dense smoke, which seemed to be rising from its every section; it needed no words to reveal to us that the hour of its doom had come.

The white flag, the citizens, the carriage, meant that Mayor Mayo was only awaiting the advance of the enemy to surrender the city, if indeed,—from the appearance of the conflagration and desolation,—anything of the devoted city would be left to surrender. For the first time during four years did the hearts of its heroic defenders sicken and sink in despair, at the desolate, hope-wrecking sight.

Our column halted a moment, then passed by the mayor and the white flag, turned into the road, and at quickened gait headed straight for the doomed city.

As the regiment passed on to the city, Jack Yarbrough, Gatewood Burnett and myself were ordered to proceed down the road in the opposite direction, with orders to keep in view of the regiment, which we were to signal, and retreat as the enemy advanced, keeping a sharp lookout to avoid capture by a flanking force. As we proceeded cautiously in the direction of the advancing enemy, three Confederate infantrymen came walking rapidly to meet us with their muskets at shoulder. When about fifty yards from us they halted, dropped their guns, and holding up their hands shouted their surrender to us. Riding up to them and asking what they meant, they answered that we were Yankees, and that they might as well surrender without ceremony, as they were hopelessly cut off; at the same time pointing to the enemy on their right and rear, from whom they were vainly attempting to escape. We assured them that we were friends, and bade them hurry forward and follow the track of our regiment.

This they did, remarking, however, that it was useless as they would be captured before reaching the city, and warning us that we would share the same fate if we did not retrace our steps immediately,—pointing to a force of the enemy on our right, which had not before been seen by us.

We retired slowly at first, and as the enemy advanced we rapidly passed these poor fellows, whom we were reluctantly compelled to leave to their fate. We signaled the enemy's advance and hurried on to avoid being cut off, reaching the rear of our regiment just as the head of the column was stopped for the time by the mob which had massed in the streets, a way through which was forced only with the use of the sabers.

Just at this juncture Burnett, whose family lived near my home, turned to me and with tremulous voice asked, " What in God's name must I do, you know how helpless my wife and children are; what will become of them if I continue with our army; they will be in the enemy's lines and I will never see them again; I cannot desert, but for God's sake tell me what to do? " I knew of the wife and several small children, for whose comfort and protection the Relief Committee of our county had to provide when necessary, and I could see the tumult of his soul, struggling to decide which in this tremendous crisis was the path of duty,—to follow our army or return to the wife and children, who would need his protection as never before. The enemy were pressing rapidly on us, the mob filled the streets and obstructed our passage to the bridge, while the flames on either side were nearly if not actually lapping over our heads. There was no time for hesitation or reflection. I answered Burnett, " I cannot advise you, as I have no wife or children as you have. My duty is plain; I shall follow General Lee, while he leads, or until I fall. You must decide this matter." A moment later, as our column moved slowly through the mob, Burnett, turning his horse to the right, said, " I have done the best I could, but I cannot forsake my family; good-by," and waving us farewell, rode off and proceeded home, where I frequently met him on my return from Appomattox. He was a good soldier, nor could we ever reproach him. When it was " all over," in referring to it he said he felt that he only did his duty.

As our column moved slowly through the mob, using sabers to clear the way, this mass of every age, sex, and color, wild with excitement, and many laden with plunder, would block our way at every turn. The streets and sidewalks were filled with boxes, barrels, timbers, and goods of every kind and description. As barrels, boxes, etc., were rolled from the stores, the mob would burst them open and scramble wildly for the contents, apparently regardless of whether they became victims of the flames, were trampled beneath our horses' feet, or fell under the blows of our sabers, in their wild greed for loot.

In one of the warehouses they found a quantity of whisky stored, and as the barrels were rolled into the street they were met by those outside, promptly burst open with clubs, the contents literally filling the gutters as from a shower of rain. Numbers of them grabbed up tubs and buckets, dipped to the brim the fiery liquid, which the more generous of them freely dispensed to our men with the tin cans, cups, etc., lying around. This served as the only breakfast we had; it was better than none, and in keeping with the surroundings.

As **W. H. Farinholt,** of Company C (who was at

the time acting as courier for General Ewell), was riding down Main Street hurrying towards the bridge he happened to see a man coming out of Mitchell & Tyler's jewelry store, with his hands full of watches and jewelry. Ordering him to stop and return his plunder, which the fellow showed no disposition to do, as he started off with it, Farinholt, not wishing to kill him, rode up on the sidewalk, and standing in his stirrups, dealt him a fearful blow on the head with his heavy army revolver, which sent him stunned and sprawling to the pavement, the jewelry falling and scattering around him. Farinholt jumped from his horse, quickly gathered up the jewelry, and opening the door dropped it in a heap on the floor, where he had to leave it, and hurried to the bridge, which he reached and crossed while it was in flames. This is only one of the almost numberless incidents of the kind which might be mentioned.

After the head of our column had reached and were crossing the bridge, Yarbrough and myself saw that from our position in the rear, as the mob passed in our front and the enemy pressed upon us behind, we were in imminent danger of being cut off from the bridge by the flames and the mob combined, and falling into the enemy's hands. We were expecting to see the bridge burst in flames every moment, which would seal our fate; nor were we mistaken. As our only hope to reach it in time, we determined to risk a short cut to the bridge out and off the main body of the mob; accordingly we turned towards the basin, and soon found our way blocked at a slip. The only way to cross the span of about twenty feet was over a plank walk about two feet wide. It was perilous, but it was too late to retrace our steps, and I determined to risk it. My horse rebelled at first, but spurring him forward I forced him on the narrow walk, which he cleared with a plunge. Yarbrough followed and we both dashed to the bridge and rushed over it as the flames were bursting from it.

Our regiment had halted on the Manchester side with the brigade, and while the bridge was burning we quietly gazed on the devoted city, which seemed doomed to destruction, the furious flames leaping from side to side as at every moment they burst out afresh. The mob was in undisputed possession now, unless checked by the enemy as they moved in, which, to their credit, I believe they did as promptly as possible, and which alone probably saved the city from total destruction.

In the river below the bridge several vessels and some small boats, along with the two ironclad gunboats which had only recently been completed, and from which we had hoped for great things, were moored about midstream with smoke rising from them, which told us that they too were to share in the conflagration. As we watched the smoke slowly rising from them, suddenly we felt the earth quiver and quake simultaneously with a deafening roar, as a column of water, fire, smoke, and debris shot skyward. As the magazines exploded the destruction of the gunboats was complete, while with the roaring flames, leaping higher and higher in their mad fury as they swept onward in their wild, unchecked career, was mingled the deafening thunder of the exploding magazines in the city.

Stunned and bewildered at the sickening sight, we felt at the moment as though the end of the world had come, while the river itself seemed to furnish fuel to the flames. The bridge, the city, the river, enveloped in fire and smoke, while at intervals the shouts of the wild-surging and now unrestrained mob reached our ears, presented a scene, and awakened emotions, which live in memory but which language is powerless to describe.

None who witnessed will ever forget or fitly describe it, while it will remain vividly engraved on memory's tablet. Beloved Richmond was lost, but would not the God of battles spare it and its heroic people from destruction? How our hearts sank within us! For four years the hostile hosts had surged around its environments, only to be hurled back in confusion and dismay by the heroic band who said, " Hitherto shalt thou come but no farther."

The flower of the world's chivalry had poured out their life-blood as a willing libation upon your altars,

when your hilltops were a sheet of defiant flame and
your valleys turned to rivulets of blood.

> Our hearts, our hopes, our prayers, our tears,
> Our faith triumphant o'er our fears,—
> Were all with thee, were all with thee!

We love best that for which we have sacrificed most;
and so we loved Richmond more than all the cities of
our Southland.   For four years it had been the coveted
prize of our foes, and the storm-center of the contending
hosts.   Our fathers and elder brothers rushed to her
rescue, and as through these years of sorrow and blood
they had fallen as fall only the brave, their younger
sons and brothers had taken their places in the cause
rendered doubly dear to them, and with deathless de-
termination to continue to the last extremity.

> For Freedom's battle, once begun,
> Bequeath'd from bleeding sire to son.

More blood, I believe, had been shed in defense of
this capital city of the Confederacy than in all the wars
previously waged on this American continent since its
discovery by Columbus.   Every battle fought by the
Army of Northern Virginia, from Manassas in 1861,
including Sharpsburg and bloody Gettysburg, to the fall
of the city on April 3, 1865, had been in its defense.
General Lee had said that " Richmond was never so
safe as when her defenders were farthest away."   Our
children can never fully appreciate our love for Richmond, sealed as it was with so much priceless blood.
Her hearts, her homes, her arms were ever open to us,
feeding us when famished, cheering us when homesick
and weary, opening her homes to receive while her
matrons and maidens became ministering angels to
our wounded and dying.   May the bonds of sympathy
which so tenderly bound together her heroic people and
her defenders be transmitted and cherished as a sacred
heritage to their children.

When the destruction of the bridge was accomplished, with emotions awakened by such memories welling up in our bosoms we turned our backs upon Richmond and left it to its doom.

It was all so sudden we could scarcely realize that Richmond had fallen, and as the men discussed the situation and the prospect before us, we took consolation in the hope that as the enemy would now necessarily be drawn into the interior and away from his fleet and base of supplies, in some way, through the matchless genius of Lee, we would eventually triumph over our foes, and the Army of Northern Virginia would yet return victorious and redeem our capital city; when Virginia would ever be the brightest star in the constellation of the Confederacy and Richmond the richest jewel in her crown.

THE MARCH

Knowing that the destruction of the bridge would prevent any rapid pursuit of the enemy, about ten o'clock on Monday morning, April 3, 1865, we proceeded on the march to join the main body of the army, which had moved up from Petersburg the previous day. Passing through a part of Chesterfield county we camped about midnight, weary and hungry, in Powhatan county. None of us (except perhaps the few who happened to have a few crusts of bread in their haversacks when we hastily left Camp Gary the previous Sunday evening) had tasted food for thirty-six hours. We camped in a pine wood, kindled fires, and hastened to search for water to mix what little flour or corn meal we may have been fortunate enough to have in our haversacks when we left camp.

After a long search in the darkness, we found a little muddy water in a small ditch. We mixed the last morsel of meal we had in a small frying pan, which I had been fortunate enough to take with me, but which I did not take the precaution to wash first, owing to the scarcity of water. Holding the pan over the fire long enough to parch a few half-cooked cakes of bread, we divided among our mess and proceeded hastily to devour. Imagine our horror when we found that in the darkness and our haste we had mixed about equal quantities of meal and horsehair (the result of failing to wash the pan, which had been hanging from my saddle since the previous day, our horses shedding their hair at the time).

Half-starved and desperate, we taxed our ingenuity to eat that bread, while the hair stuck in our teeth and throats, but our stomachs rebelled and refused to receive it. Disgusted, desperate, and anything but amiable, we cast away our last morsel and dropped on the ground to relieve in sleep the few remaining hours of the night. The language used by some in expressing their opinions of the " cause and effect " of that supper was not such as they had been taught at Sunday school.

Early in the morning of Tuesday, April 4th, we saddled up and proceeded on our march. Harkerson's Battery, which was attached to our brigade, had, before leaving its camp in the woods, thrown out a lot of shells to lighten the caissons, which the half-starved horses could scarcely pull through the mud even when empty. This battery moved on in front of our regiment and soon got stuck in the mud as usual. As many men as could be of assistance dismounted, and helped to pull the guns out of the mud, while our company, in the rear of the regiment at the time, waited impatiently for the guns to be extricated. Our venerable old Captain Allen in his impatience dismounted, and leaving his horse in the road, where we were grouped in rather careless fashion, started to walk forward to the guns in the mire.

He had proceeded but a short distance when suddenly from the woods about a quarter of a mile in our rear, which we had left a half-hour before, came the " bang, bang, bang " of bursting shells. Thinking at the moment that the enemy had come upon us and opened their guns on us, every man of us instinctively spurred his horse forward, almost riding over Capt. Allen, who stopped in the road and ordered a halt, his own horse, though riderless, following us until coming up to his rider. I shall never forget with what disgust and indignation Capt. Allen rebuked us for our thoughtlessness and disorder, as he asked us if it were possible that we could rush off with his horse following us, and leave him to his fate in the road.

Of course such a thought never entered the minds of any of us. We were simply acting from thoughtless momentary impulse, as we expected every moment the enemy's well directed shells to be tearing through our column. It was a false alarm, however: the woods had taken fire at the spot where our battery had thrown out the shells, which exploded as the fire reached them. But even in our humiliation we could not help chuckling at the ludicrous and embarrassing position of Capt. Allen, as supreme disgust usurped the place of his proverbial amiability. For a few moments it came *very* near causing a temporary stampede, as the most trivial things sometimes do under exciting circumstances.

This horse of his had made a remarkable record. His first rider had fallen dead from his saddle at Sharpsburg, the horse escaping unhurt and keeping his place in column after the fall of his gallant young master. Capt. Allen, becoming his owner, had himself been subsequently unhorsed and captured in a charge on the enemy, while the horse wheeled and escaped, and was kept ready for his rider when he was exchanged. Again, three days after this incident, if I remember correctly, one of our officers had lost his horse in an engagement and in some way at the moment borrowed and mounted this horse, when he fell from his saddle severely wounded, the horse coming out of the fight unscathed as usual, and bearing Capt. Allen safely through to Appomattox, and thence home. It seemed certain, therefore, that if his rider could keep in his saddle on this horse he was safe from capture, at least, though not from death.

Proceeding on our way as fast as we could keep the battery moving, which was continually stuck in the mud up to the hubs, we reached the Appomattox River about dark.

Shortly before reaching the river a detail of eighteen men, myself among them, in charge of a sergeant from another company, were ordered to remain behind and follow about a mile in rear of the column and arrest any of the men whom we met returning to their homes before crossing the river, as many were inclined to do from sheer hopelessness and hunger. Luther Broaddus and myself from our company were together, and soon noticed that the others were disposed to widen the breach between our detachment and our main column. Finally we urged the sergeant to move forward and keep nearer our column; then, halting, he informed us they had determined to return home, and if we were not disposed to join them we could report their movements after crossing the river. We were under his orders, and could but obey; we were powerless to do otherwise. Waving us their adieus and best wishes the sergeant and fifteen went homeward, but Luther Broaddus and myself returned hastily and reported the situation as our column halted at the bridge.

I then learned for the first time how the gnawing pangs of hunger would cause the bravest men to become hopeless and desperate. Crossing the river into Amelia County after nightfall, we soon joined the main army of General Lee and camped for the remainder of the night. Our horses had had no food since Sunday evening—forty-eight hours—and we knew could not hold out without food much longer. Therefore, before lying down to rest many of us went out in the darkness foraging, and soon found a barn well filled with corn and fodder. Against the threats and protest of the owner, who refused to open the doors, we pried off the weather boarding and loaded all we could carry across our saddles, returned to camp, and gave our starving horses all they could devour.

That forage was opportune, sustaining them through the succeeding five days, during which time neither horses nor men ever had half a feed. Our mess had exhausted our scant rations the previous night in the woeful experiment with the horsehair mixture, and had to rely upon sleep alone to relieve our hunger. Before lying down we noticed rockets shooting high into the air in quick succession, apparently a few miles ahead. We were unused to fireworks of that description, and could but be attracted by the beauty of the display; but we felt that they were more ominous than beautiful, because we knew it was the enemy's signal in our front, a foreboding which only awaited the morrow to confirm.

For two days we had not come in contact with the enemy, who did not pursue us on the march from Richmond, but we well knew from the direction of the rockets that the coming morn would open with bloody work for us, as he blocked the way.

About sunrise on Wednesday morning, April 5th, we were in the saddle and ready to move. As we formed into column we noticed a line of smoke rising about a mile to our left. The enemy's cavalry had swooped down, captured and fired our wagon train. General Gary, with his proverbial dash and celerity, led the brigade straight for them at a gallop. In about ten minutes we were upon and in the midst of them. Our prompt and sudden arrival was a surprise, certainly, to many of them who had dismounted and were pillaging and setting fire to the wagons. As they hustled out many fell in the road before our pistol fire at close range, or were captured, the others retiring hastily to their main body, which had formed in a body of woods on a hill about a half-mile distant. We pursued, following the road, and were met with a galling fire from the woods as we ascended the hill. After reaching the level the other regiments of our brigade dismounted, formed hastily, advanced through the woods and in a few minutes met the full force and fire of the enemy. Our regiment remained mounted and exposed to the fire of a part of the enemy's line, which we were unable to return effectively, while they were concealed in the woods. For about half an hour the fire was hot and furious, both sides tenaciously holding their respective positions.

The enemy's fire developed their largely superior force. We ascertained from the prisoners that our small brigade was engaging Gregg's Division of cavalry. As they gradually discovered our position, mounted in the road, which we had concealed as much as possible by leaning low on our horses and not returning their fire, they poured volleys more and more upon us.

At this juncture our regiment withdrew and, forming under the hill, broke down a fence on the roadside and charged across the open field with a yell, striking them on their flank, while simultaneously our line on foot charged them in full front in the woods.

We forced them from their position, and followed them closely as they suddenly withdrew, leaving many of their dead where they fell in the woods. Retiring about half a mile they formed again, and again our line advanced on foot, repeating the first attack with the same result. This continued through the day, the enemy forming at every half-mile or mile, stubbornly resisting our advance at every turn and yielding his position only when we forced him to close quarters. Thus we fought our way mile after mile until evening, when our men were becoming exhausted from fatigue and hunger, and our cartridge boxes were getting empty.

Without reinforcements our position was becoming dangerous, if the enemy should summon his courage, reverse conditions, and press us back. But late in the evening, when our ammunition was about exhausted as well as ourselves, a part of Fitzhugh Lee's Division came to our assistance. As our line, worn out with fatigue and hunger from the incessant fighting since early morning, dropped back about a quarter of a mile to replenish our exhausted cartridge boxes, our friends, whose arrival was so timely, took our place and prepared to continue the advance on the enemy. The changing of positions occupied about half an hour, during which time the firing ceased.

The enemy, instead of advancing on us, quickly took advantage of the situation and withdrew from our front about a mile, where our advance column soon discovered them occupying a strong position on a range of hills across from Amelia Springs, and apparently placing a battery of artillery in position. As our dismounted skirmish line advanced, led by the gallant Capt. W. C. Nunn of the King and Queen troop, Fifth Virginia Cavalry, it was met with a withering fire, and one of our officers fell from his horse dead. His lifeless body was quickly placed across his saddle and borne to the rear; as it passed us we were told, if I remember correctly, that it was Capt. Cunningham (I do not remember his regiment). About this time General Rosser rode up, and pressing to the front in full view of the enemy, joined a group of officers who seemed to be scanning the formidable force and position on the hills opposite.

At this juncture the gallant General James Dearing came up at the head of his " Laurel Brigade " of Rosser's Division, pressed to the front, and if I remember correctly, exchanged a few words with his chief, who seemed to us to point him to the enemy on the hills. Quick as a flash Dearing ordered his front column to form, and, ringing out the " charges," dashed forward, himself leading, as he always did when the foe was in front. A cavalry charge on such a position seemed desperate, but nothing daunted Dearing, and it would be a craven indeed who would not follow when he led. Dashing with a yell up the road and through a narrow cut where it pierces a hill, and swinging out on the summit, his column swept upon their flank and into their midst. The enemy broke in confusion with but slight resistance, so sudden and unexpected was the shock. In their confusion they suffered heavily as they were shot and cut down at close quarters by Dearing's men. This charge was superb and characteristic of Dearing, who was always superb. We had heard much of his splendid genius and dash, but it was the first time I had ever seen him in action, nor will I ever forget the inspiration with which we were thrilled.

Following up this charge our regiment was ordered forward to press the enemy. As we were hurrying along the narrow cut in the road between the hills we found it strewn with the enemy's dead and wounded. I shall never forget the appearance of one poor young fellow lying in the narrowest part of the road, who seemed to have literally caught a shower of bullets and was unable to move any part of his body. Pale, helpless, and apparently too weak to speak, his appealing look pleaded with us louder than words could do, not to ride over him. Instantly two of our men leaped from their saddles and tried to move him from the narrow cut to the roadside, but found both his arms and legs so broken and shattered that it was cruel to take hold of them; two more quickly went to their assistance, and jerking a blanket from one of their saddles, placed their hands under his body and slipped the blanket under him as gently as possible; then taking it by the corners the four men bore him down the hill to the roadside, where they tenderly laid him, while one of them sought a surgeon. I do not think he spoke a word, as he was doubtless too weak from loss of blood, but his pale, pleading face and appealing look was enough to stop, by common consent and without orders for the time, our pursuit of the enemy, until he could be borne to the roadside and cared for. We knew that every moment lost at such a crisis was fatal to our successful pursuit, and would give the enemy time to rally and re-form their shattered lines under cover of the neighboring woods which the delay enabled them to reach, but the enemy had better escape than brave men ride over and crush out the lingering sparks of life in a mangled and helpless foe. After removing the wounded from the narrow cut, we proceeded until checked by the enemy's fire from the woods in which they had formed, when nightfall brought an end to the hard and bloody day's work. I have never known whether or not this poor fellow's tide of life ebbed quickly out, as I imagine it did, but his memory recalls this and numerous other similar incidents on both sides. I have thought that England's poet must have caught a prophetic vision of this great struggle between American soldiers when he wrote:

> The soldier braves death for a fanciful wreath
>   In glory's romantic career;
> But he raises the foe, when in battle laid low,
>   And bathes every wound with a tear.

Seldom, I think, were the friendly shades of night

more welcomed by weary, thirsty mortals, famished almost to desperation.

For two days scarcely any of us had eaten a morsel of food, and since early morning we had been without a drop of water. The day had been spent in one continuous series of attacks and advances, always forcing the enemy from his position, but, unaided as our small brigade was, we had not sufficient force at any time to rout the heavy columns which the enemy always had in reserve to mass against us and block our way. Our reinforcements came too late; and then the incident just related and the gathering darkness prevented us from reaping the full results of Dearing's splendid charge at the close of the day.

We halted and remained by our horses about an hour, ready to meet the enemy if he should advance in the darkness. During this time some of the men started fires to cook what little rations a few had left, or had been able to secure. I had none, nor had I tasted food since Monday night in the woeful effort to masticate the mixture of horsehair and corn meal. One of the men gave me a slice of pork which he had cut from a hog he had shot on the roadside that day. While I was warming this over the fire on the end of a stick, the pickets exchanged a few shots in our front, and we were ordered to mount. I devoured the slice of raw pork without salt or bread, and in an hour was sick. My eyes had become sore and inflamed the preceding day, and the pain was now so intensified by the dust, powder, and smoke of the day that I was in agony, with fever and without water.

After an hour or two (there being no further movement of the enemy) we ventured to unsaddle our horses, as the only relief for them without food, keeping saddles and trappings ready to buckle on at a moment's notice. Sick, suffering, thirsty from fever, and exhausted, I dropped on the damp ground about midnight, almost in a state of despair. A few feet from me I noticed a man still and apparently asleep, with a large blanket spread over him and room to share it with me. Thinking it was one of our company, I quietly moved up by his side under the blanket. Just as I was about ready for dreamland I found I was lying on one of his hands, which, as I removed, I discovered was cold to the touch and stiff. Taking the blanket from his face, I found that my companion was a dead Yankee who had been covered with a blanket, as was customary when there was no time for burial. He had evidently been left there where he fell, as was the case during that day with numbers of their dead. I replaced the blanket, and moved a few feet to my former position, where I remained,—whether in sleep or delirium from fever, or both, I never knew,—until aroused about dawn on Thursday, April 6th, when, after pulling open my eyes, which were sealed from soreness, I moved forward with my company on another day's work. I think it was about noon when, as we approached the " high bridge " near Farmville, the enemy was reported in force below the bridge. We were ordered forward at a gallop, and were soon upon them. General Dearing, with his usual dash, had just led a charge into their midst, the enemy making desperate resistance at close quarters. As the fight waxed furious, General Dearing met General Read, who was in command of the Federal force, and the two engaged in a duel with pistols at close range, resulting in the death of the latter. When General Read fell from his horse and the reins from his grasp, the animal rushed wildly forward and was seized by Captain W. C. Nunn of the King and Queen troop, Fifth Cavalry, who was near the spot (as he always was in the thickest of the fight). It was a fine animal with splendid equipment, including saddle, pistols, holsters, field glasses, etc., becoming the rank of a general, and in splendid condition to bear his new rider safely through to Appomattox and thence home. In less than half an hour, I think, the enemy, after having suffered heavily in killed and wounded, surrendered, except a few who galloped off and escaped.

Our triumph was complete but dearly bought. Our loss, though much less than the enemy's in numbers, was severe, and included the gallant, chivalrous, and intrepid Dearing, who fell mortally wounded after having killed his antagonist, General Read. Also the gallant Colonel Boston of the Fifth Regiment, Virginia Cavalry, who fell with a bullet through his brain, and whose dead body was promptly placed across his saddle and borne from the field. The number of prominent officers killed on both sides before the enemy yielded testifies to the desperate character of this short and bloody hand-to-hand encounter at High Bridge. From the observations of a private, which in such a conflict as this are limited, it seemed to me to be a desperate struggle between Confederate cavalry and Federal infantry.

When the din and confusion of the shock of battle subsided, someone remarked to Captain Allen that our victory was complete, when in tones of sadness unusual for him on such an occasion, he replied: " Yes, complete, but dearly bought. Any victory is dearly bought that costs the life of Dearing." " What! is Dearing dead? " " Mortally wounded," he replied; " they have just taken him to yonder grove to die." This announcement chilled us as for the moment we bowed our heads in sorrow, and the men murmured, " What a loss, what a shame! " The loss of Dearing would have been a calamity at any time, but most of all now, when we needed most such dauntless spirits; for it was at just such a crisis as we had now reached that

> " One blast from his bugle horn
> Were worth a thousand men."

Truly knighthood lost a flower, chivalry a type, when noble, gallant, dashing Dearing fell and was borne by loving hands to the grateful shades of a friendly grove, to breathe out the only life he had to give to the cause dearer to him than life. He lingered a few days, and was borne to Lynchburg, where he died. Space forbids a recital here of the splendid and brilliant career of the young officer, which is written in lines of light and beauty on almost every page of the history of the Army of Northern Virginia, and of the Newbern expedition in North Carolina. He fell in one of the last hours of victory, before the star of the Confederacy went down to rise no more. His native county of Campbell, Virginia, would honor itself to erect a monument to this noble and brilliant son.

The battle over, the enemy in our hands, no time was lost in forming the prisoners (who I suppose were of General Read's brigade) into columns in such order as was most convenient to proceed without delay. They were necessarily a burden and source of weakness to us at this stage of our retreat, but there was nothing else to do. During this time Captain Nunn hurriedly sought a resting place for the bodies of both Colonel Boston (his late chief) and General Read, which were placed under the same tree, each wrapped in a blanket for his winding sheet, and buried in separate graves; General Read's horse meanwhile standing with empty saddle by his late master. An hour before they were mortal enemies, in deadly conflict; both had fallen at their posts, as brave men fall, life's bars and stripes with them were over now, and they sleep together in death.

Within little more than an hour, perhaps, from the time we met the enemy we proceeded on our way (I knew not in what direction). As we were passing by the prisoners, who were massed in the road, we were ordered to halt, and I noticed one of the prisoners wiping the perspiration from his face with one hand, while with the other he was still bearing a very large and beautiful and, apparently, perfectly new regimental flag, of pale-blue silk, with the coat of arms of a State in the center, surrounded by a motto in gold. Attracted by its cleanliness and beauty, I was trying to make out the motto, when a chaplain asked Captain Nunn if he might venture to offer prayer. Permission was promptly granted to proceed. Removing his hat, he raised his arm for attention, and we bowed our heads in reverence. He had scarcely reached the end of his first sentence when one of our men, more alert and less reverent perhaps than the others, interrupted by yelling to Captain Nunn: " Look, Captain, look! " We all looked—

to see a body of the enemy's cavalry approaching as they rounded a turn in the road about a hundred yards off. "Hold on, Chaplain; no time for praying! By zounds! charge 'em, men!" yelled Captain Nunn, as he drew his saber, and without further orders or ceremony headed straight for the enemy, followed by the men nearest him at full speed in pellmell fashion, there being no time for regular formation.

The effect on the enemy was instantaneous,—they changed front promptly and galloped off to avoid another collision. They had evidently not forgotten their experience at close quarters an hour before. It was doubtless a reconnoitering party who were satisfied with having "located the enemy." We on our part were satisfied to abandon pursuit and press on with the prisoners, as the enemy were uncomfortably close on us.

Passing by the prisoners we proceeded at a gallop in the direction of a heavy musketry firing a mile or two distant, which now suddenly reached our ears. As we neared the scene of the engagement we halted, dismounted quickly, and leaving our horses in the main road in charge of the leaders (every fourth man was a "leader," whose duties were to take charge of the horses and hold or lead them as occasion required when we were fighting on foot), we formed line and proceeded at double-quick about a quarter of a mile in an open field, and took position behind a rail fence. In a few minutes the heavy firing from the woods in our front, from which we were expecting the enemy, suddenly ceased, and we were ordered to rush back to our horses as rapidly as possible. These we reached just in time to escape capture, for the enemy seemed to be all around us as we dashed out in the only direction open to us. We then discovered that we were at or near Sailor's Creek, and that nearly all of Ewell's Corps had been surrounded and captured when the firing ceased so suddenly in the woods. We had arrived too late to succor Ewell in the struggle to extricate his corps from its desperate position, and barely escaped the same fate ourselves.

CHAPTER XII

The following address, historic of Company K, Thirty-fourth Virginia Volunteers, was prepared by Josiah Ryland, an officer of the company, and read at the reunion at Bruington, King and Queen County, Va., on the Fourth of July, 1884. It was published in *The Baltimore Baptist*, in order that it might be preserved by the members and friends of the old company:

The spring of 1861 saw the conservative, and hitherto quiet, State of Virginia converted into a military camp. From the mountains to the sea there was universal preparation for war. It would be needless now to give in detail the reasons that forced the conviction upon the Southern mind that the election of Abraham Lincoln to the presidency was virtually a dissolution of the Union. South Carolina, Florida, Mississippi, Alabama, Georgia, and Louisiana seceded in rapid succession. A provisional government was formed in Montgomery on the 4th of February, with Jefferson Davis as President, and Alex. H. Stephens as Vice-President. All efforts at pacification had failed, and nothing seemed to be left but an appeal to arms. If the seceded States were to be brought back by coercion, Virginians could not look on with calmness and indifference while armies from the North marched through their borders for this purpose.

Between the 20th of April and the 7th of May the company began to be organized which was first known as the King and Queen Artillery, but afterwards as Company K, 34th Virginia Infantry. On the 30th of April we had forty-six men enrolled, and the first squad drill was conducted in the yard at Stevensville Academy, under Josiah (" Pat ") Ryland and Alexander F. Bagby, both of whom had been trained at the Virginia Military Institute. There were twenty men in ranks, and for nearly an hour that morning, and another that evening, we took our first lessons in the art of war. Colonel (afterwards Captain) John R. Bagby, who was the leading spirit in getting up the company, was at this time in Baltimore on business; and as the fight had just taken place there on the streets between some of the citizens and a regiment of Federal troops, apprehensions were entertained that he might be forcibly detained.

May the 7th.—There was an immense gathering at the Courthouse for the purpose of drilling the militia of the county. Colonel Bagby had returned, and in the afternoon a meeting of our company was called in the Courthouse. We were now sixty-eight strong. Colonel Bagby was called to the chair, and John W. Ryland appointed secretary. A committee consisting of Colonel Bagby, Josiah ("Pat") Ryland, Dr. William T. Fleet, Edward Bagby, A. F. Bagby, and the writer, was appointed to draft rules for the organization of the company. This committee met that night at the residence of Colonel Bagby and discharged this duty.

May the 8th, at 3 P. M.—The company met in the Academy, and the constitution was adopted. Whereupon John R. Bagby, upon motion of the writer, was elected captain by acclamation; Josiah ("Pat") Ryland 1st lieutenant; A. F. Bagby, 2d; Josiah Ryland, 3d; Benjamin Walker, 4th; Edward Bagby was chosen secretary; George Didlake, treasurer; Dr. William T. Fleet, surgeon; and Rev. R. H. Land, chaplain. W. T. Haynes, Douglas Muire, John Bagby, Jr., and William Myer were appointed sergeants, and John W. Ryland, E. F. Acree, Boliver Lumpkin, and Joseph Cosby, corporals. The company was then divided into squads and drilled for an hour. The first and second lieutenants were sent over to Richmond to procure uniforms, and returned with a supply of gray cloth and military caps. The work of drilling was now pushed with vigor.

Tuesday, May 21st.—The company met, sixty strong, all in uniform. Under the direction of Colonel Robert Gresham, the election of officers was confirmed, the company inspected, and certificates duly sent to

Governor Letcher. The uniforms had been made almost entirely by the young ladies of the community.

Thursday, May 23d.—Virginia cast her vote for the ordinance of secession. At our precinct, Stevensville, there was not a vote against it. The same day, the writer and Sergeant W. T. Haynes left for Richmond, at the request of the company, to endeavor to secure a light battery of four guns.

On this trip the writer met for the first time Major General R. E. Lee, who was soon to become the central figure of our struggle. The General said it would be impossible to supply the demand for guns, and urged that the company should equip itself with muskets, or even with shotguns, if necessary. With much disappointment, and some hesitation, the writer suggested that shotguns would avail but little against the long-range weapons of the enemy. Looking around for a moment with a benignant smile playing over his features, he replied: "Sir, your people had better write to Mr. Lincoln and ask him to postpone this thing for a few months, until you can get ready for him." The answer was promptly made: "General, we will use the shotguns," and the modest lieutenant retired in good order. A few days after this the captain left for Richmond, and the first lieutenant for Gloucester Point, to arrange for our departure for the field.

Wednesday, May 29th.—We met at Stevensville at 3 o'clock, eighty-three men in ranks, and had a general drill. The whole community turned out to see us for the last time. Tears and ice cream flowed freely. This was our first night in barracks. Religious services were conducted at 8 o'clock by Rev. Messrs. R. H. Land and Isaac Diggs. The excitement of the occasion was not promotive of sleep.

Thursday, May 30th.—At 4:30 A. M. the roll was called; all were present and in good trim. We marched to Mantapike, and there embarked on the schooner *Way*. Loud cheers were raised as we drifted out into the channel, and then a solemn prayer was offered by Dr. S. S. Henley. At 12 we were transferred to the steamer *Logan,* and at 2 P. M. reached West Point, where we had quite a military reception given us by the two companies already there. We were duly mustered into service by Colonel H. B. Tomlin, and went into our barracks.

Saturday, June 1st.—The men were sworn into the service by William A. Spiller.

The next day, our first Sabbath in camp, we met in a sort of Sunday school and prayer-meeting, which closed with a sermon by R. H. Land.

Our time was now devoted to drilling. The King William troop arrived fifty-four strong, commanded by Captain Douglas; and on the 6th General Lee paid us a visit, and left us under the impression that we would be sent to Yorktown in a few days. News came on the 10th of the battle of Bethel. This caused quite a stir in camp.

Wednesday, June 12th.—We took the steamer *Logan* for Yorktown, but finding no accommodations for us there, we were ordered back. The next day was observed throughout the Confederate States as a day of fasting and prayer.

Friday, June 14th.—Lieutenant Whittle gave us our first drill at the heavy battery, and the next day we took charge of it.

Thursday, June 20th.—We again took passage to Gloucester Point, reaching there at midnight. Fifty of us slept that night in one small room, lying like sardines in a box. The next day we met Colonel Thomas J. Page, with whom we were to be closely associated for many months; Colonel Crump, commandant of the post; Lieutenant-colonel Page, Major Wheelwright, Lieutenant Bradford, our first drill master, and others.

Sunday, June 23d.—Captain Councill's company arrived, and on the 26th Captain Spencer's and Captain Sutton's.

Monday, July 1st.—Captain Page gave us our first drill in the heavy battery. The month was spent chiefly in this uninteresting employment, together with unloading lumber vessels, building a shell house, improving our battery, and preparing more permanent quarters for ourselves. We were now one hundred strong. The first thrilling news of the battle of Manassas reached us. We at once fired a salute of eleven guns.

The months of August and September were very trying ones to our troops. Yorktown was a perfect hospital, and Gloucester Point was not much better. We had only fifty men for duty.

September 15th.—Captain Otey's and Captain Jordan's companies arrived, and for the first time these robust men from the base of the peaks of Otter witnessed a process which, in their simplicity, they called " hulling oysters."

October 13th.—Rev. William E. Wyatt preached his first sermon as chaplain of the post. On the 31st we had a general inspection and review. The companies from the battery were marched up to the field and took their place in line. Of course Captain Page was indignant. He considered his command " on board ship," and recognized no man's right to rule over them.

November found us hard at work on our winter quarters, under the general direction of Privates Wright, Crouch, and Kemp.

November 13th.—Huckstep was reported dead in Richmond. Some of us feared he had been foully dealt with. About the middle of the month our whole battery force, strengthened by the infantry, hauled a large rifle gun to its position on the hill.

November 20th.—The Accomac refugees came pouring into our camp, and several joined our company.

Saturday, December 7th.—There was an alarm in camp. Our guard boat was fired upon, and our whole command was at once turned out. Three days afterward, Captain Joe Drudge's sloop was fired upon by the Federal gunboats. This we considered a first-class insult.

Saturday, December 21st.—The King and Queen militia reported for duty. We were now veterans and heroes, and the appearance of the militia excited no little amusement in our ranks.

Saturday, the 28th.—William Hugh Courtney died at home, after seven weeks' illness. The company was called out, and suitable action taken.

Captain Jarvis came down with Christmas supplies, causing great joy among us. The officers gave Captain Page a famous dinner, and at night we had a general reception, in which the whole company participated. Our head cook, Osborne, told us the next morning, with quite a sorrowful countenance, that he cut and served one hundred slices of cake.

So closed the year 1861. We were all in comfortable quarters. We had our drills, and inspections, and guard duties, and Sunday schools, and prayer meetings, and regular preaching on Sunday, along with the pleasures of camp life.

January 20th, 1862.—Captain Page was ordered to West Point to superintend the erection of gunboats,— a personal affliction to everyone in our command. On the 22d, our first lieutenant, Ryland, weary of the dullness of camp life, and panting for home, left for the purpose of seeking a position under General Thomas J. Jackson. It turned out, however, that the arrangement could not be made. If it had been, it is hardly probable that he would have been here to-day to take part in this reunion.

On the 25th of January our command was called out, and a parting letter was read to us from Captain Page.

Friday, February 7th.—Our men were mustered in for another term of service by Lieutenant-Colonel Page. Some changes occurred at this time. The news from Fort Donelson and Roanoke Island cast a gloom over our camp.

Thursday, the 20th.—Addison Phillips died, after three weeks' illness. The company escorted his remains to the steamer.

Saturday, the 22d, President Davis was duly inaugurated in Richmond.

Tuesday, March the 4th.—Lieutenant-Colonel Carter arrived and took command of the battery forces, and on Monday, the 10th, the company was reorganized, Captain Bagby being reëlected; A. F. Bagby, first lieutenant; the writer, second; and W. T. Haynes, third. The next sensation in camp was the naval victory in Hampton Roads. March 23d we hauled our heavy guns up to the bastion fort on the hill. On the 28th everything was astir. We moved our quarters outside the lines, dug wells, and waded in mud and sleet and darkness. The enemy was reported in heavy force at Newport News. General Lee was now in command of all the forces in Virginia.

Friday, April 4th.—Great excitement in Yorktown; our infantry were ordered over. Saturday the enemy appeared in front of the lines there, and a balloon was sent up. Firing was kept up all day, and six ships came in sight. Captain Page arrived, greatly to our relief, and took command, Colonel Carter having been relieved. News reached us of the battle of Shiloh, and the death of General Albert Sidney Johnston. Our troops returned from Yorktown, and the first shell thrown over into our lines was quickly dug up and inspected. The duel between the lines at Yorktown was kept up during the balance of the month.

Thursday, May 1st.—Orders came from General Johnson to evacuate Gloucester Point at dark to-night. The whole camp is filled with bustle and excitement. The artillerymen are equipped with muskets; three days' rations are cooked; the ammunition is moved to the vessels, and the whole command is under arms with but little time to rest, until the evening of May 4th, when Anderson goes around and spikes all the heavy guns, and we move off at 8 o'clock, the Twenty-sixth Regiment in the lead; then the militia; then an artillery battalion; and last, the Forty-sixth Regiment. We reached Gloucester Courthouse at dawn, and rested a few hours. Passing through Centreville we were met by our friends at King and Queen Courthouse, with supplies. Many of the men gave out on this heavy march. The road was strewn with knapsacks, overcoats, and camp utensils. The next night we camped at St. Stephen's Church, and the following at Mangohick. We spent the night near Old Church, and on the 10th of May moved down into New Kent and began to realize for the first time that we were a part of a large army seeking its position around Richmond. Men, tents, wagons, batteries, quartermasters, commissaries, all in inextricable confusion, and everybody in everybody's way.

Thursday, the 15th.—We crossed the Chickahominy at midnight, and had a hard time of it, making two miles in about five hours. Alas for the vexations and unaccountable delays, the marchings and countermarchings of an army. Nobody knew anything. Men went to sleep standing in the ranks. The very mules nodded between the beatings given them by inexperienced drivers for refusing to pull through bottomless roads. Everybody was mad and hungry, and worn out and unpatriotic. At last we turned into fields about six miles from Richmond, and broke into wagonloads of hardtack. The next day we moved nearer the city, and on Sunday, the 18th, our eyes were greeted with the sight of its spires. And now the doom of being finally converted into infantry seemed to settle upon us, to our bitter regret and utter disgust. Even the old battery that some of us had nursed all the way from Gloucester Point was taken away. We were quietly assigned to Rhodes's Brigade, and the addition of Captain White's company constituted us a battalion. Our former first lieutenant, Ryland, left us to try his fortune in another command.

And now we were in for it. Roll call at 4:30; squad drill at 5; company drill at 8; and battalion and brigade drill at 5 P. M., in the field near Roper's mill. For several days we were kept in constant commotion, marching and countermarching, up the road and down again, none of us knew why.

On the night of May 30th there was a heavy fall of rain. It was a fitting prelude to the storm of battle, the rain of shot and shell through which our boys were about to pass. It was evident that serious work was ahead.

Saturday morn, May 31st.—We were under arms at an early hour, little knowing what was before us. Large bodies of infantry moved with us down the road.

The command was given to halt and load; and then we made a hurried march through field and wood, double-quicking until officers and men were out of breath. We formed in line of battle, and Captain Otey, acting as field officer, in connection with Captain Bagby, addressed the command in a few words, exhorting every man to keep cool and do his duty. We then marched to the front through a pine thicket, charged through acres of felled trees, raised our first Confederate yell, and in a few minutes found ourselves in a strong horseshoe fort, from which the enemy had fled at our approach. We turned their splendid twelve-pound napoleons upon them with telling effect, and charged on through their deserted camp, under a galling fire. Five of our boys fell in a few moments,—Bacon, Butler, Courtney, Holmes, and Pynes. Sergeants John W. Ryland and William Meyer, Corporal Boliver Lumpkin, and Privates Ben Carlton, Tom Segar, John Gresham, Benjamin McLelland, H. C. Pendleton, John Willroy, George Hurt, Jim Kelly, ——— Hurt, Benjamin Sale, Tom Myrick, and others, were wounded. Falling back after a while to the redoubt, we were relieved by other troops. President Davis and General Lee appeared on the scene and were vigorously cheered by our men. Dear Otey had fallen, and the field was covered with our dead and wounded. Night closed the scene. We slept on the field, ministering to the wants of the wounded and dying. Never can the writer forget the last words of that brave boy, Jimmy Bacon. He was mortally wounded and slowly dying, and on being asked if anything could be done for his comfort, he replied: " Just leave your canteen with me, to relieve my thirst, and please take a lock of my hair and my watch for my mother, and tell her I was not afraid to die, and cheerfully gave my life for our cause." If Bacon's grave could now be found, we would erect a shaft to his memory and engrave these brave words upon it. Sunday the battle was renewed; but we were too much cut up to take part in it. The roads were filled with ambulances and wagons conveying the wounded to Richmond. We buried our dead on the field, and after lying down that night to rest for a few hours, were called up, made a forced march through mud and mire, and wagons and ambulances, to a field where we at last found some rest, and began to collect our scattered forces. General Johnson had been wounded, and General Lee assumed command in a general order. [The battle of Seven Pines.]

Monday, June 9th.—Our company, Captain Otey's, and Captain Jordan's, were ordered to report at once to Goode's Regiment, Wise's Brigade, below Chaffin's Bluff, on James River. We had now only thirty men for duty, and having pitched our tents near the Childrey house, began again the dull round of daily drill.

Wednesday, the 25th.—Jackson swooped down upon the enemy's right, and day after day we heard in the distance the seven days' battle that culminated at Malvern Hill, July 1st, and sent McClellan's forces reeling to their gunboats. We did picket duty on the river, and watched the result with intense solicitude. Great was the relief and joy in Richmond.

The month of July was without incident. Drill and guard duty, chills and mosquitoes, were the order of the day. We rarely had more than thirty-five men for duty. The captain was sick at Coyner's Spring, and the first lieutenant in Richmond. The exchange of prisoners now began, and they were constantly passing our camp on the way to Varina. McClellan " changed his base," and Lincoln called for 300,000 men. August brought its daily drills and chills, and courts-martial.

September gave us great joy over the victory at Manassas, and the march into Maryland. On the 7th of this month our company was again detailed for battery service under Captain Page, and John Willroy dryly remarked that " once more we had retired to the quiet of domestic life." Thursday, the 18th, was a day of thanksgiving and prayer.

Until the middle of October we were engaged in hauling logs and building quarters for the winter, and on through November we drilled daily at our two rifle guns, two mortars, and one eight-inch columbiad, commanding the river below Chaffin's Bluff. Regular religious services were held on Sunday and during the week.

Thursday, November 20th.—Our captain returned

from Richmond with the rank of major. Lieutenant A. F. Bagby became captain; the writer, first lieutenant; Lieutenant Hayes, second lieutenant; and at an election held on the 24th Benjamin Walker was made third lieutenant. Early in December there was a deep religious awakening in the company, and Albert Gresham and John Parks made a profession of religion. The services were conducted by Elders George F. Bagby, John Pollard, and William E. Wyatt.

Monday, December 22d.—Our young captain left under somewhat suspicious circumstances. It was given out that he was on recruiting service. We soon learned that he had captured a fair damsel near Walkerton, and mustered her into the Confederate service on Christmas day. On the 30th she was introduced at the officers' quarters as the first female recruit.

January, 1863, was a dull month in camp; rains were incessant, and we had nothing to do, nowhere to go, and nothing to eat. The excitement each day was Norvell Ryland's return from Richmond with papers and letters for the command.

February was no better. Snows and rains suspended all military operations.

March 7th.—Captain Page was ordered to Charleston, greatly to our regret. The question of supplies was now becoming a serious one. The men drew as a day's rations, one quarter-pound of meat, one quarter-pound of sugar, one and a half pounds of flour, and a little rice and salt.

April was without special incident.

Saturday night, May 2d.—Jackson was wounded at Fredericksburg, and Sunday Richmond was wild with excitement over the enemy's raid around the city. The relief was great when the news came of Hooker's defeat, but the immortal " Stonewall " Jackson died on the evening of the 10th; on the 11th his remains were brought to Richmond, and on the 12th lay in state in the Capitol, where thousands called to look upon the dead hero.

May was spent by us in camp, turfing magazines and discussing Vicksburg, now the center of military interest.

We again began our infantry drill, and this gave us more to do. Purkins took a two-horse plow from a neighbor, "just to keep his hand in," he said, and with Jim Eubank as driver, was preparing for a crop of vegetables. June was another dull month with us. Lee was in Maryland, filling the North with terror. Hooker was relieved, and Meade put in his place. Gettysburg was fought July 1st, and Vicksburg fell on the 4th. On the 16th President Davis called out all men from eighteen to forty-five.

The month of August witnessed a great revival in the Twenty-sixth Regiment, under the preaching of Rev. A. Broaddus of Kentucky. About one hundred and eighty-five professed religion, of whom Chaplain Wyatt baptized nearly one hundred. Towards the last of the month there was much sickness in camp, thirty-three being with chills at one time. The writer was separated from his command until November.

September 4th.—Wise's Brigade was ordered to Charleston, our company and Captain Montague's being included. The command passed through Petersburg, Weldon, Wilmington, and Florence, and reaching South Carolina, went into camp early in October on Wapper Creek, near Charleston.

The months of October and November gave us but little employment. An occasional change of camp, the constant shelling of Fort Sumter by the enemy, and furloughs to Virginia, were the staple of conversation.

November 28th.—Rev. R. H. Bagby arrived from King and Queen with 1200 pounds' weight of supplies for our company. We regarded him as an angel of mercy. He had followed us up through the fortunes of war, ministering to our temporal and spiritual wants. In December we were doing picket duty on Little Britain Island. Rations were small; lean beef, rice, and potatoes constituted our bill of fare. Flour was $125 per barrel, corn $60 per bushel, and neither love nor money could purchase coffee and butter.

January 15th, 1864.—Colonel Goode was assigned to the command of the second subdistrict, with headquarters at Adam's Run, the Fourth and Forty-sixth Regiments, Whilden's Cavalry, and Kemper's Battery, constituting his command. He extemporized a staff, selecting an officer and several men for duty from our company.

February 9th.—The enemy landed on John's Island, capturing our pickets. A part of our brigade went down at once, but they had left as suddenly as they came.

Wednesday, March 2d.—The writer was at home on furlough, and had the pleasure of taking part in the capture of Dahlgren's raiding party, near Stevensville. Papers found on his person were said to contain directions to capture and sack Richmond, release all prisoners there, hang Jefferson Davis and his Cabinet, and then make for the Rappahannock River.

The last of this month witnessed another religious awakening in our company.

News now reached us from Virginia that General Grant had been placed in command, and immense preparations were going on there to overwhelm us in the spring campaign. A day was set apart for fasting and prayer. Chaplain Robert gave us an excellent sermon.

April 15th.—Major Bagby left us to recruit his shattered health in Virginia. General Wise tells us he is constantly expecting marching orders; but he is busy making combs, spoons, and pipes, and working in his garden.

Tuesday, May 3d.—Our marching orders came at last from General Samuel Jones, commanding our department. All was bustle and excitement. On the 5th our regiment took its departure, filling two trains. We heard as we passed through Charleston that the enemy were moving against General Lee on the Rapidan, up the Peninsula, and on the south side. We reached Florence on the 6th, all in high spirits, cheering everyone we met, and making the woods ring with our songs. We reached Wilmington Saturday, hungry as wolves, and found peanuts $2.00 a quart, and short measure at that. Sunday we passed through Weldon, and reached Jarratt's Station at 8 that night. A raiding party of the enemy, in command of Cutts and Spears—ominous names—had just destroyed all the railroad property there.

We marched all day, to Stony Creek. Tuesday, the 10th, we passed through Petersburg, and out to the Dunlap House, where we were in arms all day. We heard that there was some reluctance on the part of General Wise to serve under General Bushrod Johnson. There was considerable activity along the lines,—shelling and picket firing and constant shifting of the few troops on the ground. We learn that General Lee has repulsed Grant every day for a week, as he shortens his line and falls back towards Richmond.

Wednesday, May 11th, 1864.—Our forces moved across Swift Creek against the enemy, but did not engage them. We were then ordered to Dunn's, three miles below the city, on the City Point road. Got——

Here the diary ended. It would be impossible now for the writer to finish the sentence, or to add a word to it. We evidently " got " into business. The siege of Petersburg began now in earnest. We had but little time for rest, and could not complain of neglect when any work or fighting had to be done. A mere handful of men kept Burnside's magnificent corps in check for days, when it really had nothing to do but to march into Petersburg. The effort to drive Butler's heavy force gave us hard work, and our company did its full share. A stirring and affecting incident occurred during one of our charges to get possession of the Osborne Turnpike. Crossfield had received a mortal wound, and was being borne to the rear on a stretcher. Meeting us, he waved his hand in triumph, and exclaimed: " Go in, boys, and give it to them. It makes no difference about me."

It is impossible now to recall dates and events during this summer. We settled down to life in the trenches, being rarely relieved, except for a day or two at a time, when we sought rest in the ravine just behind old Blanford Cemetery. Casualties were constantly occurring. We ate, slept, had our social gatherings and our religious services within the lines for many weeks. The monotony, drudgery, and constant exposure of such a life were borne with great patience and fortitude.

On the morning of July 30 the battle of the Crater occurred, and the death of Edward Bagby, while bravely defending an important part of the lines, cast a gloom over our whole company. To the gentleness of a woman he added a moral courage that knew no fear in the discharge of duty.

The fall set in with no additional activity on the part of the enemy. It seemed to be a dogged perseverance on both sides. We can never forget the faithfulness and devotion of our camp servants. With every opportunity to escape, they were as true and faithful to us as the best of us were to our cause. Being in command of a part of the lines one day, the writer said to the servant who brought him his dinner: "Jack, there are your friends, not five hundred yards distant. They say they love you, and have come to set you free. If you wish to join them, the way is open; not a musket shall be lifted upon you, and in five minutes you will be a free man." The boy's eyes actually filled with tears at such a suggestion, and he answered quickly: "I s'posed you thought mo' ob me dan dat. Gi' me a gun, an' I'll show you whar I stan'!" This seemed to be the common feeling of our old servants who followed our fortunes through the war, and endured all the hardships of camp life.

October 27th, 1864.—In the evening one hundred picked men of the enemy made a sortie upon a salient of our lines defended by a battery. It was a bold movement, and was well executed. They were soon in possession of this part of our line, killing and wounding many of the artillerymen and infantry stationed there. This was to be the beginning of a general attack.

When the firing began the writer was in the Crater, detailing a picket for the night from Colonel Tabb's regiment, the Fifty-ninth. Squads had already been sent out from the other regiments to relieve those who had been in the rifle pits on our front all day. Supposing that, through mistake, our command was firing on the relieved pickets as they came in, he ran down the trenches, ordered the companies through which he passed to cease firing, and in a few moments found himself in the salient held by the enemy. His consternation can better be imagined than described. There was no chance to escape. In a few moments he was hurried over the rampart and across the narrow field separating the two armies; and although he fell twice, hoping thus to break the hold of his captors and hide in a rifle pit, and tried to feign death by stretching out his limbs convulsively and then ceasing to breathe, the experiment failed, and he found himself a prisoner of war,—along with Colonel Harrison, Lieutenant-Colonel Wise, and Lieutenant Cox, of the Forty-sixth Virginia.

And here his humble contribution to the history of our company must close. A few days at City Point, two months at the old capital at Washington, and six in Fort Delaware, brought with them a suspense far more unendurable than the hardships and dangers of daily service in the field.

Other hands must trace the record of the hard winter that followed,—the battles of Hatcher's Run and Sailors' Creek, the retreat from Petersburg, disasters that "followed fast and followed faster," until FAILURE was written upon the Confederate cause, and the sun went down upon it at Appomattox Courthouse.

PART III

DOMESTIC AND SOCIAL

CHAPTER XII

SELECTIONS FROM THE POEMS OF KING AND QUEEN

[The following beautiful and touching lines were written by Mrs. Sarah Jane Bagby, the wife of Rev. Alfred Bagby, of King and Queen County, Virginia, on the death of her mother, Mrs. John Pollard, whose high-toned Christian character and earnest piety shed for many years a bright luster upon Mattapony Baptist Church, of which she was a member.]

MY MOTHER

There is a form now hid from view,
From which my own its being drew.
It sweetly sleeps beneath the sod,—
The darkened way the Savior trod,—
　　　　　My Mother.

There is a spirit, glad and free,
Now dwelling in eternity;
It calmly rests in Jesus' love,
Forever blest in heaven above,—
　　　　　My Mother.

I fain would tell the matchless grace,
And all the many virtues trace,
That shone in form, in face, in heart,
And made her seem of heaven a part,—
　　　　　My Mother.

But ah! 'tis vain. The sun doth light
This world of ours, and make it bright:
So she was sunshine in our home,—
A radiance reaching to the tomb,—
　　　　　My Mother.

And then above, with gentle hands,
They raised a monument. It stands
To tell, so all around may hear,
Her memory is supremely dear—
　　　　　My Mother.

And surviving daughters come to weep
O'er the cold grave where she's asleep,
And strew with flowers the sacred mound
Where peaceful rests in hallowed ground
                    My Mother.

A sister's love she never knew;
An only brother, fond and true,
Clasped her cold hand. How sweet 't will be
To clasp it in eternity!
                    My Mother!

While yet a babe upon her knee,
She spoke of Jesus' love to me,
And bade my aspirations rise
To better things beyond the skies —
                    My Mother.

In after years, when storms arose,
And trials grew, and many woes
Came thick and fast, she bade me still
" Be happy in thy Father's will "—
                    My Mother.

" As dies the wave upon the shore,"
She calmly slept, then woke no more
To this vain world, but far away
She woke to an eternal day,—
                    My Mother.

Her loving sons then sadly bore
Her body to the grave; but o'er
That precious earth, that silent tomb,
There cometh nought of fear or gloom,
                    My Mother.

Yes, she is gone! and I am left,
And earth of half its joy bereft.
As oft her empty chair I see,
The world seems empty then to me,—
                    My Mother.

Yet there is one who more doth miss
Her loving smile. His earthly bliss
Was centered there. But ah! 'tis fled;
He's lonely now, since she is dead,—
                    My Mother.

MISS SARAH JANE POLLARD
(1834–1888)
MRS. ALFRED BAGBY

But, happy thought! again we'll meet,
To cast our crowns at Jesus' feet;
To join in anthems loud and long,
Praising the Lamb with joyful song,
                    My Mother.

MY BIRTHDAY WISH

By LUTHER R. BAGBY, Stevensville, Va.

I'd like to be a boy again
And run around the farm,
And play those childish games once more
That did us all no harm.

I'd love to kneel by mother's knee
And say my evening prayer,
And look into her lovely face
While I was kneeling there.

I'd love to have that same sweet hand
Upon my shoulder laid,
As back into a little room
My boyish feet were led.

And down upon the floor we knelt
Hard by the mercy seat,
And God was asked to keep her boy
Close to the Savior's feet.

I'd love to kneel again once more
Around the fire place,
And hear my father's pleading voice
Praying for daily grace.

Sweet praises filled the very air
And heaven lit up his face,
As kneeling by the old armchair
He reached the throne of grace.

I'd love to go to Sunday School
And learn the way of life,
And spend those happy days again
So free from sin and strife.

I'd love to meet my class again
That met there by the door,
With good Judge Jones, our teacher then,
Who left us long ago.

He took us all the Bible through,
And taught us all the way
That Moses and the prophets went
And leads to endless day.

My life has been so full of faults
I fain would live it o'er,
That I might give more life, more love
To Him whom we adore.

Since this is all denied me, Lord,
Oh, give me grace to live,
So that when I am called away
A good account may give.

TO MR. AND MRS. MOORE B. WRIGHT ON THE DEATH OF THEIR BOY

By Sarah Jane Bagby

How soon the icy hand of Death did nip
    The tender flower
And cause its leaves to fade and die
    In one short hour!
Yet long enough it lingered here to fill
    Thy loving heart,
And make thee feel as if it were of life
    The better part.

Did Stranger pluck the tiny Bud within
    Thy garden fair?
Or was it He who loves and keeps thee
    'Neath his care?
Father! Mother! Thou must feel 't was
    God,—did send
An angel to transplant the rose He
    Did but lend.

Then thank Him for the fragrance shed
    Around thy way!
Bend low, " pass 'neath the rod," He'll
    Be thy stay!
When thy long day is ended, thou shalt
    Claim thine own,
And find within the pearly gates thy
    Flower, full blown.

Didst thou e'er see the eagle stir
  The eaglet's nest?
And briars place 'neath down to pierce
  Their tender breast?
That they might try their wings, and large
  Of stature grow?
Mid bracing air, mid purer climes,
  Nor look below?

Just so thy God would say to thee,
  Take staff in hand,
Rise, follow; I will lead thee to
  The better land!
Thou wilt bless the cruel thorns that
  Pierced thy breast,
Nor would not let thee rest within
  Thy earthly nest.

HER PORTRAIT

M. E. P.

As on thy face I gaze to-day,
 Thy smile seems a caress,
Thine eyes with merry, laughing light
 Again my spirit bless.
The past the present seems to-day,—
 The years behind us flung;
We stand on Love's sweet threshold, dear,
 And thou and I are young.

I've not forgot how fair thou wast,
 My bonny, bonny bride;
No envious veil of silken gauze
 Thy loveliness could hide.
But lovelier far than e'er before
 To me thou then didst seem,
And life was all, to thee and me,
 A sweet midsummer's dream.

Ah wife, I dimly knew thee then,
 Thy worth I had not guessed;
Through joy and through gloom alike,
 Thy love bore every test,

So true thou wast, so noble, dear,
　So bright, so strong, so brave;
Then waters deep of trouble came
　My sorrowing soul to lave.

No fixed gulf divides us, love,
　Only a peaceful stream;
With brightest hopes of joy beyond
　Its lucent waters gleam.
Though long the years I've missed thee, dear,
　Thou'st seemed not far to me,—
Some day the bridge that spans the tide
　Shall bear me o'er to thee.

LINES BY PROF. RYLAND

The following lines were written by Prof. Josiah Ryland when he was principal of the Stevensville Academy in 1856, and many of the King and Queen people, as well as others, will be interested in seeing them in print.—H. R. P., Jr.

1856

O age of varnish, cant and shame,
That wanteth nothing but a name!
King William throws the gauntlet down
In peerless Bessie Blanchie Brown!
Come to the rescue, King and Queen,
Produce thy Walker, Dora Deane!
Unfurl the banner of the sun;
Make way, make way, for Fenelon!
And let the glory of the day
Burst forth afresh in Ora May!
O who the matchless grace shall tell
Of her of Woodville, Floss Rochelle!
But, Bessie, Dora, Floss make way
For the last cherub, baby Gay!
Who, the last Pleiad of the skies,
With ebon hair and azure eyes,
Appears on earth, a Peri bright,
To glad our eyes and charm our sight.
Here, for a while, Dame Fortune's wheel,
Exhausted by the maddening reel,
Rests pendent while new names are found
Of would-be grace and empty sound.

When " Woman's Rights " to laws attain,
And girls go courting, might and main,
When Bloomer pants become the rage,
And high-heel gaiters strut the stage;
When boys no longer woo the lassies,
But maidens court them to their faces,
O what the luckless wights shall save
From anguish, or an early grave?
For girls (from number) must, of course,
Attack the beaux ten on a horse!
O Fenelon, my son, my son,
In such a case thou art undone!
Fly for thy life while now thou may'st,
Or cut thy throat with prudent haste.
Old times return! restore the reign
Of Polly, Nancy, Sukey, Jane,
Jemina, Phoebe, Ann, Eliza,
Abigail, Venus, Eloise.
Away with varnish, cant and gloss!
Away with Bessie, Dora, Floss!
No longer with such babies bore us.
If earth with babes must be replenished
Till the last settlement is finished,
Do give them honest Christian names,
As Matthew, Thomas, Andrew, James,
Daniel, Ezekiel, Peter, Paul:—
Apostles, prophets, martyrs all.
Such names our grandsires honored long,
On author's page, in poet's song;
Such names were towers of strength indeed
When men for liberty did bleed,
Such were the watchwords of an hour
When men staked all for Freedom's flower.
But now the time of bronze returns,
And honest cheek with flushes burns.
Cant, affectation, gloss, begone!
" Old times," old times, return, return.

THE OCEAN

G. P. B.

Who has not felt as he stood and gazed far out o'er the ocean wild,
That the moving flood was the voice of God communing with His
child?

Whose soul has not thrilled and thrilled again at this majestic scene,
The thought of lands far distant from view and the ocean lying
between?
Do the heavens declare God's glory? The firmament show His hand?
Then come with me where the sky and sea bid a long adieu to land;
Who, there, is not awe-struck and subdued, drawn close to the God
above,
Whose life is not sweet and strong, I ween, in touch with Him who
is love?

Dost doubt the existence of God and the final triumph of right?
Dost think that life speaks but of itself and death only heralds night?
Then go, I pray, to the ocean's shore 'neath a clear and star-lit sky,
And say who painted the picture sublime that greets your ravished eye.
Who orders the waves as they rise and fall with rhythm like that of
song?
The breakers dashing their foam on the sand, to whom do these
belong?
What human artist such colors could blend in picture half so grand?
What power now save an infinite one can answer your soul's demand?

But hark! a storm comes up o'er the deep, the blue sea turning to
green;
The sparkling spray on the crest of the waves enlivens and crowns
the scene.
The wind, as it rides full blast on the storm, breathes tales of magic
power;
The breakers roar and the lightnings flash, and the clouds with tempest
lower.
What law is back of wind and waves? Who speaks the storm into
being?
Whose voice sounds clear 'mid the roar of breakers arising and fleeing?
'T is the voice of God speaking to you till your soul gives answering
thrill,
The same voice that will presently say to the storm, "Now peace;
be still."

Hast stood alone by the silent grave of one you loved as your life?
Hast lost faith in the goodness of God and fallen a prey to strife?
Then stand again at the water's side as the sun sinks slow to rest,
And listen the whisper come softly, "The father above knows best."
The crimson rays from setting sun, as they mellow the water's blue,
Speak to your soul of the life to come and the Father's love for you;
Remember man only tarries here, as the waves arise and are gone,
And each one owes to God and himself to rejoice and not to mourn.

Hast wandered away from home and the right in paths of sin and
   shame?
Hast forgotten how at mother's knee you lisped the Father's name?
Then go, at the first faint break of day, Satan and sin to dethrone,
Make bare your head and kneel on the shore with God and the sea
   alone;
Now listen, O child, to thy Father's voice, " Come unto me "—the test,
Prodigal son, who hast strayed so far—" and I will give thee rest ";
Turn thy weary steps toward home at last, renew thy early vow;
The Father will place a ring on thy hand, a kiss upon thy brow.

Hast won some well-earned victory, some hard and strenuous fight?
Hast carried the day and reached the goal, turned darkness into light?
Stand e'en now at the midday hour near the ceaselessly moving tide,
As the glowing sun gilds the waves, and the waters sparkle in pride:
Then bowing thy head with humility, bid thy heart send thanks above
To Him who holds the earth in His hand, yet marks the fall of the
   dove;
As thy soul overflows with joy and peace, forget not whence they came,
But rise to still better and nobler things, e'er trusting in His name.

WHEN THE LAURELS ARE BLOOMING.

[Some five miles from Goshen station, Chesapeake and Ohio Railroad,
the North River cuts its passage through the mountains, and the pike
leading to Lexington, Va., works its way along the banks of the river,
the whole making a scene at once enchanting and sublime. It was an
object of great admiration to the late Commodore Maury. In his dying
moments he was heard to murmur, " Take me through Goshen pass,
when the laurels are blooming."]

> When the laurels are blooming,
>   When nature serene
> Is clothed in its brightest
>   And loveliest green,
>
> Bear my body then slowly,
>   Yea, gently along,
> And sing while you bear it
>   Your sweetest of song.
>
> When the laurels are blooming,
>   When mountains of blue
> Are bathing their summits
>   In bright azure hue,

Oh bear me, then bear me,
  Where they silently rise,
And speak, while they point
  To a home in the skies.

When the laurels are blooming,
  When the bird in its nest
Is waking to carol
  From winter's long rest,
When glad notes are warbling
  From leaflet and tree,
Oh, bear me where laurels
  Are blooming for me.

When the laurels are blooming,
  When the waters so wild
Are chafing and fretting
  Like yon wilful child,
As they dash o'er the lone rock,
  So well-worn and gray,
Where the laurels are blooming,
  Oh, bear me that way.

*   *   *   *

But the laurels, 'though blooming,
  Will wither and die;
Their leaves, torn and scattered,
  Forgotten shall lie;
But his name and his fame,
  To Virginia so dear,
On the page of her story
  Shall ever recur.

Thus sadly they bore him
  Where the laurels did bloom,
And tenderly laid him
  In a cold, humble tomb;
But his spirit, freed spirit,
  From sorrow and strife,
Is blooming immortal
  By the River of Life.

LINES ON THE DEATH OF ROBERT M. TABB, C. S. A.

[Written, at the request of his widow, by Sarah Jane Bagby.]

Far from the din of battle, far from the noisy strife
Of a nation's conflict, up to the better life,—
Borne by the wings of angels, soared his pure spirit away,
Far from the blood and carnage, on that calm autumnal day.

He died for home and country, none braver e'er marched to the field,
Of all that proud host of warriors that stood as their Nation's shield,
That stood,—but alas! have fallen, who nobly have fought their last
    fight,
Whose watchword, at home or in battle, was "God, my country, and
    right."

When forms that were stouter-girded, when hearts that were strong
    did quail,
On that day of unequal contest, that caused our proud banner to trail,
He rushed and with colors uplifted, he rushed to the front of the fray,
And calling on others to follow, gave his life to his country that day.

Ah! who may tell of the rapture that bursts on the astonished eye,
As earth with its tumult of passion, is exchanged for the glories on
    high?
When the ear one moment greeted by the sound of the musketry's ring,
Is tuned for the heavenly choir, to the music the angels sing.

Oh, say not in vain was the effort he made his country to save;
In vain, whether living or dying, is never the fate of the brave.
But history will write the true story, far down through the ages of
    time,
Of the deeds of the hero soldier—a record both true and sublime.

But alas! who shall comfort the mourner, dry the eye of the sorrowing
    wife,
As she clasps to her bosom in anguish his babes, now her solace and
    life?
The God of the widow and orphans bids the wild waves of sorrow
    cease,
And the heart of the sadly bereaved is calmed with heavenly peace.
    Jan. 15, 1878.

THE EMPTY SLEEVE.

By Dr. G. W. BAGBY.

Tom, old fellow, I grieve to see
The sleeve hanging loose at your side;
The arm you lost was worth to me
Every Yankee that ever died.
But you don't mind it at all;
You swear you've a beautiful stump,
And laugh at that damnable ball—
Tom, I knew you were always a trump.

A good right arm, a nervy hand,
A wrist as strong as sapling oak,
Buried deep in the Malvern sand—
To laugh at that is a sorry joke.
Never again your iron grip
Shall I feel in my shrinking palm—
Tom, Tom, I see your trembling lip,
How on earth can I be calm?

Well! the arm is gone, it is true;
But the one that's nearest the heart
Is left—and that's as good as two;
Tom, old fellow, what makes you start?
Why, man, she thinks that empty sleeve
A badge of honor; so do I,
And all of us—I do believe
The fellow is going to cry.

" She deserves a perfect man," you say;
" You not worth her in your prime? "
Tom, the arm that has turned to clay
Your whole body has made sublime;
For you have placed in the Malvern earth
The proof and pledge of a noble life—
And the rest, henceforth of higher worth,
Will be dearer than all to your wife.

I see the people in the street
Look at your sleeve with kindling eyes;
And you know, Tom, there's naught so sweet
As homage shown in mute surmise.
Bravely your arm in battle strove,
Freely, for freedom's sake, you gave it;
It has perished—but a nation's love
In proud remembrance will save it.

Go to your sweetheart, then, forthwith—
You're a fool for staying so long—
Woman's love you'll find no myth,
But a truth, living, tender, strong.
And when round her slender belt
Your left arm is clasped in fond embrace,
Your right will thrill, as if it felt,
In its grave, the usurper's place.

As I look through the coming years,
I see a one-armed married man;
A little woman, with smiles and tears,
Is helping as hard as she can
To put on his coat, pin his sleeve,
Tie his cravat, and cut his food;
And I say, as these fancies I weave,
That is Tom and the woman he wooed.

The years roll on, and then I see
A wedding picture bright and fair;
I look closer,—and it's plain to me
That is Tom, with the silver hair.
He gives away the lovely bride,
And the guests linger, loth to leave
The house of him in whom they pride—
"Brave old Tom with the empty sleeve."

CHAPTER XIII

TWO MEN DESERVING TO BE REMEMBERED, AND A BOY SENT ON AN ERRAND

BY JOHN POLLARD

Alexander Dudley was one of the most prominent men of his day. He was a practicing lawyer of King and Queen County, Va., yet was also the father of a railroad. The old people of the county can readily recall him. I knew him, though at the time he was a man and I was a boy. He came into prominence by a single step. That step was the inception and completion of the Richmond and York River Railroad, merged since his day into the Southern. He was the first to give practical shape to the enterprise, the first to believe it could be carried through thirty-four miles, from Richmond to West Point, and the man that deserves the most honor for that achievement. He floated the stock with which the road was built. With surprising enthusiasm and energy he induced men in the cities of Baltimore and Richmond, and in King and Queen, King William, Hanover, New Kent, Gloucester, and other counties to invest their money. He was made the first president, as he well deserved. The road was chartered in 1853. Three years afterwards (1856) the first passenger train was run through, as I have been informed by a gentleman who has conversed with the engineer who that day had charge of the throttle. The only marked difference between the road then and now is that at that time the train went into West Point, not on the Pamunkey, but on the Mattapony side, and here the terminus remained for a time.

But the most herculean work of Mr. Dudley had not yet been done. When the war between the States was at an end, the Richmond and York River Railroad had scarcely anything left to it but the graded track on which it had been built. What was to be done? The president might give up, might surrender to difficulties. The utterly prostrate condition of Virginia might seem to justify such a course, but the old-time energy and indomitable perseverance of the man who had begun the enterprise came to the rescue. Mr. Dudley, still president, succeeded in persuading the original stockholders to the only course that could restore the road,—to surrender their first-mortgage bonds and take second-mortgage bonds, and let sufficient bonds be sold as a first lien upon the property to rebuild and reëquip the road. This gigantic task was accomplished and the great highway of commerce was given back to the public, refurnished for work.

It has been thought that his death in 1869 (when he had by no means attained an advanced age) was partly due to the responsibility and labors taken upon himself in putting the enterprise upon its feet again.

The carrying through of the York River Railroad suggested, and paved the way for, another enterprise. That was the organization of the West Point Land Company, which project meant the purchase of five hundred acres of land at West Point at thirty dollars per acre. That purchase embraced the whole of the point itself, and all the land between the Mattapony and the Pamunkey, as far as the five hundred acres would extend. The land was bought of Hon. William P. Taylor, who once lived at West Point, though at this time he was residing on a fine estate called "Hayfield," on the Rappahannock River in Caroline County. The purpose was, of course, to build up a town at the place, in which project some had faith and some had no faith whatever. Those composing the company were substantial men of King and Queen, King William, and surrounding counties. The directors held their first meeting on the 27th day of March, 1856. At this meeting B. B. Douglas was chosen president and John Pollard (my father) secretary and treasurer. The directors usually held their meetings at West Point. It did not look much like even a small village then, to say nothing of a town. There was but one house at the place. That was the former Taylor residence, which had been turned into a tavern and was occupied as such by a Mr. New, after whom it had been named. Here the directors met. The proprietor had a well furnished table,—no wonder, as he had three rivers to provide him with what was necessary. My father took me (a boy of sixteen years) with him to the meeting of the directors at West Point to help him in his duties as secretary and treasurer, not so much because he needed my assistance as that I might be somewhat trained to the ways of business. Transactions with Mr. Taylor for land purchase occurred on April 17th, 1859. My father continued to be the secretary and treasurer as long as he lived, the last proceedings taken down by him being dated the 19th of November, 1875, and his death being noted first on the 25th of February, 1878.

I rather suppose that my employment as an occasional help to my father (in his official services to the land company) suggested the outing that now, with the reader's indulgence, I will attempt to describe. It must have occurred in the spring of 1857.

My health, though not now infirm, was then by no means superabounding in robustness. Accordingly I was stopped from school at the beginning of the session of 1856-57 and kept for twelve months at active outdoor pursuits. One of the healthful employments given me by my father was to go on horseback to Mr. William P. Taylor's, in Caroline County, and pay him $1000.00 as a creditor of the West Point Land Company. Why he was willing to take the risk of transmitting so much money by the hands of a boy of seventeen summers I cannot tell, unless he wanted a way of training me to business, and at the same time of furnishing me with the bodily exercise he thought I needed. When I got to my destination at Mr. Taylor's I would be only fifteen miles below Fredericksburg, and I asked my father if I might make my journey a little longer and see that historic town. He readily consented. I was now made ready for the trip. " Jenny Lind," my father's riding horse, was brought out and saddled up, the money

was fastened under my clothes close to my body; I
was given directions about the road; I mounted, and
was soon lost to sight. I spent the first night after
leaving home at Mr. Harry Latane's in Essex, whom
my father knew very well, he being a first cousin to
my father's mother. I found him quite an old man,
but exceedingly kind and affable. Just before I reached
his house I was overtaken by a heavy downpour of rain,
which made me quite wet. Old as he was, he took
great interest in drying my clothes, calling me all the
time " Cousin John." He was the father of Captain
Latane, who was the only man killed in the raid around
General McClellan's army and is immortalized in the
picture " The Burial of Latane." Soon after leaving
Cousin Harry Latane's I struck the river road, and
pursued that all the way. I passed Lloyds and Loretto,
and an ancient colonial church with many tombs around
it, and at length reached Port Royal about dinner time.
I went in and got something to eat. After feeding myself and horse I mounted again and went on to Mr.
Taylor's, which (if I remember rightly) was about five
miles farther on. He received me very politely, and
while he was counting the money Mrs. Taylor entertained me very pleasantly, speaking of the time when
they lived at West Point and telling me how she used to
enjoy looking out upon the bright waters of the York.
Mr. Taylor was now an old man. He had himself
been a member of the United States House of Representatives, and was a son of the distinguished John
Taylor of Caroline, a United States Senator and a
friend of Thomas Jefferson. (John Taylor was the
man that offered the Resolutions of 1798 in the Virginia House of Delegates.) Mr. William P. Taylor
and wife were childless and occupied a fine old mansion,
but it was not my plan to spend the night with them.
I was to press on that evening and reach Frank Gouldin,
whose acquaintance I had formed in attending, as a boy
delegate, the Baptist General Association of Virginia.
So when the money was paid over and Mr. Taylor's receipt obtained, and a burden of responsibility lifted from
my mind, I set off again on my way to Fredericksburg.

I soon reached the home of my friend, who received me very cordially.

Next morning I got to Fredericksburg, looked around the town, ate dinner, and started for home, fifty miles away. I cannot recall, to save my life, where I spent the night, but I think it more than likely that I put up a second night with my friend Gouldin. I started in time to reach before dinner Dr. William A. Baynham, a Baptist minister with whom I was well acquainted. He lived then in a fine mansion below Loretto; lived in affluence, and kept an open house to all his friends. On being ushered into the parlor I found that Dr. Baynham was holding an old-fashioned dinner day, and was entertaining Senator Robert Hunter and his wife and Representative Garnett and his sisters. Dr. Baynham, though a bachelor, served an elegant and sumptuous dinner. The company was very agreeable. I do not remember the subject of conversation, except that Senator Hunter told me that he knew my uncle, Judge Jeffries, and, I think, further said that they were college mates at the College of William and Mary. (As to this second statement, I begin to suspect that my memory is playing me a trick, for neither the records of William and Mary nor the life of Hunter makes any mention of his having been a student at that college.) When, after dinner, I told my hospitable host that I must go, he ordered my horse from the stable, where she had been well fed, and I mounted and proceeded on my journey. My memory does not enable me to say whether I reached home that evening; if I did it must have been quite late. I certainly got back safe and sound. I took very little account, at the time, of my mother's feelings in being called on to give me up at seventeen years of age to go alone on horseback on so long a journey with such a sum of money on my person. But I can see now that her motherly heart must have given me up with hesitation and reluctance. I can easily imagine her and my father conferring about the matter, and seeing that I was rapidly approaching manhood and ought to be thinking somewhat, at least, about taking on a man's responsibility, and that the outdoor exercise which the journey would give me was the very exercise that my health called for, they agreed I should venture. Certainly my mother made no objection, but I can now imagine what she felt then, and how glad she was that I got back without serious mishap of any kind.

CHAPTER XIV

LIFE ON THE OLD PLANTATION

We have it in mind to tell some things about how matters went on the old King and Queen plantation, for the delectation of the younger set, who never had the keen satisfaction of seeing it, and taking part in it, as the writer had. The actors here will be the master and mistress, the children, overseer, cook, hostlers, plowmen, farmhands, and house servants-at-large, all colored except the overseer. The " Great House," as the negroes invariably called it, the home of the master and family, was the seat and center of the rural scene. It was usually a building of two stories, often with dormer windows, one or likely two wings, cellar and basement,—say in all twelve rooms, with pantry, and closets ad libitum. The lawn was spacious and shady, with kitchen and meathouse in the rear, and office in front. The overseer's house stood apart, often one-fourth to one-half mile away, while comfortable cabins for the servants ran in a line on one side and to the rear. The plantation stretched around and abroad, partly open for the crops, and largely wooded. This woodland was a very godsend, for, to say nothing of rails for fencing and lumber for building, coal was yet unused here and much wood was used to cook and to keep fires aglow for master and his dependants. It ought to be added that there were ample gardens, usually in rear, for both whites and blacks.

We are up very early some fine spring morning for a purpose; and now as the gray streaks of opening day stretch upward from the eastern horizon, we are suddenly startled by the echoes of a cowhorn, which pierces the dullest ear. Instantly the whole plantation is astir. The overseer uses his bunch of keys, and swings wide open the doors of the great barn, and the less capacious corncrib, and here come Ben and Coleman, 'ostlers, and

MR. JOHN BAGBY

1791–1878; prominent as Merchant and Deacon Bruington Church; father of Drs. Richard
H., Geo. F. and Alfred Bagby, and of Maj. John R. Bagby; and Mrs. Bagby.

behind them Ottoway, Reuben, Jacob, and Carter, for not only must horses be seen after, but mules, oxen, sheep, and cows. Now all of these are comfortably groomed and fed; when all hands retire to the kitchen, and keen appetites are satisfied with coffee, cornpone, fried bacon and molasses. And here come Caroline and Big Lucy, milkpail poised on the head, to extract the white and foaming liquid from distended udder, and presently churn it into yellow butter. And now to the field! Coleman, Ben, and Carter take their respective teams, and now the mellow earth turns over fast from the sod, giving out a sweet odor as it turns. Old Isaac is off with oxen and cart for a load of wood or fence rails, or likely a load of marl from the bank to dress the upturned field. So we press on till the horn sounds for twelve, noon, when teams and men get rest and dinner. And when night's sable curtain falls, and supper is over, the young men and maids gather, banjos, and mayhap a fiddle, are tuned, and an hour or two of dancing beguiles the time; and then sweet sleep, till the horn sounds again. This with fencing, grubbing, and the gardens, fills up the week's work, and when Sunday comes, young and old of both colors in best attire flock to church, and hear the sweet story of Jesus and the Cross by Shackford, Semple, or Todd,— white and colored alike, the master and the servant. By and by Easter and then Whitsuntide, with two days' holiday each, and now the white dogwood blossoms tell that corn-planting time has come. The plows go before to open the furrows and here come the men, the boys, and a sprinkling of women. It must be borne in mind that in January and February we were largely snow- and ice-bound, and it gave us nearly as much as we could do to cut and maul and transport the wood needed to keep aglow the many fires to make mistress and the colored women and pickaninnies comfortable, and to cook the three meals a day to feed everybody. Moreover, the snow is sometimes very deep (as we remember very well, in the fearful season of 1847 with drifts fifteen or twenty feet deep); then it is more wood and more work. But the two cold months do not last forever, thanks to the good Father, and now we must make up for lost time.

And now while I have been talking and talking, the grains we have planted are alive again and shooting up all along the row. Then comes the work of replanting and thinning out, when the small plows are put in to " side " the little plants, and every one must then be brushed over with the weeding hoe. Yes, I hear you fellows of the modern cultivator and harrow call out " What a tedious and toilsome waste of time." Perhaps; but the men of that day made the corn, and that was what they were after. And now in the brighter days of May and June the four furrows are to be returned to the growing plants, and then the hoe again, to " hill up." Thus the crop is laid by.

HARVEST

We have been so busy with the corn that we had almost forgotten this matter of unfailing interest. It is now toward the second, or maybe the third week in June. The sun is hot and fast getting hotter; and look yonder! The wheat is ripe, for the stalks are taking on a golden hue, and the heads are full and ripe; for they hang low. It must be reaped, or the precious grain will waste. So here comes old Ben Braxton, his cradle, with blade keenly ground, over his shoulder, followed by Coleman, Ottoway, and Reuben of the younger set, each followed by a boy to sheave the wheat, and by others to stack it. (Reader, did you ever see a " cradle "? A stout oak handle four feet long, two inches thick at the butt end, has set into it at a right angle a steel blade, curving inward slightly, by means of a hook on its shank end, an iron ring, and a wedge. Five or six wooden fingers, curving like the blade, are attached, flanking the blade, and catching the straw when cut. This was the implement of those days, and it was much better than the primitive sickle, though it yields now to the great " harvester.")

Ben, Sr., is a veteran at this business, and knows all its ins and outs. Reaching the field he takes the lead row, returns and tackles a second, the rest following. When that is cut through and return made to the starting point, all feel need of a breathing spell; so old Ben lifts his cradle from his shoulder, lets the end of the handle fall with a thud upon the ground, pulls his little whet-blade from the ribs, shoves it into the light soil at his feet, and proceeds to whet his blade, his body swaying to and fro, keeping time to the rhythmic music of the whetting. So the work goes on till we have two hours for dinner, and then at it again till by and by the field is reaped, and the wheat comfortably shocked.

A good story is told of a King and Queen farmer who had as a head man a veteran negro named Umphrey. It was a custom of many years' standing, when the toilsome days of harvest came, to send out each day a jug of whisky from which each might get a sip now and then. This time the master had been fearfully smitten with the temperance fever which was abroad in the land at that time. As the morning work was about to begin, he called up his man and said: "Umphrey, whisky is a dreadful thing,—it kills so many people and ruins so many homes; and therefore I have determined to give you all a barrel of good, cool molasses-water in its place." It is doubtful whether surprise, disappointment, or indignation was most prominent in the old darkey's sensations. He was dumb for a moment, but rallied, and said: "Marster, marster, this here crap is too heavy to be rept on 'lasses!" Right or wrong, Umphrey got his whisky.

LOG-ROLLING

Preparation for this has been largely made in the leisure days of winter. It must be borne in mind that in that day vast tracts of land which might otherwise have been cultivated were in wood, most of it primitive and heavy. To be rid of this was the problem. So in winter the hands were set to work felling the trees and cutting trunks and limbs into proper lengths; and then rolling them into piles convenient for burning, plenty of twigs, stumps and dry wood being shoved into the chinks and crevices. Thus they would stand until the hot sun had thoroughly dried the pile, then the plows were set to turn a few furrows around to prevent the burning of adjacent stubble and grass. Now fire is applied, and all burned to ashes. Thus it was that millions of feet of lumber were ruthlessly destroyed which would now be immense fortunes to the owners. There was a surplus of labor, and many to be fed, and so the forests had to go. Very many would say now, like the boy anent the pie, "Wish I had some!" When the neighbors gathered together and began rolling there was singing, shouting and merrymaking, and by and by feasting and drinking, till the work was done,—the lassies doing the cooking and sharing the fun.

THE COTTON GIN

So far as is known to me—indeed I feel assured of it—the father of the writer, John Bagby of Stevensville, and Mr. Samuel P. Ryland and Mr. Walker, were the first men to introduce this machine into the county. This was about 1837. It was very common to see upon every respectable plantation a good-sized cotton patch; but the fiber was separated from the seed by hand, and it was a tedious process. A few developed remarkable adeptness at this, and my father was one of the few. After supper, a huge bag of cotton being brought in and spread out before the open fire, my father would spread out his large bandanna handkerchief on his lap and proceed to pick, the rest following in order. He could do it, but it was my abomination. "Peter Parley," or "Sanford and Merton," suited me much better. I was glad when the gin came, though even then my fingers were kept in training for a time. Now let us see about this famous invention of Whitney. There is a huge box with a capacious mouth at the top to receive the cotton, and an opening in front for the lint, and one smaller in the rear for the seed. Peep inside, and you see a number of fine-tooth saws embracing a wood cylinder set horizontally.

The spindle end projects outside the box at one end, arranged to receive a leather band,—this is the gin; but how are the saws to be propelled? By horse power, as we shall see. Come with me and I will show you: As we stand here on the ground, do you see that great wheel under shelter, set horizontally into a large perpendicular shaft? This shaft sets on an iron gudgeon which works in a socket at the lower end, and the same at the upper end. The wheel has cogs on its upper side; the cogs work into others set on to a spindle, which last at the other end carries a band wheel. Turn to the big shaft again: Heavy poles or scantlings, five or six, are set into it below and extend out some fifteen feet,—these are for the draft horses. Now connect the band wheel of the spindle by means of a leather band with the corresponding spindle of the gin on the floor above, hitch the horses to one or more of the sweeps, and we are ready. The horses turn the big wheel, which in turn gives rapid motion to spindle and band wheel, and that gives redoubled motion to the gin saws. Drop in a bag of cotton, old Ben, as you stand there with veiled face to save nose, mouth, and eyes from the inevitable dust, and in a twinkling you see the light fiber flying out in front, while the seeds drop at your feet. You say, reader, that this is a very heavy, clumsy machine. Yes, but it was a real godsend to the people of that far-away day; for men came from far and near, and paid toll gladly to get a benefit. Many a weary hour have my brother, the Major, and I spent in that old gin room, "vexing our righteous souls." This same horse-power threshed the wheat and oats.

A MARRIAGE IN HIGH LIFE

Next Friday, August 28th, is to be a great day at Bunker's Hill. Queen, one of the younger cooks in training, is to be married to Jim Taylor, who belongs to Mr. Bonivita, the great confectioner of Richmond; and all the country is agog,—the younger lads and lassies are quite excited. Queen has been busy making up and baking her cakes and pies; the pig for roasting is fattening in the pen; the ham, already boiled, is large and juicy; the wedding trousseau is about finished, and things are moving nicely. Peggy, the housegirl, generally called " Peg " for short, is to be first of the six bridesmaids, and is to lift the veil as the ceremony ends, for the groom to salute the bride. Parson Sparks is to officiate, and when he retires there is to be a big dance. Thomas Hoomes, the fiddler, and Sam Motley, the banjoist, are putting their strings in tune. Time, you know, does not wait for anybody, and while I am getting ready to tell you about it, the 28th has come, and so have the darkies! From north and south, from east and west, they crowd in by troops and bands.

Now Peg is pretty, winsome, and ambitious; she is especially anxious to be admired. Inasmuch as the best dress she can produce is a little worn and faded, the thought comes to her that one of the gowns of her young mistress—a handsome pearl silk—was just the thing to set off her beauty. What must Peg do but steal softly upstairs while the family is at supper, extract the pearl silk from the wardrobe, and presently don this for the marriage.

Things now go forward as had been planned,—the marriage is finally over, the groom kisses the bride; the grand supper is served, and the preacher departs. This is the signal for the dance. Hoomes calls the partners and the figures, and here they go back and forth, to right, to left, in and out, promenade all. The interest and enthusiasm are great, and increase every moment. Peg is doing her best; she is much sought after. All thought of time is forgotten, everyone is so absorbed. All at once the day breaks, the horn sounds, and consternation reigns supreme. Peg, especially, is thoroughly frightened,—she looks to right, to left, for an exit, and every avenue is blocked. To stay here was certain exposure,—go she must, for the avenger is at hand. There is but one way—the window, so drawing back a step or two, she rushed madly head foremost at the window, carrying glass, sash and all before her, and went flying to the forest, where she stayed several days; but she finally returned, a penitent, and was forgiven.

THE WORK OF THE NEGRO WOMEN

The year's work is drawing towards its end now, and someone will say, " What of the women all this time? " Bless your soul, they have found work in plenty. Bear in mind that everybody, saint and sinner, old and young, must be clothed. Yonder is an abundance of wool from the flock, but it needs to be washed, carded, spun, and woven. Then the suits must be cut out, and made up. Moreover, there are a score or two of mouths to be filled three times every day, and the cooking and cleaning to be provided for; there is bread-making and bed-making to be done—have women nothing to do? Sometimes one of the good old " mammies " has it laid upon her to look after the black pickaninnies while the mothers are at work, doing patchwork or waiting on the sick. Many a time, no doubt, our colored sisters have thought, though they may not have expressed it in language quite so classic:

> Man works from sun to sun,
> But woman's work is never done.

Then too, death, whose icy skeleton shows its horrid white teeth to white and black alike, would often invade our rural home, and for a day or two there was engrossment for all. There is a strange and weird attractiveness in death. Women are more excitable than men, and on these occasions their lamentations and moanings could hardly have been surpassed by Rachel weeping for her children. In song their voices were rich, mellow, and rhythmic. I remember well how one day, about 1858, when a really powerful meeting was in progress at Mattapony, during recess the colored people gathered outside the west door, and an old brother lined out one of the old chorus hymns. The crowd caught up the strain, and the music seemed to me as near to the seraphic as we ever hear it on earth. The best element of the whites were largely in sympathy with them in all this, bating some extravagances.

If Reuben Smith was graceful in handling the wheat

cradle, and Warner Hall deft in manipulating the hoe, surely Aunt Isabel was the most exquisite baker of bread, cake, and pies I ever knew. My mother was uniformly good and kind to the negroes, often rising from her bed at night to wait upon the sick. I personally knew a gentleman, who hearing that one of his women was sick ten miles away, mounted his horse, rode down, and stayed by her all night and saved her life.

My father bought a frail mulatto named William Ferguson. William was a carpenter, a man of quick intelligence, eager to learn; I used to sit with him by the hour, listening to his sprightly talk and teaching him arithmetic, etc. He could draw a plan, fit every post, sill, and rafter deftly to its place and finish off your house *à la mode*. I was away at college when William died, and it distressed me a good deal.

HOG-KILLING TIME

Ah, now you make the small boy's eye kindle and his mouth water, for only Christmas itself has greater charms for him. It is now the second week in December,—the atmosphere is crisp, the earth is frozen under our feet, a scum of ice has formed on the water, and it is time to make ready. This important event in the year's operations began to give signs of its coming away back in October, when the slim and crusty pine-rooters and Chesters were brought in from the fields. Then we make a floor of small saplings, and upon this build a pen, say ten by twenty feet. See that you make it strong and high, for the hog you will find very much like one of General Pickett's men captured at Gettysburg, who, when a fussy Union officer came near the pen, and began to give orders for safeguarding the prisoners, called out, "General, you give orders to have us a plenty to eat, and do it quick, or we won't stay here!" Have a good thick bed of pine-tags in the pen, and set in a large water-trough. Now throw in corn just from the shuck, with beets, or turnips, now and then. This is the process; and now that we have kept it up six or eight weeks our porkers are sleek and fat,—

they are ready for the shambles. This brings us to the gist of our story.

I heard my father tell old Isaac this morning to bring up a load of dry wood and lightwood and dump it near the hogpen. Then in the evening come Ben and Reuben, who roll up two green logs, swing up between them four large boilers and fill them with water. My brother and I are observant of all this, and lay our plans accordingly. And now to bed (after prayers and supper), till a bright light shines in at the window. This is all we ask,—we quickly don our clothes, and in stocking-feet creep downstairs, and out into the crisp night air and the darkness. Guided partly by instinct and partly by the kindling firelight, we reach our destination. The water is boiling now and the porkers must die. The boys jump into the pen, old Ben stands with butcher knife pointed and keen in hand, and as each hog is dragged out he makes one sweeping stroke across its throat, then plunges it deep toward the vitals, and as the blade is withdrawn, out gushes a stream of rich, purple blood. One or two convulsive struggles and the poor brute is dead. Then he is plunged head foremost into boiling water, after which the bristles fall away at the touch. "Cut the tail off, Reuben." And this done, we gash it in slices, rub on a pinch of salt, let it lie on the live coals a few minutes,—it will crisp and curl up, and to a boy's palate is as ambrosia to a king.

We pass by the cutting and curing, for that is commonplace; but when it comes to sausages, spareribs, and shortbones, we are there and there to stay till the prudent warn us of the nearness of Christmas, and that some space must be kept for what that happy season has in store for us.

CHRISTMAS

And so here we are now at the end of the year, and up against the day for which, to the youth of the land, all other days were made. We have had our fun in hunting old hares, shooting squirrels from the tall trees, the robins in the cedars, and the partridges as they hurtle away on the wing. We enjoyed them all, but they were only taken by the way as we looked forward to this glad fruition. And ofttimes, as we have puffed and sweated in the tiresome cornfield, we have cheered our fagged spirits by a thought of Christmas, and now here it is at last. Will the realization be as fair as hope led us to expect? The day is, as Heaven wills it, fair and frosty. It is ushered in with a sort of jingling sound,—not so very musical it must be admitted,—though so intended. The sound of a distant horn, then a bell ringing, then a chorus of a dozen tin horns, then popcrackers, with bursting of bladders, and half a hundred voices shout, "Hurrah for Christmas!" Then the children come rushing in pellmell to tell what wonderful things Santa Claus has brought to each, besides the stocking full of nuts and candy,—oblivious that pa and ma knew it before they did. Then after breakfast all hands gather on the porch, where there are piles of dresses, coats, hats, blankets, shoes (for old brother Cook has been here to dress up the leather), and whatnots for every man and woman, boy and girl,—even Peggie, yes, Peggie gets her share too. Here, of course, are the two Bens, Isaac, Davy, Coleman, Osborne, Jim, Carter, Ottoway, Reuben, Warner, Isabel, Agnes, Caroline, dear old Aunt Polly (our mammy), and a host of small fry. Each gets his share, and all, white and colored, are happy. Now a round of sports and frolics, in which colored and white are mingled, and as the clock-hands near the hour of one, carriages and buggies come laden with brothers and sisters, uncles and aunts, and cousins galore, and then comes dinner. Taking everything into consideration, the writer has nowhere seen such dinners as those. A large turkey well fatted and well roasted invariably graced the foot of the long table; a ham and cabbage the head; oysters, a roast of beef, ducks, souse, hominy, celery, etc., flanked them on either side; and after a while, when a goodly portion of these have been disposed of, comes the desert,—and whew! what an exhibit is here. There are pound-cake, sponge-cake, jelly-cake, mince pies, potato pies, cherry tarts and lemon, with custard and jelly a-plenty; sometimes a plum pudding would be substituted for one of these. Here was a feast for the heathen gods; better, if possible, it is. All hands of us, master as well as the humblest of his slaves, now have a good week's rest, and so the year comes to an end.

SUNDRY DEVELOPMENTS OF CHARACTER

One of our neighbors owned a bright mulatto boy named Thomas,—an active, intelligent, and withal a handsome youngster. Thomas was a houseboy,—reared to run errands, bring in the food, wait on the table, etc. As such he was useful, had he not developed an apparently instinctive propensity to pilfer. As he brought in the hot biscuits he would slip two or three from the plate into his pocket, and so with other viands. One day his master noticed that Thomas's pockets swelled out beyond the usual proportions, when he sprang suddenly up from the table, and with all his strength pressed the steaming hot biscuits against the poor boy's thigh, till he cried out in pain with the burning. It cured him for a time, but he soon returned to his old habits, like the sow that was washed. His master seeing this, called him up one morning, and said, "Thomas, I have warned you again and again about this thing, and I have punished you for it, but you will persist. You must go out this morning with the field hands and work with them." This was the boy's abomination, but he must make the best of it, so out he went. The hours were long, however, and the sun very hot; Thomas shirked and flunked the work whenever he could. One day the master suffered it to get out that business called him from home. So his saddle horse was accoutered for his use, and after a hasty inspection of the field he rode off. This was a ruse to catch Thomas. The master passed out into the highroad, traveled a mile or two, then turned and rode back to the field. Missing the boy from the row with the rest of the men, he inquired of the head man, and learning he had disappeared under pretext of wanting a drink of water, he rode to the spring and found Thomas sleeping soundly under the shade. Dismounting, he came near, and stooping began fanning the sleeper with his wide-brimmed straw hat. This was refreshing, and Thomas had a splendid nap; but presently, yawning and stretching himself, he opened his eyes, and at sight of his master he wilted visibly.

Notwithstanding all this, Thomas proved incorrigible, and the master sold him South.

One of our neighbors was Col. P———, a gentleman of sharp wit and keen observation, large experience, and fine conversational powers. Another was a teacher, Mr. B———, smart and well taught. The two were fond of each other's society, and conversed much together about law, politics, social matters, religion and philosophy. The former had a house-boy named Cornelius,—short, lubberly, fat, lazy, and black " as they are made "; but Cornelius, to do him justice, was politic, shrewd, and obsequious. One Sunday afternoon the colonel and the professor were discussing the capacity and characteristics of the negro race, when the colonel asserted that a negro would always do things in the inverse order of what was desired. This precipitated a hot discussion of an hour, the professor affirming that this was abnormal, unnatural, and against all reason,— hence could not be so. " Well," said the colonel, " I will test it, and you will see. In the next room here is a pair of slippers; you go in there, and see that they are arranged in proper order,—the right on the right side as usual. I will call Cornelius to bring them in here, and if he does not invert them I will yield." This was done, the boy came and brought in the slippers—cap in one hand—put them down, and at his master's word went back to his work. In some mysterious way, by some uncommon ratiocination, the slippers were inverted, the right on the left side, and vice versa.

Again, Peter Lewis was a very good worker, but slow and dull. His master sent him to the upper gate to open an old drain on the right-hand side and release some ponding water. After far more than the necessary time his master went to see about him and found him tugging away, vainly trying to carry the water off by digging a deep ditch on the wrong side.

One day when the father was sick, his little son came in saying that he had found quite a pile of corn hid under some litter in the stable. Upon inquiry it was apparent that the 'ostler had taken advantage of the owner's sickness to extract the corn from the crib, and to hide it for his own use. The authorities of the law got word of it, and Jacob was convicted after trial; but the master interceded and the sentence was very light.

GENERAL MUSTER

Monday, June 15th, 1838. To-day I am ten years old. Being at the store this morning, I heard some gentleman talking about the Fourth of July; they said it was to be celebrated at the Courthouse; that it was also General Muster day; that General Braxton was to be there to review the troops; and General Muse is coming over from Essex, and the cavalry is to charge the infantry. They said the whole county would be there and many from outside. My! what a time it will be,—we must beg Pa to let us all go.

Saturday, July 4th. Ma says she will stay to take care of the house, but the rest are all to go,—Pa on his horse, Billy Button; the girls in the carriage, and the boys in the horsecart, which Ottoway is to drive, carrying dinner for us all, and horse feed. It is only six miles, and we soon passed the Mill. When we mounted the hill and came in sight of the Courthouse green, the whole place seemed to be filled with men, horses, wagons, carts, and carriages. Here and there were little tables where men and women sold horse-cakes, cup-cakes, round-cakes, and biscuits. We boys went for these and soon spent all our money. There was great noise and confusion—men and women chatting, boys, girls, and negroes rushing about, horses neighing, and soldiers jostling everybody, with now and then an epauletted officer. Presently a shrill voice rang out: " Captain Courtney's company parade here! parade here! " Then another: " Captain Bland's company parade here!" Another: "Captain Lumpkin's company parade here!" and so on to the end. Presently the several companies were brought together and aligned; and Major Saunders, seated on his noble bay, orders: "Regiment! left face, forward march!" I have heard the raven's croak, the eagle's scream, the steam whistle, but for an ear-splitting sensation I am yet to hear the equal of the fife in the hands of Conway Courtney that day, as an accompaniment of his brother James's drum. They were in front, and each did his best—for noise they distanced everything. Now, we are in the open field, soldiers in line, the rabble hanging around, the ladies in carriages on the outskirts. Suddenly drum and fife announce the coming of officers,—Col. Boyd appears escorting two, one on each side, the generals of brigade, each dressed up in burnished uniform, with brass buttons, sword and epaulettes. The colonel rides to the front, issues orders, and the whole line passes before the great generals for inspection. This done, yet further orders are issued, and the entire line is formed into a hollow square, the field officers enclosed. Up to this time the cavalry have hardly been seen, they are hanging around in the bushes and over the hills. All at once a bugle sounds in the distance, and someone cries out: "Here they come!" Like a tornado (not quite so fiercely) they sweep down, and now try their best to break into the square. The unaccustomed horses, less willing than their riders, recoil from the stern faces and threatening canes of that square phalanx. Once more the attempt is tried, but in vain. The regiment is countermarched, and we all dispersed to our homes, tired but pleased. Ah! how little did the youthful and unmindful spectators of that scene dream of the real conflicts, the face-to-face and hand-to-hand conflicts, in which they were to bear a part in but little more than two decades from that day!

A GREAT DAY IN RICHMOND

One day in October, 1840, my father greatly surprised me by saying, " Son, I am going to Richmond to-morrow, and will carry you with me." Now I had hardly ever been out of the county in my life, and besides, there was to be a great Whig convention in the city (it was the year of the exciting campaign for " Tippecanoe and Tyler too "), the great Daniel Webster was to speak, and other notable men. My mother, early the next morning, robed me in my best bib and tucker; my father climbed to his seat in the sulky, took me between his knees, and we set our faces towards the great city. I remember that as we passed by Milan he stirred me by telling that a man named Campbell, who lived there, was cutting down a tree, and by some accident the great tree fell on him and buried him in the ground, where he was found some hours afterward.

We crossed the Mattapony at Walkerton, where my father stopped on business, and then on to Piping Tree, where we crossed the Pamunkey. Then turning westward we passed Old Church, and so, as the sun neared its setting, we drove up to a tavern at the head of Mechanicsville turnpike kept by a friend of my father, named Achilles Lumpkin, where we slept. Little did I dream that night what stirring scenes were to be enacted within twenty years around the little hamlet, wherein friends of mine were to shed their lifeblood. A son of our host that night was guide to General Longstreet at Ellyson's Mill, a half-mile away, in June, 1862. He afterwards told me that in answer to a question about crossing the swamp then, he said, " Why, General, even a hen couldn't cross there unless she used her wings."

Bright and early the next morning we were off for the city. The crowd was astir as we drove up Franklin Street and stopped at a stable. My father took me to the grocery and commission house of Lewis Webb, with whom he traded, and engaged quarters at the " Mansion House," both on Main Street. Presently there came a noise of mingled shouting, cheering, and music, which brought me to the door. A band of music led a long procession of old men, young men and boys, followed by carriages, wagons, and carts, filled with officials, speakers, and ladies,—banners and flags floating aloft and a rabble of all classes and colors crowding the sidewalks. About midway the long line and in the middle of the street came a log cabin set on wheels, and peeping in I saw coonskins and great casks of hard cider, from which last a man, by turning a spigot, was giving out the cider to every comer with can or pitcher in his hand. Thus they moved on to the Capitol square. There a great platform had been built out from the giant pillars on the southern front. After certain preliminaries and an introduction, the big figure and massive head, with a forehead I have never seen equaled (I saw him many times in after years with Clay and Calhoun in the Senate at Washington), stood before the vast crowd and began in low, measured, but sonorous tones, his address. I recall something in his opening sentence about " this bright October sun "; but a treacherous memory, and the passing years, have lost to me all beside. The crowd, however, was in sympathy with Mr. Webster, and I shall never forget the shout of " Tippecanoe and Tyler too! " It carried the election.

CHAPTER XV

COLORED PEOPLE OF KING AND QUEEN COUNTY

To form correct views of this element of our population two things must be done. It were unfair to them to put them in contrast with the whites, as a moment's reflection will satisfy us. The advantages, environments, and opportunities of the two are altogether disproportionate. Again, if one really desires to know whether the colored man has made progress, it is necessary first to observe his condition of ignorance, superstition, and bestiality while he was yet in his native home in Africa. This latter viewpoint is quite as essential as the other is erroneous. Avoid the first comparison, give due attention to the second.

From the time of the first settlements north of the York and Mattapony they have counted nearly four—at times more than four—in every ten of the whole population,—men, women, and children taken together.

In the main it is doubtful whether there ever existed a more docile, contented and happy class of people than were the colored people of this county under slavery. With some exceptions they were comfortably housed, clad, and fed. When sick they had the care of the family physician and the kind attendance of master and mistress—it was to the interest of both parties that this should be so. A general holiday was no infrequent occurrence, when everyone was free to employ his time as he willed. This was especially true at Christmas, and for the entire week, when the big backlog was rolled on the capacious fireplace, feasting and merrymaking were the order of the day. A new suit from head to foot came to men, women, and children, and often a new blanket for each bed was added. Nothing stood in the way of unmeasured joy and delight. Besides other facilities, each married couple had adjacent to their cabin a small space set off for a garden of vegetables, and in addition each man was allowed an acre or two to be cultivated for his own use, with time in which to till it. This acre or two was usually set in corn, tobacco, or cotton, and its product was at his own disposal.

As is true of the white man,—of men everywhere,—they were not all good or all bad, not all unthrifty or untidy, nor all deceitful, lazy, and thieving,—not by any means.

Everyone at all acquainted with the negro knows that he instinctively takes to religion. Not always with enlightened views, nor yet unmixed with a certain element of superstition, with extravagances, false ideals, and in some cases hypocrisy. Yet, taking him altogether, the negro is a wonderfully religious biped. Moreover, here, as elsewhere in other counties and States, the negro, as the saying goes, takes naturally to the water and is a Baptist. There are fourteen colored Baptist churches in the county, and perhaps not twenty-five negro communicants of any other denomination. Their pastors, of course, are men of color, and generally good men, not always well educated.

Before the Civil War they worshiped in the same church with their master, were baptized and attended by the same pastor, and came to the Lord's Supper along with those they served. In some places, as for instance at Bruington and Mattapony, seats were assigned them in one end of the church house. In addition, they generally had services peculiarly their own, the pastor sometimes attending, and one or more white deacons, but the colored brethren doing most of the speaking and praying. They sang remarkably well: the writer has heard as flowing, melodious, and enthusiastic music, though of course not so artistic, among them as anywhere among musical devotees. In our opinion, it is safe to say that out from among these rude and unlettered assemblages have gone hundreds of devoted souls to join the choir invisible, giving praise to Him that was slain and lives again. Such was the really religious element among the colored people. They were not by any means all religious, and of those who were so by profession some were hypocritical and used the church as a cloak for their moral deformities. These, however, were exceptional cases.

It were hard to give to our colored people more than their meed of praise for the prevailing patience, forbearance, and faithfulness amidst many opportunities and seductions of freedom during the Civil War. At that time nearly all of the white males were in the army, yet in a large majority of instances the men and women staid by their mistress and the children, and labored on to the end. They deserve a monument.

It would be going too far to claim that the negro is naturally inclined to piety, since the inspired word assures us that " the hearts of men are fully set in them to do evil "; but it is not too much to say that as slaves they were more susceptible to religious impressions and more ecstatic in their religious joys and experiences than is common among men—albeit in general not so wise and judicious as most of the other races.

Perhaps a better and more distinct view can be had by presenting the colored people of our county in types of the several classes.

1. Osborne Bowler: Was a house servant belonging to Mr. John Bagby. He made no pretense to religion, was indeed prejudiced against it, possibly because he saw it on its deformed side in false professors, and not in its reality. Yet he was an ideal houseman and a real gentleman. He stayed by his mistress to the last. After the war he bought a few acres of land and lived by himself with his family, though he never lost the attachment which bound him to the children of his old master. Osborne was a man of economy and thrift and secured a competency; but he died out of the church.

2. Washington Lewis: Belonged to Garrett Carlton near the Courthouse. He was a tall, well formed mulatto, a mechanic by trade. He paid his master so much per month and pocketed all that remained over of his earnings, his master consenting to this arrangement. He was sincerely religious and a leader among his people. Washington was a gifted speaker, being

fluent, sensible, self-possessed; and being naturally graceful, frequently spoke in their meetings for worship. During the war he disappeared and was reported as living in Washington city.

3. Beverly Sparks: Was a slave of Dr. William B. Todd at Belmont. He was carriage driver, house servant, and body servant, in a word, factotum to his master. Beverly was taught to read and write, and being bright of mind, gathered a good store of information, which eventually served him in good stead. He was a mulatto of bright color. He joined the church at an early age, and after the war became an efficient minister and pastor at Zion, a branch of old Mattapony. Beverly's work, coming at such a time, was fundamental and valuable. He left a son, Mark, who is a worthy successor of an honored father.

4. Toliver Ross: Was dark of color, cunning as a fox, and sharp as a crow. He belonged in name to old Billy Brown, but paying his master a stipend he largely controlled his time, using it for his own purposes. He married a likely girl at Col. P.'s, and there most of his time was spent. By certain blandishments and tricks of art he quite gained the confidence of the colonel, and by and by carried the keys. Soon the colonel's wheat and corn bins began to show signs of depletion, and he called Ross up and engaged him to watch for and catch the rogue. The rogue was never caught.

5. Old Uncle Killis (Achilles): Might possibly have been a native African. He was lean, stoop-shouldered, and low in stature, with the characteristic thick lips and flat nose; he was gray-headed when I was a boy. Some people around were skeptics, and some wicked, but Uncle Killis believed in " 'ligion " and in his pastor (Parson Todd), and was always in his seat on the front bench next the partition. He would sit calm and attentive for an hour, till by and by the preacher kindled into warmth, then you would be sure to hear from Uncle Killis. Beginning on a low note, but with rising inflection, he would give utterance to a peculiar strain, half moan, half groan, presently swell-

ing out and filling every niche and corner of the grand old church house, and reëchoing from the heavy walls and high arched ceiling. The venerable pastor would throw a passing glance that way, draw a long breath and proceed with his discourse until Uncle Killis waked up again. The effect, though passing ludicrous to many, was greatly impressive to the few who could rightly appreciate the situation.

6. Charlotte: Was a low, full-set, black woman belonging to R. H. B. She was very loud in her profession of santification, and sure to be at church. In times of revival—indeed she was not particular about that, any meeting would do—Charlotte could sing as loud, get as happy, and shout as boisterously as any of the saints, but unfortunately she had a bad and persistent habit, which held her all the week, and at spare times even on Sunday, of stealing whatever she could lay her hands upon, and without respect of persons.

7. Aunt Miami and her daughter Isabel: Were not French but African cooks. They could roast your pig or your turkey, boil your Old Virginia ham, bake you an oven of bread, or your apple pie, to please the palate of an epicure. I have never seen the trained colored cook of eastern Virginia surpassed in the culinary art.

8. This paper would not be at all complete were I to fail to mention "Aunt Polly," the wise though sable dominie of the cradle, the trundle bed, and the nursery. She was old when I knew her, slow of manner, dignified in demeanor, dressed in modest fashion, with the unfailing headdress of a muslin cap with ruffles in front, and was known in every "great house" as "Mammy." Mammy Polly was fond of children, having once been a child herself; though when that far-away time was, the next oldest member of the family had never understood. She knew what to do with a baby that was colicky, that had measles, whooping cough, sore throat, or the thousand and one maladies that affect children. She was about the only person I ever knew who could sit and rock a baby all day, and hardly leave her seat to eat dinner. The dear old sister

is gone now, and I fear me that no one will ever come to take her place. True, she was autocratic in her day and sphere, but she nursed my grandmother, she nursed my mother, she nursed me, and we will never forget Mammy.

9. Her counterpart was " Grannie," whose sole business it was to see after the colored brats of all colors and sizes, while the mothers spun the cotton, wove the cloth, or milked the cow. She wielded the rod too, as she was obliged to, the rascallions were so mischievous.

10. One other character we must mention, and that of some importance—at least in his own estimation. It was very common on each one of the large plantations to have a " head man," who swayed the scepter over all the rest of the slaves, himself a colored man: " Uncle Robin " was such an one. When master was on hand Robin was obsequious and humble, but Robin was not honest as the day is long, nor mild as a May morn, when master was away; and now, being a public officer, was much afield. Should one of the boys come short, or even one of the girls be disobedient, Robin was sure to threaten with and often apply the rod, and that in no measured way. Indeed, Robin was more an object of terror if possible than the dread " overseer." A head man was often tyrannical and severe.

For some years before the war, especially after the days of Nat. Turner and the insurrection in Southampton county, it was common in every neighborhood to have a " patrol," consisting of a half-dozen white men, who were to traverse the roads and plantations and see that order was preserved among the negroes. Woe then to the unlucky darky who was caught away from home after nine o'clock in the night, unless indeed he was armed with a pass from " Old Master," saying, " Tom (Dick, or whatever the name was) has liberty to pass to his wife's house," or such like. This gave rise to a noted couplet much used in that day: " Run boys, run, the patterroll er comin' ".

Aristocracy among negroes.—We talk much about English aristocracy, with its king, barons, dukes, etc., and sometimes we hear a little talk about aristocracy even in America. The old-time King and Queen negro was as aristocratic as any of them. A slave of one of the richer men and on one of the great plantations, looked down with a supreme contempt upon his neighbor who happened to be the property of a poor man. One of the latter class could not associate with the lordly family of the man of the higher estate, and if such a suggestion was made it was met with contempt. Jim Hill, who was the property of P. T., was looked upon as a "poor man's nigger," but he ventured to aspire to the hand of a daughter of Moses Brown, who was one of a large body of servants belonging to Col. F. "No, sir!" said Moses, "does dat nigger who 'longs to P. T. want to marry a darter of Col. F.'s Moses? He shan't have my darter." But Jim did get the girl and became very prosperous.—On one occasion soon after the war an old colored sister had lost some chickens, and a man named Jack, formerly belonging to a poor neighbor, had been arrested for stealing the chickens. When he was taken before the court, the good woman appeared as a witness against him. The Court, addressing the colored woman, said, "Do you know this boy?" She answered in the affirmative, saying she had known him a long time. "And what is his name?" asked the Court; she answered, "His name is Jack." "Well, who is Jack?" said the Court. "He is nothing but Jack, he is a poor white folks' nigger, he ain't got no entitle."

THE COLORED PEOPLE

By One of Themselves

A letter from Rev. M. H. Sparks, pastor of Zion Colored Church:

The colored people of King and Queen County, Va., are gradually moving up the road to civilization. As a whole they are polite and respectable. We are glad to say that in many homes family prayers are held every day; from such homes we look for young men and women with right principles.

They are buying land and pulling down the one-room log cabins and building up neat frame houses. They are buying good teams, nice buggies, farming implements, etc. A few have bought sawmills and have gone into the lumber business; a few are merchants,—but all are trying to make an honest and honorable living. The county has sent out some very able colored preachers, lawyers, and doctors, who are doing well in their line of work. The public schools have been of inestimable value to the colored youths of the county by leading the young minds from the dungeon of ignorance and superstition to higher planes of civilization. Rev. R. J. Ruffin, a very worthy man, has started a high school in the upper end of the county, which is doing much good in training young men and women to become better citizens and more useful in life.

The church has been our main source of training, spiritually, socially, morally, and financially. We have in the county fourteen churches (all Baptist). All of these churches have good Sunday schools, where the young are taught the word of God every Sunday morning. In nearly all of these churches a few faithful women have banded themselves together in Home and Foreign Mission societies which are doing much good in the Master's cause. These churches have a total membership of about 3,300 souls. They are pastored by upright Christian gentlemen who have the moral support and respect of both races. The moral condition of the county (among the colored) is largely due to the pastors who have taken high ground on all matters of morality. They do not teach that morality is Christianity, but they do hold that Christians ought to be moral in every particular,—having one wife or husband, being honest in one's dealings with all people, and obeying the civil law in every respect. They teach that Christianity is more than talk and that people who want or expect to be citizens of heaven should strive to be good citizens on earth.

We may not be considered as having gotten on the

first round of the ladder, but thank God we have our eyes looking up the ladder, and will climb it some day.

The feeling between the two races in the county is kind and friendly; there may be a few hot heads in each race, but the best people of each race have too much of the spirit of Christ to cherish any ill will towards their fellow-men. I may say here that if all of this country was like King and Queen County, I believe that the subject of the race problem would cease to be agitated, and would become as the dead things of the past. One of the best white preachers of the county said that " There is no race problem."

We pray that the people of each race who like to kindle bad feelings between the races may ever stay from the grand old county.

PART IV
MISCELLANIES

CHAPTER XVI

FAMILY AND INDIVIDUAL RECORDS

Rev. A. Bagby, D. D., Richmond, Va.:

My Dear Sir—As a lifelong citizen of the county of King and Queen, and one whose ancestors for several generations have resided there, I naturally feel a deep interest in the success of a most worthy enterprise which you have undertaken, viz.: to write a brief history of this royal old county and its most prominent families.

If a true history could be obtained of all the families of this noteworthy county, it would prove a most valuable contribution to the history of Virginia, as "history is biography" and "biography is history."

As correct data are difficult to obtain, and I am too young to have known personally many of the older heads of these families, the few incidents I am able to relate in this connection must in large measure be traditional. No county in the State of Virginia has enjoyed more, or more deservedly, the reputation for the most conservative citizenship and the highest standard of manhood as the leading characteristics of her people. Whilst they have always been most zealous advocates of religious liberty and the entire divorcement of church and state as one of the basic principles of governmental faith, yet in the line of duty they have ever been found faithful in its discharge, whether in matters pertaining to religion or the obligations of citizenship. They adhere strictly to that rule of righteousness, "Render therefore unto Cæsar the things which are Cæsar's, and unto God the things that are God's."

It will not be claimed that this is a peculiar people, occupying a higher plane than other people, but owing to the isolation of this section there have been fewer changes wrought by the influx of foreign population, and hence the blood of the cavaliers still courses in the veins of succeeding generations. The most noticeable changes now to be observed in the population of this grand old county are due to the liberal contributions that have been made to other sections by the young men, and in many instances whole families, who have gone out over this and other States, forming, as it were, streams of blessing to enrich the locality of their adoption and reflecting credit upon the place of their nativity, thus proving themselves worthy sons of noble sires. One feature of the early history of the county of King and Queen, so far as I am informed, has never been very accurately recorded: I refer to the boundaries of the parishes and the locations of the old Established churches of Colonial days.

Bishop Meade's very valuable work on the old churches and ministers of Virginia affords the only reliable data we have seen recorded touching this subject, and yet that record is incomplete.

The county of King and Queen has been called the "Shoestring County," because of its extreme length; it stretches out along the northern bank of the Mattapony and York Rivers from Caroline to the Gloucester County line, a distance of sixty-five miles, while its mean width is only eight miles. The lower portion of the county was comprised in Stratton Major parish, and the leading church in that parish was Stratton Major Church, the site of which, I have no doubt, has been located where the ruins of a church are still visible on the Milford estate, the home place of the late P. Thornton Pollard, and now owned and occupied by his granddaughter, Mrs. H. J. Dudley. When or how that church was destroyed we are unable to ascertain. A church house was built near by, but a few miles higher up the county, and called "The New Church," presumably to take the place of the one which had been destroyed. I suppose the church house now used by the Methodists, and known as "The Old Church," to be the same as the New Church above referred to. Then came St. Stephen's parish, the exact boundaries of which I have been unable to ascertain. In that parish was no doubt St. Stephen's Church—perhaps the most prominent church in the county. I take it for granted that it is the same building now used by the Baptists, the name of which has been changed to Mattapony. It is a large and substantially built church, in the form of a cross, is well preserved and in fine repair. The congregation which worships there are proud of their inheritance, and worthily use it for the glory of God.

In Drysdale parish I have traced the distinctly marked foundation of the " Park Church," located a few miles above Newtown. That church was also in the shape of a cross, and from the size of its base, I am sure was a large and important structure, though of its history I find no record. The rectory, with its walls of massive thickness, is still standing, occupied as a private residence. There was also in this latter parish a chapel located near a small stream which still bears the name of Chapel Creek, and the hill beyond is known as Chapel Hill.

You have requested me to give you some account of the most prominent families of the upper portion of the county of King and Queen, and especially of the Dew and Garnett families, from which I am descended.

The principal land-holders in the upper section of the county about the beginning of the nineteenth century were represented by the following names, to wit: Beverly, Gatewood, Pendleton, Roane, Dew, Garnett, Boulware, Lyne, Pollard, Gresham, Kidd, Henshaw, Fogg, Minor, Powers, Hutchinson, Mann, Muse, Bates, Lumpkin, and Martin, whilst a little lower down the county were Hill, Fauntleroy, Webb, Throckmorton, Merriwether, Smith, Ryland, and Fleet.

Concerning each of the above-mentioned families, whose descendants have spread out over an extended territory, much of interest might be written if correct data could be obtained and space in your book would justify.

My paternal grandfather, Thomas R. Dew, was a large land- and slave-owner, and regarded as wealthy by the estimate of that day. He was born in 1765, and died in 1849; married Miss Lucy Gatewood, who survived him for eight years. As a product of that marriage there were six sons and three daughters, to wit: Dr. William Dew, Thomas R. Dew (afterwards professor and president of William and Mary College), Philip, John W., Benjamin F. (who was my father), L. Calvin, and Mrs. Colonel Hudgins of Mathews, Mrs. Colonel Thomas Gresham, and Mrs. Temple. He was a member of the Baptist Church, exerted a wide influence in his community, and served with distinction as captain in the War of 1812. Of the ancestry of Thomas R. Dew I have been able to gain very little definite information. He was the son of William Dew, whose father came from England and settled in Maryland,—William settling in King and Queen County, Virginia, and Thomas, a brother, in the county of Nansemond, from which county he (Thomas) served as a member of the House of Burgesses. Tradition has it that Thomas R. Dew was a descendant of Oliver Cromwell,—which impression, I am told, was strengthened by the fact that in his personality and sterling characteristics he was thought to resemble that distinguished man, who played a conspicuous part and developed one of the strongest characters in English history.

Dr. William Dew, the eldest son of Thomas R. Dew, located in King and Queen County, married Miss Susan Jones of King William, became an extensive and celebrated practitioner of medicine, and died greatly lamented by his community. He was the father of three sons, Thomas R. Dew, Jr.,[1] William Dew, Benjamin F. Dew, Jr.; and five daughters, Mrs. Hord, Mrs. Robert Gresham, Mrs. Hilliard, Mrs. Gregory, and Miss Lucy Dew. Thomas R. Dew, Jr., removed to Wytheville, Va. One of his sons, H. W. Dew, is a successful physician in Lynchburg, Va., and W. B. Dew holds an important government position in the State of Wyoming.

Prof. Thomas R. Dew is the subject of a special note in another part of your book.

Philip Dew married Miss Lucy DeJarnette, and located on his fine Windsor estate in Caroline county.

* Grandson of the first and nephew of the second Thos. R. mentioned.

He left three children, Thomas R. Dew, Dr. Philip A. Dew, and Mrs. Judge Welch.

John W. Dew married Miss Pendleton and left three children, Miss Mary E. (married Judge A. B. Evans of Middlesex), Roderick Dew of Plain Dealing, and Alice, who, after the death of her sister, also married Judge Evans, and who still lives to bless the Judge's home and to be a true helpmeet in his declining years.

Benjamin F. Dew, A. M. and B. L. of William and Mary College, lawyer, farmer, and teacher, was twice married, first to Miss Mary Susan Garnett, and after her death to Miss Bettie Queensberry. His eldest son, Dr. J. Harvie Dew, is enjoying a large and lucrative practice in the city of New York, where he settled in 1868, immediately after his graduation at the University of Virginia. John G. Dew, second and only other surviving son of Benjamin F., after his graduation in the law department of the University of Virginia, settled in his native county of King and Queen, where he practiced his chosen profession of the law for many years, being Judge of the County Court for sixteen years, and is now Second Auditor of the State of Virginia. He married Miss Lelia, daughter of Dr. Samuel G. Fauntleroy of the same county.

L. Calvin Dew married Miss Boulware and died in early manhood, leaving four children, Mrs. Thomas B. Henley, Mrs. A. C. Acree, D. Boone Dew,—who yielded up his life on the altar of his country, having been killed in the first engagement after joining Company H, Ninth Virginia Cavalry,—and Robert S. Dew.

Of the three daughters of the first Thomas R. Dew, Mrs. Colonel Hudgins was the mother of Colonel William P. Hudgins, who holds an important railway position in the State of Texas; Mrs. Temple left no children; and Mrs. Colonel Gresham, had five sons, Rev. Edward Gresham (who was the father of Walter Gresham of Galveston, Texas), Colonel T. Robert Gresham, William D. Gresham, Dr. Henry Gresham, and Dr. Charles Gresham, all of whom were prominent men in their respective spheres and localities.

Colonel Reuben Merriwether Garnett, my maternal

grandfather, was the son of Reuben Garnett, and his mother was a Miss Jamison. Colonel Garnett married, first, Miss Pendleton, a daughter of Captain James Pendleton, who served with distinction in the War of the Revolution. From this marriage two sons and two daughters survived him. Dr. John Muscoe Garnett, the elder son, married Miss Hancock of Chesterfield, and lived at his beautiful country home, Lanefield, in King and Queen County. The radiating influence of his Christian life was shed over the whole community as it was most beautifully exemplified in his own home. His only surviving son, John M. Garnett, Jr., with his sisters, Misses Nannie and Fannie, still reside at the old homestead. Of the elder daughters, Mrs. Dr. C. H. Ryland resides in Richmond, Va., Mrs. Dr. W. L. Broaddus at Bowling Green, Va., and Mrs. Rev. F. B. Beale at Indian Neck, Va.

R. M. Garnett, the other son of Colonel Garnett, lived through a long and happy life at Peach Grove in King and Queen; he married Miss Bettie A. Williams of Fredericksburg, and left the following children: Muscoe H. Garnett, a prominent merchant of Richmond; James W. Garnett of King and Queen; Mrs. Gresham, the widow of Colonel William Gresham; Mrs. Fleet, the widow of James R. Fleet, Jr.; and Mrs. Rev. F. W. Claybrook.

Colonel Garnett's daughters were Mrs. Benjamin F. Dew, mentioned heretofore, and the first Mrs. John N. Ryland, who was the mother of Mrs. Joseph H. Gwathmey of King William County, and of John N. Ryland, Jr., of King and Queen. Colonel Garnett left no children by his second marriage, with Miss Hutchinson.

The Garnetts were among the best people in the land, universally respected and beloved, and were noted for their modesty and gentleness of bearing. Colonel Reuben M. Garnett was a man of unusual business qualifications, backed by a sound judgment, and his aid and advice were as frequently sought as they were freely given. Though not a lawyer by profession, such was the confidence of the people in his judgment and capacity that he was frequently consulted in regard to legal matters, and it is probable that no lawyer in the county was called on to prepare so many deeds and wills as he was, and, so far as the writer is informed, not one was ever overturned if attacked.

Of the Boulware family, there were two half-brothers, Mr. Lee Boulware and Leroy Boulware. The former had a son, John Boulware, a professor in the Columbian College, succeeded for a short time by his brother William, who afterwards served as Minister to Naples, during the administration of President James K. Polk. Mr. A. L. Boulware, a prominent attorney and president of the First National Bank of Richmond, Va., was a grandson of Leroy Boulware. Mr. J. B. Kidd, a prominent merchant, and manufacturer of the famous " Pinmoney Pickles," and Dr. W. L. Broaddus, a distinguished physician of Bowling Green, Va., are grandsons of Lee Boulware.

All the families whose names are referred to above were of the type of the old Virginia gentry, who lived in comfort on their well-tilled farms. Every such plantation was a miniature principality where slavery existed, 'tis true, in name as well as legal form, but so gentle was the discipline that it resembled in regulation a large, well-ordered family, where kindness and consideration combined to produce the utmost good feeling and contentment; which tended to the betterment of both classes. I esteem it a great privilege to have been permitted to get an insight into the habits and customs, the home life and domestic relations, which prevailed on the old Virginia plantations in the ante-bellum days. No man or set of men, who never entered into the sacred precincts of that life, can begin to appreciate, much less describe, the contentment and happiness which then prevailed on the part of the negro as well as his protector and humane benefactor. The latter, though nominally and legally his master, was in the truest sense the negro's next friend and guardian.

I can truly say that, in the abstract, I do not believe in the institution of slavery, that I am sincerely grateful for its abolition before I could become the owner of one. But from my youthful impressions of conditions as they prevailed in that section of Virginia, the leisure afforded for cultivation and improvement on the part of the whites, and the civilizing and educational advantages afforded the negro by his contact and association, even though in a menial position, with the whites, produced an interdependence and a refining influence upon both races which does not and cannot now exist. It was not unusual to find among the butlers, coachmen, and body servants of " ye olden time," in manner and deportment, a perfect model for Lord Chesterfield, a specimen of the true gentleman in grace and elegance. No system of education that has been or ever will be devised can by any possibility, with the new-issue negro, produce either a class or an individual of that degree of educational refinement.

Coming on life's stage just in time to catch some inspiration from the golden age of Virginia's history, between the years 1850 and 1860, to witness and in some measure to participate in the fiercest revolutionary struggle ever recorded in the annals of history, to suffer the pangs and humiliation of defeat, and then pass through the far worse period of reconstruction, my youthful impressions have strengthened with the passing years, that the intrepid courage and valor of the sons of Virginia and the Southland should challenge the admiration of the world. And the subsequent struggle with poverty, beset with difficulties on every hand, seeking to steer the ship of State between the breakers, to provide for the education and upbuilding of the rising generation, and at the same time carry the load of an emancipated race whose lowest passions and prejudices have been appealed to,—not for their good or elevation, but to clog and impede the progress of resuscitation and civilization and the upbuilding of the Anglo-Saxon race,—has no parallel in ancient or modern history. No people have ever met more bravely the obstacles and dangers in their pathway than the people of this Southland. No stronger evidence could be adduced of the character and manhood of their ancestors, than the chivalry, courage, and manliness exhibited by the sons in the worse than "fiery furnace" through which they have passed, yet with honor untarnished and presenting a self-sacrificing nobility unequaled in the world's history. The consciousness of duty faithfully performed is the God-given reward of the Confederate soldier, but the memory of his self-sacrificing devotion and patriotic endeavors should ever animate the Southern heart, and arouse feelings of the deepest gratitude in the breasts of all future generations. Indeed, every true American citizen, fired by the zeal of a broad-minded patriotism, will look with admiring gaze upon the most wonderful exhibition of valor and heroism ever recorded in any age.

The upper portion of King and Queen County, from an early period down to the present time, has been blessed with a succession of good schools, which aided materially in training the sturdy youth of the community in the way of truth and knowledge. The first school of which we have any information was taught by Mr. Donald Robertson, who was famous as a teacher. President Madison when a youth attended that school, and a story is related of his impressions of that section, to the effect that, years afterwards, Mr. Madison inquired of Mr. Roane, the Representative of that district in Congress, " How are the people in Drysdale parish getting along? " He further said that he was greatly impressed as a boy with the poverty of the land and the fact that the farmers traded lands every March (evidently having reference to the sandy soil and the effect on it of the March winds). Mr. Roane bore willing testimony to the prosperous condition of the people, and remarked that, if a large loan were desired, that was the only portion of his district which could readily furnish the accommodation. A succession of good schools followed continuously up to the breaking-out of the Civil War, and indeed till the establishment of a system of public free schools.

I am aware that this paper is but a rambling sort of review of a section of the county of King and Queen in which my life has been spent. By one, at least, I can say that this territory will ever be regarded as hallowed ground, and that he does and will continue to cherish a sacred memory of the noble names herein recorded, whether the same is the result of kinship, personal knowledge, historical data, or only a legend of the past.

With great respect, I am,

Yours truly and fraternally,

JOHN G. DEW.

We give here extracts from a letter from the venerable and beloved Dr. William F. Bland, who passed away in a year or two after this writing:

Glencoe Station, July 4th, 1902.

ESTEEMED FRIEND:

Your very acceptable letter of the 21st was duly received. I would have answered it sooner, but have been quite unwell. I greatly appreciate your expressions of sympathy for my wife and myself in our bereavement, and shall never forget the earnest prayer you made for the recovery of my dear Willie when he had typhoid fever. Wife and I are both feeble and have many infirmities belonging to old age. I am already older than any of my ancestors, being seventy-five, and am trying so to live that I may meet my dear children and other loved ones in the spirit world. It would give me great pleasure to meet you and talk over the past. I wish you the best of success in writing the annals of the old county, though I do not think that I can render you much help. The Laneville House (Corbin place) was built in Colonial times of brick—I think it was one hundred feet long by twenty feet wide—and was occupied by Richard Corbin, the king's deputy receiver-general. It was heired by his son, James Park, whom I can recollect. My father purchased it in 1858.

Pleasant Hill was a large two-story brick building, about fifty-two by forty feet, built before the Revolution by Augustine Moore of Chelsea for John, commonly called Speaker Robinson, who married his daughter Lucy. It was owned by the Henry family afterwards.

Newington, the birthplace of Carter Braxton and of other prominent men, was a large two-story building; was afterwards owned by the Harwood family, notably Samuel F. Harwood.

Clifton, I have heard, was owned by Speaker Robinson, and occupied by his daughters, one of whom married Col. William Boyd. Both the house here and the one at Newington were burned and each was rebuilt, the latter by Capt. R. H. Spencer.

You requested a brief sketch of my father and others. Col. Robert Bland was born May, 1800, and was twelve years old when his father, Capt. Robert Bland, served in the War of 1812. My father was an extensive farmer, colonel of militia, presiding justice of the court, and died in his seventy-first year. Dr. James T. Boyd, my uncle, was born in 1806; was a successful physician and farmer, and died in 1855. I graduated in medicine in 1849—was the oldest of twelve children. Dr. James E. Bland graduated in medicine in 1856, and died in his sixty-seventh year; was a good physician and citizen. Col. Robert M. Spencer, who lived at Clifton, was a prominent and highly esteemed citizen. Capt. Robert H. Spencer served in the Confederate army, is also a highly esteemed citizen. Alexander Dudley, a talented lawyer, was the founder of the Richmond and York River Railroad and its president when he died. There were many other worthy and reliable citizens in the same neighborhood, among them J. W. Courtney, Samuel Tunstall, Dr. Garrett, and his brother, Thomas W., W. B. Bird, Samuel F. Harwood, and others.

In regard to churches in the neighborhood, the " Old Church " must have been built in Colonial times, judging from a tombstone near it over two hundred years old. I have heard that it was sold, bought by a man named Smith and given to the Methodists. When I was a boy it was used by the Methodists and Baptists, but the latter built another house near by (Olivet).

Very truly and sincerely your friend,

WM. F. BLAND.

CAPTAIN A. F. BAGBY,

Was the second captain of Company K, Thirty-fourth Virginia Infantry, J. R. Bagby, the first captain, having been promoted major.

By himself:

"Alexander Fleet Bagby was born at Stevensville, King and Queen. Attended school at Stevensville, Richmond College, and V. M. I.; was among the first to enlist in defense of Southern rights, and was active in organizing the King and Queen Artillery—afterwards infantry; was elected lieutenant at the organization, subsequently captain; after the war, in business in Richmond, and then located in Tappahannock, Va. Married F. S. Walker."

EDWARD BENJAMIN BAGBY,

Son of the foregoing, was born in King and Queen September 29th, 1865; educated at Aberdeen Academy, ———— University, and Yale Divinity School; was located as a minister at Clifton Forge, Va., then at Newport News. In 1891 he was located at Washington, D. C.; chaplain in Congress, 1893————; pastor of ———— Church in Washington, 1891 to the present time; in eight years this church has enrolled eight hundred members. Married Virginia May Grimes of Baltimore. A second son of Captain Bagby, Richard, is also an efficient minister.

DR. RICHARD HUGH BAGBY

Richard Hugh Bagby, D. D., born June 16, 1820; married Motley; died October 29th, 1870. A son of John, 1791-1878. Educated at Richmond and Columbian Colleges; taught a session or two and studied law, but answering a higher call, was ordained at Mattapony in 1842, and became pastor at Bruington, which he served twenty-seven years; in 1869 was made field secretary of the Baptist State Mission Board, in which office he died. His body reposes under a monument at Bruington.

He was for a time president of the General Associa-

THOMAS ROANE DEW
Professor of Philosophy and President of the College
of William and Mary.

tion, and always an active participant in that and other kindred bodies. His preaching was practical, evangelical, pungent, and wonderfully forceful, acceptable, and effective, and he was in great demand wherever known. One who knew him well, himself a cultured and able man, says: "Dr. Bagby was one of the foremost men Virginia has given to the world." One of the most prominent and able citizens of Richmond says: "He was one of the two greatest men I ever met."

Dr. Bagby's sayings on his deathbed were embalmed in the *Religious Herald,* having been published more than once. He left two brothers, both having the D. D. from their Alma Mater, Columbian College, one at one time president of the Baptist General Association of Kentucky. Rev. H. A. Bagby, D. D., now of South Carolina, is his nephew, as also is A. Paul Bagby, Ph. D., of Kentucky.

CARTER BRAXTON

Carter Braxton, a signer of the Declaration of Independence, was a son of George and Mary Braxton, of Newington, whose bodies are interred at Mattapony Church, King and Queen. Mary was a daughter of Robt. Carter, President of Council. Carter was born at Newington Sept. 10, 1736, and died at Elsing Green, King William, Oct. 6, 1797. Carter graduated at William and Mary at the age of 19; married Judith Robinson of Middlesex. He was a member of the Virginia Committee of Safety named at the beginning of the Revolution. He served as a member of the Continental Congress from 1777 to 1783, and in 1785 on Commission of Public Safety with Thos. Jefferson; received vote of thanks from the Virginia Assembly. He had quite a number of descendants, notably Hon. Elliott Braxton, M. C.; Col. Carter Braxton, A. N. V., and Hon. A. C. Braxton of Staunton, member of the Constitutional Convention of 1902.

The Virginia Historical Society, acting through Mrs. R. N. Pollard, their King and Queen representative, has recently made an appropriation for restoring and relettering the tomb of George and Mary Braxton.

COLONEL JOHN M. BROOKE

(From the *Richmond Evening Leader*)

LEXINGTON, Dec. 15, 1906.—Colonel John M. Brooke, emeritus professor of physics and astronomy at the Virginia Military Institute, died here yesterday from the infirmities of old age. He was seventy-nine years old, and was one of Lexington's most distinguished citizens.

He was born near Tampa, Fla., December 18th, 1826, and was the son of General George M. Brooke of Virginia, a distinguished soldier of the War of 1812. His mother was Miss Lucy Thomas of Duxbury, Mass. At the age of fifteen he entered the United States Navy, and reported to Captain Farragut on the *Delaware*. Later he was transferred to the sloop-of-war *Cyene*. Returning home he entered the naval school at Annapolis.

He graduated in 1847, and several years later was on the coast survey. From 1851 to 1853 he was stationed at the Naval Observatory, Washington, D. C. For several years previous to 1860 he cruised in Japanese and Chinese waters, making surveys of islands in the Pacific and a part of the eastern coast of Japan. The destruction of his vessel by a typhoon occurring in 1859 while in Yeddo, Japan, Brooke remained at Yokohama until the following year. When the Japanese determined to send an embassy to the United States, Brooke was invited to accompany the vessel, which he consented to do.

His services were so highly appreciated by the Japanese that they offered him a purse of $60,000, but he refused to take anything.

Captain Brooke cast his lot with the Confederate navy in the Civil War, and in 1861 applied, in the construction of the *Virginia* (the *Merrimac*), the principle of extended and submerged ends.

His invention of deep-sea sounding apparatus revolutionized communications between Europe and America, as it made possible the laying of the first intercontinental telegraph line in the world. The *Virginia*

(*Merrimac*) was his suggestion. In 1866 Colonel Brooke was appointed professor of physics at the Virginia Military Institute.

His first wife was Miss Lizzie Garnett, sister of General Richard Brooke Garnett. His second wife, who survives, was a Miss Corbin. Two children also survive, Lieutenant George M. Brooke, of the United States Army, and Mrs. Willis, wife of Professor H. Parker Willis, of Washington and Lee University.

THE BROOKE FAMILY

Compiled from " Virginia Historical Records," by Professor St. George T. Brooke.

1. Humphrey, died 1738.

2. Colonel George, of Mantapike, born 1728; died April, 1782; was a member of the House of Burgesses, of the Committee of Safety, the Virginia Convention, and was colonel in the Virginia division of the Revolutionary army.

Robert Brooke, Knight of the Golden Horseshoe, was a brother of Humphrey. A second brother was William, who had four sons,—Richard of Mantapike, John, William, Jr., and Robert. Richard probably inherited Mantapike from his grandfather. General George Mercer Brooke, a son of Richard, entered the army in 1808, was major in battles of Lundy's Lane and Fort Erie in 1814, and was promoted to major-general.

HON. BENNEHAN CAMERON

In June, 1905, many of the people about King and Queen Courthouse were much interested by the coming into their midst of a handsome, portly gentleman, a distant relative of the Harwoods and others, whose name heads this sketch. He appeared a man of culture, refined instincts, patriotism, and high moral characteristics, and he met a most cordial reception. Mr. Cameron was born fifty years ago in Stagville, N. C. His father was Hon. Paul Carrington Cameron, one of the most valuable citizens of North Carolina. His paternal grandfather was Judge Duncan Cameron, one of the ablest jurists of his time. We are pleased to note that this gentleman is to be counted a great-grandson of old King and Queen, inasmuch as his relationship to the distinguished Chief-Justice Ruffin was that of grandson. He is a graduate of the Virginia Military Institute of July 4th, 1875; is one of the leading agriculturists and stock-breeders of the State; and has been associated with a number of the great men of the country. He served most acceptably as president of the North Carolina Agricultural Society, and was among the foremost agents in the establishment of the great Seaboard Air Line Railroad. The writer of the sketch from which this is taken adds to all this that Colonel Cameron could have had any office in the gift of his people, so greatly was he honored among them.

COL. WILLIAM CAMPBELL,

Who was a captain in the Revolutionary War, was from King and Queen County, and a close friend of Gen. Washington. He raised a quota of men in King and Queen and was assigned to duty with the First Virginia regiment. After the war he was commissioned major in the regular army, and assigned to command the arsenal at Harper's Ferry. He resigned about 1800. (See Heitman's Historical Register of United States Army.)

Judge John G. Dew—now Second Auditor of Virginia—kindly sends the following regarding his distinguished relative, that accomplished scholar,

PROF. T. R. DEW

"Thomas Roderick Dew, son of Thomas R. Dew and Lucy Gatewood, his wife, was born in King and Queen County, December 5th, 1802. His father was a large land- and slave-holder in that county, who had served for a short time in the War of the Revolution and was a captain in the War of 1812. Thomas R., the son, was graduated from William and Mary College in 1820, after which he traveled two years in Europe.

"On October 16th, 1826, he was elected Professor

of History and Political Law in William and Mary College. The chair of history, which was established for the first time under Rev. Robert Keith, in 1820, was developed by Mr. Dew into one of the first importance. At that time history and political science were scarcely known among the studies of an American college. In 1836 Mr. Dew became president, and the college, under his enlightened management, achieved a degree of prosperity never previously known. In 1840 the number of students in attendance was one hundred and forty. The time was one of great political activity, and his lectures on the restrictive system, depicting the evils of the tariff system, were very popular, not only with the students, but with the Southern public, and are thought to have had much weight in shaping the opposition to the tariff laws of 1828 and 1832. His essay in favor of slavery had a marked effect, it is said, on the slavery question. But his greatest work was his " Digest of the Laws, Customs, Manners, and Institutions of Ancient and Modern Nations," embracing lectures delivered to his class. Dr. Herbert B. Adams pronounced this work the most thorough and comprehensive course on history of which he had found any record during this early period. Mr. Dew contributed largely to the *Southern Review*. In 1845 he married Miss Matilda Hay, daughter of Dr. Hay of Clarke County, Va., and died suddenly on his wedding trip. The faculty bore formal testimony in their minutes that it was difficult to decide whether his wisdom as president, his ability as a professor, or his excellence as a man, was most to be admired.

" He died in Paris, France, August 6, 1846."

EUBANK FAMILY

Coldwater, King and Queen Co., Va.,
November 10th, 1904.

Dear Brother Bagby:

In answer to your inquiry, my great-grandfather was named William, and great-grandmother was named Jane, and my grandfather Richard was born June 11th,

1767. My grandmother was named Elizabeth, born October 23d, 1768. They raised six children, three boys and three girls. My father was the fifth child, named Philip Eubank, born May 28th, 1806; married Susan Jeffries in the year 1828. My father died the seventh day of March, 1848, some forty-two years old; left five boys, all very young. My mother lived thirty-eight years, one month and twenty-two days longer than my father; she left four sons; brother John was killed in the battle around Petersburg on the 15th day of June, 1864. She left only four sons, twenty-three grandchildren, and six great-grandchildren. My father was said to be one of the very best of men, lived and died member of the Mattaponia Church, under the pastorate of old Brother William Todd. If my good old superintendent, Colonel John Pollard, was living, he could give you the history of my father. Brother William Todd baptized me the 23d day of August, 1848. I was then only fourteen years old; afterwards you became my pastor until I moved to the neighborhood of Ware's Church. The old Mattaponia has now a dear place in my heart; there I was brought up in the Sunday school under the leadership of Brother John Pollard, superintendent, and under your pastoral care. I often think of you along with my boyhood days, and never can forget you. Whenever I have the privilege to meet you I feel like saying, Here is my first pastor and teacher in the Gospel of our Lord and Saviour Jesus Christ. I revere and reverence you as no other pastor, though I have had four since. I have loved all the pastors that have presided over me. I am quite old now, in my seventy-first year, occupying some important places in my church; deacon ever since 1857, superintendent of the Sunday school for a number of years, treasurer for twenty years. As you are my father in Gospel, is why I name these different places holding in my church, by no means in a boastful spirit. My dear brother, if I am saved it will be by the unmerited grace of God.

Your Brother I hope in Christ,

WILLIAM J. EUBANK.

CHARLES B. FLEET,

Youngest son of Dr. Christopher B. and Lucy Anne Fleet (*née* Semple), was born at Mordington in 1843. His mother—widowed—was married in 1853 to Rev. William F. Broaddus, and removed to Fredericksburg. Mr. Fleet served through the war of '61-'65 in the Fredericksburg Artillery, the first permanent officers of which were: Carter M. Braxton, captain, Edward S. Marye, first lieutenant, etc. He was in all the principal battles of the war, and surrendered with General Lee at Appomattox. His battery fired the first shot in the battle of Gettysburg and the last artillery shot at Appomattox.

COLONEL ARCHIBALD R. HARWOOD,

Was a son of Margaret Roane, a daughter of Thomas Roane; was born at Newington. He was for long years a member of the Virginia House of Delegates, and then of the Senate of Virginia. He was nominated by the Democratic party for Congress, and defeated by the late R. M. T. Hunter, who was elected by seventeen votes.

SAMUEL FAUNTLEROY HARWOOD

Samuel Fauntleroy Harwood, lawyer, son of Archibald Roane Harwood and Martha Fauntleroy, was born at the country home, Newington, King and Queen County, February 26th, 1817; educated at Rumford Academy and in Richmond; served for ten years as deputy clerk of King and Queen County. In 1847 he was elected to the State Senate and served three years, being the unexpired term of Carter M. Braxton, deceased; declined reëlection; studied law while a member of the Senate, and practiced his profession successfully up to the commencement of the war. During the period of the war he acted as secretary and treasurer of the Richmond and York River Railroad Company, and after the war was one of the directors. In the spring of 1867 he removed to Texas and for about twenty months maintained a law partnership with his brother, Major

T. M. Harwood; returned to his old home in Virginia at the end of 1868, and resumed the practice of his profession. Married Bettie Brockenbrough March 16th, 1869. He was for many years vestryman in the Episcopal Church. On Wednesday, May 23d, 1906, he died, leaving behind him a beautiful example of an upright Christian gentleman.

COLONEL THOMAS MOORE HARWOOD,

A brother of S. F., born September, 1827; died January, 1900; married ———— Brown; educated at University of Virginia and Ballston Spa, N. Y.; removed to Texas in 1850, and practiced law at Gonzales. In 1880 was tendered a seat on supreme bench of Texas, but declined. Was for years regent of University of Texas. In June, 1861, joined army of C. S. A., and was captain and subsequently colonel. Was at battles of Corinth and Holly Springs, and afterwards served in Forest's command. Colonel Harwood was a courtly gentleman and a Christian, which is the highest type of man.

DR. W. S. B. HENRY
[Falls Church, Va., Dec. 15th.]

The death of Dr. William Scarborough Braxton Henry came as a shock to his friends and loved ones. It occurred suddenly on Saturday in Falls Church, Va., at the residence of his grandniece, Miss Sallie S. Beach. He had been sick but a week, and it was thought that danger was passed, when he was stricken with heart disease.

His funeral took place this afternoon at 2 o'clock, the interment being made in Oakwood Cemetery.

Dr. Henry had lived more than the threescore and ten years allotted to man. He was " an old Virginia gentleman " in every sense of the word, and by his courteous and affable manners made many friends among both old and young. He belonged to the old generation that is fast dying out.

He was born at the old homestead, Pleasant Hill, King and Queen County, Va., August 6th, 1827, but spent about twenty-five or thirty years in Washington. His father, Colonel James Hugh Henry, son of Judge James Henry, of the Continental Congress, was an officer in the War of 1812, fought at Norfolk, Va., and also in the District of Columbia at the time of the burning of Washington by the British forces under General Ross and Admiral Cockburn. Colonel Henry was twice married; his first wife, Anne Elizabeth Braxton, was the granddaughter of Carter Braxton, signer of the Declaration of Independence. Dr. Henry was this wife's son. His second wife, Anne Catherine Temple, received from the United States government until the time of her death a pension on account of the disability of her husband contracted during the War of 1812. This pension was carried to her during the Civil War through the Confederate lines under a flag of truce. The Colonel's six sons—three by each wife—were officers in the Confederate army.

Dr. Henry enlisted in Company B, Fortieth Virginia Regiment, serving six months, when he was appointed surgeon and sent to the Fourth Division of Camp Winder, and then to take charge of Camp Lee and Batteries Nos. 9 and 10. Afterwards he was made president of the Examining Board of the Confederate States. He resigned December 22d, 1863, going to his farm, "Shellie," in Richmond County, where he remained until the close of the war. He is survived by a half-brother, General Edward Moore Henry, of Norfolk, Va., ex-commander of the Grand Camp of Confederate Veterans of Virginia.

At one time he attended Richmond College, afterwards graduating in medicine from Jefferson College in Philadelphia. He was well known in many counties in Virginia as a physician.

During President Hayes' administration he was sent as physician to the Omaha and Winnebago agencies, in Nebraska. While there he was presented with the "Sauntee Peace Pipe," by the chief of the tribe. Later he was a clerk in the Patent Office.

Dr. Henry was a member of one of the proudest and most distinguished families of the Old Dominion.

It is the same as that which produced the immortal Patrick Henry. He is a lineal descendant of Sir Alexander Spotswood, one of the Colonial governors. The family is also related to the Braxtons, Scarboroughs, Carters of Shirley, Lees, Washingtons, Moores of Chelsea, Robinsons, Nelsons, Pages, and others equally well known. He married Miss Lucy Daingerfield.

Dr. Henry had been a member of the Baptist Church since his young manhood. He was a Christian gentleman, noble, brave, and true.

JONES FAMILY

The following are extracts from a letter to the editor by Hon. Alexander C. Jones, who left King and Queen in 1859 for Arkansas with his mother (Mary Courtney, widow of Hill Jones). The children were Elonisa, Thyresa Ann, Martha Jane, Amelia, Alexander C., William, and Hill, Jr. Alexander C. was a captain C. S. A. and a member of his State legislature. Having been wounded at the Wilderness battle he came to King and Queen on furlough; was at my house when Sheridan raided us in 1864, and missed capture narrowly. He was with us at the Reunion in May, 1907. A chivalrous soldier, a fine citizen, a Christian gentleman:

"About myself there is not much to write. Wife and I are in reasonably good health for old people. I will have lived to be seventy-five on the 8th of next March, my wife two years younger.

"We have four children, two sons and two daughters. My oldest son, Courtney, lives in Oklahoma and is doing well. Laman lives with me and is our main support. I have a married daughter in Pine Bluff, Ark., with three children. My other daughter, Mary, is a trained nurse, a graduate of a New Orleans institute. She has more than she can do in her profession and so we see very little of her.

"Only a week ago we were much shocked at the sudden death of my younger brother, Hill Jones. It seems strange that he should be taken first as he was my junior by eleven years. Hill was a good man and a Christian, deacon in our Baptist Church here, and a highly respected citizen. We shall all miss him much. Four children survive him, two sons and two daughters, all married and doing well.

" You will perhaps be surprised to hear that my oldest sister, Elonisa, still lives. She is now in her eighty-seventh year and has been remarkably active and healthy up to a year ago, but is now growing quite feeble. Only we two remain of the eight, including my mother, that moved to Arkansas."

WILLIAM LYNE

Perhaps in the annals of King and Queen County we find no more distinguished man than William Lyne the 2d, son of William the 1st, who came to Virginia from Bristol, England; settled first in Granville County, N. C., and removed thence to King and Queen County. William Lyne, the second of that name, was a most distinguished man in the House of Burgesses of May, 1769, when Lord Botetourt was governor of Virginia. He was a burgess from King and Queen also in the sessions of Nov. 7, 1769; May 21, 1770; and July 11, 1771. In 1775 he was a member of the Committee of Safety from King and Queen County. He was colonel in the Revolutionary War from 1776.

William Lyne married his first cousin, Lucy Foster Lyne, daughter of Henry Lyne.

Bishop Meade's book (page 414) says of Drysdale parish: " This parish lay partly in Caroline and partly in King and Queen County. Mr. William Lyne appears during the time to have been a faithful lay delegate."

MURDOCH FAMILY

J. Ryland Murdoch, born April 10th, 1873; died January 5th, 1906, Ontario, Cal. Married Miss Gilchrist, Philadelphia., June 12th, 1901. Baptized when 13 years of age at Bruington, King and Queen, by Rev. W. R. D. Moncure. Ordained at Bruington Church, September, 1897; when the Presbytery consisted of:

Dr. Charles H. Ryland, Dr. Harry Bagby, Dr. B. Cabell Hening, Rev. J. W. Ryland, Rev. Alexander Fleet, Rev. Frank Beale.

At Berlin, New Jersey, 2 years.

At Kennett Square, Penn., 2 years.

At Winchester, Va., 2 years.

At La Junta, Col., 1 year.

JUDGE THOMAS RUFFIN

This distinguished gentleman deserves more than a passing notice. The record we shall give is taken from an address delivered by Governor William A. Graham of North Carolina, afterwards Secretary of the Navy, and from other documents relating to the same subject:

Thomas Ruffin, the oldest child of his parents, was born at Newington, County of King and Queen, Va., the residence of his maternal grandfather, Thomas Roane, November 17th, 1787. His father, Sterling Ruffin, was a planter in the neighboring county of Essex; and he in turn was a son of Robert Ruffin, who years before had established his residence at Sweet Hall, King William County. Judge Ruffin's mother, Alice Roane, was of a distinguished family. She was a first cousin of Judge Spencer Roane, Chief Justice of Virginia; also of Thomas Ritchie, the distinguished editor of the *Enquirer* at Richmond; and also a first cousin of Dr. William Brokenborough, President of the Bank of Virginia. His father, having a respectable fortune, sought for his son the best education. He lived for a while in boyhood on the farm in Essex, attending school in the neighborhood. Thence he was sent to a classical academy in the village of Warrenton, N. C., then under the instruction of Mr. Marcus George, an Irishman, and a skillful instructor. Mr. George placed great faith in the rod, and did not spare it when he thought it needed. Judge Ruffin always retained a grateful and affectionate remembrance of Master George. He was next sent to the college of Nassau Hall, at Princeton, N. J. The late Governor James Iredell was in the class succeeding that of Mr. Ruffin, and became his room-mate. Thus began a friendship between these gentle-men, which terminated only in the death of Governor Iredell. Theodore Frelinghuysen, of New Jersey, was also his college associate, as was also Joseph R. Inger-soll. Mr. Ruffin then entered the law office of David Robertson, of Petersburg, where he was associated with Winfield Scott, the future general. This was in 1806. The year following, Sterling Ruffin, the father, changed his home from Virginia to Rockingham County, N. C., and his son soon afterwards followed him. After pur-suing his legal studies yet further, he was admitted to the bar in 1808. In 1809 he established his home at Hills-borough, and on the 9th of December of that year he was united in marriage to Miss Annie Kirkland of that town.

In 1813-'16 he served as a member of the legis-lature, and became Speaker of the House. His manner at the bar was diffident and his speech embarrassed, but the vigor of his understanding soon overcame all diffi-culties. His income from his practice has hardly ever been equaled in North Carolina. In 1825 he was ap-pointed Judge of the Superior Court, and in this position had universal admiration and acceptance. In the au-tumn of 1829 he was elected a Judge of the Supreme Court, and in 1833 he was elevated to the Chief-Justiceship. Few advocates ever equaled him in pre-senting so much solid thought in the same number of words, or in disentangling complicated facts and mak-ing a demonstration clear to the minds of the auditors. He thus became habituated to abstract and exact reason-ing. With an energy that pressed the business forward, a quickness in comprehending facts, patient habits of labor, he suffered no time to be lost, and yet there was no indecent haste. While he presided it was rare that any case before a jury occupied more than a single day. He held this position twenty-three years, and in these years he delivered a greater number of opinions than any other judge with whom he was associated. These opinions are found in twenty-five volumes of re-ports, and have been cited with approbation in many courts, both State and national, and even in Westminster Hall. He has been thought by many able lawyers to rank with Judge Spencer Roane of Virginia, and with that greatest of all the Chief-Justices, John Marshall. Hon. R. T. Bennett, himself an able lawyer, says of him, " I have read every opinion delivered by the late Chief-Justice Ruffin, and when I completed these readings, I said in my deepest thought, ' Chief-Justice Ruffin is the greatest judge who ever administered justice in an English-speaking community.' " Again, Senator Graham says of him that he wore the ermine as naturally and gracefully as if he had never been divested of its folds. When the great war between the States came on, Judge Ruffin was for the maintenance of the Union until he was sent to Washington to attend a peace conference, which had been suggested by Virginia with the faint hope of saving the country from a bloody strife. After he returned, at a great public meeting called to consider the question by his own people, the venerable judge mounted the platform and exclaimed, " I know not what others may say, but as for myself, I say Fight! Fight! Fight! " On the 15th of January, 1870, after an illness of but four days, he breathed his last, in the eighty-third year of his age. His end was resigned and peaceful, and in the consolation of an enlightened and humble Christian faith. For more than forty years he was a communicant of the Protestant Episcopal Church. His venerable companion, Annie (Kirkland) Ruffin, survived him.

This is the inscription upon Judge Ruffin's tomb in St. Matthew's churchyard, Hillsboro, N. C., by Hon. Paul C. Cameron, a son-in-law:

THOMAS RUFFIN
THE FIRST BORN OF
STERLING RUFFIN AND ALICE ROANE,
BORN AT NEWINGTON,
KING AND QUEEN COUNTY, VIRGINIA,
NOV. 17TH, 1787,
DIED AT HILLSBORO, ORANGE CO., N. C.,
JANUARY 15TH, 1870.

Graduated at Nassau Hall, Princeton, N. J., 1805,
Admitted to the Bar in N. C. in 1808.
Intermarried with Annie M. Kirkland
December 9th, 1809.

A member of the State Legislature, Speaker of the House of Commons; a trustee of the University; twice Judge of the Superior Court; in 1829, Justice of the Supreme Court, in which he presided for nineteen years as Chief Justice.

Labor ipse est voluptas.

In the 83rd year of his life, in full possession of his faculties, ripe in learning and in wisdom, crowned with public honors and with confidence, rich in the affection of his kindred and friends, he closed his long, active and useful life in the consolation of an enlightened and humble Christian faith.

"A man resolved and steady to his trust,
Inflexible to ill and obstinately just."

ROBERT RYLAND, A. M., D. D.

By ———— ————

This distinguished son of the county was the child of Josiah Ryland—for sixty-five years a deacon of Bruington Church—and Catharine Peachey.

He was born in 1805 and died in his 94th year. Educated in Humanity Hall Academy and Columbian College, D. C., he was for thirty-four years the president of leading educational establishments,—first of the Virginia Baptist Seminary and then of Richmond College. The college, now the pride of Virginia Baptists, was cradled largely in his self-denying labors and prayers, and its success is in great measure due to his able administration and sound learning.

Dr. Ryland was the brother of Samuel Peachey, Joseph, and John Newton Ryland, all of whom resided in the county and were eminent for good citizenship, religious character, and usefulness. He was also the uncle of Charles Hill Ryland, D. D., son of Samuel Peachey Ryland.

REV. A. F. SCOTT

By Mrs. T. P. B.

Azariah Francis Scott was born September 14th, 1822, in Northampton County, Virginia, and died October 7th, 1898. He received a first-class education at both Richmond and Columbian Colleges, at the latter of which he took the A. M. degree. He was a close student, possessed fine discriminative powers, and was never satisfied until he had mastered the subject undertaken. He was well versed in the Scriptures and sound to the core. He never " ran after new things "; he was satisfied with the good old doctrines of the Gospel, and preached Jesus Christ as the only and all-sufficient Savior of a world ruined by sin. In early life and until after the Civil War he taught school. He was fond of this work. He loved young men and identified himself with them, and this made him very successful and popular as a teacher. Many of the most prominent men in this section were his pupils. On one occasion not very many years before his death, he paid a visit to Gloucester Courthouse, meeting a great many old friends. He was invited to sit with the judge (Fielding Taylor). A great many new people had moved to the county and curiosity was rife among them as to who this old gray-haired gentleman was on whom the judge conferred such honor. At the right time Judge Taylor introduced him as his own teacher, and added that not only had he been the teacher of the judge, but of the jury, the lawyers in attendance, and all of the officers of the court. During the Civil War he lived in Gloucester County, and being too old for the ranks, when the county was lacking in men, he served as a Justice of the Peace. To-day his portrait hangs on the walls of Gloucester Court House as a prominent county officer. Mr. Scott had very few pastorates for one actively engaged in the ministry forty-seven years. Ebenezer (of which Newington was a branch at that time) in Gloucester, Colosse in King William, Glebe Landing in Middlesex, and Ephesus in Essex, were his only pastorates.

Soon after the war he moved from Gloucester Courthouse to Stevensville, King and Queen County, and took charge of Stevensville Academy. There were several preachers in the neighborhood, and the companionship of these was highly enjoyed. They met from house to house once a week, had a good supper and

COL. SAMUEL F. HARWOOD
(1821-1906)

enjoyed conversation along lines precious to them,—such spirits as Revs. Richard Hugh Bagby, Isaac Diggs, R. H. Land, Major J. R. Bagby, and Mr. John Bagby, long since gone " up higher." The writer of this book is the only one left to tell the story.

Of the moral character of A. F. Scott it is difficult to speak extravagantly; he was one of the purest of men. He never sought honors or office, but accepted, with the modesty of a woman, his election as Vice-President of the General Association of Virginia, which office he held at the time of his death. He was known among his acquaintances as a great peacemaker, urging the spirit of the Master in loving one another. He was married when quite a young man to Miss Margaret Elizabeth Holt of Northampton County; by her there were nine children. Four are living: Mrs. Thomas P. Bagby, West Point; Va.; Mr. George Ryland Scott and Mrs. R. W. Eubank, Essex County; Mr. J. H. Scott, Portsmouth, Va. His second wife was Miss Julia Waring of Essex, and she has recently died, leaving four children: William, Mattie, Mary, and Elizabeth. His funeral was preached at Ephesus Church by his lifetime friend Elder William E. Wiatt, of Gloucester County, assisted by Elders J. W. Ryland, F. B. Beall, Alexander Fleet, J. B. Cook, and J. T. T. Hundley of the Disciples' Church. He was buried at Ephesus Church, where a handsome monument marks his last resting place on earth.

FIFTIETH ANNIVERSARY

Seldom it is that we can record the fiftieth anniversary of a wedding; yet occasionally God in His infinite wisdom grants to us this rare privilege. December 12th, 1904, Mr. and Mrs. Charles W. Porter, of Stevensville, King and Queen County, Va., having reached the fiftieth year of their married life, quietly and appropriately celebrated their " Golden Wedding." It had been their desire to have all their friends and relatives with them, but owing to the somewhat impaired health of Mrs. Porter, only the immediate family and a few others were present.

There were two rather remarkable coincidences in connection with the occasion; one was, that the fiftieth year found them in the same " old homestead " in which they were married. Another feature equally remarkable was the presence of Rev. James S. Porter, of Front Royal, Va., first cousin to Mr. Porter, who acted as his best man half a century ago.

It was a quiet but happy and joyous reunion of the family. Mr. Charles Porter's long life has been too closely identified with the affairs of his section, socially, politically, and religiously, to make it necessary for a paper in Tidewater to make comment on his worth as a Christian gentleman and a valuable public citizen, and no one who has ever been fortunate enough to meet his good wife, will soon forget her warm-hearted welcome and her lavish kindness.

Stevensville, Va., December 12, 1904.

It has been the aim of the author, and his most earnest desire, to have some loving and able pen present for our inspection that splendid line of Christian womanhood represented in this county, of whom one of the most distinguished men reared among us wrote me some years ago, that they were, *par excellence,* the finest specimens of female character he had ever known. Thus far, our efforts in that direction have been futile. We present a few characters as samples of the rest:

" Miss Priscilla Pollard—a sister of Robert Pollard, Sr., clerk of the court—was bright, intelligent, cultured, and active above others in work for her church. She was baptized by Dr. Semple into Bruington Church, and from that time forth she felt that she must be about ' her Father's business.' She was especially influential in the line of women's societies for the propagation of the Gospel at home and abroad. About 1835 she aided in organizing such societies at Bruington, Mattapony, and probably also at Beulah. It is impossible to overestimate the good which has resulted. Truly she, being dead, yet speaketh. A small flagged chair is still preserved at Mattapony marked simply ' P. P.' "

We shall trust to the kind forbearance of the reader not to regard it indelicate when we give place to the following, from the pen of one who knew and highly honored the subject of his thoughts:

SARAH JANE (POLLARD) BAGBY

" The womanhood of the Old South reached its flower about the time of the war between the States, and it is probable that, when character, native grace and attractive qualities, culture of heart and mind, high ideals, the kindness of heart that is more than coronets, and the simple faith that is more than Norman blood, are considered, the subject of this brief sketch can be rightfully considered one of its most perfect examples.

" She was fortunate to be born in a home of moderate means, but of intelligence, character, and true piety. Her education was only such as was afforded by the rural community in which her lot was cast, but as a scholar she was ambitious and diligent, being loved by her teachers and exceedingly popular among her schoolmates. There was that in her face and bearing which promptly attracted and held the pleased attention.

" When the cares of a home and a family of her own came, she loved to devote such portions of her time as could be spared to the continued cultivation of her literary instinct and she became the author of a number of poems, universally recognized for their merit. Perhaps the best known of these has reference to Commodore Maury, whose remains were carried (pursuant to his expressed wish) through Goshen Pass to their resting place at Lexington:

> When the laurels are blooming,
>   When the waters so wild
> Are chafing and fretting
>   Like yon wilful child,
> As they dash o'er the lone rock,
>   So well worn and gray,—
> Where the laurels are blooming,
>   Oh, bear me that way.

" She was devoted to her church as well as to her

children, whom she tenderly and laboriously endeavored to rear " in the nurture and admonition of the Lord."

" In a marvelous degree she was gifted with that instinct which appears to be peculiar to her sex, and on several occasions events coming subsequently to her knowledge were foreshadowed in her dreams.

" Her full spirit, like that river of which Cyrus broke the strength, spent itself in channels that knew no great name on earth, but the result of her being was incalculably diffused upon those around her; for the growing good of the world is partly dependent upon unhistoric acts; and that things are not so bad with you and me as they might have been is half owing to that number who faithfully lived hidden lives and rest in unvisited tombs.

HOW A CHRISTIAN WOMAN CAN DIE

" You would like, I know, to hear something of the last hours of dear sister. She lingered much longer than we thought she would, and Saturday sister and I both thought she was dying. Sunday morning early they thought her a little better. Sister spent the morning, indeed all of the day, with her. I went over early in the afternoon and spent the night. About 4 o'clock she thought she was dying and sent for uncle. While he stood by her bed she said, ' Come, Lord Jesus, come quickly.' Aunt Bettie came later and thought she was not dying, but by ten o'clock it was evident that she could not live long. Uncle knelt by her bed and asked, ' Sallie, my darling, do you know me?' She said, ' Yes.' ' Do you know your brother John?' ' Yes.' ' I had a letter from him and he sent his best love to you.' She said, ' Give my love to him.' Then in the midst of some incoherent talk, for her mind wandered a little at times, she suddenly said very clearly and distinctly, ' Oh, my mother!' Later in the night she said, ' Mother, mother, oh, mother!' and ' My little boy!' Also, ' I have but one trouble.' She called me frequently and asked for ice, showing that her mind was clear and that she knew I was with her.

" She spoke seldom of her hopes in regard to the future, but at different times during her illness she expressed herself as follows: ' If my Heavenly Father would but take me home, how glad I should be to go.' ' I am not afraid to die.' Once she repeated these lines:

> " Give joy or grief, give ease or pain,
> Take life or friends away,
> But let me find them all again
> In that Eternal Day."

And she tried to sing,

> " Jesus can make a dying bed," etc.

" Her funeral was largely attended. Mr. Scott preached from Psalm cxvi. 15. All of her boys were present and cousin Jim. Mr. Moncure and cousin Johnny made very appropriate remarks. The boys are all deeply distressed, and uncle very sad. I was over there yesterday helping Alice, Miss Oteria, and sister to put things in order and make everything comfortable for him; for he intends to keep house. He was sadder than I had seen him and I suppose will feel his loss more and more. I hope to be able to persuade George to come here. Alice wants to take him with her but he says it is ' too far.' His cry of distress when he first heard of his mother's death was truly affecting, but he bears his grief well.

" Can't you come down to see uncle and us sometime with Speaker? Bob is well,—is out or would send messages. Best love for you all.

" Sister died at 12 : 40 Sunday night."

CHAPTER XVII

BAGBY FAMILY

James (1), Jamestown (1628).
Isom (Isham) (1), Jamestown.
William (1), Jamestown.
William (1); Robert (2), b. 1740 (Kentucky branch).
James (1); John (2); John (3), m. Morris (Louisa branch).
John (2); Richard (3), m. Jeffries; George (4); Mary (4), m. Harwood; John (4), m. Courtney; Richard (4), m. Fleet; Baylor (4); Travis (4), m. Kidd; Susan (4), m. Haynes.
Major Thomas (3); George (4), m. Virginia Evans; Dr. Geo. W. (Moziz Addums) (5), m. Chamberlayne; Ellen (5), m. Matthews.
John (4); Richard Hugh, D. D. (5), m. Motley; Dr. John (6), m. Fleet; Richard Hugh, Jr. (6), m. Cauthorne; Luther (6), m. Johnson; Betty (6), m. Ryland; Emma (6), m. Carlton; Laura (6), m. Aderholt; Hannah (6); Virginia (6), m. W. F. Bagby, county clerk.
Emeline (5), m. Cooke; Priscilla (5), m. Ryland; Hannah (5), m. Gresham; Major John R. (5), m. Fleet; Alfred (5), m. Pollard; George F. D. D. (5), m. Courtney; Mary E. (5), m. Gresham; Martha H. (5), m. Carlton; Virginia (5), m. Pollard; Susan (5); Edward (5), killed in the war.
Richard (4); John C. (5); Capt. Alexander (5), m. Walker; Rev. Edward (6); Rev. Richard (6); Dr. Bathurst (6); Alvin (6); Alexina (6), m. Robins; Janie (6).
Sarah (5), m. White; Sue (5), m. Fleet; Dolly (5), m. Walker; Richard (5), m. Fannie Floyd.

John R. (5); Wm. F. (6), m. Bagby; Bessie (6), m. Dickinson; Nellie (6); Dr. John R., Jr. (6); Mary (6), m. Haynes.

Alfred (5); Thomas P. (6), m. Scott; Ann H. (6); Charles T. (6), m. English; Juliet (6); Alfred, Jr. (6), m. Campbell; John (6), m. Harwood; Richard Hugh (6), m. Leslie; George Poindexter (6).

George F. (5); Fred (6), m. Garrett; Theodore (6), m. Willis; George F., Jr. (6), m. Lawrence; Leslie (6), m. Halloway; Alfred Paul (6), m. Strother; Harry, D. D. (6), m. Thompson; May (6), m. Rudd (missionary).

Priscilla (5); Sue (6), m. Fleet; Nannie (6), m. Fleet; Ida (6), m. Haynes; Mary (6), m. Murdoch; Priscilla (6), m. Land; Rev. John W. (6), m. Bagby; Josiah (6), m. White; James R. (6), m. Porter; Hugh (6), m. Derieux; Joseph (6), m. Bagby; Harry (6), m. ———; Edwin (6), m. Files; Alice (6).

Emeline (5); Betty (6), m. Porter; Frank (6), m. Turpin; Mary M. (6), m. Haywood; Mordecai (6).

Hannah E. (5); Jessie (6), m. Hon. H. R. Pollard; Mattie (6), m. Pollard; Ora (6), m. Butler, D. D. S.; Susie (6); Ada (6); two sons who died young (6).

Virginia (5); Mary (6), m. Clark; Juliet (6), m. Wills; Bessie (6), m. Cox; Lallah (6), m. Smoot; Maude (6), m. Turman; Susie (6); Grace (6), m. McCaslin; Rev. Edward B., Ph. D. (6), m. Mason; John Garland, attorney (6), m. Phillipps.

Mary E. (5); Andrew (6); Albert (6), m. Jones.

BIRD FAMILY

BY COLONEL BENNEHAN CAMERON, STAGVILLE, N. C.

Janet Dickie married Bob Bird of Poplar Grove. She had two children, namely, Janet and Fannie, by first marriage. Janet died without marrying. Fannie married Col. Robert Boyd. Janet Dickie Bird married, second, Capt. Beverly Roy, about 1800, by whom there were issue two sons, Dr. Beverly Roy, born in 1802, and Dr. Dunbar Roy, born 1804. Dr. Beverly Roy married, first, Miss Abrams; by her there were two children, William and Virginia. William was killed in the Civil War; Virginia married Capt. Robert Spencer of King and Queen County. Dr. Dunbar Roy married Lucy Carter Garnett; they had issue six children,— John Beverly, Janet Carter, Gustavus Garnet, Robert Boyd, Charles Carter, Lucy Augustine.

Judith Bird, sister of Robert Bird, of Poplar Grove, married Col. Robt. Hoskins, by which marriage there were two children, Bird Hoskins and Matilda Bird Hoskins. Bird Hoskins married Elizabeth Garrett, and by this issue were four children, Robert William, John Robert, Bird, and Matilda Bird. Dr. William married Janet Carter Roy.

BLAND FAMILY

First branch: (1) Robert; (2) Colonel Robert; (3) Dr. William F.; (3) Robert; (3) Dr. J. E.; (3) Frank; (3) Mary married Savage; (3) Jennie married Dr. Grubbs; (3) Lucy.

Second branch: (1) John; (2) Major Roderick; (3) Puss married Roane; (2) Nancy married Lawson; (2) Fanny married J. D. Taylor; (J. D. Taylor then married Albright); James Redwood and Muire married Miss Albright's two sisters.

Third branch: "Gentleman John" Bland married Collins. He was a brother of Robert (1). (1) John; (2) Thomas J.; (2) Eliza married Hemingway; (2) John B. married Courtney; (2) Claiborne H.; (2) Julia married Corr; (2) Cary married Mooring; (2) Harriet A. married Morris; (2) Rev. William S. of Chesterfield married Winston; (2) Demarius married Bowden.

Fourth branch: (1) Jesse Bland; (2) Jane married Ledford Vaughan; (2) Hon. B. F., (member of Virginia Senate).

Fifth branch: (1) Major Roderick Bland married first, Clayton, and second, Goulder; (2) Buck married Corr; (2) Emiline married Sears; (2) John William married Goulder; (2) Ellen J. married Roane; (2) J. T. married Irby and Wright; (2) Hon. George C.

married Anderson; Richmond married Anderson; (2) Joseph married Courtney.

Sixth branch: (1) Rev. Archy; (1) Absalom; (1) William (Hickory); (1) Archy; (2) Tyler; (2) Schuyler; (1) Absalom; (2) Joseph F.; (2) Julizu; (1) William; (2) John H.; (2) Walter; (2) Lucy, married Roane; (2) Betty married Roane; (2) Eliza married J. F. (Tyler married two sisters,—Absalom Bland's daughters.)

Seventh branch: (1) Zachary; (2) Claiborne; (2) Thomas; (1) Edward B., Englishman, 1653. Settled at Blanford near Petersburg; (2) Giles, famed in Bacon's Rebellion; (2) Theodoric, of King's council; (3) Theodoric, colonel in Revolution; (3) Richard, of Jordan's Point, also a colonel.

(See also letter from Dr. William F. Bland. I regret my inability to show the family connections.—Editor.)

BOULWARE FAMILY

BY O. GRESHAM

Lee Boulware (1) married Catharine Miller of Caroline. They lived at Newtown, and had seven children, as follows:

John (2), educated at William and Mary, became professor at Columbian College, Washington. William (2), graduated at William and Mary, married Mary Gatewood, *née* Pendleton; was appointed Minister to Naples by President Tyler; he was killed in West Virginia at a place called Jerry's Run by the giving way of a bridge in 1870. Lee (2), graduated at Yale, died about twenty-two years of age. Caroline (2), married Rev. Andrew Broaddus, Sr.; died 1848, leaving one child, Dr. William Lee Broaddus, now of Bowling Green, Ky. Catharine (2), married Kidd; died 1867, leaving two children, John B. Kidd of Richmond, and Maria Louisa. Amanda (2), married Richardson Lumpkin; died about 1872, leaving one child, Mrs. Rosalie Bates. Susan (2), married Alexander Taliafero; died 1896, leaving four

children: Catharine L. (3), married O. Gresham; Dr.
William (3), married Kate Ryland; Charlie (3), and
Carrie (3).

Lee Roy Boulware, a half-brother of Mrs. Lee Boulware, was a man of considerable property; once owned
White Hall near Walkerton. He had a large family
of children, and all of them are dead with the exception
of one daughter in Texas. Many of his children and
grandchildren were in the Confederate army. He died
in 1860.

BROOKE FAMILY

BY COLONEL SAMUEL F. HARWOOD

Richard Brooke owned Mantapike. He had two
sons that I know of; one went into the U. S. army and
the other into the navy. The latter invented an instru-
ment for deep-sea sounding. One of the same name,
and I think a descendant of this naval officer, invented
a process used in building iron-clad battleships, and
really superintended the rebuilding of the *Merrimac*
(*Virginia*); afterwards he superintended similar work
in Richmond.

George Brooke, of the army, a son of Humphrey
Brooke and a nephew of Robert Brooke (who was with
Spotswood on his transmontane expedition), bought
Mantapike from Tunstall Banks (1764).

Richard Brooke, Sr., was a justice of the peace, and
he was impecunious. He was often on the bench when
suits came to trial against himself; in such cases he was
remarkable for his impartiality in giving judgment
against himself.—[EDITOR.]

BYRD FAMILY

The first patent of land was granted to Robert Byrd,
in 1691. I find this same tract enlarged in the name
of William Byrd in 1702.

Robert Byrd married Miss Dunbar; issue, Robert,
Judith, Barbara, and Katherine.

Robert Byrd married Janet Dickey; issue, Fannie and
Janet, born January 24, 1793; died July, 1815.

Fannie married Robert Boyd; issue, Robert Byrd.

Robert Byrd Boyd married Mary A. Pryor; issue, Fannie and Byrd.

Byrd Boyd married John Washington; issue, John Boyd, Mary A., Dolly B., Walker H., Eugene B., Fannie P., Roberta K.

Fannie Boyd married Captain Marius Pendleton Todd; issue, William Burnett, born 1855; Robert Boyd, born 1856; Henry Garland, born 1857; Mary Eliza, born 1863 (died in infancy); Fannie Boyd, born 1862; Marius Pendleton, born 1865.

Janet (Dickey) Byrd, born November 29, 1767; died September 10, 1817; married second, Captain Beverly Roy (born 1760, died 1820). (See below, under Dickey and Roy.)

COLLINS FAMILY

Tom (1) (at Ware's Bridge); William (2); Robert (2), married Gibson; Mary E. (3), married Corr; Columbia (3), married Carlton; Tommy (3); Robert (3); Martha (3), married Glenn.

Tom (2); Tom (3), married Tribble; Tom (4), married Corr; (children): George (2), married Smith; Ashton (3), married Jockson; James (3), married Corr; Dena (4), S. Burch (5); James (4).

Jane (2), married Daniel; Bob (3), married Mrs. Street; George (3); Joe (3).

Maria (2), married Jackson; Patsy (2), married Clayton; Betty (3), married Bland; Jim Polk (4), married Turner; Sarah (3), married Rev. Crittenden; Sandal (3), married Garrett; Jim (3).

Lucy (2), married Crittenden; Tom (3); George (3); Betty (3), married Yarington; Fanny (3), married Burton; (other sons and daughters, Dr. William Garland Smith among them).

CORBIN FAMILY

Major Henry Corbin of Stratton, Virginia, died 1680; had two sons, Thomas (1), who left no male descendants; his daughter, Letitia, married Richard

Lee. Garvin Corbin (2) married Miss Bassett and was president of the Council. His children were: Joan (Mrs. Robert Tucker); Jenny (Mrs. Bushrod); Alice (Mrs. Ben. Nadler); Richard, of Laneville, who married Miss Betty Taylor, ancestor of the Braxtons; John; Garvin, who married Hannah Lee; Mrs. Allerton; Mrs. Tuberville.

CORR FAMILY

James Corr (1), married Mary Corr, a daughter of William Corr; her mother was a Miss Campbell of Plymouth.

William Corr (2), married Julia Bland, a daughter of John Bland, a teacher, often called "Gentleman John." Thomas Corr (2), his brother, was unmarried, and Mary F. (2), married William Ferry; Felix Corr (2).

James F. (3), William Lycurgus, D. Fielding, Flora A., and Julia B.

James Corr (1) had a brother Jack, who went to Missouri.

Henry Corr (1) of King William had two brothers, Thomas and George. Henry (2), Mrs. Edwards, Mrs. Littlepage. Thomas H. Edwards (3), attorney.

Thomas (1) married a Miss Shackelford, and second a Mrs. Bland.

Puss (2), married Buck Bland; Catherine (2), married Jimmy Bland; Victoria (2), George (2), Milton (2), Thomas (2), married Bray.

Levi Corr of Gloucester was a cousin of William (2). Three of his sons were ministers, viz.: Watt, Thomas, and Harry.

Freling Corr (3), married first Collins, and second Crittenden. Children: Mediola (4), married Collins; Lunsford Straughn (4), Myrtle (4), married Cobb; Elsie (4), married Black; Donus R. (4), Julia B. (4), Dena (5), married Burch; James C. (5), S. Burch (6).

CRITTENDEN FAMILY

William (1), married first Bland, and second Mrs. Webley; William, Jr. (2), George (2), Carter (2),

Going (2), Mary (2), Rev. James C. (2), married four times; Charley (3), Sarah (3), married Corr; Lucy (3), married Walden; Samuel (2), married Hart; Robert (2), Matilda (2), married Webley; Cordelia (2), married Trice; Eudora (2), married Cardwell.

COURTNEY FAMILY

We compile the following, drawing largely from memoranda made by Major Alfred R. Courtney, C. S. A., of Richmond. Among the names mentioned traditionally of residents on the north side of the York and Mattapony Rivers about 1680, is that of Robert Courtney. He was apparently an English emigrant. Readers of history will recall the name Courtenay as having been prominent in England: the names are doubtless the same. Robert (1), the emigrant, had three sons, Philip, Thomas, and John. Philip, whom we mark (2), indicating that he was a son of (1), had one son, Captain Robert Courtney (3), married Campbell. His children were William P. (4), Franklin (4), Elizabeth (4), married John Bagby; Priscilla (4), married William Campbell, Sr.; Martha (4), married Haynes.

Captain Robert Courtney was a man of mark. He was captain at Norfolk during the War of 1812, first sheriff of his county, and afterwards for years presiding justice of the court. He was a man of commanding mien, fearless, outspoken, and had the unbounded confidence of his people. He was called Robert, Sr., to distinguish him from another Robert, and died in 1852. He married a daughter of Captain Whittaker Campbell (probably of the Revolutionary army), of King and Queen.

The two other sons of Robert (1), Thomas and John, became Baptist ministers. Rev. Thomas (2) had six sons and two daughters; one daughter married Taylor of Richmond, the other married Osgood. The sons were Philip (3), John (3) of New Kent, William (3), Thomas (3), Robert (3), and Nathaniel (3), who migrated west.

Rev. John (2), born 1744, died 1824, was pastor of the First Baptist Church of Richmond, Va. He was greatly honored in his pastorate, being a compeer of " Parsons " Blair and Buchanan. Though not a brilliant preacher, his discourses were powerful and won many to the faith. Both himself and his brother Thomas labored in their early days in King William.

Robert (3)—son of Thomas (2)—married Sarah Campbell, was father of a large family: Joseph Campbell (4), James Whittaker (4), Robert Mortimer (4), Martha Elizabeth (4), married Captain Smith; Lawrence Straughan (4), Thomas Lysander (4), Giles Croghan (4), Martha Lewis (4), married Patterson; Major Alfred R. (4), married Shelton. Robert (3) was in the War of 1812-'14.

The Courtney family has migrated in every direction and is represented in nearly every State in the Union. (The two Misses Campbell here mentioned as having married Robert Courtney, Sr., and Robert, Jr., were daughters of Captain Whittaker Campbell, near Bruington Church; he was probably a soldier of the Revolution.)

Another branch is as follows: William C. (Shad) Courtney was uncle to James W. Courtney of Plymouth. His sons were Conway, William, James, Thomas, and Isaac. Thomas, son of Shad, had sons: John Robert, Constantine D., Augustus A., Thomas L., Bird S., James W.; daughters: Mollie B., Willie, married Richardson; Rosie, married Shepherd.

Family records from the Family Bible of Captain Robert Courtney, King and Queen County, Va., by Captain A. C. Jones, Three Creeks, Ark.:

BIRTHS

Elizabeth Courtney, daughter of Robert and Priscilla, his wife, was born August 28th, 1794.

William Courtney, born May 29th, 1796.

Priscilla Courtney, born November 11th, 1797.

Mary Courtney, born September 6th, 1799.

Robert Hill Courtney, born November 2d, 1801.

Martha Hill Courtney, born October 30th, 1804.

Hugh Courtney, born January 12th, 1806.

William Pollard Courtney, born December 25th, 1807.

Thomas Parkinson Courtney, born May 28th, 1810.

Franklin Courtney, born June 4th, 1812.

Ann Courtney, born September 27th, 1814.

MARRIAGES

Robert Courtney and Priscilla Campbell married October 5th, 1793.

Elizabeth Courtney and Mr. John Bagby married March 15th, 1814.

Priscilla Courtney and Mr. William Campbell married September 22d, 1818.

Mary Courtney and Mr. Hill Jones married February 24th, 1819.

Martha H. Courtney and Mr. Thomas Haynes married September 22d, 1824.

William P. Courtney and Miss Martha E. Campbell married June 15th, 1828.

Franklin Courtney and Miss Adaline Pendleton married November 5th, 1835.

DEATHS

William Courtney, son of Robert Courtney and Priscilla, his wife, died August 21st, 1797.

Hugh Courtney (ditto above) died September 9th, 1814.

Thomas P. Courtney died September 26th, 1814.

Robert H. Courtney died October 17th, 1814.

Ann Courtney, died October 5th, 1823.

Martha H. (Courtney) Haynes died October 29th, 1831.

Elizabeth (Courtney) Bagby died September 29th, 1836.

Priscilla Courtney, wife of Robert Courtney, died October 7th, 1840.

Priscilla (Courtney) Campbell died July 17th, 1843.

Robert Courtney died February 24th, 1852.

DAVIS FAMILY

Hon. Robert Davis of Millers, married ————; had daughters Maggie and Mattie. Maggie married Latane.

Colonel William B. Davis, also of Millers, married first Taliaferro; issue, Martha, married Hon. Tom Winston of Minneapolis. Married second, Ella Sutton; children, Julia and James Taylor Davis.

DICKEY FAMILY

BY MRS. BETTY MONTAGUE

Adam Dickey married Miss Dunbar, who was the daughter of Hancock Dunbar, rector of St. Stephen's parish; issue: Janet, Barbara, Mary Dunbar, James.

Janet Dickey married first, Robert Byrd; second, Captain Beverly Roy. Issue, Fannie and Janet.

Mary Dunbar married Ambrose Edwards.

Barbara died.

James married Joanna, daughter of Iverson Lewis and Frances Byrd.

Judith Byrd married Colonel Robert Hoskins. Issue, Byrd, Matilda, Catherine, and William.

Byrd Hoskins, born 1800, died 1841; married Elizabeth Garrett, born 1802, died 1867. Issue, Robert Hoskins, born 1831, died 1836; Dr. William Hoskins, born December 25th, 1836; Matilda Hoskins, born October 16th, 1835, died June 14th, 1895; Dr. John Robert Byrd Hoskins, born February 2d, 1838, died December 31, 1891.

FAUNTLEROY FAMILY

The first three Fauntleroys who came to this country were John, Moore, and Samuel Griffin. The three brothers settled in the "Northern Neck" of Virginia, and were the sole owners of that section. They were French Huguenots, and had to leave France on account of the persecution. Samuel Griffin Fauntleroy, a descendant of one of the brothers, settled in King and Queen County at "Farmers' Mount." His first wife was Elizabeth Payne Todd; she had two daughters, Katherine and Betsy. The former married Mr. Lorrimer, the latter Mr. Thornton Pollard. She also had three sons, Samuel Griffin, Moore Gardner, and William Todd. The second wife was Sarah Lowry, a sister of Mrs. Robert B. Semple. She had three daughters and one son. Of the daughters, Martha married Colonel Archie Harwood, Susan Tomlin married Mr. Toler, and Lucy Garnett married Mr. James Govan. Her son, Thomas William Lowry Fauntleroy, married Fannie Todd; only one child survives them, Mary Peachey Fauntleroy.

Mrs. James Govan had four daughters: Elizabeth, who married Dr. Samuel G. Fauntleroy; Nannie, who married Dr. Griffin Fauntleroy; Susan, who married Mr. Robert Payne Fauntleroy; and Martha, who never married.

Dr. Moore Gardner Fauntleroy, son of S. G., Sr., married Ann Catherine Roberta Latane, and left two daughters, Elizabeth Payne Todd, who married Mr. John Robinson Winston, and Mary Ellen, who married William Dillard. He had five sons, John Moore, who married Annie Willis Sizer; Samuel Griffen, who married Nannie Govan; Robert Payne, who married Susan Govan; Moore Gardner, who married Flora Dillard; and William Henry, who never married. Samuel Griffen, Jr., had only one child, who was also called Samuel Griffen. William Todd Fauntleroy married Elizabeth Downing, and left two sons, Virginius H. and R. Bruce Fauntleroy. Mrs. Susan Toler left one daughter, Henrietta, who married Dr. R. Bruce Fauntleroy.

Martha, the wife of Colonel Harwood, left seven daughters and three sons, namely: Sarah, Margaret, Priscilla, Katherine, Susan, Lucy, and Emily; Samuel, Thomas, and Archie.

Mrs. Thornton Pollard of lower King and Queen, née Ellen Fauntleroy, had three daughters, Belle, Lizzie Todd, and Ella. Belle married Fauntleroy, Lizzie married Robert Roy.

Dr. Moore G. Fauntleroy was surgeon in the War of 1812.

Captain Pendleton of Revolutionary army was connected with both the Todds and Fauntleroys.

Captain Bernard Todd, who was connected with the Fauntleroys, received from the U. S. government six thousand acres of land in Kentucky.

FLEET FAMILY

We had hoped to present a more extended account of this noted family, but have been able to secure only what here follows:

They claim (and apparently with justness) to be descended from Charlemagne of France; also from several of the kings of England after William I.   Later we have William Fleet (1), Gentleman, married Deborah Scott, of Chatham, Kent.

William Fleet (2), Virginia burgess 1652.

Henry Fleet (3), sheriff of Lancaster County 1718-1719.

William Fleet (4), sheriff of Lancaster County.

William Fleet (5), born 1726.

William Fleet (6), 1757-1836, member of Constitutional Convention, 1788. Sons: Christopher B., M. D., married McKim; Colonel Alexander, justice and Virginia legislator, married first Pollard, second Mrs. Butler; James Robert, married Ryland; Benjamin, married Maria Louisa, daughter of Dr. Walker, a German.

Dr. C. B. Fleet's sons: John A., married first Maynard, second Ryland; Charles B., married Burrass; Dr. William T., married Bagby.

John A. Fleet's sons: Maynard, Charles, Dr. Bennett, McKim, Ellie.

Dr. William T. Fleet's children: Jeanette, married Vest; Brooke, married Pyles; William, Chapin, Minnie, Sydney.

Colonel Alexander Fleet's sons: Christopher B., Rev. Alexander; daughters: Betty, married Bagby; Sallie Brown.

Dr. Benjamin Fleet's sons: Colonel A. F. of Culver, Ind., David of Washington State, Judge William of Virginia; daughters: Lou, Bessie, Florence.

Mrs. Maria Louisa Fleet was a daughter of Dr. Wacken, a German physician, who located at King and Queen Courthouse and practiced his profession. He married a daughter of Robert Pollard, Sr., clerk of the court, and his daughter, Maria L., was the sole heir. In early life she married Dr. Benjamin Fleet, youngest son of Captain William and brother of Colonel Alexander Fleet. After the lapse of some fifteen years Dr. Fleet died, leaving his widow the great responsibility of seven children,—four sons and three daughters,— to provide for and educate. Nothing daunted, she took up the task. By and by she established a school known far and near as "Green Mount," of which she was herself the headmaster and inspiration. It is to Mrs. Fleet's imperishable credit that, under conditions above indicated, and by her single initiative, she impressed her own intellectual and Christian character upon her sons, Colonel A. F. Fleet of Culver Military Academy, Indiana; David of Washington State, and Judge William, and her admirable daughters, Misses Lou, Bessie, and Florence. We take pride in presenting her portrait as a representative woman of the county.

THE GAINES FAMILY AND HOMES

BY C. H. R.

The first Gaines of whom we have record in King and Queen is mentioned in the Vestry book of Stratton Major parish under date February 27th, 1766. The entry is as follows: "Harry Gaines, Gent., engaged to build the church on the old field belonging to Richard Corbin, Esq., called 'Goliath Field.'" On March 4th, 1768, the Vestry "received the church built by Major Harry Gaines, deceased." In Hening's "Statutes at Large of Virginia," February, 1759, the following appears, "Harry Gaines, Gent., is appointed trustee of the Pamunky Indians," and October 30th, 1760, "Harry Gaines subscribed £1 annually for 8 years as a premium for best wines."

A second Harry Gaines (possibly son of the above-mentioned), brother of William Fleming Gaines of "Greenway," King William County, and of Robert Gaines of "White House," King and Queen County, lived at "Providence" and died in 1789. He married Elizabeth Herndon. Their children were (1) Benjamin, (2) Harry, (3) Robert Beverley, (4) William Fleming, who died young, (5) Martha Fleming, (6) Elizabeth Herndon, (7) John.

1. Benjamin Gaines of "Plain Dealing" married Sally, daughter of Camm Garlick. Their children were Mary Ann, who married Richard Gaines, attorney-at-law, and inherited her father's residence; Mira L., who married George K. Carlton of "Carlton's Store"; William Fleming Gaines, M. D., of "Powhite," Hanover County; Sarah Jane, who married John H. Steger of Amelia County.

2. Harry Gaines of "Woodlawn" married Myra Muse. Their children were Juliet, who married Thomas Carter of King William County; Cornelia, who married Dr. Meux of Amelia County; Henry Mortimer, Martha Elizabeth, and Sarah Ann, who all died unmarried.

3. Robert Beverley Gaines of "Belmont" married Lucy, daughter of William Fleming Gaines of "Greenway," King William County. Their children were Sally, Herndon, and Lucy, all of whom died unmarried.

5. Martha Fleming married Robert Baylor Hill of "The Vineyard," and left one child, Catharine Gaines, who married Samuel Peachey Ryland of Norwood.

6. Elizabeth Herndon Gaines married Captain Thomas Miller of Powhatan County, and left no issue.

7. John Gaines resided at "Providence." He was a lawyer of ability, and attorney for the Commonwealth, and died unmarried.

Robert Gaines of "The White House" (brother of Harry Gaines of Providence), married Mrs. Jennings. Their children were (1) Richard, who married Mary Ann, daughter of Benjamin Gaines, and lived at "Plain Dealing"; (2) Harry, who married Agnes Gwathmey; and (3) Martha, who married Mr. Lee of Lynchburg.

THE GARNETT FAMILY AND HOMES

Thomas Garnett (who died in Essex County in 1748) and Elizabeth, his wife, were the parents of John Garnett, Jr.; whose son, Reuben Garnett, married Mary, daughter of James and Mary (Gaines) Jameson of Drysdale parish, and resided at " Liberty Hall," Essex County. Reuben Meriwether, son of Reuben and Mary Garnett, married Anna Maria, daughter of Captain James Pendleton (of the Continental Line) and his wife, Elizabeth Peachey (daughter of Samuel Peachey of Essex County), and resided at his wife's parental homestead " Spring Farm " near Newtown. He was high sheriff and colonel of the militia. Their children, who lived to be grown, were (1) John Muscoe, M. D., (2) Mary Susan, (3) Reuben Meriwether, (4) Anna Maria.

1. John Muscoe of " Lanefield " married, first, Priscilla, daughter of Andrew Brown of Middlesex County; and second, Anna Elizabeth, daughter of Captain Higgason Hancock of Chesterfield County. Their children were: Priscilla Brooke, Alice Marion, who married Charles Hill Ryland, D. D., of Richmond; Nannie B.; Mary Kate Macon, who married William L. Broaddus, M. D., of " Travellers' Rest "; Francis W.; Susan Harvie, who married Rev. F. B. Beale of Westmoreland County; John Muscoe of " Lanefield "; Reuben Hancock, M. A., Professor of Greek, Georgetown College, Kentucky.

2. Mary Susan married Benjamin Franklin Dew of Newtown. Their children were James Harvie, M. D., of New York; John Garnett, county judge and Second Auditor of Virginia; Mary Franklin, who married Rev. Frederick W. Claybrook of Lancaster County.

3. Reuben Meriwether married Bettie Allen, daughter of James Williams of Fredericksburg, and lived at " Peach Grove." Their children were Mary Allen, who married William D. Gresham of " Forest Hill "; Reuby Pendleton, who married James R. Fleet of King and Queen; Muscoe Harvie of Richmond; James Williams of " Peach Grove "; and Nannie M., second wife of Rev. F. W. Claybrook.

4. Anna Maria, married John N. Ryland of "Farmington." Their children were Jeannette Garnett, who married Joseph H. Gwathmey of King William County; and John N. Ryland, Jr., of "Ingleside."

GOVAN FAMILY

(1) James, (2) James, (2) Cincinnatus, (2) Moore, (2) Elizabeth married Dr. S. G. Fauntleroy, (2) Ann married Dr. Griffin Fauntleroy, (2) Susan married Robert P. Fauntleroy, (2) Martha.

GRESHAM FAMILY

BY O. GRESHAM

Samuel Gresham (1) was one of the patriarchs as far back as 1815. He married first a Miss Dudley; child: William (2), moved to Kentucky early in the nineteenth century. He has grandchildren and great-grandchildren now living in Jeffersonville, Ind.

By his second wife: George (2) and John (2), lived and died in Lancaster County; Hannah (2) also lived there, and married John Chewning; Fannie (2) married Gouldman Parker, and died about 1839 in King and Queen; James (2) died in Essex, where he married; Andrew (2) settled in Essex, practising medicine, but died young; Thomas (2) married Polly Dew, and lived in Essex, father of Edward (3), William D. (3), Robert (3), Charles, M. D., (3), and Henry, M. D., (3); Samuel (2), my father, born 1778, died 1843, father of Andrew (3), died early; Martha A. (3) married P. D. Samuel, died 1844; Samuel S. (3), born 1817, died in Norfolk 1897; John (3), born 1820, married Hannah E. Bagby, died 1884; Hannah (3) born 1822, married Thomas Motley of Caroline; Mary Susan (3) born 1825, died 1854; Benjamin F. (3) born 1828, married 1848, Anne C. Lumpkin, three children,—all dead except Mrs. Gertrude G. Samuels of Caroline,—died 1904; Albert G. (3) born 1830, married Mary E. Bagby, only one child living, Albert

G., Jr.; Virginia (3) born 1833, married William Howerton, died 1870; Sarah Ann (3) born 1839; married G. Howerton, died 1870; and Oscar (3) born 1836, married E. M. Harris; children living: Oscar, Jr., (4), Ellen Hudgens (4), W. W. Gresham (4), and Roberta Spindle (4). Oscar (3) married second, October 1882, C. L. Taliaferro; no children.

Thomas Gresham (2) was a lawyer of distinction in Essex County. His children branched as follows: Edward (3) married Isabella Mann; was an excellent citizen and minister; children: Ella (4) married Dr. Haile; Walter (4), M. C., Galveston, Texas; Philip (4), M. D., Fort Worth, Texas, married Gresham, died early; Mrs. Tyler (4) died leaving a son, Walter, a promising young lawyer; and " Bunnie " (4) ; William D. (3) married first, Campbell, and second, Garnett; leaving children: May (4) married Dr. P. Gresham; Marian (4) married Dr. Brown Evans; and Herbert (4); Robert (3) married Dew, was colonel of militia and a lawyer; Henry (3) M. D., died in Essex, leaving several children.

The Greshams are an old family with many branches. Samuel Gresham lived near Upper King and Queen Church and left an impress through his children, Samuel S., John N., Benjamin, Oscar, and Albert. Samuel married Motley, and second, Goode. John married Hannah E. Bagby. A daughter of these last became Mrs. H. R. Pollard; another, Mrs. R. N. Pollard; a third, Mrs. Dr. E. E. Butler. Their children cast a halo upon their memory. Rev. Edward Gresham was a distant relative. He was a man of virtue and intelligence; married Isabella Mann, and left sons and daughters: Hon. Walter Gresham, M. C., of Galveston, Texas; Dr. P. Gresham of Fort Worth, whose widow survives with several highly reputable sons and daughters; Mrs. Dr. Haile, Mrs. Tyler, whose son Walter is an attorney. Wm. D. was a brother of Edward, married Garnett, and second, Campbell. Thomas Gresham, an attorney of Tappahannock, the father of Edward, William D., Sylvanus, and Colonel T. Robert, was a man of ability and lucrative practice. He was a brother of Samuel Gresham of Newtown. Thomas R. Gresham and Sylvanus were men of high character,— the former a county official, father of Rev. G. T. Gresham, Richard, and Jeff. Sylvanus married Miss Cawthorne, an admirable woman. Their sons were, ————, Calvin, of Texas, and John Amos, on the Pacific coast.—[Editor.]

HARWOOD FAMILY

This family seems to be of Saxon origin, tracing back to the time of William the Conqueror. Coat of Arms, a shield with a head of antlers surmounting. Robert and Thomas were sheriffs in London about 1630. H. in America, 1619. William, chief of " Martin's Hundred," Warwick County, Va., 1620. Colonel Archibald Roane Harwood, born 1761, married Fauntleroy. The Colonel was in the War of 1812 and inherited Newington. Children: Samuel F., Margaret married Winder, Sarah, Priscilla, Thomas Moore (went to Texas), Martha C. married Bird, Archibald Roane, Lucy married McPheters, Maria S., Emily G.

A HANDSOME TABLET OF HARWOODS

(By order of Court.)

(1) " Christopher H., died 1744.

(2) His son, Captain William H., born 1734, died 1773, married Priscilla Pendleton.

(3) His son, Major Christopher H., died 1793, married Margaret Roane of Newington.

(4) His son, Captain Archibald Roane H., born 1786, died 1837; married Martha Fauntleroy of Holly Hill. War of 1812; Senate of Virginia.

(5) His sons:

1. Samuel Fauntleroy H. of Newington, born 1817; married Betty Brokenborough. Senate of Virginia; and Vestryman.*

* See biographical sketch above.

2. Major Thomas M. Harwood of Newington, born 1827, died at Gonzales, Texas, 1900; married Cordelia Brown. Willis' Battalion, Waul's Texas Legion, C. S. A. Special Judge Supreme Court of Texas, 1886. Regent University of Texas 1872-1895. Ruling Elder 1877-1900."

HENLEY FAMILY

Rev. Thomas M. Henley (first generation in King and Queen) was born in Williamsburg. Early in life he became impressed in regard to religion. His parents were Episcopalians, but upon investigation he concluded that immersion alone was baptism and decided to become a Baptist. His father, Leonard Henley, earnestly opposed his connecting himself with the Baptists, who were then a despised sect, and threatened that if he did so he would disinherit him, but in spite of this opposition and threat Mr. Henley did what his conscience dictated, and he was baptized and united with the Baptist Church. He then left Williamsburg and settled in Tappahannock and started a coach-making business, but soon began to preach. He married first a Miss Yates, the granddaughter of Bishop Yates of the Episcopal Church; by that marriage he had three children: Dr. Leonard Henley of Essex, Mary, and Robert Y. Dr. Leonard Henley had some five or six children, viz., T. M., Sally, and others whose names are unknown. Mary married first, Billups and had two children, Hugh and Sally; and then married Kemp and had one child, a daughter. Robert Y. Henley married first, Caroline Campbell, the daughter of Alexander Campbell, by whom he had two children, Dr. Thomas M. Henley and Caroline; then he married Mrs. Maria Louisa Woolfolk, the widow of John Woolfolk of Shepherd's Hill, Caroline County, whose maiden name was Magruder, by whom he had two children, Dr. Robert Y. Henley, who married Dora Walker; and Louisa, who never married. The elder son, Dr. T. M. Henley, married Priscilla Bagby and left four children, viz. Roberta Lee, Lou F., Caroline, and Winnie. Roberta Lee has never married; Lou married Richard Barclay; Carrie married ——————— Sturgis, and Winnie married A. Sidney Fitch.

After the death of his first wife, Miss Yates, Rev. Thomas M. Henley married Betty Temple, and had two children, Joseph T. and Dr. Samuel Straughan Henley. Joseph T. married Betty T. Walker, daughter of Betsy W. Todd and Temple Walker, and had eight children, viz. Virginia T., Bernard W., Charles T., Josie M., William T., Hunter H., Fannie Ellen, and Betty T., all living in 1904. Virginia married Melville Walker, and has three children, Bessie, Henley W., and Alice. B. W. married Estelle (Booth) Welsh, and has one child, Booth. Charles T. has three children. Fannie E. has four children, Temple, Samuel, John, and Emily. Hunter has four children. William Todd married Lizzie Hoskins, daughter of John T. and Hannah Hoskins, and has four children, Elizabeth, Joseph T., John Hoskins, and William Todd, Jr. Hunter married Miss Loulie Ray of Florida. Fannie E. married Samuel P. Waddill.

Rev. Thomas M. Henley, Sr., was, in consequence of his becoming a Baptist, disinherited by his father. It is worthy of note that in after years most of his father's family and their descendants became members of the Christian Church, of which church Thomas M. Henley became a member and preacher, after being for many years a preacher in the Baptist Church. Late in life he removed from Essex to Hillborough, King and Queen, which had been given to his wife by her brother, William Temple, of Rose Mount. This estate was afterwards owned by his son, Joseph T., and now by the latter's son, William Todd Henley.

Dr. Samuel Straughan Henley, the second son by his last marriage, married Robinette Pendleton, daughter of P. B. Pendleton. They left six children, viz. Thomas B., Mary Straughan, Rebecca P., Columbia, William, and Pattie. Thomas B. married Fannie Dew. Mary married ——————— Carter. Rebecca married R. S. Dew. Willie married Willis Eastwood. Columbia and Pattie never married.

HILL FAMILY AND HOMES

BY C. H. R.

Colonel Humphrey Hill, son of Thomas and Edith (Bell) Hill, of London, England, was born in 1706, and was a " blue coat " boy of Christ Church Hospital school, where the record of his matriculation is still preserved. He settled first at Hobbe's Hold (now Tappahannock) as a tobacco factor. He married Frances, daughter of Robert and Hannah (Gregory) Baylor, and built " Hillsborough," where he died and was buried in 1775. His children were (1) Ann, who married Isaac Dabney; (2) Frances, who married Baylor Walker; (3) Mary, who married Joseph Temple; (4) Baylor, who married Mary, daughter of Colonel George Brooke of " Mantapike," and became captain in the Continental Line and mayor of Norfolk; (5) John, who married Mary Elliott and resided at " Mayfair," King William County; (6) Robert, who was high sheriff of the county, and married Hannah, daughter of Samuel Garlick of " Mt. Pleasant," King William County, the immigrant; (7) William, who married Betsy Baylor and resided at " Smithfield "; (8) Edward, who married Fannie Brooke Baylor and fell heir to the homestead; (9) Elizabeth, who married Samuel Garlick, Jr., of " Beudley "; and (10) Humphrey.

Robert (6) and Hannah (Garlick) Hill lived at " Huckleberry Hall," now " Roseville," near Bruington. He was one of the County Committee of Safety during the Revolution. Their children were Humphrey of " Mt. Airy," Caroline County, who married first, Mary Garlick, and second, Betsy Minor; Richard of " Ashfield," near Richmond, who married first, Nancy Hill, and second, Molly Govan; Edward Garlick, who married first, Nancy Garlick, and second, Mary Hart; Mary, who married Owen Gwathmey of King William County; John, who married Mary Waller Lewis of Spottsylvania County; Harry, of " Mt. Gideon," Caroline County, who married first, Sally Woolfolk, and second, Mrs. Hickman, and third, Jane Burruss; Samuel, who married Miss Lewis and moved to Kentucky;

Robert Baylor, who lived at " The Vineyard " and married first, Martha Fleming, daughter of Harry and Elizabeth (Herndon) Gaines of " Providence," and second, Catharine Pollard, daughter of Robert and Martha Pollard of King William County; Esther, who married Captain Roderick Starling of King William County; and Camm, who died young. Robert Baylor and Martha Fleming (Gaines) Hill of " The Vineyard " had one child, Catharine Gaines, who married Samuel Peachey Ryland of " Norwood." The child of the second marriage was Martha Ann, who married first, James Butler, and second, Colonel Alexander Fleet of " Melville."

Edward (8) and Fannie Brooke (Baylor) Hill of " Hillsborough " had the following children: Mary, who married Robert, son of John Hill of " Mayfair," King William County; Fannie, who married Johnson of King William County; Fannie, who married John, son of John Hill of "Mayfair"; Nancy, first wife of Richard Hill of " Ashfield," Henrico County; Charles, who moved to Mississippi; Brooke, who moved to Kentucky; John, William, and Patsy, who all died unmarried.

HUTCHINSON FAMILY

Charles Hutchinson (1) married Miss Lyne

J. D. Hutchinson (2) married Miss Haile, daughter of Captain Haile of Essex.

Charles (2) married ————————————, moved to Missouri (I think), became a distinguished lawyer, and was the author of a standard legal work.

Martha (2) married Joseph L. Pollard of King and Queen.

J. D. Hutchinson (2) was a man of education and a prominent citizen; conducted a classical school for years at his residence, Liberty Hall, on the line of King and Queen and Essex near Indian Neck. He had a reputation as surveyor of lands and was the draftsman of very many deeds and wills. Liberty Hall was originally the property of the Garnetts, descended to Miss

Mary Susan Garnett, who married Benjamin F. Dew, and was sold by them to said Hutchinson. He left five sons, Edward L., Robert, William, J. D., Jr., and Charles (who is a dentist),—all active, prosperous citizens; and three daughters, Nancy, Mary, and Sally B.

Edward L. Hutchinson (3) married Miss Mary Motley, daughter of Richard Motley of Essex.

Robert (3) married Miss Clarkson, a daughter of John H. Clarkson of Essex.

J. D., Jr., (3) married Miss Lizzie Sizer, a daughter of Dr. William Sizer of King William County, and a granddaughter of Mr. Edward C. Hill of the same county.

LYNE FAMILY

Elizabeth Lyne (2), the daughter of William Lyne (1), married Jesse Carter, who was rector of Drysdale Parish (See Bishop Meade's book). They had issue, one daughter, Lucy Lyne Carter (3), married John Jameson Garrett; by whom Lucy Carter Garrett (4) (born July 8, 1816, died February 6, 1850), married A. G. Dunbar Roy (born 1804; died November 23, 1874):

Janet Carter Roy (5) (born February 14, 1838), married, December 29, 1857, Dr. William Hoskins (died June 14, 1895):

Elizabeth Lyne Hoskins (6) (born February 24, 1868), married, December 11, 1889, Andrew Jackson Montague (born October 3, 1863).

POLLARD FAMILY

To the Editor of the *Argus:*

Dear Sir: The following is so remarkable an instance of longevity, in a family consisting of five sisters and one brother, now living, that I am induced to send it to you for publication in your useful paper.

The account is taken from the Bible now in the family, recorded in the handwriting of the late venerable Judge Pendleton, who at his death, which happened on the 26th of October, 1803, in his eighty-third year, was attending his duty as president of the Supreme Court of Appeals in Richmond, Virginia:

"Sarah Pollard, born the 4th of May, 1725, was married June 20th, 1743, to Judge Pendleton. She is now in her ninetieth year."

"Anne Pollard, born the 22nd of February, 1732. She is now in her 83rd year"—married a Mr. Taylor and was the mother of Colonel John Taylor, of Caroline, the great statesman.

"Elizabeth Pollard (now Meriwether), born October, 1736, is now in her seventy-sixth year." These three ladies live under one roof—keep no housekeeper—families entire.

"Thomas Pollard, born September 30th, 1741, is nearly 73." He rode on horseback from Kentucky a year or two ago, and means to return shortly.

"Milly Pollard, now married to Colonel Edmund Pendleton, was born the 12th of May, 1747, and is now in her 68th year," and lives within two miles of her sisters.

"Jane Pollard, now the wife of Thomas Underwood, was born the 26th of May, 1744, and is in her 71st year," living in Hanover.

"Joseph Pollard, the father of the above, died December 26th, 1791, nearly 91."

"Priscilla Pollard, the mother, died July 26th, 1795, over 91."

JOHN POLLARD, JR.

By JOHN POLLARD, SR., 1870.

A chart of the Pollard family so far as I have any historical account of them, and more particularly my branch of the family:

My great-grandfather, Joseph Pollard, was born, so far as I can ascertain, in the County of King and Queen and raised his family there. In 1754, when 67 years of age, as I have been informed by my father, he moved to the County of Goochland,—consequently, he must have been born about the year 1687. He married Miss Priscilla Hoomes, of Caroline County, and had nine children, two sons and seven daughters.

Of the daughters I shall speak first.

1. One married a Mr. Watkins and left no issue.

2. Another married, first, a Mr. Dandridge, and afterwards a Mr. Underwood, and left no issue.

3. Another married Mr. Edmund Pendleton, of Caroline, a distinguished lawyer, who afterwards became judge of the Court of Appeals of Virginia, and was president of the Court for many years, and died holding that position. They left no issue.

4. Another married a Mr. Taylor of Caroline, and had an only son, John Taylor, of Caroline, who was a colonel in the Revolution of 1776, became a distinguished politician, was a member of the United States Senate, and was the author of several political works. He was one of the most successful farmers in his day and made a large fortune. He, I think, had four sons, two of whom died during the lifetime of their father. William P., one of the sons, was once a member of Congress, died during the Civil War, without issue, leaving his fortune, which he inherited from his father, to two nephews; George Taylor, the youngest of the four sons, lives (now 1870) in King William County.

5. Another married a Mr. Meriwether, who left a number of children, all of whom moved South, except one, who married a Mr. Wilson of Richmond, Virginia, and has a grandson residing there named James Winston, who is now, 1870, secretary and treasurer of the R. F. & P. R. R. Co., and a very worthy man.

6. Another married a Mr. Rogers of Spottsylvania County. She left two children, a son and a daughter. Thomas, the son, was raised a clerk in Hanover office under my uncles, William and Thomas Pollard, and afterwards moved to the State of Kentucky and married at quite an advanced age (being upwards of sixty), and left an only daughter, who married a Mr. ———, a Presbyterian clergyman, and who lives near Bowling Green, Kentucky. He obtained a large amount of property by her. The daughter married a Mr. Underwood, of Goochland County, and had several children, among whom are two sons, Joseph and Warner, who

moved to Kentucky under the auspices of their uncle, William Rogers. They are both distinguished lawyers. Joseph was first made judge of one of the State Courts of Kentucky; resigned his seat upon the bench and served one term as United States Senator.

Warner has represented his district in Congress of the United States. They both reside now, 1870, in Bowling Green, Kentucky, and have large and interesting families.

7.   The youngest, whose name, I think, was Priscilla, married Colonel Edmund Pendleton, of Caroline, nephew of Judge Edmund Pendleton. They left quite a numerous family. One of the sons became clerk of Caroline County; one of the daughters married a Mr. Turner of Caroline County; the others I have lost sight of. Thomas, one of the sons, resided for many years in Spottsylvania County, raised his family there and then moved to Kentucky. I know one of his sons, Joseph, who married a Miss Thornton of Caroline. He was a lawyer by profession. He moved to Kentucky and carried his family with him. One of his sons, Peter Thornton, returned to Virginia, and married a Miss Fauntleroy of this county (King and Queen). He has two daughters here. One married a Mr. Roy and the other is still single. The other branches of this family I know nothing of, but suppose they are scattered through the West.

Peter Thornton Pollard [elder son of Joseph Pollard], and his wife are both dead. William, the other son, who settled in Hanover County, was my grandfather. He married a Miss Anderson of Hanover. He was appointed clerk of Hanover in early life and held the office until his death. He left ten children, five sons and five daughters. Of the daughters first:

(1)   Elizabeth, the oldest, married Mr. Bernard Todd, of Charlotte County, Virginia, who for several years represented that county in the Virginia Legislature. He afterwards embraced religion and became a Baptist preacher. They had children, five sons and two daughters.

1.   Thomas, who married a Mrs. Garnett, resided

in the County of King William and died there. He was a magistrate in his county and noted for his piety.

2. William was a Baptist minister of great usefulness; succeeded his uncle, Mr. Robert Pollard, as clerk of the District and Superior Courts of King and Queen County. He was four times married, but left no issue living at the time of his death. He had an only grandson living when he died, who married a Miss Boyd of King and Queen, and died leaving four or five children.

3. Bartlett married a Miss Epps of Nottoway; died in Petersburg, Va., and left a number of children. One of his sons, Bernard, lives now, 1870, in Baltimore. One of the daughters married Augustus Robins of Gloucester County. The others I know but little of, except Kate, who lives with her brother, Bernard, in Baltimore.

4. Joseph lived in Prince Edward; married there and left a family there.

5. Garland moved to the West, and, I think, died in Cincinnati, Ohio.

1. Mary, the oldest daughter, married a man by the name of Buster and moved to the County of Kanawha; he represented the county in the Virginia Legislature; they both died in Kanawha, and I know nothing of their posterity, but suppose they are in that region.

2. Betsy married Temple Walker, and left two children, Betty and Bernard. Betty married Joseph T. Henley, and Bernard (Dr. Walker) resides near Stevensville.

(2) Mary married John Austin of Hanover, and left no issue.

(3) Priscilla married a Mr. Martin, of King and Queen, and left an only daughter, who married Walker Hawes of King William.

(4) Susanna married Robert Kelso of Prince Edward, and died leaving two children: Mary, who married a Dr. Merry, and Robert, who, now—1870—lives at Fancy Farm, Bedford County, Virginia.

(5) Jane never married.

(1) Joseph Pollard, my father (the oldest of the

brothers), married Miss Catherine Robertson of Hanover, and left four sons,—Edmund, William, John, and Joseph. Edmund, William, and Joseph died without issue. I married Miss Juliet Jeffries of King and Queen. We have several children, four sons and three daughters.

(2)   William succeeded his father as clerk of Hanover; was twice married; left three children, one son, George William, who resided in Hanover; and two daughters, Mary, who married John Daracott; and Elizabeth, who married Dr. Joseph Sheppard of Hanover.

(3)   Robert became clerk of the District and County Court of King and Queen; married a Miss Harwood and left four children, one son and three daughters: Maria married Dr. Jacob D. Wacker; Elizabeth, or Betty, married first, Thomas C. Hoomes, and afterwards Colonel A. Fleet of King and Queen. Priscilla died unmarried. Robert succeeded his father as Clerk of the County Court of King and Queen, and married a Miss Harwood, a cousin of his, but had no issue.

(4)   Benjamin lived and died at the old family residence in Hanover; was once Clerk of the District Court of Appeals of Accomac and Northampton Counties; married a Miss Winston and left three children, one son and two daughters, all of whom are now dead. The son married a Miss Winston; was Clerk of the Circuit Court of Hanover County at the time of his death. Anna, the oldest daughter, married Dr. William S. Pryor, and Catherine married Samuel Overton; both of them are now dead.

William graduated at Hampden-Sidney College; was a Presbyterian minister for more than twenty years; afterwards united himself with the Baptist Church, and died a minister in that church.

(5)   Thomas, the fifth son, married a Miss Whitlock; was for many years deputy to his brother, William, who was Clerk of Hanover and was the first Clerk of the Superior Court of Hanover, and continued so until the time of his death. He left two sons and four daughters:

Benjamin now resides in Richmond, and was for many years Clerk of the Circuit Court of Richmond.

Thomas now resides near Richmond, and is a physician of some distinction. He graduated in Paris and has twice visited Europe.

Mary married Henry Temple and left an only daughter, now the wife of Mr. Thomas of Richmond.

Fanny Bacon is now the wife of Robert Kelso of Fancy Farm.

Martha Rebecca married a Mr. Winston of Hanover, who moved to the West. She is now a widow and lives in Louisville, Kentucky.

Sarah is now the wife of Mr. William C. Winston of Hanover.

Robert Pollard, Sr., was likely a descendant of the Robert Pollard whose name will be found among the early settlers; at any rate he was a brother of the distinguished Miss Priscilla Pollard, and is found clerk of the courts about 1803. He was succeeded in office by his son Robert, Jr., who married Harwood. (In 1803-5 we find in the office as deputy William Todd, who was afterwards a noted Baptist minister.) About 1818 there came into the office young John Pollard, born in Goochland County. He was a youth of indomitable courage and high intelligence, educated and refined, and full of life. He married Juliet Jeffries, daughter of Major Thomas Jeffries, and sister of the late Judge Jeffries of the circuit court; and became the father of several of the first men of the county. The wife was one of the finest women, gentle, kindly, attractive, and a wise mother. She most happily blended the *suaviter in modo* with the *fortiter in re.* Her sons above referred to are Professor Thomas, John, D. D., James and Henry R., attorneys, and Robert N. Pollard; all now living except Thomas and James. The daughters are Mrs. P. T. Woodward, Mrs. S. J. Bagby, and Mrs. S. C. Davies. Thornton Pollard of lower King and Queen was a near relative. The Pollards are all of King and Queen ancestry.—[Editor.]

FAMILY OF C. W. PORTER

C. W. Porter, son of Samson and Catherine Porter, who came to King and Queen in 1853, married Bettie Cook December 11th, 1854. His mother was a Miss Neusom. His grandfather was William Porter and his grandmother, Mary Porter, was a Miss Sandy. C. W. Porter was sheriff of King and Queen from 1865 to 1871 and treasurer from 1871 to 1903. Children: Pendleton Cook Porter, C. W. Porter, Jr., William Franklin Porter (dead), Lizzie Lee married Brown, Mary F. married Vaughan, Gertrude married Drain, Lena P. married Bentley, Laura W. married Deshazo.

PURKS FAMILY

(1) William Purks married Mary Carlton (a sister of Benoni Carlton), and second, Deshazo; died about 1837.

(2) Dr. William (Green County, Ga.)

(2) Mary married T. W. Fogg: (3) Clay married Eubank, (3) Sarah married Tarrant, (3) Joseph W. married —————, and others.

(2) Benjamin A. married Smith: (3) Emma Hill, (3) Anne Fillmore married W. C. Adams: (4) Benjamin Alexander, (4) Anne F., (4) Mattie B., (4) Grace F.

(2) Cornelius.

(2) Alexander.

(2) John (migrated).

RICHIE FAMILY

In reply to "A Descendant," the Richmond *Times-Dispatch* of October 28th, 1906, gives the following summary on "Richie":

Archibald Richie is supposed to have been the first to emigrate from Scotland, and settled in Essex County, Virginia, previous to 1750, for we find he was a justice for that county in that year; he was engaged in merchandising on the Rappahannock River, Essex County, with his brother, Samuel Richie, from 1761 to 1791. The family were all from Scotland, and they were doubtless the sons of James Richie, of James Richie & Company, who were merchants of Glasgow, Scotland, from 1767 to 1773. Robert Richie settled in Fredericksburg, where he died March 17th, 1790; he had a sister living there, Eleanora Richie; they were children of Archibald. George Richie, who was born in Fifeshire, Scotland, April 9th, 1792, also came over, and died October 30th, 1835. George Richie and his wife, Mary —————, had two sons, William and William D. Richie, and one daughter, Georgianna Richie.

On tombstones in old St. John's churchyard the following names are found:

James Richie, died September 14th, 1838, at 24 years of age. His wife was Christina. They had children:

James Richie, Jr., died at one year old.

William Richie, born July 22d, 1800.

Thomas Richie, died May 9th, 1812.

This Thomas Richie, known familiarly as " Baldy " Richie, married Thomas Roane's sister, and was father of Thomas Richie (always called " Tom Richie "), the great writer and author, who contolled the old Richmond *Examiner and Enquirer,* for so many years the most powerful Democratic organ in the South. Mr. Richie first took the old *Examiner* after the death of Meriwether Jones, its owner; later he changed its name to *Examiner and Enquirer,* having also bought in the latter paper. For forty years his trenchant pen was a terror and affliction to the Whig party, and so influential was it that Mr. Jefferson himself would turn and say after one of his decisions, " I wonder what Tom Richie will say to that."

Mr. Richie married a daughter of Mr. Foushee, the first mayor of Richmond, for whom Foushee Street was named, being then the limit of the corporation on the west. The children of Mr. Thomas Richie and Miss Foushee were:

1.   George Harrison Richie.

2.   Thomas Richie, Jr., who unfortunately killed, in

a duel, John Hampden Pleasants, editor of the Richmon *Whig*.

3. Isabella Richie, married Benjamin Harrison, of Lower Brandon, James River.

4. Charlotte Richie, married a Gittings of Baltimore, Md.

5. Virginia Richie, never married.

6. Margaret Richie, married Dr. Stern of Washington, D. C., who was President Lincoln's family physician.

All of the above are buried in Hollywood, Richmond. The male line having run out makes the name extinct in Virginia.

ROANE FAMILY

First branch: (1) Charles; (2) Curtis, married Adams; (2) Allen, married Collier; (2) Frank, married Roane; (2) Charles, married Mitchell; (2) Elliott, married White; (2) Lilly and Sue, married Acree; (2) Spencer; (2) Warner, married Bland; (2) Joshua, married Newbill; (3) Rev. Hamilton; (3) Curtis, married Anderson; (3) Lemuel, married Bland and then Anderson; (3) Whitfield, married Bland; (3) Schuff, married Hart; (3) Emily, married Guthrie; (3) Irene, married Elliott; (3) Richard, married Bowden; (3) Luther, married Fary; (3) Charles, married two Roanes; (3) Allen; (3) Lucy, married Fary; (3) Upshur, married Roane and then Kemp; (3) Hays.

Second branch: (1) Schuyler, married Newcomb; (1) James, married Clayton.

(1) Schuyler; (2) John; (2) Austin; (2) Ruker, married Anderson; (2) Maria, married Bland; (2) India and also (2) Ginny, married Roane; (2) Sue, married Broaddus; (2) Betty, married Bowden.

(1) James; (2) James; (2) Richard, married Hudson; (2) Walton; (2) Corinna, married Callis; (2) Emma, married Newcomb; (2) Lula, married Sutton; (2) Blanche, married Douglass; (2) Ella.

ROY FAMILY

Thomas Roy settled Port Royal, Caroline County, in

BELL AIR

The old Pollard home. Early home of Hon. H. R. Pollard and of Rev. John Pollard, D. D., now of Richmond.

1744, and built the first storehouse in that place. Married Miss Judith Beverly of Port Royal; issue, Captain Beverly Roy, born about 1760; died 1820.

Captain Beverly Roy married first, July 26th, 1784, Miss Anne Corrie, of Liverpool, England; issue: Kitty Tyler, born May 6th, 1789; John Corrie, born October 9th, 1785; Jane Wiley Beverly, born March 13th, 1793; Julia Anne, born March 6th, 1795.

Anne (Corrie) Roy, died 1800, and Captain Beverly Roy married second, in 1801, Janet Dickey Byrd, widow of Robert Byrd, Poplar Grove, King and Queen County; issue, Dr. Beverly Roy, born 1802, and Dr. Augustus Gustavus Dunbar Roy, born Nov. 12, 1804. Captain Roy is said to have left home without the consent of his parents, joined the Revolutionary Army, which he entered as ensign in 1777; was promoted to lieutenant and later to captain, and served to the close of the war (Heitman's Historical Register). On his return home his face was covered with beard and his home people failed to recognize the youth that had left them. He was a charter member of the Society of the Cincinnati.

Dr. Beverly Roy married first, Miss Abrahms; issue Jennie and Willie; married second, widow Clopton, née Ritchie.

Annie Roy married Captain Robert Spencer; issue, William Roy, Sue, and Loulie.

Dr. Augustus Gustavus Dunbar Roy married Lucy Carter Garnett, March 6, 1834, Stock Hill, Essex County, Va., by Rev. Richard Claybrook; issue, John Beverly Roy, born January, 1835, at Bowlers, Essex County, Va.; Gustavus Garnett Roy, born June 8th, 1836; Janet Carter, born February 14th, 1838, Ashdale, Essex County, Va.; Robert Boyd, born Nov. 17th, 1839; Rosalie Brooke, born Feb. 9th, 1840; Charles Carter, born May 7th, 1844; Lucy Augustine, born June 26th, 1848.

Janet Carter Roy married Dr. William Hoskins; issue, Lucy Byrd Hoskins, born November 19th, 1858; Willard Dunbar, born September 2nd, 1860; Rosa Brooke, born October 27th, 1862; Charles Roy, born

Sept. 14th, 1865; Elizabeth Lyne, born February 24th, 1869; May and Blanche (twins), born January 5th, 1870; Dunbar, born March 26th, 1876; Robert Roy, born September 4, 1877; Horace Faulkner, born December 3rd, 1880.

Elizabeth Lyne Hoskins married Andrew Jackson Montague, December 11th, 1889; issue, Matilda Gay, born June 27th, 1891; Janet Roy, born October 24th, 1895; Robert Latane, born 2nd April, 1896.

THE RYLAND FAMILY AND HOMES

The progenitor of the Ryland family in King and Queen was Joseph Ryland (son of Thomas and Mary Ryland of " Beasley Cottage," England), who came to America about 1741 and settled on a farm now called " Hollywood " in Essex County near " Ryland's Branch." His first wife was Mary Dudley; the second, Elizabeth Ferguson, daughter of John and Sarah Ferguson of Essex County. The children by the second marriage were Josiah, Joseph, and Joanna. Joseph and Joanna moved to Kentucky, and Josiah lived first near Upper King and Queen Church and later at " Farmington." Josiah Ryland's first wife was Ann Semple, sister of Robert Baylor Semple, D. D. The only child of this marriage was William Semple Ryland of " Roseville," King William County. Josiah Ryland's second wife was Catharine Peachey, daughter of Samuel Peachey and Catherine Webb, daughter of John Webb), all of Essex County. The children by this union were (1) Samuel Peachey, (2) Robert, (3) Elizabeth Ferguson, (4) Martha Jane, (5) Joseph, and (6) John Newton.

1. Samuel Peachey Ryland married Catharine Gaines Hill, daughter of Robert Baylor and Martha Fleming (Gaines) Hill of " The Vineyard," and lived at " Norwood." Their children were Robert Hill, M. D., of Bayou Sara, La.; Josiah, of Richmond; Elizabeth Herndon, who married Augustus Sizer of King William County; Martha Fleming, Charles Hill, D. D.;

Mary Peachey, who married Thomas N. Walker of "Woodville"; Virginia Southwood, wife of James B. Winston of Richmond; Julia, first wife of Thomas N. Walker; Samuel Peachey of Baltimore, Thomas Miller, and Leah, wife of E. F. Acree of Danville, Va.

2. Robert Ryland, A. M., D. D., was the first president of Richmond College, Richmond, Va.

3. Elizabeth Ferguson married Thomas Hite Willis of Jefferson County, West Virginia.

4. Martha Jane married Captain James Robert Fleet of "Goshen"; their children were: Catharine Peachey, William C. of Arkansas, Elizabeth, who married John W. Garlick, M. D., of Richmond; Martha, who married George B. Steel, D. D. S., of Richmond; Lucy Ella, who married John Bagby, M. D.; James Robert of King and Queen, and J. Ryland of Ashland, Va.

5. Joseph Ryland, whose home was "Marlboro," married Priscilla Courtney Bagby, daughter of John Bagby of "Stevensville." Their children were: John William, minister, Middlesex County; Josiah, Second Auditor of Virginia, Richmond; Susan, who married John A. Fleet of "Walkerton"; Mary, who married A. Murdock of "Marlboro"; Nannie, who married Christopher B. Fleet of Richmond; Alice Peachey of Baltimore, James and Joseph of King and Queen County, Priscilla, who married Judson R. Land of King and Queen; Ida, who married George Haynes of Richmond; Edwin of Arkansas, Hugh and Harry Lee of Florida.

6. John Newton Ryland of "Farmington" married first Anna Maria, daughter of Colonel R. M. Garnett of "Spring Farm;" their children were Jeannette Garnett, who married Joseph H. Gwathmey of King William County, and John N., Jr., of "Ingleside." His second wife was Lavinia, daughter of John D. G. Brown; their children were Isabel, who married Thomas Newton Walker of "Woodville," Georgia; Brown and Mosby of Lynchburg, Evelyn, Thomas H. of New York, Annie L., and Catharine Peachy.

C. H. R.

SEMPLE FAMILY

The Semple Family came from Scotland—originally De Sempill—A. D. 1249.

Janet, John of King and Queen, James of New Kent, George, Elizabeth—all of generation (1).

John (1) emigrated and located in King and Queen 1752, m. Elizabeth Walker in 1761; John Walker (2) m. Lowry; Robertson (2) d. in Kentucky 1820; Elizabeth Baylor (2) m. Anderson, Md., Josiah Ryland 1798; James (2) m. Sarah Harwood, d. 1806; Robert Baylor, D. D., (2) b. Jan. 20, 1769, m. Ann Lowry 1793, d. Dec. 25, 1831, pastor of Bruington 39 years, president of Triennial Convention.

Robert Baylor Semple, D. D., (2); John Walker (3), James (3) of Kentucky, m. Elizabeth Garlick, d. 1866; Robert Baylor (3) m. Buckner, d. 1853; Martha (3); William Morris (3); Sarah Fleet (3); Lucy Ann (3), b. 1823, m. Dr. C. B. Fleet, and 2d W. F. Broaddus 1853; James (3); John Robert (4); Samuel Pierce (4); Elizabeth Garlick (4); William Muscoe (4); Ann Lowry (4); Mary M. (4); Mildred C. (4); Samuel Allen (4); Lucy B. (4).

John Walker (2); Elizabeth B. (3); James (3); Francis (3); John Walker (3); Robert (3); Isaac Robertson (3); Charles Donald (3); Lucy Baylor (3); Adeline Matilda (3).

TODD FAMILY

BY DR. B. H. WALKER

Early in the eighteenth century William Todd came to this country and settled first at Toddsbury, in Gloucester County. Then the family came to King and Queen County and settled at Toddsbury, near Dunkirk. They owned a very large landed estate. That William Todd died, leaving, under the law of primogeniture, all his landed estate to his son, William Todd. He left two daughters, Elizabeth Payne, who married Samuel G. Fauntleroy, and another, who married a Mr. Macon. After the death of his first wife, S. G. Fauntleroy married her cousin, Miss Lowry, the daughter of Colo-

nel Lowry of Caroline County. By his first marriage
he had three sons and one daughter: Dr. S. G. Fauntleroy, Jr., Dr. Moore Gardner, William, and Betsy,
who married P. T. Pollard. By his second marriage
he had one son and three daughters: Thomas W. L.,
Martha, who married Colonel Archie Harwood; Lucy,
who married James Govan, and Susan, who married
first Nutall and then Toler.

Bernard Todd, another member of the family, was
either a brother or nephew of William Todd 2d. He
married Betsy Pollard, daughter of William Pollard
of Hanover. He left six sons, Christopher, Thomas,
William, Bartlett, Joseph, and Garland; and two
daughters, Mary and Betsy Waring. Christopher
moved to Tennessee, where he died at the ripe age of
more than ninety years, leaving a large family. Thomas
married Eliza Pendleton, the daughter of Col. Henry
Pendleton of Newtown, King and Queen County, whose
wife was a Miss Peachey. He left three daughters,
Ellen, Frances Ann, and Mary Peachey. Ellen married
Dr. John M. Garnett and left no children. Frances
Ann married Thomas W. L. Fauntleroy and left only
two children, Garnett, who was killed at Sharpsburg,
and Peachey, who married her cousin, Captain Virginius
Fauntleroy, the son of William Fauntleroy. Mary
Peachey married Dr. George William Pollard of Hanover, and lived and died at Williamsville in the old Pollard home. She left five children: Ellen, who married
Mr. Converse and is still living in Louisville, Ky.; Bernard, who was killed in the Civil War; Mary Peachey,
who never married; Harry, who lives in Louisville, and
George William, who lives in Hanover County.

Rev. William Todd, son of Bernard Todd, left three
children: Eliza, who died young; Maria, who married
A. W. Robbins of Gloucester, and died leaving one
son, Colonel W. T. Robbins, who lived in Richmond
and died a short time ago; and Dr. William B. Todd,
who died leaving one son, Captain M. P. Todd. Robert B. Todd, son of Captain M. P. Todd, married Ellen
Garlick, daughter of Dr. Joseph Garlick. Sue Todd,
daughter of R. B. Todd, married Dr. E. J. Moseley.

Colonel Bartlett P. Todd lived in Petersburg and married a Miss Epps. He left four sons, Bernard, Joseph, Thomas, and William; and four daughters, Elizabeth, Kate, Virginia, and Susan.

Mary, daughter of Bernard Todd (as above), married Buster and left one child. Betsy Waring Todd married Walker of King and Queen County, and left two children, Bettie, who married Mr. Joe Henley, and Dr. Bernard H. Walker, who now lives in Norfolk.

WALKER FAMILY

BY B. H. WALKER

Colonel Thomas Walker, an emigrant from England, settled in Gloucester between 1625 and 1650. Colonel Thomas Walker (2) also lived in Gloucester. He was a member of the House of Burgesses in 1662. Colonel Thomas Walker (3) obtained a royal grant for land on the Mattapony River, and removing to King and Queen, he founded the village of Walkerton, and erected there a large manufacturing and grist mill, cotton gin and press, cooper shop, store, etc. The land grant extended from London Swamp above Canterbury Farm, belonging to the Gwathmeys, to Mantapike Swamp, giving a river front of ten miles, and running back some two miles. Colonel Walker (3) erected a home on the first rise from the river near Walkerton, and built also an Indian blockhouse of brick, with holes for musketry, to protect the people from Indian raids. His first house was burned, and a similar one was built immediately on the river, which was also burned. Both of these were large, square houses, with four rooms on a floor, and large halls running through from front to rear, just like the houses at Hillsboro, Rickahoc, Mantua, Mantapike, etc. He was also a member of the Burgesses and was accustomed to take his family with him to Williamsburg. His daughter, Mary Peachey (4), married Dr. Gilmer of Williamsburg, who afterwards moved to Albemarle and was the progenitor of the Gilmer family of that county.

Thomas Walker (3) left three children. The eldest,

John (4), inherited the landed estate and retained the family home. His second son, Dr. Thomas Walker (4), removed to Albemarle and became a large land-owner; he was the first white man to enter the State of Kentucky. He married first a Mrs. Meriwether, and then a Miss Thornton, her sister. They were cousins of General Washington. Dr. Walker was guardian of Thomas Jefferson. He was employed by the general government to make treaties with the Indians, and served for years. A daughter (or grand-daughter) married William C. Rives. His home was Castle Hill, afterwards owned by Mr. Rives, and still in possession of that family. The family was counted wealthy. He gave his daughter, Mary Peachey (5), at her marriage £5000. The oldest son of Thomas Walker (3) married Miss Baylor, and died leaving several children. The eldest, Baylor Walker (5), remained on the old estate near Walkerton. The other children were given estates in the Valley of Virginia. His daughter Elizabeth (5) married Henry Fleet, who was the father of Captain William Fleet and grandfather of Dr. C. B. Fleet, Colonel A. Fleet, and Dr. Benjamin Fleet of King and Queen. The other, Susannah (5), married Semple, and became the mother of Dr. R. B. Semple.

Baylor Walker married Miss Hill, the daughter of Colonel Humphrey Hill of Hillsborough. His son was Major Humphrey Hill Walker, who represented the county in the legislature many years, and died in Richmond in 1820, while a member of the legislature. In the notice of his death in the family Bible, it is stated that he was a member of "The Assembly." The night the old theater was burned, December 25, 1811, he, with another member of the Assembly, started to the theater, but called at the room of another member, who persuaded them to remain until he could make some hot whisky punch. The result was they did not go at all. (Who says whisky does no good?)

Major Humphrey Walker left four sons, John, Baylor, Temple, Robert, and Volney, and three daughters, Mary Hill, Frances, and Sukey. John, Baylor, Temple, and Volney, and their sisters, Mary and Frances, married and left families. Temple Walker was a justice many years, also high sheriff in 1844-'45. He was married four times: first, Mary Hill, daughter of Colonel John Hill of King William; second, Lucy Taliaferro of King William; third, Betsy W. Todd; and fourth, Jane Cluverius. He was the father of sixteen children.

[To give the account of Dr. Walker in full, we append this from him] :

" The Walker family came from the county of Gloucester, after they had obtained a grant from the king of ten miles river front, on Mattapony, and ten miles back into the forest. They made their residence at " Hold," as it was called—Rye Field—just below Walkerton. This place was built up by Colonel Thomas Walker, and was called after him, ' Walkerton.' They established here a large flour mill, and a gin and cotton press, a store, and a ferry. (A bridge spans the river at this point at present.) Near by their home at ' Hold ' they built a blockhouse as a resort from Indians. A part of the grant is still owned by the Walkers,—the old home, Locust Grove, by Melville Walker, and another by A. C. Walker, a justice [of the peace]. Mr. John Walker, a descendant, lived at Chatham Hill, and owned the mill and surroundings. He was the father of Watson and Melville, and had two brothers, Volney and Temple. Volney had three sons, W. H., Benjamin, and ———. Temple Walker had two sons, Dr. B. H. and A. C., as above."

THOMAS WALKER

BY MRS. R. H. LAND

My father, Thomas Walker, was the eldest son of Philip Walker of King and Queen. In early life, his father's circumstances being meager, he was thrown in a large measure on his own resources. Much of his time was spent in farm work, but whenever possible he attended such schools as the country afforded at that period, and having a keen relish for study, he acquired an education that secured for him the position of assistant teacher in a school taught by the Rev. R. B. Temple. In course of time he found himself in the Valley of Virginia, employed for four years as tutor in the family of Mr. Carven Willis of Jefferson County. Later on he returned to his native county, and entered into a partnership in the mercantile business with Mr. John Bagby, one having a store in Ayletts, King William County, and the other in Stevensville, King and Queen, and thus was established between them a lifelong friendship. Early in the last century he married Joanna Mann, and they were the parents of ten children, only four of whom lived to be grown, and only two, T. N. Walker of Richmond, Va., and Mrs. A. W. Land of Baltimore, Md., are now living. My mother, whose parents died in infancy, was raised by her grandmother, Mrs. Smith, *née* Susan Pollard, related to the Pollards of King William and King and Queen. She lived to the venerable age of seventy-two. Both she and her husband sleep in the family burying ground in King and Queen.

WARE FAMILY

From an old court record rescued from old papers found at Williamsburg when it was the capital of the State and the Supreme Court held its sessions there, I find Robert Spencer Ware files his age August 11th, 1789, "under age" (June 11th, 1791, he is "twenty-one years of age"), in an old suit brought for himself, his sister, Lydia, and his infant brother, Spencer Ware. These children are the orphans of Spencer Ware and Miss Digges, married about 1769: Robert Spencer Ware, born 1770; Lydia Ware, born 1772; Spencer Ware, born 1774, died 1804 (Spencer Ware, Sr., died 1777). From this paper we also learn that Lydia Ware married Robert Garrett of King and Queen, about 1796. Their daughter, Elizabeth Garrett (born 1802, died 1867), married Bird Hoskins (born 1800, died 1841). William Hoskins married Janet Carter Roy, December 29th, 1857.

CHAPTER XVIII

FRAGMENTS

Acree—E. Smith Acree (married Fox), a merchant at Walkerton (Turner & Acree), an estimable citizen. Father of Edward F. of Danville, A. C., Rev. R. R., Lucian, and James.

Bates, Sr.—Lived two miles north of Newtown. Sons: James T., Meredith, Dr. William, Kit, Robert, Dr. Thomas J. (married Lumpkin.)

Boulware.—William B. ("Lord"), son of Lee B. Leroy, born one mile above Newtown. Richardson Lumpkin married Amanda, daughter of Lee B., sister of William B.

Carlton, Alfred, was one of a numerous family, and himself left numerous children—Granville, Motley, Alfred, Jr., Frazer, Mrs. Oliver, Mrs. Corr, and Mrs. Vaughan.

Carlton, Cornelius H. and Walter R., were men of culture and great moral worth, who lived and died a mile or two below Cumnor.

Carlton, George K., was for years a merchant, kept Carlton's store, married Gaines. He left an interesting family—Milton, Mrs. Fox, Mrs. Powers, Mrs. Dr. Jackson, and Mrs. Steger.

Cook.—Benjamin Pendleton Cook came, a young man, into the county from Gloucester; m. Emeline Bagby.

Cosby.—Leland C. came from King William and lived for many years at Bruington. A most excellent Christian man. Children: Joseph, James, Mrs. Wright, Mrs. Pemberton, Mrs. Harper.

Councill.—Colonel J. C. Councill (married Smith) came from the vicinity of Portsmouth, attended Fleetwood Academy under Mr. White, taught there and at Virginia Military Institute; afterwards established

Aberdeen Academy; colonel C. S. A.; an invaluable citizen. Children: Mrs. Rudolph, M. Brook, George, Mrs. Pierce, Mrs. Gregory, Mrs. Dr. Gregory.

Courtney.—Captain Robert Courtney was a nephew of Rev. John of Richmond, and son of Robert, Sr.; Captain Courtney was a soldier of the War of 1812, and a man of sterling worth. Robert, Jr., was the father of Mrs. John Bagby, Mrs. William Campbell, Sr., Mrs. Captain Haynes. Captain Courtney was for years a justice—his influence powerful.

Dr. R. H. Cox, a noted physician at Centreville, afterwards West Point. He was a gentleman of high character; married Saunders. Represented the county in Virginia Legislature and member of Virginia Convention of '61. Children: Toug., Mrs. Brooks, Mrs. Dr. Smith.

Dew.—Captain Billy D., of Dewsville, a neighbor of John Kidd. Sons: Dr. William, Prof. Thomas R., John, Franklin of Newtown, and Calvin. Judge John D. is son of Franklin.

Diggs.—Rev. Isaac Diggs left an impress for good upon all who knew him. Children: Dudley, Mrs. Hart, Mrs. Allen, Mrs. T. Jeffries, and Isaac, Jr., a prominent attorney of Richmond. Elder Digges' memory is precious to many.

Dudley.—Alexander Dudley was a noted lawyer, active, strong, and public-spirited. He originated and built the railroad from Richmond to West Point, and became its first president. His sons are: Robert, married Hoskins; Harry, married Roy; Alexander, Jr.; and William R., married Spencer.

Eubank.—Philip Eubank was one of the best men of his day, His sons, who rise up to do him credit are: William, Archie, Benjamin, and Robert.

Fauntleroy.—Three brothers fleeing from France settled in the Northern Neck,—John, Samuel G., and Moore,—and these have transmitted their names to their descendants. John seems to have inspired the Indians around him with mortal terror, probably by the prowess of his arm.

Gwathmey.—Temple G. (married ———. and

Walker), was a cousin of Dr. William and R. T. Gwathmey, father of Charles B., Alfred, Llewellyn, and Archie.

Haynes.—Captain Thomas Haynes, justice, was one of the best of citizens. John R. Haynes was a mechanic, living in Exol Swamp; married two Bagbys. Sons: Cornelius, George A., and Andrew L. and John R., Jr., all of Richmond except Cornelius.

Henley, Joseph, was father of Rev. R. Y., a most excellent man and minister; of Dr. S. S. and Joseph, Jr.; grandfather of T. B. Henly, Esq., of Newport News.

Henshaw, Chaney, lived near Newtown. Children: Jane, married Kit Bates; Virginia, married Broaddus; Bob, Lucy Ann, and Thomas E. (supervisor).

Kidd.—John Kidd, Sr., lived near Munday's bridge. Children: John, Mary (Bagby), Elizabeth (Motley and Bagby), John, Jr., the father of John B. Kidd.

Latane.—Came from Essex. Harry, Sr., was a man of splendid character. His son, Dr. Thomas (married Hale and Robins), has endeared himself to the people in all his section. He is now venerable with age, but seems never to grow old. Children: Dr. Robert, Harry, Jr., of Buchanan, Dr. Thomas, Jr., Mrs. Joe Ryland, Lizzie, Blanche, Mary P., and Annie.

Governor Lumpkin's family, of Georgia, was from King and Queen; also the family of Alexander H. Stephens, for whom Stevensville is named.

Motley.—John Motley lived below Carlton's Store; father of John and Dr. M. of Richmond County, Mrs. B. T. Taylor, Mrs. Dickinson, Mrs. Major Saunders.

Nunn.—These were old citizens. One of them was a constituent member of Bruington Church. George C. was a man of fine integrity and wealth. He left two sons, Captain John R., C. S. A., of Berryville, and Dr. (also Captain) W. C., of West Point; Mrs. J. S. Purcell, Mrs. Cawthorn. William S. and Henry Nunn were brothers of George C., and leave numerous descendants.

Pendleton, Colonel, of King and Queen, had three daughters: first married Colonel R. M. Garnett; second married Thomas Todd; third married Claiborne. The third daughter afterwards married Gatewood, and then William Dew. Colonel Pendleton, I think, had a sister who married a Gatewood, father of a Joe Gatewood, who died at Milan; also of two daughters, one of whom married John Dew of Plain Dealing; the second married Christopher Baylor. The first James Pendleton was an unkind husband, and his brothers-in-law, Hugh Campbell, William Mann, William Harrison, and perhaps Captain Thomas Dew, went to his house at night and gave him a severe whipping, which act involved them in serious trouble. William, George, and Robert Ware Pendleton were sons (?) of William P., who lived and died at Pleasant Grove. They had one sister, who married Dr. John Duval.

Capt. James Pendleton was an officer in the war of the Revolution.

Porter.—C. W. Porter, married Cook, was one of the most popular men in the county. He served for years as county treasurer. Mr. Porter reared a large family: Pendleton, Charlie, Frank, who died early, but daughters married and survive.

Purcell.—James Purcell was the father of Jefferson S. and R. B. Purcell, both now dead.

Roane.—Hon. John Roane was M. C. His son John lived at Newington; in a fit of insanity killed his wife and his overseer. Judge Spencer Roane and William H. Roane have been mentioned.

Robinson.—William Robinson, of Benville, was a grandson of Speaker Robinson. Issue: William C., Needler J., and Mary, who married Sculptor E. V. Valentine.

Saunders.—Major W. C. was a well-known citizen, prominent in insurance and politics. His son, Colonel John R. Saunders (married Miss Hoskins), attorney, is a member of the Governor's Staff (1904). A rising young man.

Scott.—Rev. A. F. Scott impressed himself greatly upon the people as teacher and minister; came from Eastern Shore; taught at Gloucester Courthouse, Centreville, and Stevensville. Children: Francis, George

R., Robert, Mrs. T. P. Bagby, Mrs. Watson Eubank of Essex.

Smith.—Mr. James Smith married Fleet. Lived at Smithfield, near Clarks. Was a man of high intelligence and Christian character, an attorney much honored, the father of Mrs. Judge Jones, Mrs. Colonel Councill, Miss Priscilla, Dr. Robert, Captain James William, C. S. A., and Colonel Thomas, C. S. A., of Kentucky. The conservative influence of this family is immeasurable. The last named is now prominent in educational circles.

Street.—This is a large family living on the Dragon in Essex and King and Queen. Walker Street in 1850 lived some six miles below Carlton's Store, and was the father of Major N. B. Street, C. S. A. Major Street was for years supervisor of the county. A daughter of Street, Sr., married W. C. Hundley, and became the mother of Rev. John W. Hundley and T. Hundley, a prominent Baptist minister. One of Mrs. Hundley's daughters, Augusta, married Rev. W. A. Street. John Thurston, a man of fine character, married a Miss Street.

Muire, Thacker, a retired Methodist preacher, lived at Walkerton. He forgot the ways of peace and had multiplied lawsuits.

Todd.—Thomas Todd, of Toddsbury, in King and Queen,* had daughters: first, Ellen, married Dr. Garnett; second, Frances, married T. W. L. Fauntleroy of Holly Hill; a third married Dr. George William Pollard of Hanover (of these Dr. B. H. Walker was a cousin).

Vaughan.—There came from Petersburg about 1883 a young man named Christopher C. Vaughan. He came among strangers, but by indomitable courage and pluck won for himself a large measure of success. He is merchant, farmer, mechanic, and sawyer at Cumnor; married Miss Carlton.

Walker.—Thomas Walker was counted one of the finest singers ever known in the county. The melodious

* There was another and older Toddsbury in Gloucester.

notes of his voice have scarcely yet died away from the ears of some of the old Bruington inhabitants. Children: Thomas N. Walker, Mrs. Land, Mrs. Gwathmey, and Miss Evelina.

White.—Oliver W. (married Lawrence and Bagby), was an Irishman, who came into the county about 1840, and opened an academy at Fleetwood. In a year or two he had established himself firmly in the confidence of the people, and his school drew from all quarters. His only daughter married Josiah Ryland, Jr., Second Auditor of Virginia. Mr. White's name ought to be imperishable.

Williams.—An extensive family with many ramifications. John was the father of John, Jr., and of Henry (at Carlton's Store).

Wright.—This was a large family with various branches. Dr. John R., William G., and Moore B. were sons or grandsons of Dr. John Wright.

PURKS AND OTHER FAMILIES

BY MRS. W. C. ADAMS

During my visit [in 1907] to King and Queen County it was my pleasure to visit the home of Judge Claggett Jones, where I was courteously treated. He and his wife know by tradition that their home is the location of my grandfather Purks' old home (Woodstock).

We next drove to Mr. Theodore Courtney's store and had an interesting talk on old families; through his kindness I was enabled to visit the little burial place on the old Campbell estate, now owned and occupied by Mr. John Fleet. There are the sunken shapes of three graves. One is my grandfather Purks', and it is almost positive that the other two are those of my grandmother, Mary Carlton Purks, and Captain Whittaker Campbell, my great-great-grandfather. He owned the place when Robert Courtney, Jr. (the father of Major Courtney in Richmond), married there Captain Whittaker Campbell's youngest daughter, Sally, April 9th, 1812. Captain Campbell died between 1812 and 1814, about ninety years old. Mr. Fleet remembers my grandfather, William Purks, and described his features to me. His father, Dr. Christopher B. Fleet, was his physician in his last illness.

The next place adjoining is the old Carlton home. The place is now called Edgemont, and is owned by Mr. Benjamin Dew. Mr. Courtney told me that his sister, Virginia Courtney, married Alexander Carlton, and, at his death, married Lewis W. Smith. He also told me that Captain Robert Courtney, Sr., married Priscilla Campbell.

We then went to Mr. Albert Gresham's, where I saw Mrs. Claggett Jones, Sr., mother of Mrs. Gresham, and she spoke of the school on the Purks home, where her favorite schoolmate was Mary Purks (Mrs. Tazewell Fogg, my father's only sister). She said Benoni Carlton, Sr., married Miss Campbell, but she did not know her Christian name. (I know it was Mary (Polly), and she was the daughter of Captain Whittaker Campbell by his first wife.) She knew that Benoni Carlton, Jr., married his first cousin, Julia Ann Wood (first wife), who was granddaughter to Captain Whittaker Campbell.

I was then driven to Stevensville to see Mr. and Mrs. Joe Ryland, Jr. Mr. Ryland has a very genial way of receiving one, and it was worth the drive to just shake hands with him. Through Mrs. Ryland I located where the family Bible of the Carltons was last known to be,—in the possession of Sue. Carlton, daughter of Benoni Carlton, Jr. (by his first wife), who married Mr. Llewellyn Gwathmey of Norfolk. She died quite young, and her husband married Miss Hendren. Mrs. Ryland, who was Bettie Hugh Bagby, married first, Benoni Carlton the third (Little Ben he was called). Two of the grandsons of my great-grandfather, Benoni Carlton, Sr., married sisters, the Misses Bagby, daughters of the Rev. Richard Hugh Bagby of King and Queen. Benoni Carlton the third married Miss Bettie Hugh Bagby, and Mr. Zack Carlton, now of Luna Landing, Ark., married Miss Emma Bagby.

Mr. Pynes then drove me to Church Hill, about two

miles from Walkerton, to see three old family servants, Parthenia Allen, Nellie Jackson, and Andrew Jackson.

In King and Queen Court House I copied the following:

"In 1835 Harris Carlton was made guardian of Louisa F. Campbell, William H. Campbell, Emily Campbell, and Peter Campbell." Harris Carlton was brother to Benoni Carlton, Jr.

From a Bible owned by Mrs. S. E. Porter, Pine Bluff, Ark., I obtained the following:

"Alexander Campbell married (first wife) Lucy L. Browne, April 24th, 1828." The second marriage of this Alexander Campbell is not recorded.

"Alexander Campbell, probably a son of Captain Whittaker Campbell, died August 1st, 1829, in his 55th year.

"Sarah Campbell (*née* Courtney) died August 1st, 1827, in her 57th [or 51st] year." She was first wife to Alexander Campbell.

"Edward Fox and Emily P. Campbell were married November 30th, 1815."

Whittaker Campbell's descendants are numerous. He was a captain in the war of the Revolution. Born about 1727, died about 1814. His first wife's name is not known. His second wife was Miss Deshazo. By his first wife I know of five children (and there were others),—William Campbell the first, Alexander Campbell, Polly or Mary Campbell, Emily Campbell, Priscilla Campbell. His children by his second wife were: Peter Campbell, Jack Campbell, Elizabeth or Betsy Campbell, Sarah or Sally Campbell. Polly married Benoni Carlton, Sr., Emily married Edward Fox, Priscilla married Captain Robert Courtney, Sr., Jack died unmarried in Mississippi, Elizabeth married James Wood, and second, Robert Pendleton; Sarah married Robert Courtney, Jr., of Richmond. Captain Whittaker Campbell's daughter Priscilla and his son William the first form the first cousinship of William Campbell the second and his wife, at Essex, where now lives William Campbell the third. Captain Robert Courtney married Priscilla Campbell, a sister of William

Campbell the first. Their daughter, Priscilla Courtney, married her first cousin, William Campbell the second, who was son of William Campbell the first. So William the third is great-grandson to Captain Whittaker Campbell.

Captain Robert Courtney's son, William P. Courtney (married Martha E. Campbell) and daughter, Priscilla, form the first cousinship of Theodore Courtney and William Campbell the third of Essex. So Theodore Courtney and William Campbell the third are first cousins and each a great-grandson of Captain Whittaker Campbell.

If I am correct, Captain Whittaker Campbell is great-grandfather to Rev. Alfred Bagby, Theodore Courtney, William Campbell the third, and B. A. Purks. He is grandfather to Major Alfred Courtney, and great-great-grandfather to myself and several others. Two of his grandsons are Major Alfred Courtney and Mr. Mortimer Courtney.

I have never seen the name in print but once, and it was in a payroll of Captain Robert Courtney's company, at Smithfield, 1812 to 1813. Captain Campbell was at that time a helpless rheumatic, in a rolling chair, 85 years of age, and living on the Campbell home in King and Queen. The Marginal Remarks read:

" The time in this Pay Roll is not sufficient but it is believed that this company was also at Norfolk, in the service of the United States."

I copied it from the Virginia Militia Pay Roll, 1812 to 1813, Virginia. Reference Shelf D 35, page 437, Virginia State Library, Richmond.

The second wife of Benoni Carlton, Jr., was Miss Martha Hill Bagby.

The Alexander Campbell here mentioned was no relative of Rev. Alexander Campbell (Scotch) of the Disciples.

The Purks family came to this country from Wales, probably in 1806: the mother, two sons, William and James, and a daughter, Polly. These four are remembered by a few persons still living (the mother lived to be 94 years old). They are all buried in King and Queen except James, who died unmarried in Norfolk.

I know of 23 grandchildren to William Purks, Sr. The daughter Polly, Mrs. Prince, had three sons, who are all dead.

His son, Dr. William Purks, died recently, aged over 80; B. A. Purks is 80 [1907], and Cornelius (no children) is about 77.

Dr. William Purks and family are among the most influential in Salome, Green County, Ga. (near Atlanta), where he has lived nearly a lifetime; and a lifetime friend of his was Alexander H. Stephens, Vice-president of the Confederate States of America.

One of Dr. Purks' sons is a banker, another a professor.

The other son of William Purks, Sr., John, died in California when quite young.

DUDLEY FAMILY

BY GEORGE F. DUDLEY

4043 McPherson Ave., St. Louis, Mo., Nov. 7th, 1904.

At the request of my cousin, Miss Ann Eliza George, of No. 111 North Third St., Richmond, Va. (now here present at my residence named at the head of this paper), I make a copy of the following names of the Dudley family from whom we are directly descended. They are taken from an official copy of the will of my grandfather, William Dudley, belonging to me and now before me and my cousin (Miss George, above named), at my residence. This will was made by my grandfather, William Dudley, of the county of King and Queen, in the State of Virginia, on the 7th day of November, 1794, and admitted to probate on Monday, July 12th, 1802, at the courthouse of that county; the witnesses to the will being Thomas Metcalfe, Judith Shackelford, and Carter Braxton, Jr. The executors appointed by him in the will were his wife, Anne Dudley, executrix; his son, Henry Fleet Dudley, and William Chamberlayne of New Kent County, executors.

The only one of the executors who appears to have qualified was his son, Henry Fleet Dudley. The order of the names of his family in which the will makes the bequests is as follows:

His wife, Anne Dudley; his son, Henry Fleet Dudley; his daughter, Mary Dudley; his daughter, Anne Pinchback Dudley; his daughter, Frances Dudley (the grandmother of Miss Ann Eliza George of 111 North Third Street, Richmond, Va., above mentioned, and now present at my residence, 4043 McPherson Avenue, November 7th, 1904, attending the World's Fair at St. Louis, Mo.); his daughter, Martha Elizabeth Dudley; his son, William Dudley; and his son, George Fleet Dudley, the father of the writer of this paper, and whose name I bear in full.

It will be seen from the above list of his children that my grandfather had four daughters and three sons; a peculiar circumstance in the names of his sons is that two of them had Fleet for their middle name, Henry and George. The last survivor of his children, so far as I can learn, was Aunt Mary Dudley, known better as Polly Dudley, who never married. She died about 1862 at the residence of her niece, Mrs. Mary Frances George, then the wife of Mr. Miles George, and the mother of Miss Ann Eliza George of Richmond, Va. Miss Mary (Polly) Dudley spent much time at the residence in Richmond, Va., of Mrs. Margaret Young and sister, old friends of the Dudley family. Mrs. Young told me she saw President Washington riding out the last time he ever left his house, her father then being an overseer of the General's and living on Mt. Vernon farm.

The official copy of the will of my grandfather above referred to was made by Robert Pollard, clerk.

The home of my grandfather, William Dudley, of King and Queen County, Va., was well identified by his establishing Dudley's Ferry, which still bears his name, over York River, near the junction of the two rivers which form the York. His brother-in-law, General William Chamberlayne's residence, one of the executors named in his will, but who does not seem to have qualified, was historic socially at a very early period as the first meeting place of General Washington and the widow Custis, afterwards Mrs. Washington. My father, as he often told my mother, and his brother and sisters often visited his uncle, General Chamberlayne, and spent much time there. I often regret that in October, 1881, when I visited Mrs. Margaret Young and her sister, Miss Nellie Anderson, in Richmond, Va., they were so far advanced in age and so infirm, as they were dear friends of the Dudley family, and, had conditions been different with them, could have told me much about my relations.

Dr. George Fleet Dudley.

209 Grace Street, Richmond, Va., August 16th, 1907.—I have left out of this paper a statement made to Cousin Ann Eliza George about the time I made the foregoing (from which I have taken the above copy this day in substance), about my granduncle, Henry Dudley, brother of Grandfather William Dudley, about his service in the Revolutionary War,—for lack of time to copy it. It can be seen at Cousin Eliza's residence, 111 North Third Street, Richmond, Va.

George Fleet Dudley.

INTERESTING NOTES

From Colonel B. Cameron, Stagville, N. C.

It looks as if I can never finish the Roane chart, for constantly I am discovering some new line, and when I do this it seems like a long time to get the desired information.

I wrote you about the discovery of the Richie line, but that the lady was at the White Sulphur Springs. I finally went to Washington City to see her. Then this week I got some information about a line in South Carolina.

Then there is a line which I have not been able to trace, but now I think I have located by reason of an article in last week's issue of the *Confederate Veteran*. It gave a sketch of the life of Spencer Roane Thorp in California, who the article said was the great-great-grandson of Patrick Henry. Therefore I think he must be the child of Sallie Roane, the missing line. In other words, Chief Justice Spencer Roane married Anna Henry, the daughter of Patrick Henry. Their eldest son, William Henry Roane, was United States Senator from Virginia, and their youngest, Lafayette Roane, married and settled in Kentucky, leaving an only child, Sallie, whose descendants, if any, I have never been able to trace. I now think I have the clue, as this gentleman was born in Kentucky, and served in the Confederate army. I have written to his widow, whose address was given in the article. When I hear from her I will let you know. In the meanwhile I trust I am not delaying your work. I received the Brockenbrough lines through Mr. Stanard of your city and Mrs. Semmes of Lexington. Also from the latter about the Bernards, Dykes, and Hipkins. There are two lines still deficient, the Garnetts and the Calstons. The former will give me some trouble, the latter I think I will procure without trouble.

I have a very nice sketch of the Roane and Ruffin families, written by my kinsman, Colonel Frank G. Ruffin, whose mother was a Richie and her mother a Roane. This I thought you could use as an introduction or preface to the chart. I have sent it to a friend to edit, as it is in his own writing.

REMINISCENCES OF LOWER KING AND QUEEN

BY GEORGE S. SHACKELFORD

Richard Shackelford, son of John, was born December 18th, 1801, and died May, 1858. He was married three times. His first wife was Frances Taliaferro, who left two children, Frances and James W., both now dead. His second wife, my mother, was Mary Anne

Thornton, daughter of Frank Thornton, of Gloucester, who left seven children,—all dead, except myself. His third wife was a widow Leigh, *née* Sears, who left five children, three of whom are still living,—Laura, Lulie, and Sarah, widow of Captain James B. Pleasants of Richmond.

I was born July 31st, 1834. I have four children, George P., R. Estelle, Eva G., and Mary T. I have seven grandchildren.

There lived in the same neighborhood with my boyhood home the Anderson family. Mr. Frank Anderson had three sons and one daughter, all dead, leaving large families of children. The sons were Beverley, William H., and Hansford. His daughter married Henry Roane. There was also a Hansford Anderson, known as " Big Hansford," and Robert S. Anderson, brothers, each of whom left a family. I did not know their father.

There was also another Beverley Anderson, a near relative of the others. He left two sons, Dr. Garry and Wilbur F., each of whom has two children.

There was also a large family of Roanes in the lower end of the county. Charles Roane, born in 1776, had eight sons and two daughters: Wiley P., Ellett, Allen, Curtis, Charles A., S. F., Warner P., and Joshua. Neither of his daughters, Lillie and Sarah, left an heir, but each of the sons left a family. Wiley P. Roane is still (1903) living, and has quite a number of children. He is about seventy-six years old.

Shackelford's Church was built in the early days of Methodism. Bishop Asbury preached there, as did the early preachers. The church was rebuilt in 1823. A new church, brick, was built just across the road in 1856-'57, and is in good order.

There was a Baptist church about three miles away, called Poroporone, which has been moved four miles farther up the county to the village of Centreville. There is an old church, of that name, three or four miles farther up, which was built some time before the Revolution. It was used by all denominations, but, because all claimed it, it was ordered to be sold, and was bought by Colonel Shelton, who made a deed of it to the Methodists, and it is still owned by them.

Some time before the Old Church was sold, Mr. Corbin built an Episcopal church on his land, but failed to make a deed to them [the Episcopal society]. Mr. Peter S. Pollard bought the farm from Mr. Corbin, but there being no reservation of the church, he claimed it and sold the bricks to different parties. My father bought some of them; I know this to be a fact.

I have given but an imperfect sketch, for I can tell it better than I can write it.

Yours,

GEORGE S. SHACKELFORD.

This from Col. Fleet of Culver: "Thos. Walker, ancestor of the distinguished Dr. Thos. Walker, and Riveses of Albemarle, and Gov. Thos. Walker Gilmore, was from K. & Q."

Semple, John and James S., were sons of Rev. James Semple of England. John settled in King and Queen, marrying a Miss Walker. Their son, Robert B. A. Croghan, married Lucy Clark, and their son, Major Croghan, then a mere youth, held the fort at Sandusky against Gen. Proctor with a large force of Indians and whites. He also distinguished himself at Tippecanoe.

Col. Anderson of Fort Sumter was a son of Col. A. W. S. Anderson and Sarah Marshall Clark (Taylor and Anderson Families).

Capt. Thos. Dew served in the War of 1812; for a time he was stationed at Tappahannock, a small town on the banks of the Rappahannock River. There were efforts, and possibly repeated efforts, to effect a landing of British troops at that point, but they were successfully repulsed.

Col. Jacob Lumpkin, who died 1708, and is represented on his tomb as a " dux militum," was a prominent man in the early wars of the colony. The Lumpkin family seems to have been quite distinguished in the county. He is buried at Mattapony Church.

OTHER FAMILY NAMES:

Giles Bland, ——— Hansford, and ——— Drummond, three men of King and Queen, were among Berkeley's martyrs, *i.e.*, they were with Nathaniel Bacon in his rebellion against Berkeley, and were put to death by order of the latter.

Governor Spottswood and his knights were absent about six weeks in their transmontane expedition.

Speaker Robinson, of King and Queen County, was in the chair on the occasion when a vote of thanks was passed by the Assembly to Washington; when Washington rose to reply, and hesitated in his speech, the Speaker said: " Sit down, Mr. Washington; your modesty is equal to your valor, and that surpasses anything which I can express."

A man named Estis, living in the lower part of the county, was tall, square-shouldered, with long legs and arms—a powerful man physically. He always called himself in public, " Mr. Estis," and ventured largely upon his dignity. He had the reputation of being the biggest eater in the county, and was quite as fond of whisky as he was of Old Virginia ham. Again and again he got himself in trouble with the court when John Barleycorn got the better of him. Several times the Judge sent him to jail. A story was told of him, which I believe was true, that on one occasion at the Courthouse he bargained with an unsophisticated man who brought oysters to court to sell, to give him as many oysters as he could eat for a quarter. The man told Mr. Estis to help himself, when he forthwith devoured all that were in his bucket and took the bucket, because, he said, he had not had enough.

Fleet, Ryland, Garnett, Gaines, Hill, Bagby, Pollard, Courtney, Campbell, Wright, Shackelford, Shackford, Lumpkin, Davis, Latane, Nunn, Howerton, Dew, Boulware, Lyne, Hutchinson, Broaddus, Carlton, Evans, Haynes, Rice, Jones, Smith, Gresham, Walker, Taylor, Hoskins, Motley, Dudley, Todd, Garlick, Fauntleroy, Jeffries, Coxe, Porter, Garrett, Purcell, Bird, Harwood

(7), Street, Thurston, Hundley, Williams, Diggs, Henley, Sutton, Deshays, Gwathmey, Pointer, Spencer, Guthrie, Scott, Tunstall, Bray, Councill, Watkins, Allen, Land, Anderson, Robertson, Robinson, Mann (9), Roane, Dew, Yarrington, Burton, House, Lipscomb, Cook, Hall, Brooke, etc.

FROM BISHOP MEADE'S "OLD CHURCHES," ETC.

CORBIN FAMILY (VOL. 2, P. 14)

Henry Corbin settled in the parish of Stratton Major, King and Queen, about the year 1650. He had three children: Thomas, Garvin, and Henry. Henry, m. Bassett, was once President of the Council. Garvin had three sons and four daughters: Sons, Richard, of Laneville, m. Betty Tayloe, daughter of Col. John Tayloe; John; Garvin, Jr., m. Hannah, sister of Richard. Henry Lee was also a member of Council.

TAYLOR FAMILY (VOL. 2, P. 98)

They settled between the North (James) and York Rivers, 1698. This was James Taylor. His daughter Mary was the mother of Judge Edmond Pendleton. His son John was the ancestor of Col. John Taylor, of Caroline. John's son, James, was the father of Francis Taylor, who became the wife of Ambrose Madison, and the grandmother of President Madison. George Taylor had fourteen sons, seven of whom served in the Revolutionary Army. James Taylor, Jr., had four sons: James, George, Zachary, and Erasmus. Zachary was the grandfather of President Taylor. James Taylor, Sr., above mentioned, was for years a resident of King and Queen.

WM. C. RIVES (VOL. 2, P. 45)

Married a Miss Walker, formerly of King and Queen.

Robinson Family (Vol. i, p. 378)

John (1) was of Yorkshire, England. Christopher (2). John (3), b. 1683; President of the Council; m. Beverly, a daughter of Robert Beverly. John (4) was Treasurer, and Speaker of Burgesses, He was a defaulter to the government, but the deficit was subsequently paid over to the government. Here is the epitaph inscribed upon the monument to Speaker Robinson: " Beneath this place lieth all that could die of the late worthy John Robinson, Esq., who was a representative of the County of King and Queen, and Speaker to the House of Burgesses about twenty-eight years. With what fidelity he acted as Treasurer is well known to us. He was a tender husband—a solid Christian."

On land belonging to Melville Walker, just below Walkerton, there are marks of an old fort. We surmise that this fort was erected by whites vs. Indians at an early period, but have been able to learn nothing definite.

Messrs. Carter Braxton of Mantua, and John Gaines, neighboring lawyers, were of opposite political parties. Each represented his party on the stump, and many were the sharp thrusts given and taken. Gaines was a Whig and Braxton a Democrat.

Taylor Family

James Taylor (2d), ancestor of Gen. Zachary Taylor, the hero of Buena Vista, and afterwards President of the United States, was a Burgess from King and Queen, and was in the Spotswood (Horse Shoe) expedition across the mountains, 1716. Married Martha Thompson. These were, singularly enough, great-grandparents of two Presidents, Madison and Taylor (Robinson and Taylor families, p. 234).

Col. Richard Taylor, of the Continental Army, removed to Kentucky in 1794. When dying, he said, " The ship is foundering, but the cargo is saved " (p. 255).

Donald Robertson was born in Scotland, Sept. 27, 1717; came to King and Queen 1763; died 1783.

"Apple Tree" P. E. Church stood on land called Farmington, and was probably Robertson's Church. This is one mile below Rosemont. Cattail Church (St. David's) was a mile and a half below Ayletts, in King William.

We avail ourselves of the following from the pen of our venerable friend, Dr. B. H. Walker—himself a member of one of our first families;

"Some of the best and noblest people in the world were natives of King and Queen. Living on the farm adjoining my father's was Gen. John Young, who was Quartermaster-General under Washington. My father always spoke of him as a splendid specimen of the Virginia gentleman, independent in his words and acts, and for many years presiding justice in the county. He never married, and at his death distributed his property among his near kin. He had a favorite nephew, Charles Chilton, whom he educated and expected to make his heir, but the boy was restless and left his home for one of the South American republics fighting for independence. When he returned his uncle was dead and his property given to others. Gen. Young's former home is now owned by his great-grandnephew, John Temple, Superintendent of Schools of Westwood.

"Another prominent and noted character in the early history of the county was Col. Richard Corbin of Laneville. He was a large owner of lands, slaves, and money. People used to say, 'Rich as Dick Corbin.' He built the large hotel at the Court-House, which remained until the Civil War, when the Yankees burned it, along with the Court-House, Clerk's office, records, and private dwellings. There is a tradition that Col. Corbin was a Royalist and hid away in the subterranean cellar at Laneville many of the colonial archives. He was probably the man whom Patrick Henry, with a company of soldiers, was looking for as being Treasurer of the Colony, to recover money for the powder destroyed by Dunmore."

"I mention also," the Doctor continues, "Mr. Samuel Fauntleroy, who lived first at the Mount, and then at Holly Hill, who was the last man in the county to ride in a coach and four. He used to come in that style to Bruington Church, of which he was a member. His family was of French Huguenot extraction. He was the father of Dr. S. G. Fauntleroy, Sr., and grandfather of the late Dr. S. G. He was father also of Thomas W. L. and Dr. Moore Fauntleroy, and of Mrs. James Govan, Mrs. Arch. Harwood, Mrs. Thornton Pollard, and Mrs. Toler. Only three of his grandchildren are now living, Samuel F. Harwood, Esq., of Newington, Mrs. Susan Fauntleroy, née Govan, and Mrs. Virginius Fauntleroy of Holly Hill. Samuel F. married first, Miss Todd, daughter of William Todd of Toddsberry."

CHAPTER XIX

REPRESENTATIVES OF KING AND QUEEN IN BURGESSES, COMMITTEES, CONVENTIONS, ETC.

The following extracts are from old records found in State Library: " Thos. Walker, b. in K. & Q., 1715, able, bold and energetic, traversed mountains into Kentucky among the first. He was commissary to Braddock and present at his defeat in 1755. His son John lived at Castle Hill; was Aide to Washington, member Burgesses; U. S. Senator; d. 1809. His son Thos. a Captain in Revolution (9th Reg.) ; another son, Francis, Col. of 88th Reg. Hon. W. C. Rives married Judith, Francis' daughter, and owned Castle Hill.

COMMITTEE OF SAFETY, KING AND QUEEN COUNTY

Chosen by Freeholders Monday, Dec. 12, 1774.

Thomas Coleman, George Lyne, Gregory Baylor, Richard Tunstall, Jr., Robert Hill, Gregory Smith, Tunstall Banks, Anderson Scott, William Richards, William Todd, Henry Todd, John Bagby, George Brooke, Henry Lumpkin, Benjamin Pendleton, John Collins, Thomas Rowe, Stephen Field, William Lyne, Jos. Temple, John Lyne, and Richard and Matthew Anderson, gentlemen.

DELEGATES TO CONSTITUTIONAL CONVENTIONS

March 20, 1775—George Brooks, George Lyne.
July 17, 1775—George Brooke, George Lyne.
Dec. 1, 1775—George Brooke.
May 6, 1776—George Brooke, William Lyne.
1788—William Fleet, Thomas Roane.
1901-1902—C. B. Jones.

REPRESENTATIVES OF KING AND QUEEN COUNTY IN THE HOUSE OF DELEGATES

The following record of the County Representatives

in the House of Delegates contains some breaks which I could not fill:

1781—Thomas Coleman.

1788—Anderson Scott and Larkin Smith.

1788—Convention, William Fleet and Thomas Roane.

1789—William Roane and Larkin Smith.

1791—John W. Sample and Benjamin Dabney.

1792 and 1793—John W. Sample and Larkin Smith.

1794—Benjamin Dabney and Henry Young.

(For 1800 we find Robert Pollard a Representative from King William.)

1801—Benjamin Dabney and Larkin Smith.

1803—Benjamin Dabney and Larkin Smith.

1806—John H. Smith and Henry Gaines.

1808—John H. Smith and John Roane.

1809—Henry Gaines and Humphrey Walker.

1810—Wiley Campbell and Humphrey Walker.

1812-15—Humphrey Walker and William H. Roane (four terms).

1817—James G. Row and Charles Hill.

1818—James G. Row and Edwin Upshaw.

1821—Thomas G. Smith and Humphrey Walker.

1822—Archibald R. Harwood and Edwin Upshaw.

1823 and 1824—Archibald R. Harwood and Benjamin Pollard.

1826—John Mason and Benjamin Pollard.

1827 and 1828—Edwin Upshaw and Benjamin Pollard.

REPRESENTATIVES IN LEGISLATURE

1829—John Gaines and William Armistead.

1830—Benjamin Pollard and ———.

1832 and 1833—A. R. Harwood and ———.

1834—Benjamin Pollard and ———.

1835—John W. Robinson and Alexander Fleet.

1836, 1838, and 1839—David P. Wright and ———.

1840-1842—William B. Davis (three terms).

1843—John Lumpkin and ———.

1844—William B. Davis.

1844 and 1846—John Gaines and ———.

1847—David P. Wright and ———.

1848-1850—James R. Howser (three terms).

1846—Carter M. Braxton (Senator).

1847-1850—Samuel F. Harwood (Senator, four terms).

1849—Littleberry W. Allen (Sergeant-at-Arms).

I find the name of James Smith of King and Queen on payroll for 1850—a Senator; also those of M. R. H. Garnett (Essex), B. B. Douglass and H. B. Tomlin (King William), and Robert McCandlish (Middlesex); also Henry A. Wise, John R. Chambliss, John M. Botts, Tazewell, Taylor, etc., as of the General Assembly in 1850; also Andrew B. Evans (Middlesex), 1859, King and Queen, is omitted for some years here—probably associated with Essex.

1859 and 1861—Thomas W. Garrett (Essex and King and Queen).

1862-1864—George T. Wright (Essex and King and Queen, three terms).

1865—T. J. Christian (King and Queen and King William).

1869 and 1870—J. W. Bullman.

1872 and 1873—John N. Gresham.

1874—William Hoskins.

1876—Richard H. Cox.

1876—For King William, Philip Gibson.

1877 and 1878—Richard H. Cox.

1877—King William, R. S. Ryland.

1879—J. W. Bullman (H. D.); J. G. Cannon (Senator).

1880, '82, '84, '86, '88—H. R. Pollard (five terms).

1889, 1891, 1893—James S. Jones (three terms).

1895 and 1897—G. C. Bland.

1899—J. W. Fleet.

KING AND QUEEN OFFICERS, 1714

Sheriff: John Madison.

Coroners: George Braxton, T. Pettitt.

Justices: John Holloway, Wm. Bird, James Taylor,

G. Braxton, T. Pettitt, J. Madison, L. Orill, Robert Pollard.

Burgesses: John Holloway, William Bird.
County Clerk: C. C. Thacker.
Parishes: St. Stephens and Stratton Major.
Ministers: Ralph Bowker and John Skaife.
1702. Ed. Portlock.
(Historical Society Papers, Vol. II., page 7.)
(Historical Society Papers, Vol. IV., page 381.)

For many years prior to the Civil War, the enforcement of justice in the county was, by constitutional enactment, in the hands of the Justices of the Peace, one of their number being chosen as presiding justice, a given number constituting a court. The compensation was very small, there was only the honor of the position, and the consideration that a presiding justice, after so many years serving, was to succeed to the shrievalty, which paid very well. Such men as those whose names are here given served as presiding justice from 1830 to 1860, and gave luster to the office: John Lumpkin, Alexander Fleet, Thomas Haynes, John R. Bagby, Samuel Tunstall, Robert Courtney, Robert Bland, Robert Spencer, John Pollard, and others. Very many of the older citizens regarded this county court system as unsurpassed in the equitable administration of justice, and never ceased to regret its downfall under the " Underwood Constitution " after the war.

EXTRACTS FROM RECORDS OF KING AND QUEEN COUNTY
COURT

Monday, December 5th, 1831—William Browne, Esq., Judge (also presided April, 1832).

James Smith and John Pollard appointed Commissioners in Chancery.

On motion of William Todd, Clerk, Robert Pollard, Jr., was appointed Deputy Clerk.

John B. Christian, Attorney for Commonwealth; Hugh Campbell, Sheriff.

Tuesday, September 20th, 1832—James Semple, Judge.

Grand Jury: Temple Walker, Foreman; Thomas Garnett, Banks Garnett, Thomas Wyatt, Robert Bland, Jr., Robert Courtney, Jr., Philip B. Pendleton, Josiah Ryland, David P. Wright, Carter B. Fog, Henry G. Segar, Leroy Boulware, John B. Martin, James C. Roy, Peter T. Pollard, Robert Ware, John Williams, Elias R. Wattlington, and Isaac Hillyard.

April 25th, 1833—Francis Row, Sheriff.

September 21st, 1833—William Todd resigned as Clerk; Robert Pollard, Jr., appointed Clerk.

June 11th, 1835—A. P. Upshur, Judge; Lee Boulware, Sheriff.

November 3d, 1835—John B. Christian, Judge; James D. Halyburton, Attorney for Commonwealth.

May 4th, 1837—John Motley, Sheriff.

May 11th, 1839—Thomas F. Spencer, Sheriff.

November 10th, 1841—Joseph Pollard, Sheriff.

May, 1843—John Mann, Sheriff.

November, 1844—James M. Jeffries, Attorney for Commonwealth.

May, 1845—Temple Walker, Sheriff.

May, 1847—Robert Courtney, Sheriff.

May, 1849—John Lumpkin, Sheriff.

November 9th, 1849—Joseph Christian and Samuel F. Harwood qualified as attorneys at law.

May, 1851—John Pollard, Sheriff.

November, 1852—John Tayloe Lomax, Judge.

November, 1854—Robert M. Davis, Sheriff.

November, 1857—Richard H. Coleman, Judge.

April, 1858—John H. Watkins, Sheriff.

November 18th, 1859—A meeting of Judge, members of Bar and officers of the Court. Robert L. Montague announced the death of James Smith. Addresses also by Alex Dudley, James M. Jeffries, B. B. Douglas, and C. G. Griswold.

November, 1861—Peter D. Samuel, Sheriff.

Militia in 1781: Caroline, 805; King William, 436; King and Queen, 500; Essex, 468; Middlesex, 210; Gloucester, 850.

The records show the following King and Queen men in the War of 1812:

4th Reg. Va. Mil., Col. Elliot Muse, Capt. John Bagby, 1st Lieut. John Gill, 2d Lieut. Geo. Hill, 3d Whit Campbell, 1st Sergt. Baylor Temple, 2d Thos. Walker. Privates, John Didlake, Edw. Fox, Asa Gresham, Hart, Haskins, John Lumpkin, I. Lewis, Lipscomb, Nunn, Motley, Ro. Pollard, etc.

9th Reg., Col. Wm. Boyd, Surgeons John Haskins and M. G. Fauntleroy, Adj. John G. Garnett, 1st Sergt. Harris Carlton, Q. M. Sergt. Henry Bagby.

9th Reg. Artil., Col. Boyd, 2d Lieut. Jas. Gresham, A. R. Harwood, T. C. Holmes, Capt. Privates, Eubank, Walden, Jeffries, Haskins, Muire, Pendleton, Trice, Thurston, etc.

21st Reg., Capt. Wm. Harwood.

KING AND QUEEN BURGESSES

The following will be found interesting as presenting names of representatives from King and Queen in the House of Burgesses up to the Revolution. (From Stanard's " Colonial Virginia Register," Albany, N. Y., 1902:)

March 2, 1692—William Leigh, John Lane.
Sept. 24, 1696—William Leigh, Joshua Storey.
May 13, 1702—William Leigh, James Taylor.
June 18, 1702—William Leigh, James Taylor.
March 19, 1702-3—William Leigh, William Bird.
April 20, 1704—(In place of Leigh, deceased) William Bird.
April 24, 1706—Robert Beverley.
Nov. 7, 1711—John Holloway.
Nov. 16, 1714—John Holloway, William Bird.
April 23, 1718—John Baylor, George Braxton.
Nov. 2, 1720—George Braxton, Robert Beverley.
May 9, 1722—George Braxton, Richard Johnson.
May 9, 1723—George Braxton, Richard Johnson.
May 12, 1726—George Braxton, Richard Johnson.
Feb. 1, 1727-8—George Braxton.
Aug. 5, 1736—John Robinson, Garwin Corbin.
Nov. 1, 1738—John Robinson, Garwin Corbin.

May 22, 1740—John Robinson, Garwin Corbin.
May 6, 1742—John Robinson, George Braxton.
Sept. 4, 1744—John Robinson, George Braxton.
Feb. 20, 1745—John Robinson, George Braxton.
July 11, 1746—John Robinson, George Braxton.
March 30, 1747—John Robinson, George Braxton.
Oct. 27, 1748—John Robinson, George Braxton.
April 10, 1749—John Robinson, George Braxton.
Feb. 5, 1752—John Robinson, Philip Johnson.
Nov. 1, 1753—John Robinson, Philip Johnson.
Feb. 4, 1754—John Robinson, Philip Johnson.
Aug. 22, 1754—John Robinson, Philip Johnson.
Oct. 17, 1754—John Robinson, Philip Johnson.
May 1, 1755—John Robinson, Philip Johnson.
Aug. 5, 1755—John Robinson, Philip Johnson.
March 25, 1756—John Robinson, Philip Johnson.
April 30, 1757—John Robinson, Philip Johnson.
March 30, 1758—John Robinson, Philip Johnson.
Sept. 14, 1758—John Robinson, George Braxton.
Nov. 9, 1758—John Robinson, George Braxton.
Feb. 22, 1759—John Robinson, George Braxton.
Nov. 1, 1759—John Robinson, George Braxton.
March 4, 1760—John Robinson, George Braxton.
May 19, 1760—John Robinson, George Braxton.
Oct. 5, 1760—John Robinson, George Braxton.
March 5, 1761—John Robinson, George Braxton.
Nov. 3, 1761—John Robinson, George Braxton (died before taking seat).
Jan. 4, 1762—John Robinson, John Pendleton.
March 30, 1762—John Robinson, John Pendleton.
Nov. 2, 1762—John Robinson, John Pendleton.
May 9, 1763—John Robinson, John Pendleton.
Jan. 12, 1764—John Robinson, John Pendleton.
Oct. 30, 1764—John Robinson, John Pendleton.
May 1, 1765—John Robinson, John Pendleton.
Nov. 6, 1766—John Robinson (died during session), George Brooke, and Richard Tunstall (in place of Robinson, deceased).
March 12, 1767—George Brooke, Richard Tunstall.
March 31, 1768—George Brooks, Richard Tunstall.
May 17, 1769—William Lyne, John Tayloe Corbin.

Nov. 17, 1769—William Lyne, John Tayloe Corbin.
May 21, 1770—William Lyne, John Tayloe Corbin.
July 11, 1771—William Lyne, John Tayloe Corbin.
Feb. 10, 1772—George Brooke, John Tayloe Corbin.
March 4, 1773—George Brooke, John Tayloe Corbin.
May 5, 1774—George Brooke, John Tayloe Corbin.
June 1, 1775—George Brooke, George Lyne.

PORTRAITS IN KING AND QUEEN COURT HOUSE, OCTOBER, 1905.

William Lyne Wilson,
Judge Jones,
Judge Jeffries,
Judge Foster,
Clerks Pollard,
Major N. B. Street,
Major J. R. Bagby,
Rev. R. B. Semple,
Rev. William Todd,
Speaker Robinson,
Hon. Carter Braxton,
Colonel John Pollard,
Colonel Smith Acree,
Colonel Alexander Dudley,
Colonel R. B. Bland,
Major Roderick Bland,
Robert Courtney,
Thomas Garnett,
Dr. J. Muscoe Garnett,
Judge Wright,
Judge Thomas Ruffin, of Newington, Court of Appeals of North Carolina,
Judge Spencer Roane, Va. Court of Appeals,
Captain Archibald Roane Harwood, of Newington,
Hon. Watt Gresham,
Dr. Richard H. Cox,
Dr. William Hoskins,
Dr. B. F. Dew,
Dr. J. N. Gresham,
T. R. Gresham,
Prof. T. R. Dew,
Rev. A. Broaddus,
Rev. Robert Ryland,
Dr. Samuel Griffin Fauntleroy, J. P.,
Samuel Tunstall, J. P.,
James Parke Corbin,
Colonel Robert Spencer, J. P.,
Colonel Alexander Fleet,
William Boulware, U. S. Minister to Naples,
Captain Campbell Fox, C. S. A.,
James Southgate,
Colonel William B. Davis,
———— Hutchinson,
Author of this Book,
David P. Wright, J. P.,
Judge John G. Dew.

INDEX

INDEX

Richmond, evacuation of, 202-210; great day in, 275-276; operations from, to Appomattox, 192-202

Richie family, 352-354, 375

"Rickahoc," 73

Rights, Bill of, 121

Rives, William C., 380

Roane family, 68, 69, 73, 85, 354, 375, 377
  Hon. John, 367
  John, 68, 69, 76, 85, 367
  Judge Spencer, 69

Roy family, 354-356

Robinson, William, 367
  family, 77, 381
  John (1664), 24

Rogers, George, 37
  Giles, 36

Rolfe, John, 24

Rowe family, 77

Ruffin, Judge Thomas, 312-315

"Rye Field" ("Locust Grove"), 70

Ryland family and homes, 356-357
  Robert, A. M., M. D., 315

Saint Stephen's parish, 60, 61, 290; act dividing, 46; bequest to, 68, 82; sale of glebe lands, 46, 47, 49

"Sandy Point," 74

Saunders, Major W. C., 367

Second Kilpatrick raid, 136

Scott, Rev. A. F., 315-317, 367

Semple family, 368, 378
  Robert, 35, 113-115

Shackelford, 35

Shackelford family, 376-378

Shackford, Jos. W., letter of, 103, 104 (footnote)

Sheridan's raid, 136

"Shoestring Country," 290

Skaife, Rev. John, 63

Slavery in Virginia, 295-296

Smith, Captain John, 17, biography of, 21 (footnote); explorations of, 21

Smith, James, 368

Southgate family, 88-91
  James, letter of, 84, 85

Southerland family, 77

Spears raid, 132, 133

Spottswood, Governor, 65, 83, 379

"Statutes at Large," Hennings, quoted, 42-55

Stephens, Hon. Alex. H., 82, 223

Steth, Rev. (1646), 24

Stratton Major parish, 43, 60, 290; empowered to sell glebe lands, 48; old parish church of, 79; register of, 79

Street, Major N. B., 368
  Walker, 368

Taxation, indiscriminate, of citizens for Church of England, 56

Taylor family, 380, 381

Temple, Joseph, 67, 71
  Sir William, 67
  Robert, 71
  William, 69

"The Mount," 65

"The New Church," 290

"Tippecanoe and Tyler too," 276

Todd family, 65, 358-360
  Rev. William, 59, 64, 113
  Thomas, 368
  William, 66
  William, 2d, 66

Toddsbury, 65

"Todd's Meeting House," 64

Tunstall family, 71, 72

Varina, place of residence of Pocahontas and Rolfe, 24

Vaughan, Christopher C., 368

Virginia, Church of England in, 56
  colony of, divided into eight shires, 42
  journal of trip from Detroit to, 80, 81
  loyalty of, 24
  negroes imported to, 24
  population of, in 1609, 23; in 1625, 23; in 1648, 23; in 1701, 23; in 1782, 24; population of, in 1701, compared with Connecticut, Maryland, Massachusetts, New York, 23, 24
  slave population of, in 1648, 23